For
Alex Giltner and Stephen Lawson—
friends lately found,
and in a dark season

THE HIDDEN AND THE MANIFEST

David Bentley Hart (signature)

The Hidden and the Manifest

Essays in Theology and Metaphysics

David Bentley Hart

WILLIAM B. EERDMANS PUBLISHING COMPANY

GRAND RAPIDS, MICHIGAN

Wm. B. Eerdmans Publishing Co.
2140 Oak Industrial Drive N.E., Grand Rapids, Michigan 49505
www.eerdmans.com

23 22 21 20 19 18 17   2 3 4 5 6 7

ISBN 978-0-8028-6596-0

Library of Congress Cataloging-in-Publication Data

Names: Hart, David Bentley, author.
Title: The hidden and the manifest : essays in theology and metaphysics /
    David Bentley Hart.
Description: Grand Rapids : Eerdmans Publishing Co., 2017. |
    Includes bibliographical references and index.
Identifiers: LCCN 2016053091 | ISBN 9780802865960 (pbk. : alk. paper)
Subjects: LCSH: Philosophical theology. | Theology. | Metaphysics.
Classification: LCC BT40 .H343 2017 | DDC 230—dc23
    LC record available at https://lccn.loc.gov/2016053091

Contents

CONTENTS

Preface

This collection spans the better part of my scholarly career, as well as the better part of my theological interests. Even those pieces that concern topics at something of a tangent from the broad main courses of my work touch, for the most part, on themes quite near my heart. Two are the texts of public addresses produced for very specific occasions and have not been published before; one, a somewhat eccentric essay on the topic of "thrift," was intended for print in a volume arising from one of the more peculiar projects I have participated in, but proved somewhat thematically incongruous with the rest of the book and was withdrawn (the book was intended as a hymn of celebration to thrift as a virtue, I believe, but my remarks struck a number of discordant notes); the rest have all been printed previously, and their provenances are named in the footnotes. All pieces are reprinted with permission. And I should record my thanks to my research assistant at St. Louis University, Jacob Prahlow, for his diligence in obtaining those permissions and in assembling this volume from so many disparate manuscripts.

I have altered very little, for better or worse, but I have attempted to remove from those articles that appeared in larger collections most cross-references to the articles of other contributors in the same volumes, lest I produce a one-sided impression of the discussions from which the pieces arose (and unfairly give myself the last word). I have also decided not to attempt to soften some of the more immoderate or provocative remarks in these essays, despite my new resolve to strike a more emollient tone whenever I can, because it would be wrong to change the record now, and would in any event probably be quite insincere. I ask readers only to believe that everything intemperate herein is offered in a spirit of good humor, without malice and in full expectation of reciprocal treatment in kind, and any lack of proper restraint on my part below is not *really* my fault, but that of the teacher of my literary infancy, H. L. Mencken (to whom any complaints should be addressed). I should mention that, in some cases, various of these essays cover some of the same ground in the same language (indeed, verbatim). In fact, the seventh essay collected here was written as a kind of distillation and reconsideration of various aspects of the essays that precede it in these pages. I might have changed the texts to avoid redundancy, and so spared the reader the tedium of grimacing more than once at the same obnoxious formulations, but each essay has its own integrity, and there is a point in time past which one cannot go back and change what one has written without doing more harm than good. So I hope readers will pardon the pleonasms.

I should also note that I have made no attempt here to bring earlier pieces into conformity with my later prejudices and predispositions. I suppose there have been fewer changes in that regard than I sometimes imagine—at least, in reviewing some of these pieces, I have found that I had already said things in them that I had not remembered already thinking—and in general I expect the only true difference of significance is one of candor. I am much more comfortable now than I once was with an open avowal of a kind of "Christian Platonism" (with a few Aristotelian inflections) as the imprecise but satisfactory description of my metaphysical predilections. In the past, and then only very occasionally, I thought I had to pay pious lip service to the anxieties and apprehensions of those less at ease with that designation than I was and am (much as I used to feel I was obliged to be guarded and hesitant in confessing my universalism, so as not *épater le bedeau*). Now I realize that this was not necessary, that Christian Platonism is not a metaphysics that dare not speak its name, and that I can trust in the intelligence, good will, and prudence of my readers. In fact, I really cannot imagine an alternative metaphysics for theology that does not ultimately collapse under the weight of its own contradictions; and I certainly have no patience for the dangerous fantasy that theology could or should be done without metaphysics. Then again, I do not really believe that much of anything can be done without metaphysics, either explicit or implicit, and so the truly liberating future course for theology in that regard (and for every field of humane reflection) should be to seek a way to get beyond getting beyond metaphysics.

Every blessing. *Orate pro me, Fratres et Sorores.*

ONE

The Offering of Names

Metaphysics, Nihilism, and Analogy

[A]s the cause of all and transcendent of all, God is truly without name, and yet he bears the names of all the things that are. Truly he reigns over all things, and all things revolve around him who is their cause, their source, and their final end. He is all in all.

— Dionysius the Areopagite

How is Logos the fateful . . . which sends each thing into its own? The gathering laying-out assembles all destining in itself, by bringing beings to us and letting them lie before us, keeping each being, whether absent or present, in its place and on its way, and by its assembling it secures all things in the all.

— Martin Heidegger

I. Attributes and Names

I want, in what follows,[1] to ruminate on the principal issue Janet Soskice

1. Much of this essay, especially in sections II–IV, is very close—in substance and manner of exposition—to arguments made at various junctures within my *The Beauty of the Infinite: The Aesthetics of Christian Truth* (Grand Rapids: Eerdmans, 2003). This is not surprising, as the initial draft of this essay and the final draft of that book were written at the same time, as fruits of the same research and meditation. While this essay has, for me, the virtue of concentrating those arguments into a single stream of "ontological" reflection, some may perhaps wonder—not without some understandable impatience— how I would situate my claims here in a broader theological frame, subject to scriptural

raises in her essay:[2] that is, her elegant distinction between the theological enunciation of the "divine names" and the philosophical enumeration of the "attributes of deity." The difference between the two practices, it seems clear, is nothing less than the difference between two ontologies: between a metaphysics of participation, according to which all things are embraced in being as in the supereminent source of all their transcendental perfections, and a "univocal" ontology, which understands being as nothing but the bare category of existence, under which all substances (God no less than creatures) are severally placed. The former permits practices of theological nomination—in liturgy, metaphor, metaphysics, and so on—because, even in asserting that there is an infinite qualitative difference between the coincidence in God's simplicity and plenitude of all the transcendental moments that compose the creature (goodness, truth, beauty, unity, etc.) and the finite, multiplicit "prismation" of being's light in the creature, it allows for a continuity of eminence between those moments and the transcendent wellspring from which they flow; thus one may in some sense name God from creatures, even though the infinite disproportion between divine being and finite beings places the truth of those names infinitely beyond the capacity of finite reason properly to grasp. Naming God, then, always has the form of analogy, an irresoluble tension between the cataphatic and apophatic, a language of likeness chastened by the pious acknowledgment of an ever greater unlikeness. The problem this would seem to raise, though, is that of the immense epistemological caesura that one must of necessity tolerate between the attributive use of a word "here below" and its properly nominative use in regard to God—for how much is really said (or known) when one speaks "names" whose "truthfulness" is certified precisely by their transcendence of finite comprehension? The latter ontology, it would then certainly seem, offers thought a more obvious and substantial form of "analogy": a direct proportionate similitude between attributes inhering in discrete beings (albeit between finite and infinite instances); thus to say "God is good" is to say much the same thing as "Henry is good," but with far greater certainty, and with no ambiguity. The metaphysics of participation, one could argue, precisely insofar as it regards God not as a being but as the source and ultimate truth of all beings, places an abyss between God and creatures that neither thought nor language can traverse without losing its moorings in human under-

---

and dogmatic constraints and imperatives; to answer such concerns, I would refer the curious to the book.

    2. In the volume from which this essay is taken.

standing; but a univocal ontology allows the essences of our attributions to remain intact, even when they are modified by the addition of the further attribute "infinite."

The problem, though, with identifying the divine attributes univocally, as features of the divine substance in much the same way as they are features of created substances,[3] is that the God thus described is a logical nonsense. A God who is a being among beings, who possesses the properties of his nature in a composite way, as aspects of his nature rather than as names ultimately convertible with one another in the simplicity of his transcendent essence, is a myth, a mere supreme being, whose being and nature are in some sense distinct from one another, who receives his being from being as such and so is less than being, who (even if he is changeless and eternal) in some sense becomes the being he is by partaking of that prior unity (existence) that allows his nature to persist as the composite reality it is. He is a God whose being has nonexistence as its opposite; he is not, that is to say, the infinite *actus* of all things, *id quo maius cogitari nequit*, but only an "ontic" God. There simply is no such God. Atheism is not the mirror inversion of this sort of theism, but both its inmost secret and its most necessary corrective. If God is thought of in such terms—if his true transcendence as the being of all beings is forgotten, hidden behind the imposing spectacle of a more conformable "supreme being"—then the longing to know the truth of God cannot help but lead to the rejection of God as truth; the inevitable terminus of "theism," so conceived, is nihilism.

In a sense, this is merely to repeat a claim that one school of modern Continental philosophy (call it the "ontological-hermeneutical") regards as a truism: that nihilism is the hidden "vocation" of the Western intellectual tradition, that the will to "positive" truth that is the unique passion of Western thought must finally—in what Nietzsche called the inversion

---

3. Soskice adduces perhaps the best example: Locke's formula for arriving at a rational understanding of God: we begin from various simple ideas derived from finite reality and appropriate to God, which we then multiply by infinity and combine to fashion for ourselves the complex idea of a supreme being (*An Essay concerning Human Understanding*, book 2.23, §33). A more guarded and austere example, though, would be that of Kant (*Prolegomena to Any Metaphysics That Will Be Able to Present Itself as a Science*, trans. P. G. Lucas [Manchester: Manchester University Press, 1962], pp. 121–80), who allowed that analogy might be used of God, but only insofar as it remains rhetorical and quadratically proportional (a:b::c:d), and does not take the form of a simple comparison between two discrete things, or between two things in relation to a third thing held in common (which sounds quite reasonable till one grasps how utterly vacuous the knowledge of this proportion is if there is not an *ontological* participation of one of the two sets in the other).

of the highest values—give birth to a discourse of absolute truthlessness, or the "truth" of innumerably many perspectives. Nihilism was first described by Jacobi, in the course of his critique of Kant, and it was he who first discerned a necessary liaison between its spiritual pathos and the intellectual ambition embodied in metaphysical systems. But it was Nietzsche who first argued that the "death of God" has come about as the result of the Christian (which is to say the vulgar Platonic) will to power, that pitiless, ascetic, ultimately life-denying hunger for absolute possession of the "most high principle" that must pursue God till it has killed him.[4] For Gianni Vattimo, the prophet of "playful nihilism" or "weak thought," nihilism is not simply the destiny of all Western metaphysics, but its solution, inasmuch as metaphysics is itself (he says) violence: the wresting of first principles from the intractable multiplicity of experience, the construction of a "hierarchy within totality" meant to contain and control the unmasterable flow of "difference," a subordination of life to some supreme lifeless value (*ousia, kinēsis, eidos, ego, Geist . . .*).[5] But the most interesting (and infuriating) theorist of metaphysics' nihilistic vocation is Heidegger, and it is his treatment of the matter that, in an unexpected way perhaps, makes an explicit connection between the "question of being" and the question of naming God.

To formulate the argument I want to make very simply: the forgetfulness of the difference between naming God and describing his attributes, characteristic of Western thought since—let us say—at least the early modern period, is one and the same with the forgetfulness of the "onticoontological difference." Admittedly, there is a certain irony in resorting to Heidegger's rebarbative patois in order to argue (as I shall) that only classical Christian metaphysics escapes such forgetfulness; for Heidegger himself, Christian metaphysics is nothing but a strikingly intense form

4. This, obviously, would not be a cause of grief for Nietzsche were Christianity not a particularly depraved collusion of inhuman desire and all-too-human pusillanimity, a product of the resentment of the spiritually and physically debile, who do not possess the resources, in the wake of God's death, to affirm the whole of being in all its prodigality, creativity, and destructiveness (and so forth and so on, *in taedium maximum*).

5. See Gianni Vattimo, "Towards an Ontology of Decline," in *Recoding Metaphysics: The New Italian Philosophy*, ed. Giovanni Borradori (Evanston, IL: Northwestern University Press, 1988), p. 60. In recent work, Vattimo has come to claim that the peaceful annunciation of nihilism and the death of metaphysics are the result of the announcement of the *kenōsis* of God in Christ. See, for instance, Vattimo, *Belief*, trans. Luca D'Isanto and David Webb (Stanford: Stanford University Press, 1999), and Vattimo, "The Trace of the Trace," in *Religion*, ed. Jacques Derrida and Gianni Vattimo (Stanford: Stanford University Press, 1998).

of *Seinsvergessenheit*; but my use of the term is appropriate. The event of modernity within philosophy, after all, consisted for Christian thought in the death of a certain vision of being: it was the disintegration of that radiant unity where the good, the true, and the beautiful coincided as infinite simplicity and fecundity, communicating themselves to a world whose only reality was its dynamic participation in their gratuity; and so consisted also in the consequent divorce between this thought of being—the supereminent fullness of all perfection—and the thought of God. In this "moment" (which occurred over several centuries), "being" somehow became the name of what formerly would have been regarded almost as being's opposite: a veil or an absence, explicitly or implicitly invoked, but in either case impenetrable—the veil veiling itself, the empty category of sheer uniform existence that adds nothing to the essence of things, and whose only "determination" is an absolute privation of all determinacy. And God's transcendence, so long as philosophy suffered any nostalgia for "that hypothesis," came to be understood as God's absence, his hiddenness behind the veil of being, breaking through, if at all, only as an explanatory cause. However hostile, then, Heidegger's own diagnosis of the "oblivion of being" may be to Christian thought, it nevertheless proceeds from a sadness quite familiar to theology in the post-Christian era; Heidegger recognizes that the particular pathology of modernity lies—to some very large degree—in the loss of a certain kind of wonder or perplexity, a certain sense of the abiding strangeness of being within the very ordinariness of beings. Not, it must be said, that he really desires to reverse the course of this decline: for him the nihilistic dissolution of every transcendental structure of being—every metaphysics—is something both good and bad, both a promise and a risk, and something that must be followed to its end. Following Nietzsche, he reads the history of nihilism as the story of the Western will to positive truth, which must—before it can be transcended—exhaust itself, and so bring metaphysics to its ultimate collapse. And, in this account of things, the theological understanding of the transcendence of being over beings appears as merely a particularly acute instance of a duality intrinsic to every metaphysics: like every speculative "system," Christian philosophy is subordinate to that original forgetfulness that allows metaphysics its fruitful but erring reign over Western thought, and so while theology possesses a kind of understanding of the ontological difference, it arrives at that understanding only by abstracting some general characteristic of beings and projecting it as the "ground" or "principle" or "truth" of beings—which it then identifies with God. This is what Heidegger calls the "double founding" of "onto-theology," the grounding of beings in being, and then the further grounding of being in some supreme being. Thus Christian philosophy is, at the end of the day, merely "metaphysics" once more, oblivious of the utter qualitative distinction between being and beings; and while metaphysics may illuminate the ontological difference for thought in some measure, it does so necessarily by way of a more original obscurity, a withdrawal or hiding of being behind one or another ontic exemplar—behind one or another of the masks being wears in the drama of its passage through successive metaphysical epochs and regimes.

Thus Heidegger's genealogy of nihilism is perfectly seamless: after that first lightning flash, that blissful dawn, when being originally manifested itself for thought in the West, in the naïve but for that very reason pure language of the pre-Socratics, the West's initial moment of philosophical wakefulness necessarily began to harden into fixed and rigid forms. Whereas the pre-Socratics, immersed in the "lighting" of being, enjoying a "poetic" immediacy of language to event, understood being as *alētheia* or *physis* or *logos*—as, that is, the unveiling of being in beings, the temporal arising and passing away of beings, and the "gathering laying-together" of the event that grants beings and being to one another—thought could not long endure the mystery of these *names* for being, and soon had to begin to substitute for them the inert conceptual *properties* of being. This is the apostasy of Plato, for instance, in turning his gaze away from the silent mystery of being's "yielding hiddenness" and toward the visibility of original essences, *eidē*, the frozen, eternalized "looks" of things. Here the search for truth as a positive possession of reason—a thing among the things of the world—takes hold of reason, and here the history of metaphysics is inaugurated in earnest, and—no matter what new concept will displace *eidos* (*ousia, actus, ego, Geist*)—the entire course of this epochal "destinal sending" is set in motion by this always more essential oblivion. Now, in the twilight of the metaphysical age, we find ourselves in the time of realized nihilism, of the technological *Gestell*, in which reality is understood as just so many quanta of power, the world as nothing but the representation of the self-established subject, and the things of earth as mere material, a "standing reserve" awaiting exploitation by the merciless rationality of technology. The ancient nuptial ecstasy of word and world—of poetic saying and ontological unveiling—has now become all but impossible. This is the moment of highest risk. But if in this moment we reclaim the more essential truth of this nihilistic destiny—that truth is not an object to be possessed, that the world is not reducible to the "sufficient reason" for its existence, that we should not press toward foundations and principles but should rather dwell in the "worlding of the world" and find the truth of things in their limpid *Anwesen*—we can perhaps heal ourselves of the positivist passion, await the world in a state of poetic and passive expectancy, look for a new dawning of the light of being, speak thoughtfully the names of that nameless mystery as it shows itself to us . . .

All of which has an undeniable charm about it; but it is at just this point that one should pause and ask whether the sweet, melancholy quietism in such language does not dissemble a certain kind of metaphysical ambition. For Heidegger's account of nihilism, and of what stands beyond nihilism, is dictated not simply by a scrupulous honesty regarding the history of Western thought, but much more by his own ontology—which itself could well be characterized as nihilistic. For Heidegger, whose earliest attempt at a "fundamental ontology" transcribes into ontological terms Husserl's phenomenological collapse of the distinction between "it is" and "it appears," being is so entirely pure of determination as to be convertible with nothing. It is simply the manifestation of the manifest, the inexhaustible movement of manifestation itself, the silence whose self-effacement allows beings (in their absolute difference from being) to sound forth. Being's generosity—its *es gibt*, its withdrawal or "nothinging," which lets beings come to presence in the "juncture" of being and, in due order, give way to other beings—is merely its nothingness among beings, its "refusal" to appear as the absolute. Here, certainly, the "metaphysics" of light (of being as the overflowing fullness of the transcendentals) has been "overcome" (or, more accurately, abandoned), but only in favor of a "metaphysics" of darkness. For being is, in a sense, darkness itself, the *dialectical* negation that indifferently grants all beings their finitude. Its every "mittence" is, as Heidegger says, an "errance"; it gives "light" only by *being* dark, by hiding and leading astray; as much as truth is a peaceful letting-be-manifest, it is also a struggle of obscurity and light, *Erde* and *Welt*, in which peace and strife are inseparably joined. *Logos* forces *physis* into a gathered containment. No less than the Stoic image of the cosmos as a finite totality in which every form is continually displaced by another, the whole under the irresistible sway of *anankē*, the later Heidegger's understanding of the destinal epochality of being's temporality ever more absolutely identifies the event of being not only with the "presencing" and "whiling" of beings, but with their annihilation. Like Hegel, Heidegger thinks of truth as also, intrinsically, destruction. *If* this is indeed how being must be conceived in order for the thinker to escape the oblivion of being that lies at the heart of "metaphysics," then indeed theology has no name for being—or, it would seem, for God.

This *if*, though, is precisely the question I want to raise: Is Heidegger's ontology genuinely an alternative—*the* alternative—to "onto-theology," or does Heidegger himself perhaps fail adequately to think the difference between being and beings, and so the difference between nomination and attribution? This is worth asking for many reasons. For one thing, Heidegger's thought gives powerful expression to the deepest impulse of modern Continental philosophy in its interminable struggle to liberate itself from theology, and thus it is a particularly transparent instance of philosophy functioning as a theology evacuated of transcendence. In Heidegger's attempt to ask the question of being anew, free from the heritage of metaphysics, he presents us with an exquisitely poignant image of the descent of thought into an absolute and self-sealing discourse of immanence. And this by itself makes it profitable to ask whether his understanding of the "oblivion of being" is one to which theology must pay heed; for the "ontologist" and the Christian metaphysician alike may concur that something has been forgotten, but it also remains the case that what each regards as forgotten is what the other regards as the most extreme form of forgetting. More to the point here, however, our question is worth asking simply because Heidegger's thought is very much concerned with naming (with the poetic *logos*, in which the silence of being peals forth, veiled in its very unveiling, with the naming of the "gathering" of the "ring-dance" of the "fourfold," etc.), because he wants so desperately to free the discourse of truth from the morbid mythology of grounds and of sufficient reason, which finds the truth of the world only in the world's barest and most meager possibility or featureless principles, and which must in some sense erase the event of the world to establish the ground of the world. For Heidegger the truth of an apple (say) lies not in the metaphysical principles that secure it within the rationality of being, but in the event of the apple in its appearing, in all the richness and poverty of its transient particularity, and the language of truth that alone can "correspond" to this truth is a "poetic speaking" that allows the event of the apple within the world to show itself within words. Such a view of things certainly attests to a quite earnest desire to free thought from the destructive passion of instrumental reason, in order to "return" philosophical reflection to a condition of peaceful dwelling in the givenness of the world; and there is moreover a clearly discernible theological pathos in Heidegger's longing to see a peaceful belonging together and intimacy between *res* and *signum*, sustained by their coincidence in the event (or act?) that embraces them both. But the most important reason for asking our question is that, in Heidegger's terms, the naming of being in beings is impossible: for if beings show forth being only in the occlusion of being, in being's "nihilation," then the names we speak are—at the end of the day—so many "opaque signifiers"; if being shows itself only through the immemorial event of its self-effacement, upon which thought (bound as it is to static representations) can then only supervene with a quaint anachrony, then being is silence itself, absolutely different from all saying, a nothingness against which all beings are "set off," and the "naming of being" (or the naming of the God who is not a being among beings) is an empty paradox; this is the Derridean "vocation" of Heideggerean ontology.

Happily, though, when it is disentangled from Heidegger's *Seinsgeschichte*, Christian philosophy proves to possess resources for understanding and overcoming the "nihilistic terminus" of modernity in a way that does not arrive at this hopeless *impasse*; and it can moreover provide an account of the ontological difference far more cogent than any Heidegger ever enunciated. For Heidegger was in error, and for the most surprising of reasons: because he, perhaps more than any other philosopher in Western thought, was oblivious of the difference between being and beings. In taking phenomenological "givenness" to a dialectical extreme, and abstracting from it an ontology, he hid from himself the true question of being— which was raised uniquely in theological tradition, and answered there in a way beyond every nihilism (nowhere more perfectly than in Denys's *Divine Names*). And in constructing his genealogy of metaphysics as one continuous decline from philosophy's first moment of ontological wakefulness to a final eclipse of being in the "age of the world-picture," Heidegger succeeded in concealing from himself the most remarkable aspect of the history of Western metaphysics: to wit, its Christian interruption.

II. *Ereignis* and *Actus*

I should note, I suppose, that Heidegger's purblindness is in some great degree willful, and even a little perverse. As I have said, his early journey from phenomenology to ontology was made possible by—and so was confined to—phenomenology's collapse of any meaningful distinction between "it is" and "it appears." At some level, perhaps, this represented a kind of transcendental restraint on his part, or critical sobriety, but it by no means purged his thinking of "metaphysical" presuppositions. How, after all, can one elect such a point of departure unless one has arrived, in advance, at a decision—a conjecture—that has foreclosed the very question of the relation between being and manifestation? More importantly, how much sense does it make to attempt to extract a fundamental ontology from a philosophical discipline from which the question of being has been scrupulously and necessarily "bracketed" out? Inasmuch as Heidegger was obliged, at the beginning of his project, to argue toward the legitimacy of any ontology at all, and then had to do so only in terms that the phenomenological realm of inference (the economy of appearance and hiddenness) permitted, there was no point in the early development of his thought at which it became possible to think of being outside of the closed circle of what appears and what does not appear. Not that Heidegger was in any way discomfited by the epistemological limits he thus imposed upon himself. In truth, the acceptance of such limits was, more than anything else, a decision taken in the service of a rather transparent play for power—one nowhere more evident than in the essay of 1927, "Phänomenologie und Theologie."[6] It was here that Heidegger attempted to seize away from theology the high ground of "metaphysics," discourse on being, by drawing an absolute distinction between philosophy's properly ontological sphere of inquiry and theology's "ontic science" of faith—the science, that is, of something called "Christianness," and of the special comportment of belief toward the cross of Christ (which, when all is said and done, reduces theology to a purely psychological and "local" pursuit). Heidegger could easily, it is true, have called upon a well-established tradition of Protestant dogmatics to defend the peremptory division of prerogatives for which he argued, but to any attentive reader it should be clear that his only genuine concern was to secure for his philosophy an inviolably unique claim upon ontology, and to do so precisely by despoiling theology of the language of being and beings that—contrary to Heidegger's account of things—had become available to human reflection only when the Christian doctrine of creation assumed, but altered, antique metaphysics. Granted, Heidegger claims that he discriminates between the spheres of faith and philosophy not so as to accord one priority over the other (the ontic and the ontological, or the empirical and the theoretical, he argues, simply belong to different orders), but he no sooner makes this assertion than he demonstrates its duplicity: the philosopher, for example, is able to see that the theologian's special language of sin falls under the more original, ontological determination of *Dasein*'s guilt (*Schuld*), and thus the analysis of guilt can clarify

---

6. In Heidegger, *Wegmarken* (hereinafter *W*), *Gesamtausgabe* 9 (Frankfurt am Main: Vittorio Klostermann, 1976); in English, *Pathmarks* (hereinafter *P*) (Cambridge: Cambridge University Press, 1998).

and correct the concept of sin, but never the reverse.[7] "There is no such thing as a Christian philosophy,"[8] Heidegger helpfully informs us.

However—and there is a piquant irony in this—it is precisely Heidegger's assiduous struggle to begin his project from a vantage pure of theology that ultimately renders his project incoherent, and in fact makes it impossible for him genuinely to contemplate being *in its difference* from all beings. This is obvious from the period of *Sein und Zeit* onward. By denying himself any stirring of reason's necessarily ecstatic movement toward a horizon continuous with and yet transcending the scope of experience, and by seeking to capture the truth of being (or meaning of being) entirely within the horizon of *Dasein*'s being-in-the-world, Heidegger condemns himself to circling interminably between the two poles of the ontic process of arising and perishing, within which ambit he can do no more than arbitrarily isolate certain "existentiell" structures of experience and treat them as "existential" openings upon the question of being. It scarcely matters, then, how comprehensive or thorough his "phenomenology" of this being-in-the-world may be, because any conclusions he may draw therefrom regarding being (or even regarding how *Sein* appears *for Dasein*) are little more than intuitive—indeed, oracular. Nowhere does this essential mystification in the early Heidegger's thought disport itself more flagrantly than in 1929's "Was ist Metaphysik?" It is tempting to allow oneself to be carried away by this essay's beguiling treatment of the "nothing's" power to awaken us to beings *as* beings, or by its lovely meditation on boredom, or especially by its treatment of anxiety as a *Stimmung* possessed of a unique ontological probity;[9] but, if one succumbs, one will in all likelihood fail to note how many baseless assertions throng each of Heidegger's moves. To take the most striking example: it may be true that anxiety apprises us that all things are "set off" against the nothing, but to cross from what is after all a simple recognition of ontic contingency to any conclusion concerning being as such requires either that one abandon to some degree the ontic economy of existence and nonexistence (of finite determination), or that one treat this economy as the sole truth of being (which leaves the real question of being, as distinct from all beings, unaddressed). Heidegger chooses the latter course, but one should not be deceived that in doing so he is fleeing the "metaphysical" and embracing the "scientific." Simply said, it does not matter which fundamental mood—boredom or anxiety,

---

7. *W* 64/*P* 51–52.
8. *W* 66/*P* 53.
9. *W* 110–12/*P* 87–88.

happiness or wonder—reveals to us the uncanniness of existence; the only "nothing" made available within this experience is merely the opposite of existence. Thus, to do as Heidegger does, and argue for a kind of secret synonymy between the "nothing" and "being" (following a rather impressionistic logic: being discloses beings as beings, the nothing discloses to us that beings are beings, thus in the being of being the nothing nothings . . .), is simply to avoid the question actually at issue. That is to say, in this obviously dialectical scheme, the "nothing" can be taken as "ontological" only if being is to be conceived as the opposite of the existence of (ontic) things. But this is vacuous. If being is really, *ontologically* different from all beings—even if one grants that it is the ontic oscillation between existence and nonexistence that first wakens us to this difference—then being cannot be the opposite of anything;[10] it stands over against neither existence nor nonexistence within finite reality, but is the "is" both of "it is" and of "it is not," and so the difference of one from the other is something utterly distinct from the difference of being from both. The simple opposition of "is" and "is not," understood as the simple functioning of noncontradiction within finite things, is not an ontological determination, but is merely what raises the ontological question in the first place. To confuse being with the simple nonexistence that anxiety has the power to reveal is as much a species of *Seinsvergessenheit* as it is to confuse being with simple existence; one has simply mistakenly identified being with one moment in the determination of finite "essences"—with, that is, the ontic "not this" rather than the ontic "this." It is true that the distance between beings and nonbeing reveals to us that being is not a being among beings; but, at the same time, if we resist lapsing into dialectic, it should also reveal to us that being is as mysteriously beyond nonbeing as beyond everything that is. After all, it is the synthesis within beings of *what* they are and *that* they are (and so of what they are not) that makes it impossible, within the grammar of ontic process, to speak properly of being *qua* being. The ghost of Leibniz still haunts us with his maddening question: How is it that there are beings at all, and not much rather nothing? And no obscure conflation of being and the nothing will suffice to dispel philosophical perplexity here, as the question might just as well be phrased thus: What permits beings and nonbeing to be distinct from one another, such that beings are the beings they are while nothing (*ex quo nihil fieri potest*) remains nothing? How can there *be* such a distinction and such a unity?

I think that, at some level, Heidegger can be accused of a very basic

10. See Maximus the Confessor, *Chapters on Love* 3.65.

logical mistake. Granted, it is not always easy to follow Heidegger's logic well enough to identify either its strengths or its flaws, especially in his earlier period, where it is often annoyingly difficult to assign any clear meaning to his use of the word *Sein*; there it is even occasionally possible to read him as being concerned solely with something like *esse commune*—a general existence, which is nothing apart from what exists. In his mature work, however, after his so-called *Kehre*, Heidegger supposedly turns his eyes from *Dasein* to *Sein*, and then to the *es gibt* of the event that grants the "ontico-ontological difference" (albeit in the form of a forgetting) to every age of thought. Here we discover—so says John Caputo[11]—that the abstract "beingness" of beings is clearly not what Heidegger means by *Sein*.[12] At some level this is certainly so: when he speaks of being, Heidegger does indeed mean more than the "existence" of "existents"; he clearly means the possibility or event of such existence. That said, he confines the concept of being to a finite economy of "presencing" that is nothing but the process of "beingness," of becoming and passing away, and as a result his ontology remains a reflection only upon how beings appear within this economy. This is a problem, because properly speaking the question of being is: Why is there an economy of existence at all, and not, much rather, nothing? And this would seem to mean that no moment within this economy, at the end of the day, can account for the economy as a whole. Nor does Heidegger escape the realm of the merely ontic by turning from the question of being to that of the *Ereignis*. As Caputo points out, Heidegger came to argue not that metaphysics is utterly oblivious of the ontological difference as such—philosophy has always known something of the difference, even where it reduces being to a being—but that metaphysics always fails to grasp the distance of the difference between being and beings:[13] being and beings are imagined as a circle of mutual grounding, between two separate kinds of "thing," which blinds the metaphysician to the mystery of being's purity from beings, and so to the mystery of the eventfulness of the passing over of being to beings and of beings to being. The mystery is hidden from view behind the splendid machinery and intricate hierarchies of rigid presence, substance, structure; the givenness of beings in their *Anwesen*—their arrival, their tremulous "whiling," their passing away again into concealment—goes unremarked in its self-effacing silence.

11. John Caputo, *Heidegger and Aquinas: An Essay on Overcoming Metaphysics* (New York: Fordham University Press, 1982).

12. Caputo, *Heidegger and Aquinas*, p. 143.

13. Caputo, *Heidegger and Aquinas*, pp. 155–56.

For this reason, Heidegger claims that we must begin the thinking of being anew, not merely from the vantage of the difference, but from the vantage of the event of the difference. In 1957's *Identität und Differenz*, he takes two "steps back" from beings: the first is a step into the "ontico-ontological difference," of which metaphysics is conscious, but only according to some generalized model of a characteristic proper to beings; but the second is a step into the still more original *differing* of the difference, the *Austrag* (*auseinander-zueinander-tragen*) that grants being and beings to one another and opens for each epoch of thought the possibility of its forgetful thinking of the difference.[14] This appropriating event (*Ereignis*) must not be confused with "creation," according to Heidegger; it is a letting-be-seen, not a kind of causality or *actus*; it is the giving that gives by withdrawing itself. And what it gives is the process of *alētheia*, or *physis*, the surging-up and whiling of beings in the "juncture" of the event. In 1946's "Der Spruch des Anaximander," Heidegger had described this juncture as lying between two concealments—the future "to-come" and the past "having-been"[15]—a twofold absence that it holds apart so as to allow things to come to presence.[16] Nor is what the juncture makes present some kind of discrete perduring substance poised between these absences; the present "presences" only in allowing itself to belong also to the absent[17]—and here we glimpse something of the essence of tragedy.[18] In a footnote added to the text in 1950, Heidegger says that the discrimination (*Unter-Schied*) of which he is here speaking "is infinitely distinct (*unendlich verschieden*) from being, which remains the being *of* beings."[19] This event may also be called *Logos*, which Heidegger takes to mean, originally, a "laying-out before that gathers together":[20] *Logos* gathers all destining (*Schicken*) to itself, keeping each being, whether absent or present, "in its place and on its way," sending each into its own, and by its assembling, *Logos* "secures all things in the all."[21] Heidegger's "temporalization of being" consists, then, simply in this: being and beings are

---

14. Heidegger, *Identität und Differenz* (Pfullingen: Günther Neske, 1957), p. 65.

15. In Heidegger, *Holzwege* (hereinafter *H*), *Gesamtausgabe* 5 (Frankfurt am Main: Vittorio Klostermann, 1977), pp. 334–36.

16. *H* 355.

17. *H* 357.

18. *H* 357–58.

19. *H* 364, note d.

20. Heidegger, "Logos (Heraklit, Fragment 50)," in *Vorträge und Aufsätze* (hereinafter *VA*), *Gesamtausgabe* 7 (Frankfurt am Main: Vittorio Klostermann, 2000).

21. *VA* 226–27.

given to one another by an event that opens a finite juncture between the arrival of the concealed future and the departure of the concealed past, where beings waver into presence, linger, and waver away into nothing. Time is being's passage from nothing to nothing, surmounted by a mysterious, noncausal event that assembles, limits, apportions, and sustains the economy of nihilation. And this event, as *Logos*, occurs for us in language, and then in the thoughtful hearing of language's gathering saying of the world's "worlding"—as is nowhere more powerfully expressed than in the almost incantatory conclusion of "Brief über den Humanismus": as clouds are the clouds of the sky—making it visible, distinctly, as sky precisely by obscuring it—so language is the language of being; and, as the vast depths of the earth are barely scored by the inconspicuous furrows drawn by the farmer's plow, so thought is a humble laboring at the surface of language, whose immensity it scarcely touches.[22]

Again, I would not care to deny how seductive and impressive Heidegger's "vision" can be: so seductive and impressive, indeed, that only the most humorlessly pertinacious reader is likely to notice the little man hiding behind the screen, working the levers. Nevertheless, I reiterate my earlier charge: however much Heidegger may have succeeded at producing the appearance of a new kind of ontology, he never succeeded in understanding being as truly *ontologically* different from beings. Even his tortuous meditations upon the *Ereignis* serve only to confirm the event of the world in its own immanence, its ontic process, and all the while the real question of being fails to be posed. How is it that becoming is? This is never truly Heidegger's question; and one passage in "Anaximander" seems to me perfectly to express why it cannot be:

> Whatever has its essence in arrival and departure we would like to call becoming and perishing, which is to say, transience, and therefore not what has being (*das Seiende*); for we have long been accustomed to opposing being (*Sein*) to becoming, as if becoming were a nothingness and did not even belong to being, which one habitually understands only as sheer perdurance. If, though, becoming *is*, then we must think being so essentially that it not only comprises becoming in some empty concept, but that, rather, being ontologically (*seinsmäßig*) supports and characterizes becoming (*genesis—phthora*) in its essence.[23]

22. W 364/P 276.
23. H 343: "Was jedoch dergestalt in Ankunft und Abgang sein Wesen hat, möchten wir eher das Werdende und Vergehende, d.h. das Vergängliche nennen, nicht aber das

I must say, it seems to me that there is almost nothing in these sentences that is not obviously wrong. To begin with, to say that, in distinguishing between becoming and being, "metaphysics" customarily treats becoming as a kind of nothingness is to say something simply false; it sounds like one of those silly slanders of Platonism for which a serious scholar should have no patience. Surely it is more correct to say that the problem of philosophy has always been that of the synthesis of "nothingness" and "essence" within becoming, the persistence of unity within change, and so—quite logically—Western metaphysics has traditionally recognized that nothing that is (including becoming) is able to account for itself; hence being and becoming are not to be accounted synonyms. But that is a mere cavil compared to what one should say regarding the far graver problem bedeviling Heidegger's central argument: "if becoming *is*. . . ." Not to be too cavalier here, but I must observe that one could just as easily argue that being has always been characterized as altogether different from any number of things—lampshades, armchairs, clever ideas, lizards, passion fruit—but *if these things are*. . . . In every case, it is the "is" *of* the thing—whether it be becoming, a lampshade, a clever idea, or what have you—that proves irreducible *to* the thing. It would be convenient, of course, if one could dissolve the verb—the mysterious "to be"—into its subject, but one cannot. And "becoming" is no exception to this rule: it refers to the ontic "how" of finite existence, which means it *cannot* refer, of itself, to the ontological "that" of existence. Moreover, while it is an article of faith for Heideggereans that being has been understood, throughout metaphysical history, simply as sheer enduring presence, it is a belief gaily unencumbered by evidence.

This is not to deny that eternity has traditionally, in Western thinking, been regarded as an aspect of that which is other than all beings, but certain things must be kept in mind. To begin with, the difference between timeless eternity and substantial perdurance is an absolute difference, a qualitative difference, rather like that between truth and truths, or between being and beings, and so it is no more correct to speak of eternity as sheer presence than to speak of it as sheer absence—which any garden-variety Neoplatonist could tell you. Moreover, even if the metaphysical

---

Seiende; denn wir sind seit langem gewohnt, dem Werden das Sein entgegenzusetzen, gleich als ob Werden ein Nichts sei und nicht auch in das Sein gehöre, das man seit langem nur als das bloße Beharren versteht. Wenn jedoch das Werden *ist*, dann müssen wir Sein so wesentlich denken, daß es nicht nur im leeren begrifflichen Meinen das Werden umgreift, sondern daß das Sein das Werden (γένεσις—φθορά) seinsmäßig im Wesen erst trägt und prägt."

certitude that becoming is not being might occasionally take the form of a crude distinction between changing things and a great changeless substance (though nowhere in Platonism or Christianity, as far as I know), it is a certitude that arises from the recognition that nothing in the ontic play of existence and nonexistence (not even becoming, or the process of "unhiddenness") is its own "is," and that the "is" cannot be something that becomes, that has an opposite, or that contains potential. And, perhaps most importantly, as a negation, "eternity" is an absolutely necessary and entirely benign moment in prescinding from beings to being, to which there is no alternative that is not nonsensical. For Heidegger, the incorrigible tendency of metaphysics is to isolate some general characteristic of beings, convert it into a concept of being *qua* being, and then treat beings as though they were mere instances or reflections of this supreme, changeless abstraction. Curiously enough, though, this is precisely what Heidegger himself does: he chooses to make the world of finitude the ground of the "truth" of being, and does so by taking the ontic characteristic of temporal change, of becoming and transiency, generalizing it as the process of hiddenness and unhiddenness, and abstracting from it various names for being; this process he then mistakes for the ontological difference itself, which means that he can conceive of being only as a reflection of our own "beingness." Then, over this entire dialectic of existence and nonexistence, he erects an arch of fate, of a "destining" that apportions finite things to their placement and displacement in a cycle of interminable immanence,[24] and so confirms beings in their potentiality (their nothingness) as the "ground" of being.[25] In scholastic terms, Heidegger has merely elevated possibility over actuality.[26] What he certainly has not done is address the

24. See Heidegger, "Moira (Parmenides, Fragment VIII, 34–41)," in *VA* 235–61.
25. See 1930's "Vom Wesen des Grundes," in *W* 123–75.
26. ". . . possibility is always higher than actuality, *sicut Martinus dicit*"— Caputo, *Heidegger and Aquinas*, p. 284. This touches upon an issue that requires more space than I can grant it here. Heidegger claims that the language of *actus* and *actualitas* in Thomas reflects a "Roman" distortion of Aristotle's *energeia*, characteristic of the ancient Latin world's culture of force, fabrication, technology, and conquest, a culture whose governing motif was one of efficiency. I find this worse than unconvincing, however: not only is it the case that Thomas carefully discriminates between a crudely univocal use of the language of cause or act and his properly analogical use (a fact that would not really make any difference against Heidegger's essentially intuitive argument here), but it is also the case that *actus* is neither philologically, semantically, nor historically bound to the connotations Heidegger assigns it (after all, one can *agere gratias*, *poenitentiam*, or *pacem*, and it is very important *se agere* as well; but one must *aedificare* or *condere pontem*). It is true that Heidegger reportedly believed that earlier Greek patristic language might be more elusive

essential mystery: How is it that either possibility or actuality *is?* Whence comes the "is" in "it is possible"?

Does it, after all, make any particular sense to grant possibility priority over actuality? Obviously, at the level of the ontic, the possible is always in excess of whatever is, in any moment, actual; but, once again, this merely restates the problem. It is precisely *because* this is the case at the level of the ontic that thought is obliged ultimately to seek, beyond the ontic supremacy of the possible, the ontological truth of the actual. For, in itself, an economy in which the possible is higher than the actual is, manifestly, *impossible.* What Heidegger calls *Anwesen* consists, necessarily, in a dialectic between "this" and "not this"—between what is and all that might be, that has been, that will be, all that is concealed, potential, and that *is* not. But this is precisely the dialectic that must remain an inert impossibility if the difference between possible and actual is not enfolded within a prior actuality. Not to sound too doctrinaire, but the nothing cannot magically pass from itself into something; *fieri* simply *cannot* precede *esse.* Heidegger obviously makes a vague gesture in the direction of this rather elementary impasse by distinguishing between the "ontico-ontological difference" and its event, but here too, unless this event is understood as the donation of being from a plenitude of actuality, such a distinction is little more than a revision of the problem it pretends to address. One must either be willing to speak of something like an *actus essendi subsistens* or cease speaking of being altogether; and to misrepresent talk of this transcendent act, that infinitely and simply is all that the possible might possibly be, as simply "ontic" discourse, concerned with some efficient cause or power, is to trade

---

of his critique, but I for one resist taking comfort from this, as I believe that Thomas's language is entirely continuous with the language of the Cappadocians, Dionysius, Maximus, etc. Perhaps it is interesting to ask whether Heidegger could have read Dionysius or Maximus, speaking of God as the fullness of being, "leading" (to use the Dionysian term) beings into being, or as the light shining in and on all beings, drawing them to himself, or as the infinite source of beauty that "excites" the "*erōs*" of beings out of their nonbeing, and interpreted this simply as a discourse of double founding, a mere causal economy between a supreme thing and derivative things. Could Heidegger have read Dionysius's language of the divine ecstasy that calls forth and meets our ecstasy, and so gives being to beings, or of the Good's supereminent "no-thing-ness," and treated this too as a form of ontic causality infinitely magnified, without significant analogical ambiguity? Such questions are pointless, though, as Heidegger's commitment to his own metaphysics of process, epochality, language, and "thought" was chastely resistant to any discourse of transcendence, which is what—in any event—the patristic language is; and to ask such questions, moreover, is perhaps to have conceded that scholastic *actus* was indeed what Heidegger said it was—which it was not.

in empty caricature. From the high patristic period onward, Christian thought had developed an ontology of the infinite, which Aquinas perhaps brought to its most lucid Latin expression (though I am not a partisan among the various schools): being is not reducible either to essence or to finite existence; "infinity," which for Aristotle was to be ascribed only to the inchoate potentiality of matter, became now a name for the fullness of *esse*, which is the transcendent act in which essence and existence alike participate; and thus being differs from beings more or less as does goodness from anything good. *This* language of participation, however much one may wish to resist its logic, is no naïve "essentialism" or "causalism," nor certainly is it the "reciprocal grounding" of "onto-theology." Nor is the concept of *actus* it presumes some pale reflection of one or another general characteristic of beings. Rather, indeed, it is this approach to ontology alone that makes it possible to conceive of the distinction between being and beings as something other than an ontic economy. Even if, in the realm of the ontic, the possible is in some sense the fountainhead of the actual, this obviously finite order still must be conceptually inverted (which involves an appeal to the infinite) if one is to be able to think of being as such, for possibility—however one conceives of it—must first *be*.

This is, I readily confess, an argument for "necessary being." It may seem that, in turning away from Heidegger's ontology only to retreat to so antique and "metaphysical" a redoubt, I am behaving rather like a French soldier fleeing to the shelter of the Maginot Line after the German armies have already circumvented it; but I can see no coherent alternative. In the defense of such a move, I can only observe that "necessary," in this context, cannot mean a first cause in any ontic sense (in any sense, that is, appropriate to the order of secondary causality); rather, it indicates the transcendent "possibility of possibility," which must be infinite actuality: in the language of Nicholas of Cusa, infinite transcendent *Posse*, which is at once infinite possibility and infinite act. This is a logic that no "ontologist" can really escape. Even Heidegger, by thinking of possibility as "higher" than actuality, is really only transposing his terms; he is thinking of the possible *as* the actual, as possessing greater (albeit indeterminate) "eminence," which must be forcibly distributed into temporal determinacy and definite manifestation by the apportioning hand of destiny. Heidegger sees the no-thing-ness of being not as an infinite purity from all limit, but as a mirror inversion of ontic presence in the ontic absence of past and future, and so he sees the withholding of being in beings not as the qualitative transcendence of the infinite, but (almost) as the restrained immensity of the "there," the absolute compresence of the totality deferred into temporality. Even, then, if we concede that Heidegger's *Sein* is not *esse commune* (which clearly it is not), we must also recognize that, in its complete dependence upon the dialectic of existence and nonexistence, Heidegger's "ontology" is a species of "double founding"—of, that is, metaphysics, and of the most "causal" variety. Heidegger's second step back from metaphysics is not a step into a more original distinction than the "ontico-ontological difference," but merely a stepping away from the infinite into the finite, so as to complete metaphysics' decline by a descent into a passive self-sealing immanentism, reflecting the world's transitoriness to itself in the fixed, anonymous mirror of the "event." And, having thus failed to think his way toward being's real difference from beings, Heidegger accomplishes nothing by differentiating the *Ereignis* "infinitely" from all being but to confirm—through negation—the totality in its finitude. This, though, is the fate of every "metaphysics" (at least, according to Heidegger): in that it considers the ontological difference from the vantage of the ontic, it can do no other than arrive at (in the univocal sense) a cause. Only the theological understanding of being's infinite act, neither determined in beings nor lacking anything in their absence, comprehends the difference as belonging first to being, not beings; which is to say, only theology views ontology from the place of a gift received.

None of which is to deny the brilliance of Heidegger's diagnosis of nihilism; no one else ever laid out with such compelling clarity the pathology of modernity. Nor would I even wish entirely to reject his suggestion that nihilism is a fate written in the history of metaphysics from its earliest dawn. And surely no theologian can take exception to Heidegger's desire to free philosophy from the arid, and ultimately nihilistic, reduction of "truth" to sufficient reason or positive ground. However, no less than Nietzsche, Heidegger was a creature of the history he sought to understand, to "retrieve," and in a sense to conclude: coming when he did, in the dying twilight of Western philosophy's long, sedulous suppression of its memory of Christian philosophy, he was rather like a man standing on a vast level plain as night falls, gazing into the distance, entirely unaware that, lying midway between him and the horizon to which he is turned, is an immense chasm, veiled in shadows; he was able thus to look back to the birth of philosophy, construct a genealogy of nihilism that very plausibly (if not always convincingly) tells the story of thought's decline from its first glimpse of being's mystery, and even bring nihilism to its consummation, while all the time remaining abysmally oblivious of how deep theology's "interruption" of that genealogy was. It was possible, therefore, for Heidegger to ask the question of being anew, without any fear of his philosophy gravitating back into the environs of theology (thus forfeiting its precious and hard-won autonomy), because the forgetfulness of the question's meaning had by his time become so entirely complete. Hence the philosopher whose idiom was the most robustly and indefatigably "ontological" ever was the philosopher who most signally failed to ask—or even grasp what it would mean to ask—the question of being.

III. *Ad Nihilum* and *Ex Nihilo*

If, as my argument implies, modern philosophy's forgetfulness of being is nothing other than a forgetfulness of Christian thought, and if Heidegger is the first philosopher in whose work this forgetfulness has become so forgetful even of itself as to mistake itself for the one thing it cannot possibly be—an ontology—then perhaps Heidegger's greatest significance as a philosopher lies in his value as a kind of cautionary epitome. What matters most is not what he rejects—say, an ontology of infinite actuality that he simply does not understand—but what he is moved, in consequence, to embrace. After all, the special genius—or, at any rate, special charm—of Heidegger's thought is its recovery of a genuinely pagan vision of being: the muscular naïveté of Heracleitus and Hesiod, but steeped in the lugubrious, effete, cosmopolitan fatalism of late antiquity and fringed with opulent Romantic embroideries; the languid "thinker," weary with the burden of history, discovers among Attic ruins the hidden traces of a truly tragic—which is to say, sacrificial—ontology. Within such an ontology, obviously, certain issues cannot be raised: the baffling truth that every "this" is "this" on account of that transfinite unity that shows itself in every thing, every part of every thing, and every series of things; or the clarity and intelligibility of discrete forms; or the persistence of things in themselves, in recognizable integrity, across time; or the way in which desire and knowledge each seem to precede the other; and so on. Such questions are, by definition, questions of the "transcendentals," and bespeak the Platonist's servile fascination with the "looks" of things. But being, for Heidegger, is an original alienation from form, the movement of an original "not." One might wish to ask how it is that all things are unities within change, how order and thought and beauty are one and yet distinct, how the world and perception are inseparably joined in a circle of love and knowledge, and so forth, but for Heidegger—absurdly enough—these are not properly ontological questions at all. The only answer he could provide would be that the world appears thus because it must so appear: for being to disclose itself in beings, it must be forced or "nihilated" into the limits of the ontic, its power must be wrested into the juncture as limited and transient forms of "presencing," *Welt* must be ripped from the depths of *Erde*, the thing must gather from the four regions in order to be set off against being's nothingness; the truth that a thing is, and is what it is, follows from the necessary reduction of the nothing to something, according to the determinations of an empty but irresistible "destining." One must rest content with the metaphysical dogma that what is must be, and cease to ask how it could be so. Actually, in treating questions regarding the transcendental moments in which all things subsist, and by which knowledge receives the world, as mere "ontic" questions, more or less on the same level as questions concerning causality, Heidegger makes all too obvious how very oblivious of the ontological difference he really is; but it is only by way of such an oblivion that he can make his pilgrimage back to the pre-Socratic immersion in *physis* with a pure heart. A vision of being as a closed finite order of placement and displacement, life and death, presided over by fate, is simply the aboriginal pagan vision of being as sacrifice: as order won through strife, as an economy of destruction and reviviscence, as the totality of beings sealed within itself. It is an ontology with no horizon but beings, which can do no more than abstract from nature, violence, and transience to a dark, inexhaustible reservoir of ontic possibility, and to an inescapable process of coming to pass and passing away.

In some sense, I want to endorse Vattimo's talk of the "violence of metaphysics" (though not quite in his apocalyptically dramatic terms): Western philosophy has never, insofar as it has functioned as a self-sufficient discipline distinct from theology, been able to think of the being of the world except in terms of a kind of strife between order and disorder, a certain set of tragic limits to being's expression of itself, and so an inescapable structure of deceit within the fabric of the finite. Every "metaphysical" ontology presumes that, in some way both primordial and ultimate, difference *is* violence, even (indeed, especially) when it is an ontology of the postmodern variety that thinks it has freed itself of the "totalizing" tendencies of "onto-theology." There is nothing startling or blameworthy in this, given that all nontheological philosophy is, by definition, a discourse concerning necessity—not, that is to say, *necessitas* in the theological sense, the utter fittingness with which divine freedom expresses the goodness of its nature in the generosity of its act (being itself the *actus* of all that is); but necessity in the sense of being's finitude, its absolute limitation to the condition of the world in its "worlding," its fatedness. However well a "pure" metaphysics may be able to conceive of ontological dependency, it can never, by its own lights, arrive at the thought of true contingency. Even a Heracleitean metaphysics of chance is anything but a philosophy of the freedom of either the ontic or the ontological, but is—as Nietzsche so well understood—a doctrine of the absolute necessity of the being of this world; even the most etherealizing "idealism" can at best conceive of the ultimate as the apex or "absolute" of the totality of beings, the spiritual resolution of all the ambiguities of the immanent, but can never really think in terms of true transcendence. If the ambition of metaphysics is to deduce from the features of the existence of the world the principles of the world, then it must see all the characteristic conditions of the world as manifestations of its ground. Thus metaphysics must embrace, not merely as elements but as principles of being, all the tragic and negative aspects of existence: pain, ignorance, strife, alienation, death, the recalcitrance of matter, the inevitability of corruption and dissolution, and so on. And it must respond to such sad necessities according to one or another wisdom of the immanent: joyous affirmation, tragic resignation, heroic resolve, Dionysian anarchy, the "rational love of God," the "negation of negation," or some form of nihilism, tender or demonic. Being, conceived in terms of the totality, is a pitiless economy, a structure of sacrifice in which beings suffer incompletion and destruction in order that being may "be." The world and its principles sustain one another in a dialectic of being and beings, a reciprocal movement of fulfillment and negation, the completion of finitude in the mystery of the absolute, and the display of the absolute in the violence of its alienation. The land of unlikeness is explicable only in the light of the forms; but where else can the forms shine forth? But it is just this—the tragedy of being in its dispensation—that is the wellspring of philosophy's power; for thought can move from the world to the world's principles only in such measure as what is, is what must be; only because being is constrained by necessity to these manifestations, and only because being *must* show itself in beings, is an autonomous metaphysics possible. Once necessity is presumed, every merely human philosophy is possible. Thereafter, it is not so much discernment as sensibility that draws any given thinker to the crystalline intricacies of the Platonic cosmos or to the delirious abandon of the Dionysiac; to the great epic of the Concept or to the tediously uniform debris of "difference"; to the dry clarity of a logic of substance and accidents or to the poetic irrationality of a mysticism of the "event."

If this is so, though, then perhaps one could rewrite Heidegger's genealogy of nihilism, preserving many of its features intact but casting it anew as the story of the persistent, polymorphous myth of metaphysi-

cal necessity—its fabulous birth in the age of the pre-Socratics, its protean passage through innumerable schools and systems, its defeat at the
hands of a powerful and seemingly victorious champion, and its rebirth
in a new, more terrible, more invincible form. Such would be, obviously,
a subversion of the Heideggerean tale, but not an absolute rejection; it
might, in fact, make the story more coherent. According to Heidegger,
again, being has reached its eschaton, the most extreme limit of its decline,
its fated gathering to its ultimate essence,[27] in the time of the technological *Gestell*;[28] but, having achieved this, the vantage of ultimate extremity,
thought can now look back over the history of *Seinsvergessenheit*, understand what has brought us to this moment, glimpse that flash of light that
illuminated being in thought's "first beginning," and prepare ourselves,
with a certain pious *Gelassenheit*, for another beginning. In a sense he is
right: "systematic" philosophy, as an independent enterprise of critical
reason, has reached the point of collapse; Christian thought's interruption and rescue of Western metaphysics has been followed by a revolt of
reason whose ultimate form cannot now be anything but nihilism made
transparent to itself; so Heidegger, the last metaphysician (or the first of
the last metaphysicians), who can see the shape of nihilism but who—as
that increasingly otiose thing, a philosopher—cannot step back from this
destiny, instead attempts to press through it to a resignation that somehow "anticipates" and so overcomes nihilism, and that thus returns to
metaphysics' origin. However, again because his move is the final reactive
agitation of a revolt, the thought of being available to him is still nihilistic, still a finite ontic economy, stripped even of the soothing mirages
of modern metaphysics: *Geist*, ego, positivity, etc. Ultimately, Heidegger
succeeds only at returning to an oblivion of being as profound as his own,
the pre-Socratic inability to separate wonder at being from brutish awe
before nature and fate, part and whole, becoming and totality—that is,
the pre-Platonic indistinction between being and sacrifice.

Western thought had attempted to rise from this superstitious subju-
gation to the world's mere event: Plato and Aristotle, however imperfectly,
were both shaken by that effulgent moment of wonder that can free reflection from mere animal dread; perhaps the one could not quite transcend
the dialectic of change and changeless essences, the other the dialectic of
finite form and unrealized potency, nor either the still "sacrificial" econ-

---

27. *H* 327.

28. See Heidegger, "Die Kehre," in Heidegger, *Die Technik und die Kehre* (Pfullingen:
Neske, 1962).

omy of finitude, but both stood within an opening in Western thought that theology could transform into a genuine openness before the transcendent God. Still, Heidegger may be somewhat correct in seeing, even in this openness, the inauguration of Western reason's long journey toward technological mastery as the highest ideal, toward instrumental control as the governing model of all truth, toward—in short—nihilism. Perhaps there truly was, precisely in the birth of philosophy as a self-conscious enterprise of rising above the ephemerality of the phenomena to take hold of their immutable premises, a turning away from the light toward the things it illuminated, a forgetfulness of being within philosophy's very wakefulness to being. And perhaps in this fateful moment of inattention to the mystery of being's event, the relentless search for being's positive foundations commenced, and then proceeded along a path that, in the end, would arrive at the ruin of philosophic faith. All of this may be— indeed, in some obvious sense, is—quite true. But the Platonic *erōs* for the beautiful, good, and true was also a longing for something more than mere "grounds"; it was a desire for being's fullness, though one not yet able to understand being as gift. Other ancient schools of thought were generally less precocious in their advances toward Christian theology. Stoicism, for instance, however magnificent, humane, and sophisticated it was in its most developed forms, was still somewhat retrograde in this regard, and was bound to a vision of the cosmos as a fated economy of placement and displacement, and to a more transparently sacrificial cosmic mythology of eternally repeated *ekpyrōseis* (the universe as an eternal sacrificial pyre); but Stoicism too was profoundly marked by philosophical wonder before the goodness and loveliness of cosmic and divine order. The syncretism of late antiquity may often have produced monstrosities of occult "wisdom" and grotesque aberrations of philosophy and religion alike, but in the case of the Platonic tradition it also made it possible for a philosopher like Plotinus to reflect upon the generosity of the good and the convertibility of the good and being, and thus press against the boundaries of the totality. But it was only when Christian thought arrived, and with it the doctrine of creation, that the totality was broken open and, for the first time ever, philosophy was granted a glimpse of being's splendid strangeness within its very immediacy and gratuity.

With this "Christian interruption" of metaphysics, every principle of necessity was made subordinate to the higher principle of grace. Christian thought, then, in its long history of metaphysical speculation, far from constituting just another episode in the genealogy of nihilism, was in fact so profound a disruption of many of the most basic premises of philosophy, and so audacious a rescue of many of philosophy's truths from the impotent embrace of mere metaphysical ambition, that it is doubtful yet that philosophy can grasp what has happened to it, or why now it cannot be anything but an ever more indignant and self-tormenting flight from that interruption. The language of creation—however much it may be parodied as a language regarding efficient causality and metaphysical "founding"—actually introduced into Western thought the radically new idea that an infinite freedom is the "principle" of the world's being and so for the first time opened up the possibility of a genuine reflection upon the difference between being and beings. And the Christian understanding of God as Trinity, without need of the world even for his determination as difference, relatedness, or manifestation, for the first time confronted Western thought with a genuine discourse of transcendence, of an ontological truth whose "identity" is not completed by any ontic order. The event of being is, for beings, a pure gift, into whose mysteries no *scala naturae* by itself can lead us. And if the world is not a manifestation of necessity, but of gratuity—even if it must *necessarily* reflect in its intrinsic orderliness and concinnity the goodness of its source—then philosophy may be able to grasp many things, but by its own power it can never attain to the source or end of things. If being is not bound to the dimensions prescribed for it by fate or the need for self-determination or the contumacy of a material substrate, then the misconstrual of the contingent for the necessary constitutes philosophy's original error.

It is for this reason also that theology's interruption of the "history of nihilism" was philosophy's redemption, immeasurably deepening its openness to being and increasing the intensity of its highest *erōs*. Within Christianity's narrative, the world acquired a new glory; for all that it had been robbed of the imposing dignity of metaphysical necessity, it had been imbued with the still more extraordinary dignity of divine pleasure; the world had become an instance of what could only be called beauty— beauty of a kind more absolute and irreducible than any known to pagan Greek culture. A God whose very being is love, delight in the glory of his infinite Image, seen in the boundlessly lovely light of his Spirit, and whose works are then unnecessary but perfectly expressive signs of this delight, fashioned for his pleasure and for the gracious sharing of his joy with creatures for whom he had no need, is a God of beauty in the fullest imaginable sense. In such a God, beauty and the infinite entirely coincide; the very life of God is one of, so to speak, infinite form; and when he creates, the difference between worldly beauty and the divine beauty it reflects subsists not in a dialectic between multiplicity and unity, composition and simplicity, shape and indeterminacy, but in the analogy between the determinate particularities of the world and that always greater, supereminent determinacy in which they participate. Thus it is that theology alone preserves and clarifies all of philosophy's most enchanting prospects upon being: precisely by detaching them from the mythology of "grounds," and by resituating them within the space of this peaceful analogical interval between divine and worldly being, within which space the sorrows of necessity enjoy no welcome. Thus, for Christian thought, knowledge of the world is something to be achieved not just through a reconstruction of its "sufficient reason," but through an obedience to glory, an orientation of the will toward the light of being and its gratuity; and so the most fully "adequate" discourse of truth is worship, prayer, and rejoicing. Phrased otherwise, the truth of being is "poetic" before it is "rational" (indeed, it is rational precisely because of its supreme poetic coherence and richness of detail), and thus cannot be known truly if this order is reversed. Beauty is the beginning and end of all true knowledge: really to know, one must first love, and having known, one must finally delight; only this "corresponds" to the Trinitarian love and delight that creates. The truth of being is the whole of being, in its event, groundless, and so, in its every detail, revelatory of the light that grants it. In a strangely impoverished and negative way, Heidegger—the apostate from theology—almost understood this, but ultimately proved to be only a "metaphysician" after all. Then again, Heidegger, like Nietzsche, was unable to see that his own revolt against metaphysics was itself really nothing but a necessary moment in metaphysics' recovery of itself from theology. Philosophy could not, after all, accept the gift Christian thought extended to it and remain what it had been—a science of mastery, an interrogation of the "ground"—but neither could it ignore Christianity's transformation of its native terms: once the splendor of truth had been assumed into the Christian love of beauty, its *philokalia*, once the light of the world had been taken into the discourse of ontological analogy and divine transcendence, and once the difference between being and beings had entered thought and disrupted every attempt to "deduce" from the world its metaphysical identity, philosophy could not simply reassert itself as an independent project, but had to discover a new foundation. Philosophy, like a king in exile, would have to suffer the most extreme divestment and privation before it could reclaim its lost privileges. This is the true sense in which theology is part of the history of nihilism: it leaves nothing good behind in the philosopher's hands; it plunders all of philosophy's most powerful interpretive instruments for its own uses (despoiling the Egyptians, to use the classic metaphor), and so makes it necessary, in the aftermath of theology's cultural influence, that philosophy advance itself ever more openly as a struggle against the light, an ever more vehement refusal of the generosity of the given.[29] If nihilism is indeed the hidden core or secret vocation of metaphysics, in the post-Christian age nothing but that core, that vocation, remains: and so it must become ever less hidden, ever less secret.

Christian tradition, in making the eternal beauty of ancient philosophical longing so much more prodigal in its availability, and in urging philosophical *erōs* toward a more transcendent end, deprived the world of any grounds within itself and so further gilded the world's glory with an additional aura of gratuity and fortuity; the shining forth, the *phainein*, of the phenomena now belonged to another story, and so no longer provided irrefragable evidence of reason's ability to gain possession of the world's principles. To free itself from theology, then, philosophy had to discover a new order of evidences, one not "compromised" by collaboration with Christianity's complex discourse of divine transcendence. This could be accomplished only by way of an initial refusal of the world's alluring and terrifying immediacy; through a simple but peremptory act of rejection, the order of truth could be inverted, moving truth from the world in its appearing to the subject in its perceiving. Thus reason's "freedom" would be secured anew. At the same time, however, such a rejection could not but unveil, with unceremonious suddenness, the "nihilistic" terminus that Nietzsche and Heidegger saw as being inaugurated in the eidetic science of Platonism. Descartes phrases the matter with exquisite precision: "Now will I close my eyes, I will stop up my ears, I will avert my senses from their objects, I will even erase from my consciousness all images of things corporeal; or, at least . . . I will consider them to be empty and false."[30] If this austerely principled act of self-abnegation (or self-mutilation) was not

29. This is not to deny that Christian theology had a part to play in the transition from the implicit nihilism of antiquity to the explicit nihilism of modernity: late medieval voluntarism, the rise of nominalism, a late scholastic tendency to insulate the spheres of theology and philosophy from one another; the occasional triumph in Catholic and Protestant discourse alike of a concern for God's sovereignty over a concern for God's goodness; flirtations with occasionalist epistemology and, simultaneously, univocal ontology; the ever more pronounced tendency to understand divine freedom as pure, unconstrained *arbitrium* (which an earlier theology would correctly have seen as a limitation on the liberty of God's *voluntas*), and the consequent tendency to understand human freedom as pure spontaneity of will and unpremised choice; and so on. But this is only to say that secularization begins in theology's apostasy from itself, and that Heidegger—the failed theologian—is the perfect emblematic figure of Western philosophy in its sad senescence.
30. Descartes, *Meditations* 3.

modernity's founding gesture, it was at any rate the perfect crystallization of its untender logic. Thereafter, the verity of the world was something to be found only within the citadel of subjective certitude, through an act of will. Philosophy's transcendental turn made instrumental reason its own foundation; the truth of the world would no longer be certified by the *phainein* that gives things to thought, but only by the adjudications of the hidden artificer of rational order, the ego. Understanding, indiscerptible from the power of the will to establish and negate, could not now be understanding of a prior givenness, but only a reduction of the exterior to something conformable to and manipulable by reason. Philosophy may begin in wonder, the *thaumazein* of a gaze enraptured by the radiance of the world, striving to ascend to the source of that radiance, but it ends, it would seem, in an anxious retreat from world to self, from wonder to suspicion, from light to will. It was Christianity's rescue of the world's light from the myth of necessity that forced philosophy to take the transcendental turn; and Christianity's story of transcendent freedom made possible its own distorted reflection in a discourse of truth premised upon the subject's rational reconstruction of experience from its own freedom of will; but only a conscious project of immanent reason, not dependent on a transcendent source of truth, could decisively liberate philosophy from theology's narrative of being as gift. The phenomena had to be conformed to our gaze, rather than the reverse; indeed, in no genuine sense could they be taken as "phenomena" at all—the shining forth of being in beings, inviting vision to a movement beyond itself. Wakefulness to transcendence had to be replaced by the "clear-eyed" disenchantment of a controlling scrutiny. And when the wakened gaze was forsaken for a gaze that establishes its own truthfulness, thought could possess no world that was not its own artifact; and that world could be no more than the passive and indifferent realm of thought's investigations and scientific adventures.[31] Thereafter the phenomena, when again admitted into philosophy's calculations, could be no more than mensurable objects of curiosity or use. Natural light—impotent to produce propositions or "clear and distinct ideas," able only to offer the world to recognition or illuminate it as mystery—could

---

31. This is not, let me be clear, a kind of primitivist protest against science and technology, with all their plenteous goods and plenteous ills (though I am quite sympathetic to such protests and read William Morris insatiably). My concern is the "ideology of knowledge" or "mythology of understanding," so to speak, and the question of whether some form of nominalist disenchantment, combined with some form of transcendental epistemology, was necessary for the advance of the sciences (which I do not believe) is not one I mean here to address.

prove nothing, but was now seen as itself needing transcendental probation and authentication.

Descartes, admittedly, did not intend to confine thought within an
inviolable interiority; indeed, he found the surest confirmation of the
trustworthiness of his perceptions in the presence within his mind of
the thought of the infinite, which must, he claimed, have been placed in
him by God, inasmuch as it cannot in any way be abstracted from finite
experience. But it is just this divorce between empirical knowledge and
the concept of the infinite, as Descartes understood them, that makes it
obvious that, from the transcendental vantage, immanent and transcendent truth are dialectically rather than analogically related; the former
concerns a world of substances that exhaust their meaning in their very
finitude, while the latter can appear among these substances only in the
form of a paradox—a "knowledge" whose only evidence and condition
is itself. God's infinity, thus conceived, is not truly the infinite; it is not
qualitatively other than every finite thing precisely by being "not other,"
but instead the possibility and "place" of all things, the unity and fullness
of being in which all beings live and move and are; rather, it is merely the
negation of finitude, the contrary of limit, found nowhere among my finite cognitions. This "modern" infinite is not only beyond finite vision; it
is without any analogous mediation—any *via eminentiae*—within the visible. A world certified by my founding gaze, and then secondarily by God
(the postulated *causa efficiens et causa sui*), can admit the infinite into its
calculus only as the indivisible naught that embraces every finite quantity,
the "not-this" that secures every "this" in the poverty of its particularity.
However, the power of such an "infinite" to disrupt the ordered internal
universe of the ego, as Descartes thought it must, is an illusion. The distinction between God's featureless, superempirical infinity and the palpable limits of the perceiving ego functioned for Descartes as proof that the
"I" does not constitute its experience in any original way, but rather is itself
constituted by the creative will of an invisible God; but it required only the
next logical step of distinguishing the empirical ego from the transcendental ego to collapse the distinction between the infinite and subjectivity
altogether. This was Kant's greatest triumph. The transcendental project
in its inchoate, Cartesian, insufficiently "critical" form could escape the
circularity of knowledge—the ceaseless oscillation of epistemic priority
between understanding and experience, between subject and object—only
by positing, beyond empirical ego and empirical data alike, a transcendent
cause. But Kant clearly knew that this is simply to ground the uncerti-
fiable in the unascertainable. Moreover, he certainly felt no impulse to

retreat to an alternative that was anything like the premodern language of illumination, which would resolve the question of the correspondence between perception and the perceived by ascribing that correspondence to the supereminent unity in which the poles of experience—phenomena and gaze—participate. Now that every standard of validity had been definitively situated within the knowing subject, within the self's assurance of itself, such a "metaphysics" was a critical impossibility, as it could never be established by the autonomous agency of reason; indeed, it could be seriously entertained as a satisfactory answer only by a mind resigned to a certain degree of passivity, a trust in a transcendent source of truth that is, by definition, elusive of the scrutiny of the independent ego. And so Kant was more or less compelled to ground the circle of knowledge in a transcendental capacity behind empirical subjectivity, the "transcendental unity of apperception" that accompanies all the representations available to the empirical ego; this was, manifestly, a metaphysical conjecture, but it was one to which the limits of modernity's conjectural range permitted no alternative. Not, that is, that an alternative would have been desirable: Kant thus gained for subjectivity not only a mastery over the realm of the "theoretical," but a "supersensible freedom" so profound that even the moral law—once the exclusive preserve of God, the gods, the good beyond being—could be regarded as its achievement. Bliss was it in that dawn to be alive, no doubt, when the Christian universe was inverted and philosophy knew the exhilaration of breaking free from dependency upon God—either the Christian God or his shadowy Cartesian surrogate—to claim for itself an autonomy greater than any it had ever yet possessed.

And yet, when the first frisson of excitement subsided, it became obvious—to some, at least—that it was an autonomy curiously devoid of freedom. There was undeniably a kind of Promethean rebellion in philosophy's turn to the transcendental ego, but also a fate not unlike that of Prometheus bound to his pillar in the Caucasus. And while Hegel might seem an implausible Heracles, it was he more than anyone else (more even than Fichte) who saw that a liberty that consisted in resting secure in the impregnable citadel of the self, peering out through its machicolations at a landscape purged of all metaphysical mystery, never hoping to take possession of the lands beyond its walls, was scarcely distinguishable from incarceration. He understood that philosophy would always be in retreat if it could not actually overcome theology's metaphysical tradition, provide an account of theology that could cogently portray the Christian story as an unrefined foreshadowing of a story that only philosophy would be able to tell fully, and so assume theology into itself; thus it was that he went

31

about recovering the largely forgotten rationality of classical Trinitarian doctrine (modern theology's most irksome irony), so that he could rethink it, subvert it, and bring its disruptive force back under the governance of philosophical reflection. Hegel was willing to surrender some real measure of the isolated ego's independence because he was engaged in the near impossible task of bringing under speculative control the radical contingency that Christian theology had introduced into the "absolute," and—more—in an attempt to overcome a final irreducible difference that Christian thought had imagined within God; by "historicizing" Spirit, Hegel sought at once to "spiritualize" history and to "idealize" the Trinity, making God and history a mutually sustaining process. What Hegel could not tolerate was the notion either of a God who possesses in himself difference, determinacy, plenitude, and perfection independent of any world, or of a world thus left devoid of meaning in the ultimate speculative sense of "necessity" and so reduced to the status of something needless, something thoroughly aesthetic, not accomplishing—but merely expressing—a love God enjoys in utter self-sufficiency. Divine infinity, conceived as Trinitarian, always infinitely "determined" toward another, does not require time's tragic probations and determining negations; all created being is an unnecessary, *excessive* display of God's glory, and thus the world of things is set free in its "aimless" particularity. The Christian infinite is its own "exteriority," without need of another, negative exteriority to bring it to fruition. And without the majestic mythology of necessity governing the realm of the absolute, philosophy enjoys no sure authority over the contingent.

Nor is this any less intolerable a state of affairs for "postmetaphysical" forms of philosophy than it is for Hegel. The most radically anti-idealist thinkers, from Nietzsche to Derrida, tend to possess an inflexible conviction that being is finite; that what is must be; that death is the possibility of life, and absence is the possibility of presence; and that the world's most terrible limits are being's indispensable conditions. Heidegger, especially, cannot do without a firm faith in the necessity of being's event, its necessary limitation within the dispensations of its epochal sending, its finitude. Being *must* be thus: manifestation as obscuration, truth as duplicity, mission as "errance." Here the ambiguous Platonic wakefulness to wonder is submerged again in brute passivity, the full Christian awakening is entirely purged from memory, and philosophy becomes a crepuscular and elegiac meditation upon its own death. And Heidegger's postmodern epigones are ontological fatalists of the purest water. For all of them, the event of world and thought can be understood only as an order of sacrifice, an original economy sustaining order over against (but in dependency on) chaos, absence, the invisible excess, the "unpresentable"—but it must not be conceived as gift, as the donation of form from an always more eminent splendor that *limits itself*, not out of necessity, but according to the kenotic and ecstatic love of the *summum bonum*. Thus there can be no names for what exceeds the representable order; it is the dissimulation of this excess that gives us the illusory world of presence; and this unnamable sublimity, far from having any analogy among the phantasms that issue from it, is the terrible night into which all things are offered up by time as a perfect offering, and in which all light has always been and always will be extinguished.

In any event, this is merely the barest sketch of a revised genealogy of nihilism, which could take a far fuller and more varied form. Here it is best simply to remark that, in the case of Heidegger, there is a peculiar poignancy in the impossibility of his position: he is animated by a theological hunger, in the service of which he pursues an entirely unsustainable, antitheological logic of immanence—which makes him, really, a very late Romantic. It makes perfect sense that his thought should then—as his late essays amply attest—dissolve into a kind of Arcadian nostalgia, an almost Rousseauian yearning for the pure word that can speak the event in its immediacy, an innocent and pristine tongue, uncorrupted by duplicity or dead metaphor (a language to which, with an aching proximity, Greek and German alone are nearly transparent). The perpetual flight from metaphysical "attribution" to poetic "naming" is an interminable descent to the poverty of "simple saying."[32] Interminable because Heidegger's own ontology—which is clearly a univocal ontology—must frustrate such a yearning utterly: the *Ereignis* is always the same event, invariable and without metaphysical height or depth, and so all words equally manifest and dissemble it: they say and "unsay" the same thing. In short, nothing is said, of being or of God. At most, one can sit on the bank of the Ister, alongside the shade of Hölderlin, attempting to speak the world's worlding by naming beings in their momentariness: "river" . . . "sky" . . . "grass" . . . "more river." This is not, I make bold to assert, profound. If truth is to be understood as simply a more lyric species of tautology, what is this but the nihilism of modernity in its all but purest form? And would it not be wise then at least to *seek* another kind of speaking, one that is neither simple metaphysical attribution nor "simple saying," but a language that can name the difference between being and beings in a movement of simultaneous disjunction and union, of names at once descending and ascending: the language, that is, of analogy?

32. W 364/P 276.

IV. The *Oculus Simplex* and the *Analogia Entis*

I do not believe in Heidegger's famous *Kehre*: there may be the appearance of a more "objective" tone in his later writing, but Heidegger himself (contrary to his assertions) remained to the last a prisoner of the transcendental perspective, refusing—not from critical scruple, really, but from a sober calculation regarding over what territory thought could now plausibly assert its sovereignty—to look beyond his gaze, toward his vision's natural horizon or toward the more original (or more transcendent) distance that makes that horizon possible. The "turn" of his idiom from "authenticity" and "resolve" to talk of "destinal" historical epochs probably had more to do with his political degeneracy than anything else: the later language has an exculpatory impersonality about it that might provide a decrepit and impenitent Nazi, hiding in the *Schwarzwald*, some small shelter. Hence, it is perfectly legitimate for us to return to his earlier point of departure and ask whether phenomenological rigor really ever required of him that he abandon a "transcendent" ontology, or that he remain fixed in the difference between existents and nothingness, or even that he step away from this opposition to circle back to it from the vantage of the "event."

Why, for instance, should the "correct" *Stimmung* prompting our investigations, and opening them to being, be that of anxiety, rather than of wonder, or even *erōs?* Anxiety enjoys no better claim to ontological probity, simply because of the vacuity with which it regards particular objects, than do moods that encompass and yet somehow exceed these objects, moods that perhaps "rise" toward a fullness that can account both for the splendid "thereness" of particular things and also for the hunger that they animate in us for their source. Why should the inward retreat of anxiety command our assent more forcefully than the outward abandon of desire? It may be that love's appetite, excited by the beauty, sublimity, or simple existence of things, is uniquely able to press on to their wellspring, the supereminent plenitude of the transcendentals, where unity, beauty, goodness, truth, knowledge, and desire are convertible with one another. And it may also be that what discloses itself within this mood is being's inexhaustible self-outpouring in beings, an infinite act at once gathering all things together in transcendent peace and prismating its own infinite determinacy in the endless diversity, here below, of finite combinations of its transcendental moments. What one sees, and the "more" that one sees within what one sees, is always determined by prior intentions (both simple eidetic intentions and hermeneutically richer linguistic and cultural prejudices), and no mood escapes this necessity. It is simply false, therefore, that the nothingness disclosed by dread is less "metaphysical" or "onto-theological," or more immediately available to reflection, than the no-thing-ness of being—the transcendent fullness of determinacy disclosed by love. The "ontologically erotic" gaze that loves and desires being is more attentive to what constitutes or "en-acts" the seen than is an anxious awareness of the nothingness that shyly hides itself behind the seen; love sees each thing's fortuity, its mystery, its constancy within a "transfinite" unity, its immediate particularity, its radiant inherence within its own "essence," its intelligibility, and its way of holding together in itself the diversity of its transcendental aspects as a realized unity amid, and in unity with, multiplicity and change. The gaze of love seeks the being of things in the abiding source in which they participate; it is a way of seeing that is acquainted with moments of enchantment, which awaken it, however briefly, to a recognition of the persistence of being's peaceful and sustaining light (utterly unlike either the violence of time and nature or the stillness of an ultimate ground) and of this light's "gratuitous necessity"; and these moments, however fleeting or imperfect, compel thought to risk a conjecture toward the infinite.

This gaze of love, that is to say, sees being as an infinite font of manifestation, showing itself in the existence and essences of things, kenotically allowing (and so without alienation from its own diffusive goodness) the arrival in itself of what is, in itself, nothing: the pure ontic ecstasy of contingent existence. It is a gaze that necessarily strives to pass beyond the ontic play of negativity and positivity, and so sees—or expects to see— how ontic negation must be inverted, so as to reveal that it is the effect of a prior plenitude. Heidegger calls being "eschatological," but does so in a vein of etiolated Hegelianism, which leaves the word's meaning suspended between the historical-dialectical and the existential. There is, however, a genuinely ontological sense in which being can be called eschatological: for finite beings, every instant is eschaton, each moment is an arrival from nothing (not from the concealed, or the "ultimate ground," but from nothing at all) into the infinite, a birth into its uttermost end; each moment is a call and a judgment, issued across the ontically impossible distance between nonexistence and existence (not just between possibility and actuality), by which beings receive a vocation and a verdict at once, and so are "adjudged" with an ontological justice, which brings them to their ultimate encounter with being. For finite beings, forever becoming, being is absolute futurity. Finite being is an *erōs* in its very essence, an ecstasy out of itself and toward an infinity of beauty known both as concrete immediacy and as transcendent mystery.

It may seem that I am doing nothing here, myself, but recommending a mystifying relapse into a second philosophical naïveté, simply to cast off the burden of sober critical reason; I would say, however, that what I want to urge is a theological reappropriation of what might be called the "covenant of light"—that is, a trust in the immediacy of the given, a view of knowledge as an effect of the *erōs* stirred by the gift of the world's truth—and so an emancipation of theology from any superstitious credulity before the arid dogmatisms of (modern or postmodern) transcendental logic. I can imagine no objection to Heidegger's attempt to arrive at ontology by way of phenomenology (in a sense, this is simply the path blazed by Platonism), but what I would like to advocate is a phenomenology liberated from transcendental stricture: one can begin from the phenomenological presuppositions that being is what shows itself, and that the event of the phenomenon and the event of perception are inseparable, and still say that only a transcendental prejudice would dictate in advance that, in the event of manifestation and in the indiscerptibility of phenomenon and perception, one may not and cannot see a light exceeding them as an ever more eminent phenomenality: not merely an object's hidden sides, or the interplication of the visible and the invisible in one another, but the descending incandescence of the infinite simplicity that grants world and knower one to the other. Not that one can merely deduce Christian metaphysics from empirical perception, obviously; but such a metaphysics is certainly not a fabulous founding of the visible in the invisible, or of the immanent in a merely posited transcendence. It is, rather, a way of seeing that refuses to see more or less than what is given (including givenness itself). Even were it not my contention (which, quaintly enough, it is) that this "metaphysics" is intrinsic to Christianity, and that without it neither theology nor biblical hermeneutics can be fully prosecuted, still I would say that the Christian philosopher should proceed in obedience to such a "transcending" phenomenology: an initial trust in being's goodness and veracity, a surrender of self to the testimony of creation (embraced, naturally, within and consummated by an essential faith in God revealed in Christ). The experience of the beautiful, for instance, is a sudden intimation of the fortuity of necessity, and of the contingency of a thing's integrity; it is an awe awakening one to the difference of being from beings, and of "existence" from "essence," allowing one to see within the "nonnecessary" concord of a phenomenon and its event a fittingness that is also, manifestly, grace. In this moment of agitation, one discovers a surfeit of splendor that commands one's wonder. One then sees that though the "what it is" of a thing is never commensurate to the surprising truth "that it is," it is always good that this is *this*, and that this *is* (however sin and death distort an object and our perception of it). This mysterious coherence of the wholly fitting and utterly gratuitous then urges reflection toward the proportion of their harmony, which is to say toward the infinity where "essence" and "existence" coincide as the ontological peace of both a primordial belonging-together and an original gift; neither of these (neither the belonging-together nor the gift) is nameless, but neither can be grasped according to the discrete properties of finite reality.

It has become common in some quarters to call the tradition of Christian metaphysics that evolved from the time of the New Testament through the patristic and medieval periods the *analogia entis*, and this term I shall adopt. This tradition succeeded in understanding (in ever greater depth) the liaison between the biblical doctrine of creation and the metaphysics of participation that is announced obscurely by the New Testament, and in integrating it into Trinitarian dogma, and thus made it possible for the first time in Western thought to contemplate both the utter difference of being from beings and the nature of true transcendence. The general preference for the term *analogia entis* was sealed in the last century by the remarkable Erich Przywara, and by his compelling interpretation of patristic and medieval metaphysics as a systematic ontology.[33] His arguments defy any easy summary, and the various nuances that he and other authors have given the phrase "analogy of being" are far too complex and subtle to treat of here; but I can say that, at the most fundamental level, the term *analogia entis* means only that being can be neither univocal between God and creatures (which would reduce God to a being among beings, subject to a higher category) nor equivocal (which would, curiously enough, have precisely the same result), and so the only coherent understanding of the relation of created being to uncreated must be analogical. *In him* we live and move and have our being. Every creature exists in a state of tension (as Przywara likes to put it) between essence and existence, in a condition of absolute becoming, oscillating between what it is and that it is, striving toward its essence and existence alike, receiving both from the movement of God's grace while possessing nothing in itself, totally and dynamically dependent, sharing in the fullness of being that God enjoys in infinite simplicity, and so infinitely other than the source

33. See Erich Przywara, *Analogia Entis: Metaphysik; Ur-Struktur und All-Rhythmus* (Einsiedeln: Johannes-Verlag, 1962). It is a term, admittedly, that some theologians have rejected—in the most notorious case, that of Karl Barth, with a vehemence bordering on the silly. But Barth's misunderstanding of the term, and of Przywara's project, and of the theological consequences of rejecting it, renders his complaints largely vacuous.

of its being. Thus the analogy of being does not analogize God and creatures under the more general category of being, but is the analogization
of being in the difference between God and creatures; for this reason, it is
quite incompatible with any naïve "natural theology": if being is univocal,
then a direct analogy from essences to "God" (as the supreme substance)
is possible, but if the primary analogy is that of being itself, then an infinite analogical interval has been introduced between God and creatures,
precisely because God is truly declared in the "essence" and "existence" of
all things. Conversely, the rejection of analogy, far from preserving God's
transcendence, can actually only objectify God idolatrously as an "over-
against": such a duality inevitably makes "God" and "creation" balancing
terms in a dialectical opposition, thus subordinating God to being after all.

In the *analogia entis*, however, the term above all terms is "God," the
full act of being, in whom all determinacy participates, but himself beyond
all finite determination, negation, or dialectic: not one of two poles, not
the infinite "naught" against which all things are set off (which would still
be a "finite infinite"). And it is not possible to regard this transcendent
act as a primordial convertibility of being and nothingness, requiring its
tragic solution in the finite—by way of Hegel's "becoming," or Heidegger's
"temporalization," or what have you—as such a convertibility would already comprise an ontic opposition, a finite indetermination subordinate
to its own limits, and so would still be in need of an ontological explanation, some account of the prior act of simplicity in which its unresolved
and essential contradiction would have to participate in order to constitute
a unity (in order, that is, to be). Being can neither be reduced to beings
nor negated by them; it is peacefully expressed and peacefully withheld in
its prismation in the intricate interweaving of the transcendentals. Even
the transcendental moments of "this" and "not this" have their source in
God's triune simplicity, his coincidence within himself of determinacy (as
Trinity) and "no-thing-ness" (as "the all"—Sirach 43:27—in whom we live,
move, and are). The analogy thus permits the very difference of creatures
from God, their integrity as what they are, and their ontological "freedom"
to be understood as manifestations of how the Trinitarian God is one God.
The analogy allows one to see being as at once simplicity and yet always
already difference, not as a result of alienation or diremption, but because
the fullness of being is God's one movement of being, knowing, and loving
his own essence; to be is to be manifest; to know and love, to be known
and loved—all of this is the one act, wherein no "essence" is unexpressed,
and no contradiction awaits resolution. The analogy thus stands outside
the twin poles of the metaphysics of the necessary: negation and identity.

After all, purely dialectical and purely "identist" systems are ultimately the same; both confine God and world within an economy of the absolute, sharing a reciprocal identity. If God is thought either as total substance or as total absence, foundation or negation, "ground of Being" or static "Wholly Other," God is available to thought merely as the world's highest principle rather than as its transcendent source and end.

For us, the analogy of being—the actual movement of our being's likeness to God within an always greater unlikeness—is the event of an endless becoming; and this means that, for Christians, becoming is not to be understood according to the tragic wisdom of any metaphysical epoch ("Platonism's" melancholy distaste for time, change, distance, despite their necessity, or Hegel's dialectic, or Heidegger's resolve, or any other "*Stimmung*" that can grasp becoming only "backward" from death). Our being and our essence alike perpetually exceed the moment of our existence, lying always before us as gratuity and futurity, mediated to us only in the *erōs* and fear of our life *in fieri*. Finite existence, far from being the dialectical labor of an original contradiction or an oblivion of the hyperouranian forms, is a pure gift, grounded in no original substance, rising from nothingness into God's infinity, absolute fragility and fortuity, impossible in itself and so actual beyond itself. Becoming is a pure ecstasy *ex nihilo*, a constant and living tension between what a thing is and what it is not, between its past and its future, between what is interior to it and what is exterior, and so on. It is nothing but the rapture of its own arrival, and while its contours are always necessarily defined by the shadows of what no longer is and what is not yet, it is only because of sin that these are sources of sadness or anxiety (mourning for the lost, lust for the unattained) rather than faith, hope, and love ("remembrance" of our true end, *erōs* for God's infinity, the love of all things in God). Creation is, in every moment, a liberation that sets us free either to love all things in the love of God or to turn toward things and away from God (the true *Seinsvergessenheit*),[34] and is, consequently, always a moment of judgment. The event of our being is already emancipation from metaphysical necessity; it is the ontic ecstasy of the *ex nihilo*, the primordial impulse of prayer and worship, an awakening, a displacement of nothingness by openness, a reflex of light; and our response to this original ontological vocation can be, in any moment, obedience or rebellion (in which we experience God's gift as either election or dereliction). In this sense, becoming must be a "crisis" for sinful creatures, but the original and ultimate truth of becoming is peace,

---

34. See Bonaventure, *Itinerarium mentis in Deum* 5.3–4.

39

birth, life. One is always called to "become what you are," to be born into one's end; as Maximus the Confessor says, our end is our beginning, our *logoi* are found in God's Logos, we come to be in God by participation.[35] That which is most interior to us, "essence," is the most exterior: we become what we are by entering ever more into the infinitely accomplished "exteriority" of God, the plenitude of his triune act of love and knowledge, appropriating what is "ours" only through an original surrender of every ground. Our very nature and essence exceed our grasp, and our hunger for the Good above us is our feasting upon being, our ontological delight (rather than a morbid embrace of our own substance or foundation). This primordial ecstasy never need fold back upon itself in a dialectical recovery of "self" from "other" or of *anamnēsis* from the phenomena; our perpetual oscillation between actuality and possibility, our striving toward our "essence," is how we partake of God's love and knowledge of us in his Logos. This alone is our being, and is all of our being; for we belong to him, not to ourselves.

It is the analogy of being between God and creatures that alone liberates beings from the tragedy of identity, which is at the heart of any metaphysics or theology (whether dialectical and dualist or idealist and monist) that fails to think being analogically. As the analogy is situated not between discrete substances sheltered under the canopy of being—between "my" essence, to which existence is superadded, and God's essence, to which existence attaches simply as a necessary attribute—but between the entire act of my being and the transcendent act of being in which it participates, the event of my existence, in its totality, is shown to be good and true and beautiful in its very particularity. Being may be understood as at once the truth of essence (the transcendental determinations that are imparted and mediated to us throughout time in the event of our existence, as continuously we become what we are) and of existence (the gratuitous event of our participation in the triune dynamism of God's life as we are called, every moment, into unmerited being). In God, being is one perfect act of self-manifesting love, while in us it is always a dynamic synthesis of the incommensurable "what" and "that" of our being. This is the difference that both divides and unites, the distinction between infinite and finite that allows finite being to subsist in infinite being's single act. Our likeness to God, which is our end and so calls us into being, is embraced in an ever greater unlikeness—and this is the difference that truly lets us *be*. When the difference between being and beings is truly forgotten, and with it the

---

35. Maximus, *Ambigua* 7. See especially Patrologia Graeca 91:1077C–1080C.

analogy between being and beings, it is this interval that is forgotten: then we think of the most eminent truth of our being not as transcendent mystery, but as the ground of the I, and from this fatal inversion spring all the grandeur, melancholy, and cruel futility of metaphysics in its "nihilistic vocation." When metaphysics has its premise in an analogy of identity, or in a continuity of identity between what one is and the eternal "I am," "I know," "I see," or "I will," it does not matter whether one's grammar is monist or dualist; all reality subsists in the interval between two vanishing points: the supreme principle or substance and the bare, featureless, changeless essence of "my" most proper "self." This is even true of the most spiritually elevated achievement of Western metaphysics, Neoplatonism, when left unredeemed by the doctrine of creation and by, in consequence, the *analogia entis*. For if the truth of things is their pristine likeness in substance (in positive ground) to the ultimate ground, then all difference is not only accidental but also false (though perhaps probatively false): to arrive at truth, one must suffer the annihilation of particularity, a pitiless reduction of the exterior to an absolute interior without any outward contour; the calculus of identity is absolute zero, destitute of form. The reduction of truth to identity (no less than its currently more fashionable reduction to absolute alterity) is nihilism from the first: the most high is the utterly desolate, truth is nothingness. And so, once again sounding the Nietzschean alarm, one can say that the abolition of truth as a value was always already secretly inaugurated in the search for truth as positive ground. The elations of Neoplatonism are so very instructive here because they are still not quite capable of freeing themselves from the pathos of every epoch of Western philosophy: the interval discriminating the most high from the here below is the tragic moment of exteriority, alienation, probation, which is nonetheless the necessary distance of reflection, *theōria*, *anamnēsis*, and return. But the movement from there to here is one of division, reduction, contamination, and oblivion, and the converse movement, from here to there, is a repetition (though inverted) of this same impoverishment: reduction, decortication of the world, oblivion of the flesh, a flight of the alone to the alone. Truth's dynamism is destruction, a laying waste of all of finite being's ornate intricacies, erasing the world from the space between the vanishing point of the One and the vanishing point of the *nous* in their barren correspondence. This is why the potentially tragic "dualism" haunting Platonism could give rise so naturally to the potentially tragic "monism" of Plotinus—for dialectic and identism are finally the same. Which is also why, incidentally, the postmodern dread of eternity and recognition in no way escapes the melancholy of "Platonism's" dread of "dissemination":

these are merely the two extremes of one ontological vision, fixed in the same interminable dialectic of Same and Other.

The doctrine of creation, however, escapes this dialectic altogether: it asserts that all things live, move, and are in God not because they add to God, or in any way determine his essence, but as gracious manifestations of his fullness. This alters metaphysical thought radically: it binds beings to being precisely by breaking the bond of necessity between them. The *maior dissimilitudo* of the ontological analogy means that the *similitudo* between God and creatures, rather than dwelling merely in a thing's flawed likeness to some higher essence, distorted in the mirror of space and time, consists rather in each thing's pluriform and dynamic synthesis of its transcendental moments and the particular event of its existence, which synthesis is what constitutes it as a being. Each actuality, in differing from God, testifies to the fullness of God's actuality. Indeed, the "ever greater unlikeness" of the proportion means that the "likeness" is itself ever greater the more fully anything is what it is, the more it grows into the measure of its difference, the more profoundly it drinks from the transcendent moments that compose it and allow all its modes of disclosure to speak of God's infinite goodness. All beings, inasmuch as they are intrinsically *ex nihilo*, become what they are by drawing on an infinite wellspring of determinacy, particularity, and actuality. Whereas an analogy of identity finds truth in the ever less particular emptiness of a simple and absolute singularity, the analogy of being finds truth in the ever greater particularity that each thing acquires as it enters ever more into the infinite that gives it being.[36] This means also, one should then note, that there is a far greater intimacy between God and creatures granted by the *analogia entis* than by identist thought: the most high principle does not stand over against us (if secretly within us) across the distance of a hierarchy of lesser metaphysical principles, but is present within the very act of each moment of the particular. The infinite nearness of the *interior intimo meo* is possible precisely because of the infinite transcendence of the *superior summo meo*.

It is a phenomenological (and, for Heidegger, ontological) maxim that, for anything to appear, there must indeed be a more general hidden-

---

36. Thomas Aquinas writes that "veritas fundatur in esse rei magis quam in ipsa quidditate": this means, he argues, that the "adequation" that truth is consists in an assimilation of the intellect to the *esse* of any given thing, whereby it accepts each thing as it is (*Scriptum super libros sententiarum*, I, d. 19, q. 5, a. 1, *solutio*). This is an elegantly succinct formulation—truth is the fullness, not the impoverishment, of a thing's modes of being; judgments are true if one accepts beings as beings in the fullness of their determinations.

ness: the unseen sides of an object that, in being hidden, allow a distinct form to emerge from "total" presence; the obscuration of everything the object shields from view; the hiddenness of past and future that allows the object to disclose itself in the exteriority of its temporal "ecstases"; and indeed, the invisibility of being itself, the deferral of its absoluteness in its gracious giving way to the finite. However, it makes all the difference whether one sees this movement of hiddenness within manifestation in terms of an original negation or in terms of a self-outpouring that flows from the plenitude of full Trinitarian manifestation. The analogy allows one to see in the difference of being from beings, and the "withdrawal" of being that permits beings to stand forth—which involves a seeming "constriction," "occlusion," or "withholding" of being—not a negation or nihilation, but a *kenōsis*. After all, if the continuity between being and beings is not univocal, but truly analogical, then being need not be conceived as somehow ontic—as, say, an inexhaustible reservoir of possibility that must be apportioned by the nothing's "nothinging"—but can be understood entirely as the transcendent act of self-outpouring love, which is full in being utterly "exposed"; being can be understood as the immediate act of the entire circle of manifestation in the realm of the ontic, granting actuality at once to both visibility and invisibility, presence and absence, out of its own self-manifesting, self-knowing, self-loving abundance. Being is not negated by the "negative" because the entire economy of manifestation is its good gift. The concept of ontological analogy instructs the pure eye, the *oculus simplex*, to see the gracious *kenōsis* of the supereminent in the finite, and the exaltation of the finite in the peaceful simplicity of the infinite. The analogy teaches vision to see the supereminent convertibility of the transcendentals not as the savage blaze of "total light," a substance rent apart in the diversity of existence, but as the embracing unity that allows difference to be, by giving it space in which to differ. Apart from the analogy, the eye fails to see that in the very coherence of the moments of experience there is a prior act of grace in which unity and difference both subsist; one might not see that the great sea of possibility that is fitfully actualized as "world" is still infinitely distinct from the actuality—the unity—that allows even the possible to be. For all things—all the words of being—speak of God because they shine within his eternal Word. One may name God from beings.

Every metaphysics, simply said, that does not grasp (or at least adumbrate) the analogy of being is a tower of Babel, attempting to mount up to the supreme principle rather than dwelling in and giving voice to the prodigality of the gift. It is the simple, infinite movement of analogy that constitutes everything that is as a being, oscillating between essence and existence and receiving both from beyond itself; and it is the movement of analogy that makes everything that is already the return of the gift thus given, the offering of all things by the Spirit up into the Father's plenitude of being, in the Son. *Ex nihilo in Deum*—and there is no other "place." By this movement, each thing comes to be as pure event, owning no substance, made free from nothingness by the unmerited grace of *being* other than God, participating in the mystery of God's power to receive all in giving all away—the mystery, that is, of the truth that God is love. If indeed there is a sacrificial logic to metaphysics, as Vattimo and others say (the world and its highest principle sustaining one another in an economy of mutual founding, each in some sense both affirming and negating the other, each bound to the other by the logic of necessity), then the analogy of being that first appears in Western thought in the doctrine of creation is the only true "overcoming of metaphysics," the end of the myth of sacrifice: creation and salvation are gifts adding nothing to the being of God, and so nothing of the world needs to be destroyed to give glory and sustenance to the ultimate principle. Instead, our piety is one of rational worship, bloodless sacrifice, thanksgiving for a gift, liturgy, the offering of names.

TWO

No Shadow of Turning

On Divine Impassibility

Every good gift and every perfect gift is from above, and cometh down from the Father of lights, with whom is no variableness, neither shadow of turning.

—James 1:17 KJV

I. Divine Suffering, Divine Becoming

Time, of course, is not a transparent medium; of the future we can glimpse only the shadows of possibilities, and whatever we can discern of the past recedes incessantly into an ever greater distance, and is visible usually only through the distorting atmosphere of the preoccupations of the present. At times it proves practically impossible to forge between ourselves and an earlier epoch those ties of imaginative sympathy that would allow us to understand it from within something like its own language and sensibilities; at that point we are no longer able credibly to represent to ourselves the spirit of that other age, but only to preserve the relics of a lost and irrecoverable world. This is always a cultural and intellectual bereavement, of course, as understanding is a precious thing, but when such a rupture between ages occurs within a supposedly continuous and internally consistent tradition of discourse, such as Christian theology, it constitutes something potentially far worse: it calls into serious question the intrinsic stability of that tradition, and hence the validity of its claims to probity and truthfulness. Of course, the loss of the past never occurs suddenly or convulsively; a catastrophist model of change can never capture the

45

slow but relentless process that transforms the stable and even apodictic truths of one age into the quaint and curious debris by which another at best diverts itself; the change occurs discretely, as one element of a coherent whole becomes detached from the context that made it intelligible or necessary, and then another, until integral order has dissolved into a mere collection of monuments.

If the evidence of twentieth-century literature on the matter is rightly weighed, the topic of this essay—God's impassibility, the venerable patristic and medieval doctrine that the divine nature is in itself immutable and immune to suffering—may well prove to be a piece of conceptual furniture for which fewer and fewer theologians can find or remember a proper use. That the Christian God is possessed of impassibility, or *apatheia* (to employ the proper Greek term), that he is impervious to any force—any pathos or affect—external to his nature and is incapable of experiencing shifting emotions within himself, seems to many an impossible proposition now to affirm, one certainly that is prima facie incompatible with the biblical portrait of the God of Israel and that, even more certainly, is wholly irreconcilable with what Christians believe occurred in the suffering and death of Christ on the cross. Surely, it is now often asserted (with a confidence whose increase is exactly proportionate to understanding's withdrawal), this word *apatheia* is the residue of an obsolete metaphysics and a sign that, however necessary it was for the early church to employ the resources of pagan philosophy to articulate Christian doctrine, the baptism of Hellenism was never entirely complete.

This is not to say that the doctrine is altogether moribund: many a metaphysically canny modern theologian still knows to insist on its necessity, at least as a grammatical restraint, a negative moment in our theology that reminds us that, as Rowan Williams writes, "we should not delude ourselves that God's difference is merely that of one thing from another: we need to put down those formal markers (immutable, impassible, omnipotent, etc.) as a way of insisting that we cannot write a biography of God."[1] But even here, two observations should be made. The first is that, stated thus, *apatheia* is a purely apophatic term, serving simply as a safeguard against the theologian's speculative ambitions; and this in itself demonstrates something of the distance we have traveled from earlier ages of theology when the teaching of divine impassibility was not simply a

---

1. Rowan Williams, "Trinity and Ontology," in Williams, *On Christian Theology* (Oxford: Blackwell, 2000), p. 160. Williams is describing the view of D. M. MacKinnon here (it should be noted), but with approbation.

limit placed upon our language, a pious refusal to attempt trespass upon God's majesty in his light inaccessible, but was in fact very much part of the ground of Christian hope, central to the positive message of the evangel, not simply an austere negation of thought, but a real promise of joy in God. And the second observation is that it is indeed a "biography" of God, in some sense, that certain theologians now think we should write—or rather should find already written for us in Scripture. After all, it might reasonably be asked, in the story of God's dealings with Israel and of the Son's incarnation, death, and resurrection, have we not been given, quite concretely, the narrative of God's identity? Have we not seen the story of God unfold before our eyes, and is it not a story in which divine love and wrath, pity and suffering, are clearly substantive elements of God's presence with us? Have we not, in short, seen the wounded heart of God, wounded by our sin in his eternal being and wounded to death at Golgotha? And these questions, for some, become immeasurably more pressing in the wake of the twentieth century—in the wake of death camps, and gulags, and killing fields, and the fires of nuclear detonations; in this age in which we have seen such unutterable horrors, can we really believe in a God essentially untouched by pain, removed by nature from all suffering, beyond all change? Can we vest our hope in such a God, or believe he loves us, or love him in turn?

Not that the church fathers were not aware of the profound difference between the God of the philosophers and the God of Scripture, between the serenely abstract and remote deity who, in late antiquity, had become the object of "rational worship"—or, at any rate, admiration—for many a refined soul, and the loving and wrathful God of the Bible, who shook with jealousy at the infidelities of his people, who created out of the depths of his love, and for his pleasure, and who finally poured himself out in Christ, even unto death, in pursuit of those who had forsaken him. And, indeed, *apatheia* is not an entirely univocal concept in the theology of the church's early centuries. But it is nonetheless striking that, in the course, say, of the great disputes of the fourth and fifth centuries concerning Trinitarian dogma and Christology, divine impassibility was a principle that all parties concerned accepted without serious reservations, even though it was a principle that, on the face of it, better served the causes of what came to be viewed as the heterodox schools of thought. Arians and Eunomians quite plausibly argued against the essential divinity of the Son on the grounds that real generation within the changeless Godhead is unimaginable and that the adventure of the incarnation and death of the Son is obviously impossible for a nature truly divine; "Nestorians" could insist upon a real and inviolable distinction within Christ between the activities of the Logos and those of "the man" because, as God, the divine Logos was beyond suffering and change altogether. Still, the orthodox were every bit as adamant as their opponents. Athanasius, the Cappadocians, Cyril of Alexandria—all were equally certain that God is immutable by nature, eternally the same, and beyond every perturbation and pathos to which a finite nature is subject, even though this unyielding commitment to the metaphysics of divine impassibility could produce what look like very odd formulations indeed. Cyril, for instance, who insisted with more fervor and ferocity than any other theologian of the early church upon the absolute unity of Christ, the perfect simplicity of the identity of the incarnate Logos in all his acts, could write, without any sense of contradiction: "When the only-begotten Word of God became a human being, he did so not by discarding his being as God, but by remaining, within the assumption of the flesh, that which he was. For the nature of the Word is changeless and unalterable, and can suffer no shadow of turning."[2] And this indeed was the pattern of Christian discourse from the earliest period of patristic theology: more than three centuries earlier, Ignatius of Antioch, who could anticipate his own martyrdom as his opportunity to become "an imitator of the suffering of my God,"[3] had nonetheless exhorted Polycarp of Smyrna to "[w]ait for him who is above every season, the timeless one, the invisible, made visible for us, the intangible one, who suffers not, who suffered for us, who in every way endured for us."[4] Even Origen, who was at least on one occasion willing to speak of a passion suffered by God before the incarnation, even of a kind of passibility of the Father,[5] ultimately refused to allow such language anything more than metaphoric status; though indeed we may and must speak of divine rejoicing over our virtues and divine grief over our vices, "The divine nature is entirely removed from every affect of passion and change, remaining ever unmoved and undisturbed upon the summit

2. Cyril of Alexandria, *Homiliae diversae*, Homilia 2, Patrologia Graeca (hereinafter PG) 77:985–89 [γέγονε δὲ ἄνθρωπος ὁ μονογενὴς ὁ τοῦ θεοῦ Λόγος, οὐκ ἀποβεβληκὼς τὸ εἶναι Θεὸς, ἀλλ' ἐν προσλήψει σαρκὸς μεμενηκὼς, ὅπερ ἦν. Ἄτρεπτος γάρ ἐστι καὶ ἀναλλοίωτος ἡ τοῦ Λόγου φύσις, καὶ οὐκ οἶδε παθεῖν τροπῆς ἀποσκίασμα].

3. Ignatius, *Epistle to the Romans* 6.3 [. . . μιμητὴν εἶναι τοῦ πάθους τοῦ Θεοῦ μου].

4. Ignatius, *Epistle to Polycarp* 3.2 [τὸν ὑπὲρ καιρὸν προσδόκα, τὸν ἄχρονον, τὸν ἀόρατον, τὸν δι' ἡμᾶς ὁρατόν, τὸν ἀψηλάφητον, τὸν ἀπαθῆ, τὸν δι' ἡμᾶς παθητόν, τὸν κατὰ πάντα τρόπον δι' ἡμᾶς ὑπομείναντα].

5. Origen, *Homiliae in Ezechielem*, Homilia 6.6, in Origène, *Homélies sur Ézéchiel*, ed. Marcel Borret, SJ (Paris: Les Éditions du Cerf, 1989), pp. 228–30. See especially p. 230: "Ipse Pater non est impassibilis." One must, of course, recognize that for Origen such a pronouncement is a homiletic hyperbole, not to be taken too literally.

of blessedness."[6] Surely, one might be justified in protesting, there is an essential incoherence in this language; what purpose does the language of *apatheia* serve, anyway, if it must always accompany every affirmation of God's love and suffering as a sudden disorienting paradox?

Even if it is the case (as it is with me) that one's sympathy with such complaints is small—that one entirely rejects the suggestion that the language of divine impassibility is inconsistent with the story Christians tell of the acts of God in Christ, and regards such a claim as evidence only of misunderstanding filtered through emotion—still one must acknowledge that *apatheia* does generally tend to appear within Christian discourse now, if at all, as a metaphysical predicate only, necessarily implicit within certain quite classical philosophical definitions of the "divine," but in no real sense part of the rational coherence of the Christian narrative, or certainly of the "good news" it has to offer. Moreover, as speculative grammars and intellectual fashions have changed, versions of theology have taken shape in which the teaching of divine impassibility enjoys no welcome; indeed, there are now alternative theologies aplenty that insist upon not only a capacity for suffering in the divine nature, but a necessity for it. Some, of course, like the various forms of process theology, stray far beyond the identifiable boundaries of the Christian story in their pursuit of metaphysical completeness (though not, apparently, in pursuit of a cogent ontology), but others hew nearer the straight and narrow of dogmatic tradition.

One species of modern "pathetic" theology that seems particularly pluriform and perdurable is a kind of Trinitarian reflection within modern systematics that attempts—in a variety of ways, but always in some sense as an effort to repristinate the "trinitarianism" of Hegel—to collapse the distinction between God's eternal being as the triune God and the temporal history of God's unfolding presence with his creatures as Father, Son, and Holy Spirit: that attempts, that is, to read the story of God in Christ not simply as the revelation of God's identity, but as the actual event of that identity, of how God becomes the God he is. After all, the prejudice holds, the distinction between being and becoming—between timeless and eternal reality and the ceaseless transience of finite and mutable existence—is a Greek prejudice, is it not, a metaphysical fable written by pagans who could imagine time only as a prison and eternity only as absolute stillness? And is not then any distinction between the immanent

---

6. Origen, *Homiliae in Numeros*, Homilia 23.2; PG 12:748 [Aliena porro est divina natura ab omni passionis et permutationis affectu, in illo semper beatitudinis apice immobilis et inconcussa perdurans].

and economic truths of the Trinity an artifact of Platonism rather than an interpretation of Scripture? Thus, for the various theologians one might place in this school, Trinitarian discourse is that place within Christian theology where the history of the world and the story of God are one narrative, where God's radical intimacy with us in time is affirmed, and where creaturely finitude is shown to belong to God's eternal being. For each, the story of God in Christ is the story of how God becomes the God he is through his free determination that he will identify himself with the man Jesus, even to the point of death, and through the love whereby this identification is preserved and elevated in the Spirit. God's "eternal" being is the dramatic history of God's encounter, in Christ, with the horizon of abandonment and death and his triumph over it. None of the painful particularities of the incarnation, then, are exterior to the internal movement of God's identity; the pathos of the Son is related to a pathos within the Father, both of which are taken into the love of the Spirit. And this means that, as the pathos of finite existence constitutes God as God, sin, suffering, and death are the horizon God has elected along with his own identity in Christ, for God's redemptive actions are not simply gracious, but definitive of his nature, and so evil is present in creation as the shadow accompanying God's decision to be this God and not another.

Of course, a story laid out in such broad terms corresponds exactly to the system of no one theologian, and many of those to whom something like this story can be attributed differ from one another quite radically. In the realm of theological celebrity, one can identify a very serious engagement with Hegel's logic, worked out in quite a rigorous and biblical fashion, in the thought of Wolfhart Pannenberg and Robert Jenson (neither of whom allows the language of divine passion to displace from their theology the reality or centrality of Easter); but one can also find a far more incautious and vulgar "Hegelianism" prodigally displayed in the loose, rhapsodic, paraenetic discourse of Jürgen Moltmann, with all its chaotic sentimentalism, or a Hegelianism saturated with a palpable metaphysical nihilism in the altogether different and immeasurably more systematic (and yet paradoxically even more incoherent) thought of Eberhard Jüngel. For Moltmann, the event of Christ—in particular, the event of the cross—is that "crucial" moment in which God's identity is achieved: on the cross, Moltmann says, God constitutes himself as suffering love;[7] there he

---

7. Jürgen Moltmann, *The Crucified God: The Cross of Christ as the Foundation and Criticism of Christian Theology* (Minneapolis: Fortress, 1974), pp. 244-45; Moltmann, *The Trinity and the Kingdom: The Doctrine of God* (Minneapolis: Fortress, 1981), pp. 82-83.

inaugurates the Trinitarian history of divine suffering,[8] there he takes all godforsakenness and rejection into his eternal being,[9] there he truly exposes himself to the dark annihilating Nothingness over against which he affirmed creation in the beginning,[10] and so "becomes the God who identifies himself with men and women to the point of death and beyond."[11] And Jüngel, sounding the rich, dark Wagnerian chords of his strange and quasi-mystical discourse of putrescence (*Verwesung*) and death, sees the event of the cross as God identifying himself with the dead man Jesus, thus constituting himself in relation to transience, to nothingness, as the unity of life and death in favor of life;[12] in the absolute opposition between Father and Son on the cross,[13] the struggle between possibility and nothingness, God makes "room for nothingness in the divine life" and, "suffering annihilation in himself . . . shows himself to be victor over nothingness"[14] by remaining one God, both life and death, in the love of the Spirit.[15]

It is possible to treat of none of this adequately here, though one must observe, if only in passing, that it is unlikely that such approaches to Trinitarian theology can withstand very close philosophical scrutiny. Perhaps that should always be a subordinate concern for theology, but still it should be remarked that, when all is said and done, the idea of a God who becomes through suffering passions, whose being is determined in a history, according to "encounters" with other realities, even realities he creates, is simply a metaphysical myth, a mere supreme being, but not the source of all being. To wax vaguely Heideggerean, he is a God on this side of the ontological difference. For one thing, it is an oddly quixotic expectation that one could rescue Hegel's "insights" from Hegel's metaphysics by shifting the narrative from the generality of the system's universal horizon, whereupon the constant play of the Concept's diremption into finitude and recuperation into *Geist* shows itself as the sublime logic of all human labor, struggle, and reflection, to the particularity of the identity and fate

8. Moltmann, *The Crucified God*, p. 255.

9. Moltmann, *The Crucified God*, pp. 276–77; Moltmann, *Trinity and the Kingdom*, pp. 81–83, 118–19.

10. Jürgen Moltmann, *God in Creation: A New Theology of Creation and the Spirit of God* (Minneapolis: Fortress, 1993), p. 102.

11. Moltmann, *Trinity and the Kingdom*, p. 119.

12. Eberhard Jüngel, *God as Mystery of the World* (Grand Rapids: Eerdmans, 1983), p. 299.

13. See Eberhard Jüngel, "Das Sein Jesu Christi als Ereignis der Versöhnung Gottes mit einer gottlosen Welt: Die Hingabe des Gekreuzigten," *Evangelische Theologie* 38 (1978).

14. Jüngel, *God as Mystery*, p. 217.

15. Jüngel, *God as Mystery*, p. 328.

of Jesus of Nazareth, who is now understood as the one historical object of God's self-defining determination. Hegel's logic cannot work that way, and the system is not something to be trifled with: it is too well thought out, and one step toward it is complete capitulation. The only way in which the distinction between being and becoming can be overcome (if this is at all possible or desirable) is by way of a complete collapse of the difference. Being must be identified with the totality of becoming as an "infinite" process. Otherwise one cannot avoid some version of Heidegger's onto-theological critique (and, frankly, Heidegger's critique almost certainly holds against the complete system anyway): one is identifying being with a being among beings; one's God is an ontic God, who becomes what he is not, possessed of potential, receiving his being from elsewhere—from being. And, as a being, he is in some sense finite, divided between being and being *this*, and so cannot be the being of creatures, even though he is their cause.[16] Among other things, this means that this God fails the test of Anselm's *id quo maius cogitari nequit*: a standard whose provenance may not exactly be biblical, but whose logic ultimately is, and that teaches us to recognize when we are speaking of God and when we are speaking of a god, when we are directing our mind toward the transcendent source of being and when we are fabricating for ourselves a metaphysical fable, when we are being Christians and when we are being mere theists.

But the greatest problems with such approaches to Trinitarian theology are as much moral as metaphysical, for once the interval of analogy between the immanent and economic Trinities (between God in himself and God with the world) has been collapsed into simple identity, certain very unsettling conclusions will become inevitable. Moltmann and Jüngel both, for all their differences, attempt to avoid depicting God, in his history of becoming, as merely the passive creature of his creatures: freely, they insist, he chooses his course. But this idea of God as a finite subject

16. See E. L. Mascall, *He Who Is: A Study in Traditional Theism* (London: Longmans, Green, and Co., 1945), p. 112. Having argued that while a God who is determined by the world can provide a metaphysical explanation of the course of worldly history, he can still never actually provide an explanation of the sheer "that it is" of the world, Mascall concludes that "nothing less than a strictly infinite God can provide the explanation of the world's existence, and that, in consequence, the world must be, in the fullest sense, contingent and altogether unnecessary to God. Various objections . . . complain that, on such a view, God could not have the intimate interest and concern with his creatures that is manifested in the Christian Religion. . . . [W]hile this would certainly be true if God was a finite being, it is not true if God is infinite." I do not believe that this is a logic that theology can intelligibly forsake.

writ large, who elects himself as a project of self-discovery, only compounds the problem; in place of the metaphysically necessary "God" of the system, this sort of language gives us only an anthropomorphic myth, a God whose will enjoys a certain indeterminate priority over his essence, in whom possibility exceeds actuality, who is therefore composite, ontic, voluntaristic . . . and obviously nonexistent. More to the point, as many of the fathers would have argued, a God who can by nature experience finite affects and so be determined by them is a God whose identity is established through a commerce with evil; if the nature of God's love can be in any sense positively shaped by sin, suffering, and death, then sin, suffering, and death will always be in some sense features of who he is. Among other things, this means that evil must enjoy a certain independent authenticity, a reality with which God must come to grips, and God's love must—if it requires the negative pathos of history to bring it to fruition—be inherently deficient, and in itself a fundamentally reactive reality. Goodness then requires evil to be good; love must be goaded into being by pain. In brief, a God who can, in his nature as God, suffer cannot be the God who is love, even if at the end of the day he should prove to be loving, or the God who is simply good, or who is the wellspring of being and life. He, like us, is an accommodation between death and life.

Nor is it enough to say that, as God's identity is infinite, the conditions of the finite do not determine its ultimate nature, for while a truly transcendent infinity might be able to assume the finite into itself without altering its nature, an "infinite" that realizes itself in and through finite determinations can in no sense remain untouched by the evils it passes through, even if the ultimate synthesis of its identity is, in its totality, "infinite" in the circular Hegelian sense; such can be only the infinite of total repletion, the fullness of ontic determinations in their interrelated discreteness and dialectical "yield"; only thus can being be one with becoming. Again, one simply cannot say that God finds himself in the one historical object of Jesus *tout court*; in specifying this one historical object, God must also specify the entire web of historical and cosmic contingencies in which this object subsists; no worldly reality can stand apart from the entire reality of the world. And so, if one pursues the logic of divine becoming to its proper end, one will find that all things are necessary aspects of God's odyssey toward himself; every painful death of a child, every casual act of brutality, all war, famine, pestilence, disease, murder . . . all will turn out to be moments in the identity of God, resonances within the event of his being, aspects of the occurrence of his essence: all evil will become meaningful—speculatively meaningful and so necessary—as the crucible in which God is forged. If, metaphysically, Hegelian trinitarian theology fails Anselm's test, morally it fails the test of Ivan Karamazov: if the universal and final good of all creatures required, as its price, the torture of one little girl, would that be acceptable? And the moral enormity of this calculus is obviously in no wise mitigated if all of creation must suffer the consequences of God's self-determination. The God whose identity subsists in time and is achieved upon history's horizon—who is determined, however "freely," by his reaction to the pathos of history—may be a being, or indeed the totality of all beings gathered in the pure depths of total consciousness, but he is not being as such, he is not life and truth and goodness and love and beauty. God belongs to the system of causes, even if he does so as its total rationality; he is an absolute *causa in fieri* but not an ultimate *causa in esse*. And so he may include us in his story, but his story will remain both good and evil even if it ends in an ultimate triumph over evil. How can we tell the dancer from the dance? The collapse of the analogical interval between the immanent and economic in the Trinity, between timeless eternity and the time in which eternity shows itself, has made God not our companion in pain, but simply the truth of our pain and our only pathetic hope of rescue; his intimacy with us has not been affirmed at all. Only a truly transcendent and passionless God can be the fullness of love dwelling within our very being, nearer to us than our inmost parts, but this "Hegelian" God is not transcendent—truly infinite—in this way at all, but only sublime: a metaphysical whole that can comprise us or change us extrinsically, but not account for or transform us within our very being. And this is a fearful thought, especially if, like Moltmann, one seeks in the passions of the divine an explanation for the suffering of creatures: what a monstrous irony it would be if, in our eagerness to find a way of believing in God's love in the age of Auschwitz, we should in fact succeed only in describing a God who is the metaphysical ground of Auschwitz.

Let us at any rate be certain we truly understand what is at stake when the tradition says that God is by nature impassible, immutable, and timeless, and how all these words have been refined and transfigured by the story of what occurred in Christ and by the proper grammar of Trinitarian dogma. I shall attempt at least, in what follows, to give a brief account of these things, under the form of a kind of "patristic synthesis," drawn from the writings of various fathers and arranged in a very simple sequence of three distinct moments: *apatheia* as love; *apatheia* as Trinitarian love; and *apatheia* as Trinitarian love seizing us up into itself.

II. *Apatheia* as Love

Apatheia entered Christian thought not only as an attribute to be ascribed to God, but as a virtue to be pursued, and in this latter acceptation, the term was borrowed primarily from the Stoics, for whom it signified chiefly a kind of absolute equanimity, an impassive serenity so fortified by prudent self-restraint against any excesses of either joy or sorrow as to be virtually indistinguishable from indifference. Not that it was not an ethical quality: one who could become truly free from the passions could also learn to treat others, whatever the accidents of their births, with regard, concern, and justice; but it was also most definitely conceived of as a kind of regal inactivity of the will. When Christians adopted the term, however, it became something much more. According to Clement of Alexandria, for instance, true *apatheia* consists in the cultivation of understanding and charity,[17] and as we are drawn to God in Christ, we are being conformed to a God who is without *pathē*—devoid of pain, free from wrath, without anxious desire, and so on—not as a result of having mastered the passions within himself, but from his essence, which is the fullness of all good things;[18] and ultimately the Christian who has so advanced in understanding as to be purged of emotions is one who has become entirely love:[19] a single inexorable motion of utter *agapē*. Far from being mere Stoic detachment, then, *apatheia* is in fact a condition of radical attachment. And Clement is in no sense unusual here. In the "Letter to Anatolius" with which he prefaces his *Praktikos*, Evagrius of Pontus states that "*apatheia*

---

17. Clement of Alexandria, *Stromata* 3.5; PG 8:1144–48.

18. Clement of Alexandria, *Stromata* 4.23; PG 8:1360–61.

19. Clement of Alexandria, *Stromata* 6.9; PG 9:292–300. See especially pp. 293–96: "But [those who believe that one cannot be impassible and still desire the good] obviously do not know the divinity of love [*agapē*]. For love is not passionate longing on the part of the lover. It is rather a loving act of appropriation, restoring the gnostic to the unity of the faith, notwithstanding time and place. But he who has already, through love, entered into these things, advancing beyond hope by knowledge, does not long for anything, possessing, as far as possible, the thing longed for. He naturally, therefore, remains in one changeless condition, loving knowingly ['gnostically']. Nor, therefore, will he fiercely crave to be assimilated to the beautiful, as he already possesses beauty by love." [Ἀλλ' οὐκ ἴσασιν, ὡς ἔοικεν, οὗτοι τὸ θεῖον τῆς ἀγάπης. οὐ γάρ ἐστιν ἐπὶ ὄρεξεις τοῦ ἀγαπῶντος ἡ ἀγάπη. στερκτικὴ δὲ οἰκείωσις, εἰς τὴν ἑνότητα τῆς πίστεως ἀποκατεστηκυῖα τὸν γνωστικόν, χρόνου καὶ τόπου μὴ προσδεόμενον. Ὁ δ' ἐν οἷς ἔσται δι' ἀγάπης ἤδη γενόμενος, τὴν ἐλπίδα προειληφὼς διὰ τῆς γνώσεως, οὐδὲ ὀρέγεται τινος, ἔχων, ὡς οἷον τε, αὐτὸ τὸ ὀρεκτόν. εἰκότως τοίνυν ἐν τῇ ἀμεταβόλῳ, γνωστικῶς ἀγαπῶν. οὐδ' ἄρα ζηλώσει ἐξομοιωθῆναι τοῖς καλοῖς εἶναι δι' ἀγάπης ἔχων τοὺς κάλλους.]

has a child called *agapē* who keeps the door to deep knowledge of the created universe."[20] In the text itself, moreover, he defines *apatheia* as the very health of the soul,[21] at which we arrive only to the degree that true spiritual love has conquered our soul's *pathē*.[22] He even insists that this is in no sense a suppression of the soul's vital energies—its irascible (*thymos*) and concupiscible (*epithymia*) elements—but is simply their conversion toward natural integrity: a ferocity directed against evil and a desire directed toward divine virtue.[23] This tradition reaches its most profoundly developed form in the thought of Maximus the Confessor, whose *Chapters on Love* is a virtual manual of instructions for the cultivation of *apatheia*, which is to say, for him, the cultivation of a spiritual vision that—having divested itself of all the fantasies summoned up by self-love,[24] pride, the desire for power, and all other sins—can see all things with a pure heart, as images and reflections of the Logos who shaped them,[25] and so love them without restraint, with a love so perfect that no perturbation or pathos can obviate its intensity. The mind's life of illumination, he says, is born only of love,[26] which is possible only for a mind purged of all hatred for others,[27] because God is love itself and can be known and possessed only in love.[28] Again, the attainment of this love is a refinement of the soul's innate dynamisms, so that concupiscence is transformed into divine desire and irascibility into divine love,[29] and this grants us a true delight in divine beauty.[30] And this state of mind is, for Maximus, properly called *apatheia*.

Obviously, at this point, one is not talking about the sort of austere impassivity or want of feeling one would ascribe to Aristotle's or Plotinus's "God," much less some sort of pure and dispirited indifference. Augustine, for instance, who believed perfect impassibility to be impossible for us in

20. Evagrius, *Praktikos*, in Evagrius Ponticus, *The Praktikos and Chapters on Prayer*, ed. and trans. John Eudes Bamberger (Kalamazoo, MI: Cistercian Publications, 1981), p. 14. See also ch. 81, p. 36.

21. Evagrius, *Praktikos*, ch. 56, p. 31.

22. Evagrius, *Praktikos*, ch. 35, p. 25.

23. Evagrius, *Praktikos*, ch. 24, p. 23; chs. 84–86, p. 37.

24. See also, and in particular, Maximus the Confessor, *Epistola II: De charitate*, PG 91:392–408.

25. Maximus the Confessor, *Capita de charitate* 2.100, PG 90:1017; 4.72, PG 90:1068.

26. Maximus the Confessor, *Capita de charitate* 1.9; PG 90:964.

27. Maximus the Confessor, *Capita de charitate* 1.15; PG 90:964.

28. Maximus the Confessor, *Capita de charitate* 1.23, PG 90:965; 1.38, PG 90:968; 4.100, PG 90:1074.

29. Maximus the Confessor, *Capita de charitate* 2.48; PG 90:1000.

30. Maximus the Confessor, *Capita de charitate* 1.19; PG 90:964.

this life, and probably undesirable, says that "if [*apatheia*] is taken to mean . . . a freedom from those affects that are contrary to rationality and that perturb the mind, then it is plainly a good thing and most desirable. . . . But if by *apatheia* is meant a state in which no feeling can touch the mind, who would not adjudge such insensibility to be worse than all vices? . . . that perfect future beatitude will be without any goad of fear or any sadness; but who except him who is wholly lost to the truth would say that neither love nor joy will be there?"[31] For Gregory of Nyssa, it is possible even to say that nothing that does not lead to sin is properly called a pathos.[32] But, one might ask, at this point has not the meaning of the term "impassibility" been so thoroughly altered as to have no real use? Is it not the case that once we have admitted love into our definition of the word, we have thus rendered it unintelligible, inasmuch as love is a reaction evoked by what one suffers of another?

To state the matter simply—no: love is not primordially a reaction, but the possibility of every action, the transcendent act that makes all else actual; it is purely positive, sufficient in itself, without the need of any galvanism of the negative to be fully active, vital, and creative. This is so because the ultimate truth of love is God himself, who creates all things solely for his pleasure, and whose act of being is infinite. And this is why love, when it is seen in its truly divine depth, is called *apatheia*. If this seems an odd claim to us now, it is largely because we are so accustomed to thinking of love as one of the emotions, one of the passions, one of those spontaneous or reactive forces that rise up in us and spend themselves on various objects of impermanent fascination; and of course, for us "love" often is just this. But, theologically speaking, at least according to the dominant tradition, love is not, in its essence, an emotion—a pathos—at all: it is life, being, truth, our only true well-being, and the very ground of our nature and existence. Thus John of Damascus draws a very strict distinction between a pathos and an "energy" (or act): the former is a movement of the soul provoked by something alien and external to it; the latter is a "drastic"

---

31. Augustine, *De civitate Dei* 14.9.4; Corpus Christianorum: Series Latina 48:428. [. . . si ita intelligenda est . . . ut sine his affectionibus vivatur, quae contra rationem accidunt mentemque perturbant, bona plane et maxime optanda est. . . . Porro si ajpavqeia illa dicenda est, cum animum contingere omnino non potest ullus affectus, quis hunc stuporem non omnibus vitiis iudicet esse peiorem? . . . perfectam beatitudinem sine stimulo timoris et sine ulla tristitia futuram; non ibi autem futurum amorem gaudiumque quis dixerit, nisi omni modo a veritate seclusus?]

32. Gregory of Nyssa, *Contra Eunomium* 3.4.27; Gregorii Nysseni Opera (hereinafter GNO), ed. Werner Jaeger et al. (Leiden: Brill, 1958–), 2:44.

movement, a positive power that is moved of itself in its own nature.[33] And love, certainly, is a movement of the latter kind. Or—to step briefly out of the patristic context—as Thomas Aquinas puts it, love, enjoyment, and delight are qualitatively different from anger and sadness, as the latter are privative states, passive and reactive, whereas the former are originally one act of freedom and intellect and subsist wholly in God as a purely "intellectual appetite."[34] Thus Gregory of Nyssa portrays his sister Macrina as teaching that the soul joined to God, who is beauty itself, will have no need of the energy of that appetent desire (*epithymia*) that arises from need or anxiety to unite it to divine goodness and loveliness,[35] but rather will "attach itself thereto and mingle with it through the movement and energy of love (*agapē*)"[36]—which she defines not as a reactive agitation of the will, but as a habitual inward state oriented toward the heart's desire.[37]

Logically prior to any pathos we encounter, even the pathos of sin that confines our nature from the first, love is active in us as the very power of our existence, the truth of a nature that is in its essence sheer yearning, summoned out of nothingness toward union with God, who is the source and consummation of every love. It is a patristic commonplace, which one could illustrate copiously from Gregory of Nyssa, Augustine, Maximus, and many others, that the true freedom of the rational creature is a freedom from all the encumbrances of sin that prevent us from enjoying the full fruition of our nature, which is the image and likeness of God; when sin is removed, when we are restored to the condition in which God called us from nothingness, our entire being is nothing but an insatiable longing for and delight in God, a natural and irresistible *erōs* for the divine beauty.[38] We spring up into God. This is that ultimate liberty that Augustine places above the mere voluntative liberty of being able not to sin: it is the condition of being so entirely free from sin and death, so entirely transformed in the love of God and of, in God, one's fellow creatures, as to

33. John of Damascus, *De fide orthodoxa* 2.23; PG 94:949–52.

34. Thomas, *Summa theologiae* I.20.1a.

35. Gregory of Nyssa, *De anima et resurrectione*, PG 46:89 [. . . οὐκέτι ἔσται χρεία τῆς κατ᾽ ἐπιθυμίαν κινήσεως, ἢ πρὸς τὸ καλὸν ἡγεμονεύσει]. The relation of charity to desire becomes increasingly complex in Gregory's work, the word *erōs* coming at last to assume the latter into the former.

36. Gregory of Nyssa, *De anima et resurrectione*, PG 46:93 [. . . προσφύεταί τε αὐτῷ καὶ συνανακιρνάται διὰ τῆς ἀγαπητῆς κινήσεώς τε καὶ ἐνεργείας . . .].

37. Gregory of Nyssa, *De anima et resurrectione*, PG 46:93 [τοῦτο γάρ ἐστιν ἡ ἀγάπη, ἡ πρὸς τὸ καταθύμιον ἐνδιάθετος σχέσις].

38. To offer one example, almost at random, Gregory of Nyssa, *De vita Moysis* 2; GNO 7/1:112–13.

be incapable of sin altogether.[39] Or, to use the language of Maximus, it is natural freedom, restored in us by Christ, who frees us from the false passions of our "gnomic" freedom (the power of the finite will to consent to love or to bind itself to destructive desires).[40] It is that state, as the Pseudo-Dionysius phrases it, in which our ecstasy meets the ecstasy of God.[41] Once this bond of love is forged, no transitory impulse of resentment, fear, or selfish appetite can sever it. And precisely because it is prior to and—in God—ultimately impervious to any contrary power (hatred, pride, anger, pain, death), such love as this is the only true impassibility. For, as Christ showed on the cross, God's love is an infinite act, and no passion can conquer it: "Father, forgive them, for they know not what they do."

III. *Apatheia* as Trinitarian Love

Of course, an understanding of divine *apatheia* as the absolutely inextinguishable vehemence of infinite love, what the Pseudo-Dionysius calls divine ecstasy or divine *erōs*, which therefore—precisely as impassibility—is ceaselessly active and engaged in creatures, was unimaginable for much of pagan philosophy. This image of God's immutability as *semper agens* rather than *semper quietus* would obviously have made no sense within a tradition that understood divine purity as a cold, remote, perfectly immobile simplicity, not mindful of us at all, even if—in some sense—it is a wellspring of being, bliss, and beauty for us. But not only did Christian theologians have it on scriptural authority that God is love, as doctrine developed they had an ever richer and more concrete way of understanding this truth: the doctrine of the Trinity. That is to say, for Christians even the simplicity of the divine nature is the simplicity of utter fullness, including the fullness of relation and differentiation: the interior life of God is also an infinite openness, for in his eternal being he is God always as an infinite gesture of self-outpouring love, the Father's entire gift of his being in the generation of the Son and the breathing forth of the Spirit. This is the eternal event that is God's being, and so he is never a purity of essence withdrawn from every other, but is entirely the utter generosity and joy of self-giving. This is why, also, God creates. According to the Pseudo-Dionysius, the flow-

39. Augustine, *De correptione et gratia* 2.12.33, in Divi Augustini, *De correptione et gratia*, ed. C. Boyer, SJ (Rome: Pontifical Gregorian University, 1931), p. 46.

40. See Maximus the Confessor, *Opuscula* 3, PG 91:45–56; *Opuscula* 7, PG 91:69–89; *Ambiguum* 5, PG 91:1045–60.

41. Ps.-Dionysius, *De divinis nominibus* 4.12–13; PG 3:772–76.

ing forth of God's goodness in finite beings is not simply the irrepressible ebullition of sheer divine power (as it perhaps is for much of Neoplatonist thought), but is the act of one who lovingly shares himself with all, who in his transcendence over all beings leads all things into being, and who is full within his self-emptying act of differentiation.[42]

More than that, God's is a life of real pleasure in the other, always already full of delight, fellowship, feasting, responsiveness, and love. For Gregory of Nyssa, what we see in the economy of creation and redemption is true of God's eternal being: that in God's acts, the Father inaugurates, the Son effects, and the Spirit perfects their one indivisible movement[43] (though, of course, in God this is not a successive or composite reality). God is the fullness of an infinitely completed, and yet infinitely dynamic, life of love, in which there is regard, knowledge, and felicity; writes Gregory, "the divine nature exceeds each [finite] good, and the good is wholly beloved by the good, and thus it follows that when it looks upon itself it desires what it possesses and possesses what it desires, and receives nothing from outside itself."[44] And thus: "the life of that transcendent nature is love, in that the beautiful is entirely lovable to those who recognize it (and the divine does recognize it), and so this recognition becomes love, because the object of his recognition is in its nature beautiful."[45] No one expresses this better, or in more luminously exquisite Trinitarian terms, than Augustine, for whom the mystery of God's being lies in the boundless depths of a perfect love, whose dynamism is the Father's eternal generation of his image, the full likeness of his imperishable glory, and the absolute delight—*delectatio*—by which the light of the Spirit, in whom the Son is seen, makes perfect the eternal drama of this love.

> [T]he Son is from the Father, so as both to be and to be coeternal with the Father. For if the image perfectly fills the measure of him whose image it is, then it is coequal to its source. . . . He has, in regard to this image, employed the name "form" on account, I believe, of its beauty, wherein there is at once such harmony, and prime equality, and prime similitude,

42. Ps.-Dionysius, *De divinis nominibus* 2.11; PG 3:649–52.

43. Gregory of Nyssa, *Ad Ablabium: Quod non sint tres Dei*, GNO 3/1:47–50.

44. Gregory of Nyssa, *De Anima et Resurrectione*, PG 46:93. [Ἐπεὶ δὲ οὖν παντὸς ἀγαθοῦ ἐπέκεινα ἡ θεία φύσις, τὸ δὲ ἀγαθὸν ἀγαθῷ φίλον πάντως, διὰ τοῦτο ἑαυτὴν βλέπουσα καὶ ὃ ἔχει, θέλει, καὶ ὃ θέλει, ἔχει, οὐδὲν τῶν ἔξωθεν εἰς ἑαυτὴν δεχομένη.]

45. Gregory of Nyssa, *De Anima et Resurrectione*, PG 46:96. [ἥ τε γὰρ ζωὴ τῆς ἄνω φύσεως ἀγάπη ἐστὶν, ἐπειδὴ τὸ καλὸν ἀγαπητὸν πάντως ἐστὶ τοῖς γινώσκουσι (γινώσκει δὲ αὐτὸ τὸ θεῖον), ἡ δὲ γνῶσις ἀγάπη γίνεται, διότι καλόν ἐστι τῇ φύσει τὸ γινωσκόμενον.]

in no way discordant, in no measure unequal, and in no part dissimilar, but wholly answering to the identity of the one whose image it is. . . . Wherefore that ineffable conjunction of the Father and his image is never without fruition, without love, without rejoicing. Hence that love, delight, felicity or beatitude, if any human voice can worthily say it, is called by him, in brief, use, and is in the Trinity the Holy Spirit, not begotten, but of the begetter and begotten alike the very sweetness, filling all creatures, according to their capacities, with his bountiful superabundance and excessiveness.[46]

And so we say: "In that Trinity is the highest origin of all things, and the most perfect beauty, and the most blessed delight. Therefore those three are seen to be mutually determined, and are in themselves infinite."[47] This last sentence is crucial, for it means that the triune God stands in need of no determination in the finite, no probation of the negative, no moment of becoming: nothing can give increase to that fullness of community and joy. God enjoys a peace that is absolute, never needing to define itself over against death or violence (for then it would not be essentially peace, but only final armistice). With or without creation, as Athanasius so often insists, God would be fully God as he eternally is.[48]

This, again, is why God's love is called *apatheia*. For us, of course, as finite beings, our every expression of ourselves and sense of what we are—in word and will, knowledge and love, form and recognition—is fragmentary, the frail emanation of a confined subjectivity, present to itself only as a play of presence and absence, light and darkness; but as God is not a finite

---

46. Augustine, *De Trinitate* 6.10.11; Corpus Christianorum: Series Latina 50:241–42. [Imago enim si perfecte implet illud cuius imago est, ipsa coaequatur ei, non illud imagini suae. In qua imagine speciem nominavit, credo, propter pulchritudinem, ubi iam est tanta congruentia, et prima aequalitas, et prima similitudo, nulla in re dissidens, et nullo modo inaequalis, et nulla ex parte dissimilis, sed ad identidem respondens ei cuius imago est. . . . Ille igitur ineffabilis quidam complexus patris et imaginis non est sine perfruitione, sine charitate, sine gaudio. Illa ergo dilectio, delectatio, felicitas vel beatitudo, si tamen aliqua humana voce digne dicitur, usus ab illo appellatus est breviter, et est in trinitate spiritus sanctus, non genitus, sed genitoris genitique suavitas, ingenti largitate atque ubertate perfundens omnes creaturas pro captu earum.]

47. Augustine, *De Trinitate* 6.10.12; Corpus Christianorum: Series Latina 50:242. [In illa enim trinitate summa origo est rerum omnium, et perfectissima pulchritudo, et beatissima delectatio. Itaque illa tria, et ad se invicem determinari videntur, et in se infinita sunt.]

48. See Athanasius, *Orationes contra Arianos* 2.11, PG 26:168–69; *Epistola ad Serapion* 1.14–17, PG 26:536–49; 2.2, PG 26:609–12; 3, PG 26:624–37; 4.1–6, PG 26:637–48.

being, but infinite being, his expression of himself and knowledge of and delight in that expression are, in each moment, completely and infinitely God: God's Word is the perfect expression of God and so is God; the living Spirit of God is God's life and joy, and so is God. An infinite and infinitely full distance is here, an infinite capacity, that is also infinite unity; in God, in these hypostatic distinctions, there opens up that infinite "place" that is the possibility of every place—of creation and in creation (as Hilary of Poitiers says, there is no place but is in God).[49] No created interval could possibly add to or subtract from that distance, which is the distance of an eternally accomplished act. And in that distance there is always more than mere difference: there is the infinite longing of desire and the infinite peace of satiation, for the Spirit—the desire, love, power of the Father—comes to rest in the Son, there finding all the delight he seeks. As the light and joy of the Trinity's knowledge and love, the Spirit reinflects the distance between Father and Son not just as bare cognizance, but as perfected love, the whole rapture of the divine essence. To call this infinite act of love *apatheia*, then, is to affirm its plenitude and its transcendence of every evil, every interval of sin, every finite rupture, disappointment of longing, shadow of sadness, or failure of love—in short, every pathos.

Another way of saying this is that God has—indeed is—only one act: the single ardent movement of this infinite love, delight, and peace. Indeed, so insistent are many of the fathers on the simplicity and singleness of the divine essence—that is, the Trinitarian event—that they will not acknowledge that God in any literal sense ever tastes of any other "feeling" than this love. Even the wrath of God in Scripture is a metaphor, suitable to our feeble understanding, one which describes not the action of God toward us, but what happens when the inextinguishable fervency of God's love toward us is rejected; according to Origen, Gregory of Nyssa, Maximus the Confessor, Isaac of Nineveh, and others, even hell itself is not a divine work, but the reality we have wrought within ourselves by our perverse refusal to open out—as God himself eternally has done—in love, for God and others, for when we have so sealed ourselves up within ourselves, the fire of divine love cannot transform and enliven us, but only assail us as an external chastisement:[50] for our God is a consuming fire, and the pathos of our rage cannot interrupt the *apatheia* of his love.

---

49. Hilary, *De Trinitate* 1.6, in Hilaire de Poitiers, *La Trinité* I, ed. G. Pelland (Paris: Les Éditions du Cerf, 1999), p. 216.

50. See, e.g., Origen, *Contra Celsum* 4:72, PG 11:1141–44; *Homiliae in Ezechielem* 3.7, in Origène, *Homélies sur Ézéchiel*, pp. 138–42; *De principiis* 2.10.4, PG 11:236–37; Greg-

Does such divine self-sufficiency, though, in some terrible way leave us out (to resort to the emotive terms in which this complaint is often framed)? If the fecundity of divine love is an infinitely achieved act, do all the dark passages of history and pains of finitude then have no ultimate meaning? How could such a God want us, if he has no intrinsic need of us? But, again, love is not need, is not lack, but is itself creative, and so is always gracious; and because God's is a Trinitarian love, one that is always open to the other, it can include us in itself without changing in its nature: indeed, love us with an ardor that no mere finite passion could evoke. *Apatheia*, defined as infinitely active love, "feels" more than any affect could possibly impress upon a passive nature; it does not require our sin and death to show us "mercy": God loved us when we were not, and by this very "mercy" called us into being. And this is the ground of all our hope.

IV. *Apatheia* as Trinitarian Love Seizing Us up into Itself

Of course, at the end of the day, the modern theologian who wants to reject the language of divine immutability and impassibility is generally one who is attempting to do justice to the story of God's incarnation in Christ and death upon the cross. It seems simply obvious that here we must be talking about a change within the being of God, and of a suffering endured by God, and so in both cases of a capacity endemic to his nature. From the vantage of the cross, so to speak, how can the traditional metaphysical attributions of divine transcendence not appear to obscure a clear understanding of who God has shown himself to be? What does it profit one to assert, along with Cyril of Alexandria, that Christ "was in the crucified body appropriating the sufferings of the flesh to himself impassibly"?[51] Or, with Melito of Sardis, that "the impassible suffered"?[52] Rather than trading in paradoxes, why not lay down our metaphysics at the foot of the cross?

The truth is, however, that we err when we read such phrases principally as paradoxes; they are actually intended as simple formulae for

ory, *De Anima et Resurrectione*, PG 46:97–105; Maximus the Confessor, *Quaestiones ad Thalassium* 59, PG 90:609.

51. Cyril of Alexandria, *Third Epistle to Nestorius* (Ep. 17) 6, in Cyril of Alexandria, *Select Letters*, ed. and trans. Lionel R. Wickham (Oxford: Clarendon, 1983), p. 20. [τὰ τῆς ἰδίας σαρκὸς ἀπαθῶς οἰκειούμενος πάθη.]

52. Melito of Sardis, Fragment 13.15, in *Méliton de Sardes, Sur la Pâque et fragments*, ed. and trans. Othmar Perler (Paris: Les Éditions du Cerf, 1966), p. 238 [impassibilis patitur . . .].

explaining, quite lucidly, the biblical story of our salvation in Christ. To begin with, the denial that the incarnation of Christ is a change in God's nature is not a denial that it is a real act of the living God, really coming to partake of our nature, nor certainly is it an attempt to evade the truth that, as the Second Council of Constantinople put it, "one of the Trinity suffered in the flesh."[53] The divine person of the Logos has really, through his humanity, suffered every extreme of human dereliction and pain and has truly tasted of death. What the fathers were anxious to reject, however, was any suggestion that God becoming human was an act of divine self-alienation, an actual *metabasis eis allo genos*, a transformation into a reality essentially contrary to what God eternally is: for this would mean that God must negate himself as God to become human—which would be to say God did not become human. Hence, a strict distinction must be drawn between the idea of divine change and that of divine *kenōsis*. When Scripture says, "the Logos became flesh," says Cyril of Alexandria, the word "became" signifies not any change in God, but only the act of self-divesting love whereby God the Son emptied himself of his glory, while preserving his immutable and impassible nature intact.[54] God did not, he says (here following Athanasius),[55] alter or abandon his nature in any way, but freely appropriated the weakness and poverty of our nature for the work of redemption.[56] And Augustine makes precisely the same distinction: "When he accepted the form of a slave, he accepted time. Did he therefore change? Was he diminished? Was he sent into exile? Did he fall into defect? Certainly not. What then does it mean, 'he emptied himself, taking the form of a slave'? It means he is said to have emptied himself out by accepting the inferior, not by degenerating from equality."[57]

This may appear at first to be a distinction without a difference, but it is in fact a quite logical—and necessary—clarification of terms, which can be justified on many grounds. To begin with, there is a qualitative dis-

53. Anathema 10.

54. Cyril of Alexandria, Ὅτι εἷς ὁ Χριστός, in Cyrille d'Alexandrie, *Deux dialogues Christologiques*, ed. G. M. de Durand (Paris: Les Éditions du Cerf, 1964), pp. 312–16.

55. Athanasius, *Epistola ad Epictetum*, PG 26:1064.

56. Cyril of Alexandria, *Scholia de incarnatione Unigeniti*, PG 75:1374; see also the *Third Epistle to Nestorius* 3, in Cyril of Alexandria, *Select Letters*, p. 16.

57. Augustine, *Enarrationes in Psalmos* 74.5; Corpus Christianorum: Series Latina 39:1028. [Sicut formam servi accepit, ita et tempus accepit. Demutatus est ergo? deminutus est? exilior redditus? in defectum lapsus? Absit. Quid ergo *semetipsam exinanivit, formam servi accipiens*? Exinanisse se dictus est accipiendo inferiorem, non degenerando ab aequali.]

proportion between infinite and finite being, which allows for the infinite to appropriate and accommodate the finite without ceasing to be infinite; or, to put it in more strictly ontological terms, if every being derives its being from God, and so all the perfections that compose a creature as what it is have their infinite and full reality in God, then the self-emptying of God in his creature is not a passage from what he is to what he is not, but a gracious condescension whereby the infinite is pleased truly to disclose and express itself in one instance of the finite. Indeed, in this sense, to say God does not change in the incarnation is almost a tautology: God is not some thing that can be transformed into another thing, but is the being of everything, to which all that is always already properly belongs. Simply said, there is no change of nature needed for the fullness of being to assume—even through self-impoverishment—*a* being as the dwelling place of its mystery and glory. If one finds such language unpalatably abstract, one may prefer to adopt more obviously biblical terms: as human being is nothing at all in itself but the image and likeness of God, then the perfect dwelling of the eternal image and likeness of God—the Logos—in the one man who perfectly expresses and lives out what it is to be human is in no sense an alien act for God. The act whereby the form of God appears in the form of a slave is the act whereby the infinite divine image shows itself in the finite divine image: this then is not a change, but a manifestation, of who God is. And, finally, the very action of *kenōsis* is not a new act for God, because God's eternal being is, in some sense, *kenōsis*: the self-outpouring of the Father in the Son, in the joy of the Spirit. Thus Christ's incarnation, far from dissembling his eternal nature, exhibits not only his particular *proprium* as the Son and the splendor of the Father's likeness, but thereby also the nature of the whole Trinitarian *taxis*. Christ is indeed the lamb slain from the foundation of the world. For God to pour himself out, then, as the man Jesus is not a venture outside of the Trinitarian life of indestructible love, but in fact quite the reverse: it is the act by which creation is seized up into the sheer invincible pertinacity of that love, which reaches down to gather us into its triune motion.

On the other hand, even in affirming the appropriateness of divine incarnation, the fathers still insist, in Gregory of Nyssa's words, that in Christ "that heavenly *apatheia* proper to the divine nature was preserved in the beginning and in the end of his human life."[58] And this is most definitely not the result of a failure to think the gospel through to its end:

58. Gregory of Nyssa, *Epistle* 3; GNO 8/2:26. [φυλασσομένης τῇ θεότητι καὶ ἐν τῇ ἀρχῇ τῆς ἀνθρωπίνης ζωῆς καὶ ἐν τῷ τέλει τῆς θεοπρεποῦς τε καὶ ὑψηλῆς ἀπαθείας.]

it is in fact, for them, the very substance of the gospel. After all, as a rule, the patristic narrative of salvation begins from the Pauline language of the glorification of creation through Christ, and achieves its most perfectly coherent form in the Christology of the fourth, fifth, and subsequent centuries: it is the story, that is, of *theōsis*, divinization, God becoming human that humans might become God. And it is in Christ that this economy occurs: for insofar as the person of the eternal Word can at once comprise divine and human natures in himself, we too, by dwelling in Christ, come to partake of the divine nature without ceasing to be human. Which means that the formula "the impassible suffered" is one whose terms must not be dissolved into one another. Only because, in Christ, our nature came into intimate contact with the eternal vitality of the divine nature, which no passion or interval of alienation can disrupt or alter, and through that contact death and sin were slain, can we be saved from all that separates us from God, and brought into the radiant shelter of his eternal peace, his *apatheia*. So Gregory can say that, in Christ, "What is by nature impassible was not changed into what is possible, but what is mutable and vulnerable to passions was changed into impassibility through its participation in the changeless."[59] And Cyril—for whom the unity of Christ is so profound and the union of natures so intimate that we must posit a *communicatio idiomatum*—nonetheless, in perfect consistency with his Christology, asserts that "According to his own nature, [Christ] suffers absolutely nothing; as God he subsists incorporeally, and is entirely beyond suffering."[60] This is the essence of the miracle of the incarnation, for patristic theology as a whole, and indeed is the good news Christians proclaim; for in the sufferings that the incarnate Word feels in his human nature, and so experiences even as the divine person he is, a marvelous transaction is accomplished. In the words of Gregory of Nazianzus: "[W]e do not separate the man from the Godhead, but say that he is one and the same, who was formerly not a man, but God and the only Son, eternal . . . who in these latter days has assumed humanity for our salvation: passible in his flesh, impassible in his divinity; circumscribed in body, uncircumscribed in the Spirit; one and the same, earthly and heavenly, tangible and intangible, comprehensible and incomprehensible, so that in this one and

59. Gregory of Nyssa, *De vita Moysis* 2; GNO 7/1:42. [τότε οὐ τὸ ἀπαθὲς τῆς φύσεως εἰς πάθος ἠλλοίωσεν, ἀλλὰ τὸ τρεπτόν τε καὶ ἐμπαθὲς διὰ τῆς πρὸς τὸ ἄτρεπτον κοινωνίας εἰς ἀπάθειαν μετεστοιχείωσεν.]

60. Cyril of Alexandria, Ὅτι εἷς ὁ Χριστός, pp. 482–84. [Πάθοι μὲν ἂν αὐτὸς εἰς ἰδίαν φύσιν τὸ σύμπαν οὐδέν. Ἀσώματος γὰρ ὑπάρξων ὡς Θεός, ἔξω που πάντως κείσεται τοῦ παθεῖν.]

the same who was at once wholly human and also God, the whole of humanity, fallen through sin, might be created anew."[61] This is the economy whereby, as Maximus phrases it, God gives us, in exchange for our destructive passions, his healing and life-giving passion on the cross[62]—which is worked by deathless love.

Indeed, it is fair to say that it is in this sense—before any other—that salvation is a matter of exchange for many of the fathers. It is the transaction, that is, the *admirabile commercium*, of divine and human natures that occurs in the incarnation of the Word, the miraculous reconciliation of God and humanity that simply is the very *communicatio idiomatum* of Jesus's identity, and that opens out to embrace us within its mystery in the death and resurrection of Christ when, as Cyril says, he accomplishes in himself the exchange of our slavery for his glory[63] and, having assumed our sufferings, liberates us from them through his unconquerable life.[64] The great Alexandrians, especially, tended to see salvation in terms of the atonement offering of Israel, whose central action was the bearing of the blood of the sacrifice—the blood of the people, as it were, dead in sin—into the holy of holies, where it came into contact with the deathless indwelling glory of God, so that Israel might be purified of its sins and made alive by God himself, the fountain of life. Just so, Athanasius[65] and Cyril like to speak of Christ's body as the temple wherein this immortal glory encounters our humanity and, by a divinizing contact, makes it live eternally. Following Hebrews 10:19–20, Cyril speaks of the veil of Christ's flesh—like the temple veil that hid the holy of holies—concealing the transcendent supereminence and exceeding glory of the Logos,[66] so allowing Christ "both to suffer in the flesh and not to suffer in his Godhead (for he was at once himself both God and human)" and thus to show through the resurrection "that he is mightier than death and corruption: as God he is

61. Gregory of Nazianzus, *Epistola ad Cledonium* (Ep. 101), PG 37:177. [Οὐδὲ γὰρ τὸν ἄνθρωπον χωρίζομεν τῆς θεότητος, ἀλλ' ἕνα καὶ τὸν αὐτὸν δογματίζομεν, πρότερον μὲν οὐκ ἄνθρωπον, ἀλλὰ Θεὸν καὶ Υἱὸν μόνον προαιώνιον . . . ἐπὶ τέλει δὲ καὶ ἄνθρωπον, προσληφθέντα ὑπὲρ τῆς σωτηρίας τῆς ἡμετέρας, παθητὸν σαρκὶ, ἀπαθῆ θεότητι, περιγραπτὸν σώματι, ἀπερίγραπτον πνεύματι, τὸν αὐτὸν ἐπίγειον καὶ οὐράνιον, ὁρώμενον καὶ νοούμενον, χωρητὸν καὶ ἀχώρητον, ἵν' ὅλῳ ἀνθρώπῳ τῷ αὐτῷ καὶ Θεῷ ὅλος ἄνθρωπος ἀναπλασθῇ πεσὼν ὑπὸ τὴν ἁμαρτίαν.]

62. Maximus the Confessor, *Mystagogia* 8; PG 91:688.

63. Cyril of Alexandria, Ὅτι εἷς ὁ Χριστός, pp. 366–68.

64. See Cyril of Alexandria, *Apologeticus pro XII capitibus contra orientales*, XII Anathematismus; PG 76:337–80.

65. See Athanasius, *Epistola ad Epictetum* 10; PG 26:1068.

66. Cyril of Alexandria, Ὅτι εἷς ὁ Χριστός, p. 456.

life and the giver of life, and raised up his own temple."[67] And this is in fact the consummation of the miraculous commerce that occurs in Christ: the perfection of our nature in Christ's resurrection body, a body entirely divinized and so entirely without pain.

To put the matter somewhat differently, the saving exchange that occurs for us in the incarnate Word is perfectly expressed for Cyril in John 20:17, when the risen Christ says, "I am going to my Father and your Father; to my God and your God," for here we see how the Son's Father by nature has become our Father by grace, precisely because our God by nature has become his God through condescension.[68] Indeed, for Cyril, whenever Christ calls upon his Father as "my God," he does so on our behalf and in our place: especially in the cry of dereliction from the cross.[69] And this is our salvation: for when the infinite outpouring of the Father in the Son, in the joy of the Spirit, enters our reality, the *apatheia* of God's eternally dynamic and replete life of love consumes every pathos in its ardor; even the ultimate extreme of the *kenōsis* of the Son in time—crucifixion—is embraced within and overcome by the everlasting *kenōsis* of the divine life. Because divine *apatheia* is the infinite interval of the going forth of the Son from the Father in the light of the Spirit, every interval of estrangement we fabricate between ourselves and God—sin, ignorance, death itself—is always already exceeded in him: God has always gone infinitely further in his own being as the God of self-outpouring charity than we can venture in our attempts to escape him, and our most abysmal sin is as nothing to the abyss of divine love. And as the Word possesses this Trinitarian impassibility in his eternal nature, and so as God cannot suffer, as a man he can suffer all things, bear any wound—indeed, bear it more fully than any other could—as an act of saving love: as Easter. And while God's everlasting outpouring, which is for him a life of infinite joy, in assuming the intervals of our estrangement from God, appears for us now under the form of tragic pain and loss, the joy is the original and ultimate truth of who he is, is boundless, and cannot be interrupted—and so conquers all our sorrow; our abandonment of God, and the abandonment of the Son and of every soul in death, is always already surpassed by the sheer abandon with which the Father begets and breathes forth his being. And the terrible

67. Cyril of Alexandria, Ὅτι εἷς ὁ Χριστός, pp. 474–76. [. . . καὶ τὸ σαρκὶ μὲν ἐλέσθαι παθεῖν, θεότητι δὲ μὴ παθεῖν ἦν γὰρ ὁ αὐτὸς Θεὸς τὸ ὁμοῦ ἄνθρωπος. Ὅτι γάρ ἐστι θανάτου κρείττων καὶ φθορᾶς, ζωὴ καὶ ζωοποιὸς ὑπάρχων ὡς Θεός, μεμαρτύρηκεν ἡ ἀνάστασις· ἐγήγερκε γὰρ τὸν ἑαυτοῦ ναόν.]

68. Cyril of Alexandria, Ὅτι εἷς ὁ Χριστός, pp. 334–36.

69. Cyril of Alexandria, Ὅτι εἷς ὁ Χριστός, pp. 442–44.

distance of Christ's cry of human dereliction, despair, and utter godforsakenness—"My God, my God, why hast thou forsaken me?"—is enfolded within and overcome by the ever greater distance and always indissoluble unity of God's triune love: "Father, into thy hands I commend my spirit."

V. Final Remark

Whether one is moved to embrace as warmly as one ought the doctrine of divine impassibility, it remains the case that the doctrine was never simply a philosophical mistake on the part of patristic and medieval tradition, the anomalous trace of an alien metaphysics, a fragment of paganism floating in the wine of faith; nor certainly was it the result of a failure to pay heed to the narrative of Scripture. But neither, one must acknowledge, was it so great a subversion of metaphysical rationality as to detach it utterly from its philosophical origins. For though Christians altered many of the nuances attached to the word *apatheia* radically, still they preserved its most essential speculative elements intact: immutability, eternity, simplicity, and so forth. This was a laudable and necessary thing: for the affirmation of God's impassibility is also an affirmation that God is truly good, that creation is freely worked and freely loved, that evil and violence and all the cruelties of human history enjoy no metaphysical or divine warrant, but stand under the everlasting damnation of the cross; that God simply is the fullness of charity, and so remains as he ever is in creating and redeeming and joining to himself creatures whom he summons into being not out of need, but for the much higher purpose of serving his delight. (And what dignity could be greater or gift more utterly gracious than to exist solely for the pleasure of an infinite charity that needs no increase in its joy, but freely gives?) This strange word *apatheia* allows us to say not only piously, but also meaningfully, that we belong to the lamb slain from the foundation of the world, that love is as strong as—and stronger than—death, that God loved us even when we were not, that in him there is no shadow of turning, that indeed God is light and in him there is no darkness at all, that in Christ all was Yea and Amen. . . . It allows us to say not only that God loves, that is, but that, simply enough, God is love.

THREE

The Writing of the Kingdom

Thirty-Three Aphorisms
toward an Eschatology of the Text

Introduction: The Question of the Text

Quaeritur: Who is the author of the text and who the reader? In the text, is one confronted by another, or is the text merely bare exteriority and irrecuperable dissemination? Are author and reader two autonomous selves who, in a medium of extraordinary transparency, mirror their depths each in the other, or is the text only the occasion of an interpretive event whose sheer fortuity is necessarily an alienation from (and denial of) all subjectivity? (Is this a theological question, and in what sense?)

I. Three Prolegomena

§1 For theology, this question (like every question of significance) can be answered only eschatologically.

§2 It is also a question that has perhaps become tediously familiar to us in recent decades, and the alternatives it comprises are perhaps so needlessly stark that it requires only a slight refinement of terms—obedient in all likelihood to a subtler, more Hegelian logic—to reconcile them. But the question also traverses the entire history of Western philosophy; its resolution, or at least the reconciliation of its antinomies, can occur variously, according to many different grammars, and it is a question that seems inevitably to invoke the name of God: either as the author whose infinite voice accompanies the entire "text" of creation, as the absolute source and absolute recovery of meaning, or as the sublime absence whose abyssal withdrawal provokes a mad and insatiable desire for what lies beyond the vagrant syllables of being (the inaccessible other who speaks and the inexpressible self who hears) and so evokes the text as the tragic form of this desire, the ever more exterior body of the exile, seeking an immemorial and impossible city. Whether the text grants, then, the interiority of self *and other* (as *known* to the self) or only the seductive shape of a desire incapable of satisfaction is a question—however inadequate its terms—that theology can (and should) address.

§3 However construed, the text is the exterior; all exteriority is the text.

II. Transcendental Reflections: The Self in the Text

§4 Of course, the question of author and reader is, in its earliest critical moments, the more original question of the self. Our "postmodern" disenchantment with the "self," however, is curiously bitter, and testifies to the ardor with which (in our transcendental and idealist naïveté) we made the self the chief object of our passion. The infatuated devotion of youth yields to the disillusioned recriminations of age. But this estrangement from what once we loved above all else was ineluctable, and was foreshadowed in certain ambiguities within our original fascination. Idolatry's vain adoration is always already faithlessness; it is the rejection of what is truly given. Modernity's discovery of the "self" coincided from the first with a loss of the self; we desired a self beyond all perturbation and exteriority, and so abandoned every particularity and contingency— every aspect of the living person—to an irredeemable finitude. If the first sacrificial victim of our perverse devotion was the other, the last and most precious ("thine only son, whom thou lovest . . .") was the empirical ego; the transcendental ego in whom self and world were unshakably certified could be only a self beyond subjectivity, a self born and preserved only in the forsaking of every self. No love founded upon so singular an act of betrayal, or animated by so peremptory a division, could long persist without inverting itself as hate or morbid resentment. We were urged on from the beginning by a specular passion—the desire to see and know ourselves pellucidly, reflected in a radiant surface that would capture every depth visibly—and the world was made to serve as a mirror answerable to this appetent gaze; but visibility itself, paradoxically, had first to be excluded from this vision, because the visible—stable representation—is always only appearance, and cannot validate itself, and the empirical ego (as another representation) is at best *doxa*, and can only deepen our despair. And so truth is first withdrawal into an inner sanctuary; the phenomena are rescued and restored only thereafter, not now in the eloquence of their mute appeal, of course, but in the lucid regularity with which they repeat the stable integrity of thought's pristine and featureless identity. This becomes explicit for us, reflectively, in the Kantian completion of the Cartesian transcendental project, when the substantiality of the "Ego" is displaced by the activity of the "cogito," in the transcendental unity of apperception. Nature, as construed regulatively by understanding and reason, may ultimately function "outwardly" in harmony with the "inward" law, reconciled in the free élan of judgment, and in the momentary probations of the sublime (which may grant some distant premonition of nature's infinity, lying beyond the impenetrable "veil of Isis," but which ultimately serves only to assure one of reason's supersensible freedom); but the other, irrecuperable exteriority, the unanticipable surd of the occasional, of historical contingency (the place of covenant, the time of revelation . . .), yields nothing of worth that this transcendental ego has not determined a priori. Such was the form the self—the object of our love—assumed when we captured it in our first embrace, as the reward for so many sacrifices so faithfully performed; how could we escape the idolater's inevitable disappointment on finding our fervent attentions met by such unresponsive and adamantine coldness?

§5 The pathos of modernity was deepened troublingly (though with impeccable consistency) by absolute idealism's final capture of the exterior (what speculative shadow of it remained, that is, in the form of the *Ding an sich*) in the play of the Ego, in its positing of ego and nonego; this Fichtean completion of the Kantian transcendental project redeemed the exterior by denuding it of exteriority, dissolving it into the Ego's primordial unity, deferring it toward infinity's horizon. A passion excited to frenzy: no finite identity was thus assured, the transcendental became transcendent again (even as it became, finally, irreducibly, self), and so desire still did not abate. The most extreme expression of this hunger here took shape: the insane immolation of all exteriority, so that our speculative passion could rest fixed upon a mirror within, securely possessed. But it was a shattered mirror, of course, an irreconcilable division of transcendental self from empirical, where each self was made to die to the world even at the moment when each had been discovered. In the silence of its pleromatic depth, the self was infinitely self, and infinitely secret. The speculative serenity of this vision, however, perhaps conceals the subtle agitations of a growing madness; absolute interiority is infinite exile, and the finite ego, in its loneliness (within itself, unknown to itself, and outside itself, as a shadow of itself), can assert itself only through transgression.

§6 The question of the text appears here, then, as the question of a concrete occasion for the display of a universal *exitus* and *reditus*, the adventure of speculation. The Hegelian completion of the Fichtean transcendental project (by way of Schelling) made the matter exquisitely clear: the text (the world, the exterior) gives the truth of the other (the author who negates and completes the reader, the alterity that disrupts and so forms identity) neither as immediacy (for immediacy is impossible; one cannot reach another as wholly other nor resolve another into what is wholly the same) nor exactly as mediation, except as a kind of self-mediacy (for all strangeness and difference is a provisional alienation, within the oscillating dialectic of a profounder recognition and identity), deferred toward ever greater fulfillment through constant negation and recovery, diremption and recuperation. It is true that the autonomy of the Fichtean Ego is displaced by the drama of thought's great labor to attain recognition through the consciousness of another, but the displacement (however vast in terms of the rationality of *history*) portends a still greater homecoming (and greater sacrifice). The seduction of the mirror gives way to the intoxication of transparency; all is bathed in an entirely pellucid medium: rational Spirit. This is a beautiful and majestic economy, but one served only to the degree that author and reader both die in the text—both *die*. Flesh and blood cannot inherit the kingdom that rational reflection glimpses afar. The devotion is given over to history now, and a languid detachment elevates thought above the tragic welter of the particular. In the system, of course, which can recover the self, in a sense, only through the recovery of all knowledge (assuming this is not simply a mad desire), the division between absolute and particular is—theoretically—abolished. But, even if the empirical ego is given back a little space to live and breathe, it is because the unity of history has reduced the unity of apperception to an ephemeral instance of what transcends any self, and the empirical disunity of the self to a necessary but negative probation. History belongs to Spirit, to thought, and truth is ultimately an infinite forgetfulness of empirical selves.

§7 The Kierkegaardian rejection of the Hegelian project (by way of Schelling) is resonant with a self's desperate demand that it be accommodated; the Nietzschean rejection of transcendentalism and transcendence alike arrays itself in heroic and tragic dignity, and converts self into spectacle, into achievement and triumph; but, in one fashion or another, as constancy or exuberance, the only medium for this rebellion is subjectivity, whose condition of irreparable fragmentation ultimately reduces rebellion to mere insolence.

§8 When idolatry grows wearisome, and the devotion that required so many and such extravagant sacrifices begins to wane, the victims rendered up cannot then simply be recalled. With the collapse of the great transcendental project (or, more precisely, its completion), we are left with two disenchantments: two selves have been lost, the transcendental and the empirical. But so has the exteriority that was laid upon their altar: the exteriority of an articulate world, whose orders of eminence and splendor spoke in us before the discrete self was fully formed in our reflections, a world that disclosed itself in an intelligible or divine grammar. This order of truth cannot simply be recovered for us. (Nor should theology simply desire such a recovery: the Word is always poured out in words, present to and in excess of our "truths," expressing its infinite richness by assuming every privation without estrangement; any recovery of "analogy" hereafter lies at the end of a *via negativa*, along whose course any simple metaphysical scale of resemblances must be abandoned. Theological analogy, though, never was such a metaphysics.)

§9 A "postmodern condition" is one in which there must be a recoil to bare subjectivity and alterity, but an ironic recoil, in which each requires and resists the other, and each is both absolute and nonsensical. A shapeless ego troubled by "proximity," self contaminated by otherness, but otherness uncontaminated by the same. A self still remains—this is the heritage of modernity, which cannot simply be rejected—but a nameless, fortuitous self, disturbed by externality (by the text), which arrives always as provocation, accusation, persecution, or equivocal (even sinister) invitation. The self is made singular only by anonymity and secrecy and an irrepressible motion away from itself, and the other is made doubly secret, known by a disjunctive and transgressive (but necessary) analogy, or known as unknown through the "trace." No matter whether one speaks with the disruptive exuberance of Deleuze or the moral pathos of Levinas, or (in fact) the aporetic prudence and delicate suspicion of Derrida, we remain in a Kantian place, and the world of textuality (insofar as it appears to us as intelligible) belongs to the shimmering veil of the theoretical, suspended between two sublime and unrepresentable things: self and other (whether analogizable or not). The edifice of the transcendental project—resting upon the slightest of supports—collapsed, but its ruins remain our grammar.

§10 The text confronts the self and the self confronts the text, in either case as *mere* interpretation, fabulous invention, bewilderment, anger. The author—the other—is impossible: as is the reader. To have awakened from our delirium, from the enchantment of the mirror, is to have inherited the solemn and moral—or, then again, heroic and poetic—*labor* of the opaque. The exteriority of the text does not mediate, neither does it present the other; author and reader do not *appear*. It serves, rather, either as spur to a joyless desire for what is beyond, for an unapproachable good (though here the word "good" often seems only pious convention), or as a provocation and aggression that demands a reciprocal act of overcoming and creativity (though here these words often seem only heroic convention). Traces upon traces, alluring or infuriating arabesques and ellipses: a surface of impenetrable inscription upon impenetrable inscription, "redeemed" only in its continuous, irreparable disruption. The equivocal metaphors with which we began—transparency or mirror, either or both—are rendered otiose: neither self nor other is given. A limitless obligation and mourning are demanded, or the savage ecstasy of psychotic and nomadic flight is inaugurated, but in either case in defiance of visibility and legibility alike. This, at least, is one reading of our condition; its gravity cannot be dispelled too easily, nor merely distorted into the levity of a "playful" nihilism. But it is a condition already known to theology, in a sense always already answered.

III. Prophetic Dissemination: The Inscription of the Text

§11 What is the condition of textuality? Ideally, it is the inscription of intelligibility upon an unintelligible substrate (passive *materia prima*, brute and intractable *hylē*, the fallow void of the *chōra*, the blank page); this essay's third prolegomenon is susceptible of many interpretations, from the most unashamedly "metaphysical" to the most fashionably "nihilist," and it will return below in thoroughly theological form, but it is perhaps best to consider it here in the context of the history of this ideal economy of inscription, this confluence of meaning and meaninglessness, order and chaos. For, in one sense or another, text and substrate—intelligibility and "matter"—are always inseparable for us; the history of Western philosophy since Plato perhaps consists in a sequence of epochal collapses of the distinction between text and world. Whether this elevates the indomitable givenness of the exterior to the level of analogical articulacy or reduces language to the accidental play of inchoate energies or of *différance*, whether it abandons absolute exteriority to the ineffable *beyond* of transcendental cognition or dissolves it in the depths of infinite consciousness, depends upon the age; but always the distinction of text from world arrives at a point of indifference, and remains undecidable. The world is known to us only as an interpreted world, always received according to an "intention"; nor is interpretation simply a matter of phenomenological adequation, the indiscerptible coincidence of *noēsis* and *noēma*, but is also governed in every instance by a hermeneutical history, by a tradition of reading and inscription whose origins and ends are equally unsearchable. In Plato's thought, of course, the ideal economy of the inscribed appears in its purest form: the substrate (matter, the "here below") receives—albeit imperfectly—the impress of the forms, and one can "read" the text of the world because, in a moment of anamnetic retreat, the mind can consult its innate foretext; two surfaces compose the world—one featureless, bare, abysmal, and dark, the other beautiful, luminous, and clear, the latter surface superimposed upon the former—and the divergence of one from the other can be remarked, at least theoretically, only because the mind's recollection of the forms allows one to see where and how their reflections, here in the land of unlikeness, deviate, depart from their models, and consort with *simulacra*. While it is true that the distinction between text and substrate is always sustained in the Platonic scheme, the condition of all exteriority as one of textuality as such is everywhere assumed; compared to this always more primordial indistinction between the world and the economy of inscription, the simple distinction of what is written from the surface that receives its traces is as nothing. All exteriority is the text. And truth is that which *shines*: truth is always radiant, a distinct shape illuminated by the light of the good beyond beings, an intelligible finitude conquering the inexpressive darkness of the infinite (the "*apeiron*," which, in Platonic terms, can mean only the "indeterminate," chaos, the eternally meaningless). The transcendental tradition of modernity alters, but does not abandon, this economy: the Kantian distinction of theoretical cognition from the thing in itself repeats this logic of textuality, though, by resituating the home of the "forms" in the understanding, Kant deprives reflection of that transcendent index that made the Platonic distinction between form and substrate meaningful (or, indeed, possible); the collapse of the distinction between text and world is complete, and later idealism's talk of the absolute immanence of the world within thought merely makes this explicit. Even the later return to a more chastened transcendentalism in the thought of Husserl can no longer think what exceeds thought as an unintelligible noumenon, but only as an ever more eminent phenomenality, an as-yet-undisclosed surfeit of textuality. Now, in our "postmodern" state, the world of forms long since departed and our confidence in the stability of the categories of understanding now quite shaken, text and world remain inseparable, but no longer under the regime of the understanding: text and world, as one, have reverted to the rule of the aleatory and impenetrable; the intelligible is always a fragile and conditional accommodation with chaos, fissured by innumerable contradictions and ambiguities; the exterior belongs to force, to the capture of force, or to dissemination. But still, always, as text.

§12 The question that at present governs reflection upon this condition is whether the text (every text) is always "written." Derrida's reading of Plato's *Phaedrus*, even if many of its more extravagant claims regarding Western thought as a whole (including theology) are best overlooked, provides theology with a certain opportunity for rearticulating (albeit in a postmodern idiom) a critique of pagan philosophy common in the patristic age. The Platonic distrust of writing, the mysticism of immediate address, the "gnostic" myth of the soul's preincarnate vision of the hyperouranian mysteries and subsequent fall into the "foul tomb" of the body, the teacher's anxiety that his authority over his words (and his disciples) not be lost in the interminable and ungovernable dissemination of texts, the Socratic claim of the philosopher's special power of recollection and insight, the Platonic politics of enclosure, exclusion, pedagogical autocracy, and "ideal" law—indeed, all the elements of the *Phaedrus* that "Plato's Pharmacy" addresses, either directly or by implication, appear in Derrida's essay under the form of a profound unity; and this is an accomplishment few other exegeses of this text can boast. The cult of *anamnēsis* can certainly be seen as *also* the regime of pedigree and privilege; the mysticism of the immediately spoken invokes a rule of silence, a Word that lives in the death of words. The self and the city partake of a single interior, a single garden fecundated and preserved by the simultaneous domination and exclusion of the exterior; truth is an always more inward retreat to the absolutely past, a glance into the "dark backward and abysm of time," but a retreat that requires the ambiguous service of an ever-present *pharmakon*, an always recused *pharmakeus*: writing, at once poison and cure. One can, of course, read Plato in quite an opposite direction; a theologian of Platonic disposition might claim that the "good beyond beings" is—like the creator God of the Bible—a disruption of this rule of inescapable immanence and metaphysical totality, and might be tempted to contest the distinction between Platonic *anamnēsis* (which seeks the unchanging *archē*) and Augustinian *memoria* (which opens out upon the dynamic eternity of God), or show that this is a difference that does not constitute an antinomy; but such a course might risk rendering much of the *Phaedrus* not only contradictory but also incoherent. Derrida's reading, if nothing else, does describe the dialogue's pervasive metaphysical pathology, at least in part: the Platonic anxiety before the "chaos" of dissemination operates at every level in the *Phaedrus*, and colors with a certain poignant duplicity the valedictory prayer to Pan with which the dialogue closes, imploring the great god for a unity of the outward self with the inward. Having thanked Derrida for his reading, however, insofar as it is appropriate (that is, insofar as it addresses—specifically and solely—the discourse of Platonism), theology can move beyond it. For it is surely the case for theology that what Plato seeks by way of *anamnēsis* must actually be regarded as also an inwardness that opens out onto radical, indeed infinite, exteriority: a *creature*, considered solely as creature, has no recollection of an eternal identity, does not emanate from an eternal ground, but receives its identity always, in every moment, as the repeated gift of an infinite God, who gives all to what is eternally other than himself. The Word theology hears and responds to is profoundly— infinitely—written; it must come to the surface—where it is impressed—in an act of reading; and so the true depth of the "self" that hears and responds to this Word is an ever greater exteriority: may my inward self, then, be as one with this outward text, may I be written again and again by grace. The soul is a surface composed of writing and reading, address and response. And "writing"—mediation, but also dissemination—belongs properly to theology's Logos, because it offers no retreat into an anamnetic silence, an imperturbable and heroic inner wisdom, but always ventures forth as future, the truest exterior: "writing" is the proper name for "memory" once theology has reinscribed memory as hope and promise.

§13 Derrida, of course, implicates Christian "creationism" and "infinitism" in the story he tells (especially in *Of Grammatology*) of a pathetic metaphysical nostalgia for perfect presence; he carelessly conflates theology with idealism, and so reduces all talk of creation to talk of a "closed totality of signifiers," "finite or infinite," the grand circuit of the transcendental signified into which all signifiers can be dissolved. It is permissible somewhat to elide Derrida's distinction between "writing" and "creation," however; the created is precisely that which cannot be made subordinate to a metaphysical scheme of closed signification, because while its only significance is indeed deferred toward a transcendence it can never embody, it is so only as the *free* play of God's glory, the "meaningless" excess of God's graciousness. This is the "textuality of the world" that theology proclaims: neither an epistemic index delivered over to the rational agency of a substantial subjectivity ("metaphysics"), nor the provocative clamor of chaos ("postmodernity"), but an address that necessarily awakens a response, a glory that elicits either praise or a hiding of the eyes in shame. Any complaint raised against the presence of a "transcendental signified" can be ignored here: it is a complaint that is compelling only to those who share the prejudice that prompts it. Creation speaks of God, but not as an intrinsic order of essential signification; it speaks only when received and narrated according to a desire for and love of God. Hence the language of analogy in theological tradition, which (contrary to certain "postmodern" prejudices) has always resisted any simple binary economy of signification, or any simple metaphysical scale of ontologically continuous emanation. The art of analogy, for theology, is the art of a certain irreducible and fruitful interval, a certain distance—the distance of the gift (but "interval," "distance," and "gift," all understood in ways that Derrida's work has consistently not allowed). More of this below; here, suffice it to say that theology, no less than certain of the discourses of magisterial postmodernism, starts from an awareness of a world of signifiers disseminating endlessly, irrecuperable within any grand metaphysical scheme of correspondence or signification. The humble estate of the word, spoken or written, is a condition of provisionality, vagary, and semiotic peregrination. But this awareness is not scaffolded within any *transcendental* dogmatism that confines the thought of dissemination to a discourse of erasure or of absence.

§14 The question from which this essay set out remains: Who is the author, who the reader? If one can and must presume an ultimate indistinction of textuality and exteriority, if the "self" consists in a surface of interpretation, of reading and response, and if every sign eludes both the logic of correspondence and the structuralist fixity of a synchronic system, can this question be asked? But, then again, need the question be confined to the level of the sign, or even of the syntagma? More original than the sign—which can be isolated only secondarily, in a reflective moment—is a certain kind of *narration*: understood as that continuous and creative act of discourse that, in being spoken, speaks the speaker, invokes and invites the hearer, delivers a story to interpretation. Whether narrative as such is always a category contaminated by metaphysical nostalgia is an unimportant question here: narration need only mean that continuous act of arranging the surface—the text—that allows signs to appear, that can order them according to a memory that is also a desire for a future, that interprets by reconciling disparate moments according to a certain creative ordering of passion. Apart from this ordering, this always prior and active narrative, could language occur? How could we think of it? How could we speak? And so it constitutes something other than "metaphysics" to allow the question of the self to arise again as a question concerning the narrated self: What shape can desire impart to what is spoken and its response; how does the next moment of reading "recall" and restate what has been read? In the midst of all that disseminates—more original than the flight of the sign, or than *différance*—is an irreducible narrativity, and both self and other (both reader and author) subsist in the narration that, at any moment, composes and recomposes the surface of their "encounter." Reader and author are told, are recounted and invented (which is to say, at once found and fashioned) upon a textual surface. Theology is, of course, animated by the belief that only God tells and has told the tale correctly, and by the hope that the self narrated in "me" by God's creative Word is a story to which "my" telling can conform itself in love, and so theology is always, precisely, attention to the text.

§15 No telling is simply "mine": "I" appropriate what is told in me; "I" am narrated and so, in reading, become, or occur. To say this differently, I am not I before (*avant*) the text, but only before (*devant*) the text. I am I in hearing a word, in the evocation of a response; I emerge only in that I am addressed, as the event of the text in one to whom it is addressed (in me), as one who must reply and who, therefore, is. The author, then, is always before me as a prophetic utterance, as the one who prophesies my coming, my hearing, and who is pledged to me, promised to me. Author and reader appear for the first time in the event of the text as the one promised and the one prophesied: neither is given as an immediate presence, neither is recalled or recognized in the light of an eternal identity, but each is given to the other as a future. As with every promise, a certain anxiety (at times terror) constitutes the event, but also a certain rejoicing; dissemination, in the event of the text, becomes also hope, not only endless retreat from an immemorial past, but a pilgrimage toward a desired future. And in this event I appropriate and am appropriated, I take the text upon myself, I am taken by the text as the surface upon which it inscribes itself. In the arts, we experience this often with particular vividness—Shakespeare, Vermeer, Bach—but it occurs with a special claim on us in the text of Scripture, in the address of He Who Is (of He Who Will Be as He Will Be).

§16 All language is sibylline: it invokes—it foresees—a hearer. And every text is oracular: it evokes, anticipates, announces, and supplicates a reader, even one who, at the moment of writing, is immeasurably remote, unimaginable, hoped for at the extreme limit of possibility. All writing calls out for, anticipates, and longs for a reader. *Every text*, to one degree or another, embodies this prophetic saturation of language, which is language's very life; even across vast intervals of time, the author is the one promised, given over, to be received by another who has not yet appeared to view, who can be only prophesied, hoped for. Author and reader *eventuate* in the text, as promise and hope, a single surface composed from two ecstasies, in the third moment (which is also the first moment) of the text itself. A beautiful and terrible pledge is made—that we, author and reader, will one day meet there, in that place, upon that surface, in its final radiance, and will know, and will be known—but it is made irrevocably. This illimitable attendance upon the mystery of a promise is the essence of prophecy, and the price of calling out longingly for the arrival of the one in whom the text will impress itself: for a flesh that will bear the marks of covenant.

§17 But for this hope, no text would appear, none could be written, nor any read; I could not speak, I would not be I, if not for the economy of a promise. Simply said, there would be no text apart from this expectation, for every reading responds, however obscurely, to a promise, and every text is legible only in the light of hope. Every text comes, all exteriority appears, not only according to the reader's "intention," but as the embassy of one who is yet to come. For reading is impossible—no soul could bear the labor—but for the anticipation of fulfillment, but for the futurity of the written, the outward, word. To write is always to call to an unseen other expectantly; to read is always to await an unseen other, pledged in an intimacy found upon a single shared and indivisible surface.

§18 To speak of covenant is not to speak of an ideal hermeneutical feat, a fusion of horizons, an interpretive triumph, or even an understanding (except of a fragmentary variety, hidden under the mantle of the prophet); nor to speak of a retrieval of a past intention in a present, divinatory act of reading. For now, the text comes as promise, is read as hope, and points toward an eschatological fulfillment in which we—author and reader—will at last see and be seen, the both of us brought finally and entirely to the surface. Every text—every utterance—presumes a covenant, but it is the *written* text in which this is most beautifully expressed, because the deferrals of the written word—the Torah, the Gospels—uniquely forbid resort to the comforting circularity of "dialogue" and its often sterile mythos of the immemorial, the autochthonous, the ideal. The text as covenant is eschatological promise, futurity, an exteriority without the "dialectic" of selves (which is also to say, without their sacrifice).

§19 Theology must say that one is only because one is addressed by God. God's utterance cannot be without response, and hence I am; I have always been called forth, as reader, as hearer of God's address in creation. And creation (*qua* creation) is a free utterance, the work of grace, the open declaration of God's glory, fashioned from nothingness; creation is an infinite semiosis, a text, the exterior, below which lies no abiding substance, no constant and autonomous substrate. Again, this is not to imagine creation as merely a system of correspondences and resemblances, a closed book, or a hierarchy of metaphysical sympathies, and nothing more; it is to say, rather, that the world everywhere speaks glory, that its signs (which may admit of no ultimate division within themselves between signifier and signified) disseminate and yet, in their very irreducible openness, constitute (when received according to a particular desire) pledges of the one who calls forth hearers of his covenant.

§20 If the event of the text embodies two ecstasies—writing and reading—it also displays each as an ecstasy that never simply folds back in again upon itself (recovering the "self" from the negative "moment" of the other, recovering a primordial memory from the evanescence of the phenomena, and so forth). Precisely because its structure is, of necessity, eschatological, it sets the signs it comprises free from the silence of the absolute past. The text—the exterior—shines in its every instance, without any moment of its particularity being sacrificed to the total saying of the unshaken origin: for all is given anew in every moment from a future where all signs (it is promised) will shine together in the perfect accord of the kingdom. The signs of being speak the radiance of God's glory because they are freely given as what they are, freely called, in the extravagant needlessness of their particularity, to the wedding feast; they do not depart from an idea, to which they must return to attain the condition of "truth," but venture toward an infinite freedom, an infinite rejoicing (the liberty and joy of God, imparted to creation), and only thus are they *true* (that is, their surface *is* their depth). For the eschatological—as a structuring *pathos*—is a longing not for the closed totality and imperturbable splendor of a system, but for the dispensation of an ultimate peace, a dwelling together of all things in harmony. Of course, as—for instance—Nicholas of Cusa understood, a longing for ultimate peace (as opposed to simple, undifferentiated unity) requires a very particular calculus of the infinite.

IV. The Distance of the Kingdom: The Place of the Text

§21 What is the distance in which the text occurs? Where is it inscribed? For the question that precedes every other question concerning text or self—or indeed, any question concerning being—is the question of distance, of distantiation and difference. This is the primordial reduction, the structure or intention more original than the "pure intuitions" of space and time, or than the distinction of the same from the other, or even than the distance of the ontological difference. *Where* does being occur, according to what dispensation? What grants the distance in which difference eventuates? A curious condition of our postmodern situation is the dependence of even our most audacious nihilisms upon the structures of our most monolithic metaphysics. When Plato was forced to consider the problem of the *chōra*—the outside, the placeless place where the forms give shape to the land of unlikeness—his language equivocated between metaphors of fecundity and sterility; but, however aporetic his discourse became at this point, clearly he could never think the *chōra* except in terms of a certain formlessness, darkness, and alienation. For the distance that makes room for what differs is, of necessity, the outside, the distance of an exile, an abandonment, and a violent dissimulation, and the labor of philosophy is to recover from a "fall" into the abyss of the exterior (the tragedy of distance, which is also the possibility of thought). But at the "end" of the metaphysical fable, when Derrida again considers the *chōra*, on the far side of every idealism, his thinking is still governed by the metaphysics he has abandoned: for him, as well, being's distance is one of estrangement, formlessness, emptiness, *exile* (and this precisely because the *chōra* is neither force, nor principle, nor idea, nor place); his thought differs from Plato's in that he gives priority to the *chōra* and its intractable indifference to every form, but not in how he conceives of distance. Similarly, when Deleuze attempts to place the thought of difference before every thought of identity, he can do so only by reversing the order "metaphysics" supposes between the intelligible and the formless, between idea and chaos. The destiny of Western thought, perhaps, has always been to think distance according to these oppositions, and the question must be asked whether this determines in advance the *speculative* distance in which the "postmodern" takes shape—or, rather, the specular distance: Is the postmodern merely the mirroring inversion of the metaphysical? Is thought now to be confined to a perpetual oscillation between *eidos* and *chōra*, unable to decide which is prior or which is "true"? We have not, then, advanced beyond a certain frantic trepidation, a vertiginous dread before being, which pervades philosophy; philosophy, thus constrained, is indeed a meditation upon death: death as the return from the untruth of the phenomena, whether this means regaining the vision of the forms or disappearing into the night of difference. Wherever this speculative continuum is entered, one thought persists: the exterior is an exile, birth emerges from death, the ontic is a violent departure from the ontological, all language dissembles what enables it (Logos, *chōra*, presence, absence). If this is the distance in which the text is inscribed, it can promise only death.

§22 Theology begins from another account of distance, one native to the scriptural narrative. The moment within Western thought that philosophy has never adequately understood is the arrival of the language of creation, which makes all distance originally the distance of a gift—absolutely a gift, compelled by no metaphysical necessity, continuous with its source not firstly by way of substance but simply according to the gesture with which it is bestowed. When, for instance, Heidegger dismisses the language of creation as a "grounding" of Being in a first being and as the reduction of the world to a mere *factum*, he merely demonstrates the degree to which he has failed to think the interval that the thought of creation opens up. For, certainly, if the Being of beings is where the "Nothing nothings," if this Being which *is* only in its veiling and unveiling—in the luminous arising and "whiling" of its disappearance, at the "juncture" of presencing, according to the *logos* that gathers beings, disposes them, and sends them on their way—*is* Being, without the outward contour of yet another difference, then the thought of the creator God can be only an onto-theological error, a failure to think the difference, a forgetfulness of the fold of Being-beings (or of what "gives" this difference to every age of thought); but the Heideggerean account can never be anything but a metaphysical presupposition, a certainty that the Being of beings—which his thought discerns in each being's event, where it occurs, in the fissure between Being and Nothing—is simply the Being of all that is, and that the "appropriating event" (*Ereignis*) composes being only according to the "justice" of arising and disappearing. But if, on the other hand, the distance of the ontological difference is contained within a greater and more original distance, which gives it room, and if the difference constitutes only an analogy of that giving, thought cannot yet say how a thinking of Being (or of its "dif-fering") could foreclose the thought of the God who gives being, from beyond this fold. To be clear, this is not to place God simply "beyond being" in the fashion of Levinas, for whom creation's distance is imagined too much on the order of a gnostic abyss, posing the good over against the ontological; nor even to repeat the gesture of Jean-Luc Marion, who similarly thinks the distance of God from creation as all but completely alien to the distance, within creation, of the ontological difference (in either case, the question of the *chōra* must return, more violently and unanswerably, until being itself becomes convertible with the "profane" or the "evil," and a certain metaphysics is revived in its most malign form). Rather, it is to say that the distance of creation is a gift that participates in a distance that is always gift, always love and joy and peace, and the distance of the fold is an analogy of the distance that gives Being needlessly to beings; for analogy here is an interval that—always preserved within itself—marks the interval of the gift as irreducible. To phrase this in more explicitly Christian language, the distance that gives the distance of being is the infinite interval of the Trinitarian *perichōrēsis*, a distance that is always given as delight in another, as a sharing, a receiving, an address and a response, always an "exteriority" (but without alienation or violence); a distance, moreover, in which the couplet of Being and presence is unfolded from eternity, as an infinite coincidence and infinite peace; creation, the giving of the gift, falls within the interval of this giving, and the distance of creation from God, and all distances within creation, are analogies of this infinite gift. Thought thus, distance is, most originally, peace and life; and inscribed thus, within this distance, the text may genuinely promise (and give) another. For the text, if it bears the shape of the gift (and to the very degree that it is so given), discloses the exterior as just this peace, and the surface as a place of meeting.

§23 There is still no theological need at this point to resort to the myth of autonomous subjectivity, or to one of idealist fusion; but neither can theology rest content with the language of community without communion (after the fashion of Levinas or Jean-Luc Nancy), as though exteriority were of necessity an absolute alterity or (at most) a *partage*, where love is subordinate to an economy of death (the death of the Other, glimpsed in the Other's eyes as an infinite prohibition, or my death, as the limit where I transcend myself in a freedom that also frees every Other to die apart from me). For while it is true that, as Nancy insists, we are born upon the surface, emerge into freedom only at the limit, and live only upon that exterior of bare existence, it is not true that this *writing* (existence itself, "infinite finitude," exteriority without reserve, the pellicle of the momentary and passing event) gives and will give nothing. The structure (the *Wesen*, it is perhaps better to say) of the written is the event of a promise (both a prophecy and a pledge); we would know nothing of writing if this were not so, we would be unaware of "existence," we could not read. And, if so, perhaps the moment of existence that gives us the fleeting passage of presencing belongs to a distance that is *full*, a "musical" distance, in which all that passes is also recalled, restored, born into a fuller music; perhaps this is the surface of being's inscription: the ever more open circumincession of the Trinity. For theology, therefore, the exterior may be thought otherwise.

§24 It was Gregory of Nyssa who first reconceived the "infinite" in Christian terms, as the distance of God himself, which we traverse in an ontic ecstasy, an *epektasis*, a "stretching out"; for him, ultimately, all distance is the distance of God, and we—while remaining creatures—traverse that distance in love, are taken into it, and grow into it. The ceaseless energy of our passing, if guided by love, never effaces our finitude, but shows it capable—through movement—of the infinite that loves us. The *apeiron* of this thinking is not chaos or a Dionysian riot, but an infinite expanse of ever more superabundant beauty and reconciling peace; the infinite of the Platonic economy is abandoned, and the infinite of postmodernity's tragic wisdom is forestalled. This is the distance where we are written, the surface upon which we pass.

§25 Given this account of distance as infinite plenitude, opening itself to infinite traversal, there is no need for any heroic *pathos* (tragic or joyous) before the fact that the self possesses no stable identity or essence, can never retreat into a dialectical recovery of itself, is always exterior to itself in an otherness lying ahead; this is simply the condition of the creature, to whom all is always being given anew, and whose being therefore never comes to rest upon any foundation. It is the knowledge of distance, as the most primordial of ontic conditions: distance, which is the most original phenomenological intention, and which is transcendental in the critical sense, as the very structure of subjectivity, is the being "I" am given. Or, rather, "I" denominates a distance, an interval *of response* that is always constituted as a distance-from. "I" am a particular distance from the call, and a particular distance in which the call resonates, and a particular traversal of an infinitely given distance (which only in this traversal becomes for me an "interiority," a *diastēma* of my "stretching out"). "I" am never simply an object set at a distance, but the effect of the distance, its creature, called forth from nothingness by the one who gives room and time, the one in whose triune life presence is always given over, *deferred* (a deferral whose analogy is, for us, futurity).

§26 Nor is there any need to embrace the philosophical prejudice that finitude is originally violent, that the ontic is essentially strife, and that all linguistic mediation (all writing) partakes of a necessary and inevitable reduction, aggression, or alienation (a prejudice born before Plato, persisting on into the discourse of "postmodernity"); self and other—in the event of the text, of the exterior—occur to one another as phenomena, representations, interpretations, but it is not necessary to think that this is *essentially* a violence (even a necessary and fruitful violence), or that this condition of exposure is simultaneously an incarceration of each by the other, where each is bound by the negativity of knowledge's labor. Violence is perhaps secondary to the encounter, parasitic upon its being, the effect of sin; for, as there is no self to reduce apart from the encounter, no otherness that is not born in the moment of the text, the most deeply folded interiority is still only a gift of the surface, evoked and shaped by the encounter; to grant priority to the reduction, rather than to this miraculous parturition, is a metaphysical decision, and nothing more. The text is a nuptial revelation of each to the other, which occurs in a medium that is both intimacy and estrangement, proximity and separation, but perhaps one that is governed first not by the violence of a dialectical reduction or negation, but by the peace of an eschatological promise. Such, at least, is the substance of faith.

§27 The infinite is being's luminous distance, in which the ontic participates, but it is disclosed only by the style of the motion that traverses it; it can be measured by every moment of brokenness, "displayed" as violence in sin's estranging movement; or its surface can be crossed in such a way that every aporetic interval, every pause, is received as a caesura within a continuing movement toward the God whose radiance pervades being (though the disruptions of sin cannot, of course, be entirely overcome this side of the kingdom). The course of the motion, its cadence, discloses the surface upon which it occurs, and what guides this motion is a desire, a hunger for the wedding feast; and so the motion is also a sabbatarian suspense, sustained by love, which alone can interpret the distance, as the distance gives itself to traversal.

§28 The exterior—the text—is disclosed for us as language, as an address and the possibility (and grammar) of a response: disclosed, that is, entirely as language. Language—the textual address that always evokes an "I" who can answer, and that promises the writer to the reader—does not mark one pure depth of subjectivity mysteriously imparting itself to another, two selves somehow prior to the event of the text; rather, the depth of all things is just this infinite surface of language, endlessly enriching and articulating the distance of this being that is spoken, and reflecting the infinite depth of that Trinitarian discourse of love—the eternal eventuation of the Persons to one another in an address of love, one to another, opening out to a third, always being perfected by being given back with a new intonation—by which God is God. This is known to Christian thought because we see ourselves—indeed, are given selves—only in the body of Christ. Here the metaphor of the mirror acquires new meaning: the specular detaches itself from the speculative; the transcendental scheme (for which the world serves as a mirror of the self and its powers) is inverted; it is we who, according to our desires, reflect the motile glory that confronts us in all creation and in every other, and that shapes us. Language is not the transparent medium by which a prior presence reveals itself, nor the reflective surface in which a subjectivity returns to itself; but it is the surface of the event, on which "selves" take shape in one another, in the specular play of invocation and answer, pledge and prophecy. This infinite play of light, in which we are born to one another and within one another, and in which we are given to ourselves as the gift of others, is how the surface of inscription gives us depth: the depth of mirrors that capture a light from beyond themselves and give it back again. The textual event—the linguistic occurrence of the exterior—is a coinherence in which persons donate one another, receive from one another, are given to one another by the God who gives his distance as the place where creatures—born from nothingness—come to pass.

§29 Profounder (and more original) than the speculative urge to possess oneself as an indomitable substance is the desire to know oneself as known by God, to become the surface in which God's beauty appears; we see now as in a glass darkly, but then will see face-to-face, seeing God in all bodies (as Augustine says), seeing God as the infinite vision whereby we see (as Nicholas of Cusa phrases it), and loving ourselves only in God's love for us (to use the terms of Bernard of Clairvaux). As mirrors mirroring ever more, infinitely more, we "see" God. As I *am* only in that I am evoked by another, only by knowing the one who addresses me am I known to myself; and him I know only in response to that address, in being born outside of myself in the exteriority of that text.

§30 Herein should lie the romance of Judaism for the Christian, the deep allure of (in particular) the rabbinic tradition. Ceaseless labor over the minutiae of the law is the supreme act of gratitude to a lover on the part of a beloved. For the law is a language of love: its every nuance calls for a response, its secret splendors must be sought out, each syllable summons forth a rapt and lingering attentiveness. This is not in any sense a tragic labor, a shoring up of fragments of the past, or the frantic recovery of debris, but is the joyous art of perfecting a reply to a lover's embassy. Only the people to whom the law was delivered can enjoy this particular dialect of intimacy, this nuptial colloquy; but the Christian who catches any glimpse of it, and in whom it does not excite a eucharistic hunger, has not yet understood the gifts of grace.

§31 For Christians, the fruit of the law is given in the Word, to whom one must return again and again in a ceaseless feeding that at once has the savor of fulfillment and provokes an ever deeper hunger for the feast of the kingdom. In the Eucharist, the text that supremely addresses and evokes me is discovered; the story of Easter—which is God's true telling of the world—is told in me and I in it. I am given the flesh of the author of my flesh, who feeds me. In the prophetic saturation of *all* language, a rising up was always promised; but in Christ, the entire address of God and response of creation are perfected, and all words are raised up in the Word. The obscure promise—as evocative of desperation as of hope—that animates every text and delivers it to a reader, becomes clear in Christ, and becomes real joy, real feasting. Every Eucharist is a Passover, in which a liberation from death is given, and the one who calls me forth pledges me to himself and to all others, and promises an appointed time and place (Zion) where the pledge will be consummated. The promise that is the very possibility of all language and every text is a hunger that can be filled only at the wedding feast, when the other will be given; and in the bread and wine of communion, this promise is made explicit as the coming of the kingdom. Until then, as we traverse the distance he metes out, he has become for us the waybread that nourishes us.

§32 Again, but for this anticipation, hope, and love, no reading would be possible, no word heard. No desire, but for this eschatological desire; nor any love possible, but for this love of God. If a resurrection of bodies were not promised, even in the simplest exchange of words, the body of the text would never rise up in me, nor I in the text; the hope of this redemption, this meeting of purest exteriority, beyond the estranging interiority of death or the disembodied soul, is the hope that allows attention to the text's sequences, to the openness of their every moment to a greater fruition in the next, and gives rise to the expectation (and so apprehension) of a meaning imparted (a meaning that is, though, the entire body of the text itself, given back again beyond its ending). This eschatology is the structure of writing and reading, the form of the text, and so every text—given and received—is potentially a passing over from death to life. Every text is known only insofar as one expects to be known; every feast is joyous only because it promises that feast that lies beyond all weeping; every address awakens me to a response because it faintly echoes the address of the one who summons me in language and in all of being; every text cries out for redemption. Until then, we continue failingly in the economy of the text, and move fitfully in that specular infinity where all surfaces acquire their depths from the other surfaces they enfold, and that enfold and reflect and reinflect them, and from the infinite light in which they are placed and that enfolds all things in itself forever. The Word that calls us forth from nothingness out into this radiant distance is eternally spoken, and this we know because the Word has dwelt among us, and nourishes us still, and draws us on. Even so, come quickly.

§33 Next year in Jerusalem.

FOUR

From "Notes on the Concept of the Infinite in the History of Western Metaphysics"

Part I

1. There is not—nor has there ever been—any single correct or univocal concept of the infinite. Indeed, the very word by which the concept is named typically—and appropriately—possesses a negative form and is constructed with a privative prefix: *a-peiron, a-perilēpton, a-ōriston, a-peranton, a-metrēton, in-finitum, Un-endliche*, etc. In order, therefore, to fix upon a proper conceptual "definition" of the infinite, it is necessary to begin with an attempt to say what the infinite is not.

2. Before that, however, one ought to distinguish clearly between the "physical" (or mathematical) and "metaphysical" (or ontological) acceptations of the word "infinite." The former, classically conceived, concerns matters of quantitative inexhaustibility or serial interminability, and entered Western philosophy at a very early date: even in pre-Socratic thought, questions were raised—and paradoxes explored—regarding such imponderables as the possibility of infinite temporal duration, or of infinite spatial extension, or of infinite divisibility; and mathematicians were aware from a very early period that the infinite was a function of geometric and arithmetical reasoning, even if it could not be represented in real space or real time (that is to say, a straight line must be understood as logically lacking in beginning or end, and the complete series of real, whole, even, odd—etc.—numbers must be understood as logically interminable). The paradoxes of Zeno, for example, apply entirely and exclusively to this understanding of the infinite, and concern the apparent conceptual incompatibility between the logical reality of infinite divisibility and the physical reality of finite motion (inasmuch as the infinite divisibility of space would seem

to imply the necessity of an infinite, ever more "local" seriality within all actions in space or time).

3. The metaphysical concept of the infinite is rather more elusive of definition and, as a rule, must be approached by a number of elliptical and largely apophatic paths. Perhaps its most essential "negative attribute" is that of absolute indeterminacy: the infinite is never in any sense "this" or "that"; it is neither "here" nor "there"; it is unconditioned; it is not only "in-finite" but also "in-de-finite." Granted, in the developed speculative traditions of the West, pagan and Christian alike, this indeterminacy—when ascribed to the transcendent source of being—came to be understood also as a kind of "infinite determinacy"; but even here, this determinacy consists in an absolute transcendence of finite determination. The rule remains indubitable: only that which is without particularity, definition, limit, location, nature, opposition, or relation is "infinite" in the metaphysical sense. Hence "matter"—in the sense of *hylē* or *materia prima*—is understood by classical and medieval philosophy as infinite precisely because it is utterly devoid of the impress of *morphē* or *forma*, and not because it is in any sense limitlessly extended or divisible. Neither extension nor divisibility, in fact, applies in any way to prime matter; in Aristotelian terms, prime matter belongs entirely to the realm of *to dynaton*, the possible, so long as no *energeia* supervenes upon it to grant it actual form; its infinity, therefore, is purely privative. Thus space and time are not "metaphysically" infinite, despite their interminabilities. Neither, moreover, is any arithmetic series: the set of even numbers, for instance, while endless, is nevertheless definite; it includes and excludes particular members; it is a particular kind of thing; it is bounded by its own nature. In the purely metaphysical sense, in fact, the mathematical infinite remains within the realm of the finite.

4. This distinction between the mathematical and metaphysical concepts of the infinite was not obvious to the earliest thinkers of the Greek tradition, and was often at best only a tacit distinction within their reflections. Even in the classical age of Greek thought, the difference between the interminability of "number" and the indeterminacy of "possibility" was not much remarked, though it is obviously implicit in Aristotle's observations (in *Physics* 3.6–7) regarding, on the one hand, spatial extension and divisibility and, on the other, the purely *potential* existence of the infinite in the realm of discrete substances.

5. Aristotle's distinction—however undeveloped it may be—leads toward the rather striking (but more or less inevitable) conclusion that the infinite, metaphysically conceived, is invariably and necessarily related

to the question of being: How is it that anything—any finite thing, that is—exists? To resort to a somewhat Heideggerean idiom, whereas the mathematical infinite is an essentially "ontic" category, the metaphysical infinite is thoroughly "ontological." It is that over against which the finite is (phenomenologically) set off, or out of which it is extracted, or upon which it is impressed, or from which it emanates, or by which it is given. This is true at both extremes of the metaphysical continuum: at the level of prime matter or at the level of the transcendent act or source of being; at the level of absolute privation or at the level of absolute plenitude.

6. From this one can draw a very simple metaphysical distinction between the finite and the infinite. The realm of the finite is that realm in which the *principium contradictionis* holds true. In an utterly vacuous sense, the more "positive" *principium identitatis* holds true in all worlds and at every level of reality; but the more "negative" *principium contradictionis* describes that absolute limit by which any finite thing is the thing it is. In a very real sense, finite existence *is* noncontradiction. Neither infinite potentiality nor infinite actuality excludes the coincidence of opposites, inasmuch as neither in and of itself *posits* anything; only when, on the one hand, potentiality is realized as a single act (and so becomes "this" thing rather than "that" thing) and, on the other hand, actuality limits itself by commerce with potentiality (and so becomes the particular existence of "this" thing rather than "that" thing), does any particular thing come into being. Only that which is posited—only that which has form and can be thought—"exists." Or, to phrase the matter purely in phenomenological terms, existence is manifestation, and manifestation is finitude; the *Sache* of thought is that object in which a certain set of noetic intentions are realized and by which an endless multitude of other intentions are frustrated.

7. Thus we can say that the "infinite"—at least metaphysically speaking—is not merely that which lacks boundary or end (despite the word's etymology), but is rather that wherein the *principium contradictionis* does not hold true. In a very real sense, therefore, the infinite does not "exist." It is devoid of *morphē*, it has no mode, it cannot be thought. This, in fact, is essentially what Aristotle says in the *Physics*, though there he is still thinking principally in terms of potentiality and unformed *hylē*. One may also, however, say that what later Christian metaphysics would call *to ontōs on* or *actus purus* is infinite in much the same sense: it too does not have a finite mode; it too does not, in the common sense, exist. Of *potentia pura*, one may say that it does not *exist* but nevertheless *is* insofar as it *is* possible; of *actus purus*, one may say that it does not *exist* but nevertheless *is*.

8. We see here, then, that between the mathematical and the meta-

physical senses of "infinite" there exists not merely a distinction, but very nearly an opposition. In the realm of the mathematical infinite, the *principium contradictionis* remains of necessity inviolable. And thus, between the two acceptations of the word "infinite," any apparent univocity is illusory, and any possible analogy is at best pictorial, affective, and immeasurably remote.

9. The two models under which the metaphysical infinite was "classically" conceived—before the Christian period, at least—were those of "indeterminacy" and "totality." And in both the pre-Christian and post-Christian metaphysical epochs, these two models functioned often each to the other's exclusion, or were only imprecisely distinguished from one another, or were implicitly at odds with one another. In Hegel's thought, however, they were placed in explicit opposition to one another, as (on the one hand) the "bad" infinite of endless and meaningless particularity and (on the other) the "good" infinite of dialectical sublation. It is tempting to describe this entire tradition of reflection upon the infinite as "idealism," though its most fundamental premises were present in Western thought from the very beginning, well before any "idea" ever floated free of the cosmos.

10. These two "masks of the infinite" appear with almost archetypal perfection at the very dawn of the Western philosophical tradition, in the two great "systems" of the pre-Socratic age, the Heracleitean and the Parmenidean. Neither Heraclitus nor Parmenides enunciates any particular metaphysics of the infinite as such, of course, but each provides a conceptual form for such a metaphysics: in the thought of the former, it is that of indeterminacy, the fecundity of chaos, the sheer boundless inexhaustibility of becoming and perishing; in the latter, it is that of the totality, absolute closure and enclosure, the simple and eternal fixity and fullness of the whole, the eternal actuality of all possibilities.

11. For pre-Socratic thought as a whole, however—if indeed any general categorization is possible here—the "infinite" is conceived principally as the antinomy of order, and as therefore both unthinkable and dangerous. For Anaximander the *apeiron* is a kind of eternal and limitless (though perhaps in some sense spherical) elemental plenum from which the finite and bounded cosmos has been extracted and against which the cosmic order is continuously preserved. For Empedocles also the universe is a kind of small, fragile, local island of order amidst the boundless flux of material being, a sort of city liberated and walled off from chaos. For the Pythagoreans it is *peras*—born of number—that subdues the limitless and gives dimensions (and thereby existence) to finite things. At this point,

however, the distinction between the metaphysical and the mathematical infinite has not been clearly drawn. The finite is set off against the infinite, but almost entirely in the fashion of a stable concrete object set off against an unstable and fluid, but nonetheless material, "first element." The Pythagorean mysticism of number is still not the abstract Aristotelian metaphysics of form, or of the actual and the potential.

12. For Plato—and, really, for the entire classical philosophical tradition of Greece, including Stoicism—the infinite was solely a negative concept. Words like *apeiron*, *aperilēpton*, *aōriston*, and so forth were more or less entirely opprobrious in connotation; they were used to designate that which was "indefinite" or "indeterminate" and hence "irrational" or "unthinkable." The infinite is that which lacks form, that which reflects no *eidos* and receives the impress of no *morphē*. As such, it is pure deficiency. Hence, Plato would never have called the Good beyond being "infinite." And Aristotle's ontology was entirely concerned with finite substances (a category that included even God, the supreme substance), and had no room for anything like a concept of "infinite being."

13. Of the entirety of classical Greek thought, from Plato onward, it may fairly be said that this "Platonic" (or perhaps "Pythagorean") prejudice remains constant: the highest value and the only ground of rational meaning is intelligibility, and so the highest good can never be conceived as lacking rational limit. Only that which possesses eidetic dimensions and boundaries is thinkable; all else is chaos, formlessness, pure irrationality, and therefore malign. One sees this not only in Plato's epistemology, but also in his cosmology. In the *Philebus*, for example, the universe is considered as the product of four primordial forces: limit, the limitless, the mixture of these two, and the first cause of this mixture; the infinite in itself is an aboriginal tumult of oppositions—such as the dry and the moist or the hot and the cold—which can come to constitute a living world only when it is brought under the governance of number and harmony. And, in the *Timaeus*, it is only in imposing the limiting proportions of distinct ideas upon chaos that the demiurge brings about a world.

14. Stoic metaphysics, needless to say, is a tradition unto itself, and though there was a constant cross-pollination of Platonic, Aristotelian, and Stoic thought over the centuries before and after the rise of Christianity in the empire, whatever distinctive concept of the infinite one might ascribe to Stoicism surely cannot be said to be "idealist" in its guiding premises. Nevertheless, the model of reality peculiar to Stoicism is, if anything, even more intransigently, aboriginally Greek than that of the other developed schools; it might almost be described as a remarkably refined

and embellished, but essentially pure, expression of a certain pre-Socratic vision of the whole. The "Stoic infinite" obeys the logic of totality rather than that of indeterminacy. The entire cosmos—which is, viewed transcendentally, convertible with the divine mind—is an enclosed and finite order, spatially and temporally determined, endlessly recurrent and yet invariable in its parts and processes. It is a perfect plenum, possessed of perfect order, a "cosmopolis" in no respect deficient and in every respect admirable; it is at once both the material plenitude and the harmonious city of cosmic order described in the thought of Anaximander and Empedocles. As such, its "infinitude" is also its limitation; as both an ideal order and the whole of all that is, it can contain its plenitude only in the form of a distribution of parts and succession of events. In this perfectly sealed order of arising and perishing, advancement and retreat, the whole must always and again "make room" for what it contains. Death is necessary so that new beings can arise within the divine plenitude; and, in its fullness, the whole of the spatial and temporal order is destined for *ekpyrōsis*, a return into the primordial fire of divine mind, only that it might arise once more and repeat the same circuit again and again, identical in every detail, throughout eternity. No more astonishing, sublime, or terrible vision of the world as totality—and none more perfectly sealed within itself—can be found or imagined. But, in this system, the thought of the infinite in a truly transcendent metaphysical sense—as that which is absolved of all finite determination while giving being to the finite—remains unthought.

15. The first evidence of a purely "positive" metaphysical concept of the infinite in Western thought might be found in Plotinus. At least, one should note his willingness to speak of the One as infinite, or of Nous as infinite and the One as inexhaustible. According to W. Norris Clarke, at least, this is not mere apophasis: by "infinite" Plotinus means, *inter alia*, limitless plenitude as well as simplicity, absolute power as well as absolute rest. Plotinus even asserts that love for the One must be infinite because its object is (*Enneads* 6.7.32). The infinity of Plotinus's One, then, is no longer mere indeterminacy, as the infinite was for earlier Greek philosophy, but is rather the indeterminate but positive wellspring of all of being's virtues, possessing those virtues in an indefinite (and so limitless) condition of perfection and simplicity. Yet, even so, for Plotinus the infinity of the One is perhaps in some sense only dialectically related to the totality of finite beings; it is the metaphysical reverse of the realm of difference, its abstract and formless "superessence," at once its opposite and its substance, the absolute distinction and absolute unity of being and beings. The infinite, then, is the ground of the finite precisely in that it is "limited" by its inca-

pacity for the finite; the One's virtues are "positive" only insofar as they negate, and so uphold, the world. Thus Plotinus's thought comprises, if only implicitly, a kind of diremption and recuperation (to speak in Hegelian terms): the ambiguous drama of *egressus* and *regressus*, *diastolē* and *systolē*, a fortunate fall followed by a desolate recovery. As the world's dialectical counter, its "credit" or "treasury," sustaining its totality, the One is of necessity the eternal oblivion of the here below; it is not mindful of us, and shows itself to us only in the fragmentation of its light, shattered in the prism of Nous, dimly reflected by Psyche in the darkness of matter. So the bounty of being is pervaded by a tragic truth: the diffusiveness of the good is sustained only by the absolute inexpressiveness of its ultimate principle. At the last, the "infinite" in Plotinus is still a concept governed by the α-privative.

16. There was no reason for any of the classical pagan schools of thought to move beyond this concept of the infinite; no principle indigenous to pagan thought demanded that they do so.

FIVE

The Destiny of Christian Metaphysics

Reflections on the *Analogia Entis*

I. The Analogy as a Principle of Christian Thought

In that small, poorly lit, palely complected world where the cold abstractions of theological ontology constitute objects of passionate debate, Erich Przywara's proposal regarding the *analogia entis* is unique in its nearly magical power to generate inane antagonisms. The never quite receding thunder of Karl Barth's cry of "antichrist!" hovers perpetually over the field of battle; tiny but tireless battalions of resolute Catholics and Protestants clash as though the very pith and pulp of Christian conviction were at stake; and, even inside the separate encampments, local skirmishes constantly erupt among the tents. And yet it seems to be the case that, as a rule, the topic excites conspicuous zeal—especially among its detractors—in directly inverse proportion to the clarity with which it is understood; for, in itself, there could scarcely be a more perfectly biblical, thoroughly unthreatening, and rather drably obvious Christian principle than Przywara's *analogia entis*.

What, after all, are the traditional objections to the analogy? What dark anxieties does it stir in fretful breasts? That somehow an ontological analogy between God and creatures grants creaturely criteria of truth priority over the sovereign event of God's self-disclosure in time, or grants the conditions of our existence priority over the transcendent being of God, or grants some human structure of thought priority over the sheer *novum* of revelation, or (simply enough) grants nature priority over grace? Seen thus, the *analogia entis* is nothing more than a metaphysical system (which we may vaguely denominate "Neoplatonist") that impudently imagines there to be some ground of identity between God and the creature susceptible of human comprehension, and that therefore presumes to lay hold of God in his unutterable transcendence. But such objections are—to be perfectly frank—total nonsense. One need not even bother to complain about the somewhat contestable dualities upon which they rest; it is enough to note that such concerns betray not simply a misunderstanding, but a perfect ignorance, of Przywara's reasoning. For it is precisely the "disjunctive" meaning of the analogy that animates Przywara's argument from beginning to end; for him, it is the irreducible and, in fact, *infinite* interval of difference within the analogy that constitutes its surprising, revolutionary, and metaphysically shattering power. Far from constituting some purely natural conceptual scheme to which revelation must prove itself obedient, the *analogia entis*, as Przywara conceives of it, is nothing more than the largely apophatic, almost antimetaphysical ontology—or even meta-ontology—with which we have been left now that revelation has obliged us to take leave of any naïve metaphysics that would attempt to grasp God through a conceptual knowledge of essences or genera. A more plausible objection to the analogy might be the one that Eberhard Jüngel attributed (unpersuasively) to Barth, and that even Hans Urs von Balthasar found somewhat convincing: that so austere and so vast is the distinction between the divine and human in Przywara's thought that it seems to leave little room for God's nearness to humanity in Christ. This is no less mistaken than other, more conventional views of the matter, but at least it demonstrates some awareness of the absolute abyss of divine transcendence that the analogy marks.

At its most elementary, what Przywara calls the *analogia entis* is simply the scrupulous and necessary rejection of two opposed errors, each the mirror inversion of the other: the equally reductive and equally "metaphysical" alternatives of pure identity and pure dialectic. For neither approach to the mystery of God—neither the discourse of God as the absolute One nor the discourse of God as the absolute "Wholly Other"—can by itself truly express the logic of divine transcendence; both resolve the interval of difference between God and creation into a kind of pure and neutral equivalence, somehow more original and comprehensive than that difference, and so more original and comprehensive than God in himself *as God* (though this is perhaps easier to see in the case of the metaphysics of identity).

As Przywara understands the analogy, it is first and foremost an affirmation that creation comes about *ex nihilo*, and that God therefore is not merely some "supreme being," but is at once utterly transcendent of all beings and also the only source of all beings. Thus the analogy presumes what no self-sufficient and perfectly systematic metaphysics could ever properly admit into its speculations: the radical contingency and nonnecessity of the created order. One cannot begin to understand the principle of the *analogia entis* unless one first grasps that, before all else, it is the delightful and terrible principle of the creature's utter groundlessness; it is the realization that we possess no essence, no being, no foundation that is not always, in every moment, imparted to us from beyond ourselves, and that does not therefore always exceed everything that we are in any moment of our existence. Or, said differently, essence and existence never coincide in us as they do in God, but subsist, from our perspective, only in an altogether fortuitous synthesis, and are given to us at once, separately and together, in a movement of purest gratuity, from a transcendent source upon which we have no "natural" claim. Thus the sheer dynamism of creaturely existence (which is the constant and guiding theme of Przywara's thought) can never be resolved into the stability of any ground of identity belonging to us; only in him do we live, and move, and have our being. Of course, to understand even this much, one must avoid falling into any of the common misunderstandings that have attached themselves to the concept of the *analogia entis* since at least the days of Barth. Before all else, one must grasp that, for Przywara, the ontological analogy does not treat "being" as some genus under which God and the creature—or the infinite and the finite—are placed as distinct instances. Quite the reverse, in fact: it is precisely *being* that is to be understood as analogous; and it is precisely any univocal concept of being—any notion that God and creatures alike are "beings" comprehended by "being as such"—that the *analogia entis*, as a principle, denies. The proper proportion of the analogy, after all, is that of the *maior dissimilitudo* (or, as Przywara would prefer, the *semper maior dissimilitudo*) that separates God from any creature. So transcendent is God, one might say, that *even being*—that barest, most basic, most primordial of attributions—is *only analogous* between him and his creation. And this is an absolute impoverishment for any traditional metaphysics that would hope to lay hold of God within human concepts, for there is no discrete being called God, within the fold of "being as such," whose nature we can conceive *per analogiam essentiarum*.

Nevertheless—and this touches upon the other "false path" to transcendence—the being of the creature must indeed be *analogous to* God's pure act of being; otherwise, all talk of God would be confined within an arid dialectical theology of the "Wholly Other" so extreme as to posit— even if only tacitly—a logically absurd equivocity of being. Absolute otherness is not transcendence, but merely a kind of "negative immanence"; for true transcendence must be beyond all negation. If creation were somehow something simply "outside of" or "other than" God, like one object outside another, then logically one would have to say that there is something more than—something in addition to—God; God, thus conceived, would be a kind of thing, less than the whole of things, a being embraced within whatever wider abstract category is capacious enough to contain both him and his creatures under its canopy, without confusing their several essences (and inevitably that category will be called "being," in the barren univocal sense). It is one of the great oddities of most debates concerning the *analogia entis* that those who reject the principle in order to defend God's sovereign transcendence against the encroachments of human reason are in fact effectively denying God's fully ontological transcendence and replacing it with a concept of mere ontic supremacy. If being is not susceptible of the interval of the analogy (even though it is an interval of ever greater unlikeness), then God and creation exist in a reciprocal real relation to one another, which means an extrinsic relation between two mutually delimiting objects; not only is this a degrading concept of God, but inevitably it must presuppose the mediations of some *tertium quid*, some broader context of "reality" that somehow exceeds the difference between God and creatures. Nor is it enough to answer such concerns with the essentially magical claim that the "divine will" alone mediates between God and world; for, unless God is understood as the ontological source and ground of creation, creation itself must be understood as a thing separate from God, founded upon its own potentiality, and the creative will of God must then be understood simply as the spontaneous and arbitrary power of conjuration possessed by a very impressive—but still finite—divine sorcerer.

The actual terms of the analogy, moreover, are of a sort that could not possibly give offense to any Christian, however piously and proudly certain he or she might be of his or her own nothingness before God. The proportion of likeness within the analogy subsists simply in the recognition that God alone is the source of all things, while we are contingent manifestations of his glory, destined for a union with him that will perfect rather than destroy our natures; entirely dependent as it is upon his being—receiving even its most proper potentiality from him as a gift—our being declares the glory of He Who Is. The proportion of unlikeness, however, which is the proportion of infinite transcendence, subsists in the far more vertiginous recognition that God is his own being, that he depends upon no other for his existence, that he does not become what he is not, that he possesses no unrealized potential, that he is not a thing set off against a prior nothingness, that he is not an essence joined to existence, and that he is not a being among other beings; and that we, in our absolute dependence upon him, are not timeless essences who "demand" existence or who possess any actuality of our own; neither essence nor existence belongs to us, and their coincidence within each of us is an entirely gratuitous gift coming to us from beyond ourselves; we have no power to be, no *right* to be, no independent ground that gives us some sort of natural claim on being.

Of all the accusations laid against the *analogia entis* by its most redoubtable foes, none is more peculiar (nor, in my experience, more common) than the claim that the analogy is simply a pagan—specifically Neoplatonist—metaphysics of participation, to which Christian motifs have been at best cosmetically applied. I am not entirely certain, however, what reply to make to such an indictment. It is so thoroughly irrelevant to Przywara's argument that it is not even clear that it could be characterized as wrong; one must simply assume at this point that the very concept of an "analogy of being" has become equivocal, since those who reject it on these grounds are clearly talking about something altogether different from what Przywara means when he uses the same words. It is true that Przywara presumes some sort of "metaphysics of participation," as any clear theological concept of the contingency of finite existents must involve some idea that all finite things "partake of" being rather than intrinsically possess it, and that God alone—and in himself—is the source of all being as such. And it may be perfectly fair to describe many of the philosophical premises of Przywara's thought as—in a very general and excruciatingly imprecise sense—"Platonist" or "Neoplatonist," since some such metaphysical scheme has been part of Christian discourse since the days of the New Testament itself. But this most definitely has nothing to do with the distinct and distinctive principle of the *analogia entis*, which no one (at least, no one who actually understands the concept as Przywara does) could possibly mistake for some metaphysical system of natural likenesses established upon and sustained by the supposition of a prior identity between the absolute and the contingent. In fact, it is precisely this that the analogy is not and can never be.

I say this with some care, I should add, since—anxious though I am to do full justice to Przywara's insight—I am equally anxious to avoid conceding any legitimacy to the terms in which this particular rejection of the analogy is couched. Speaking entirely for myself, I am quite happy to embrace a metaphysics that might loosely be called the metaphysics of traditional Platonism, or even the metaphysics of certain kinds of Vedanta philosophy; indeed, I would argue that, as far as a philosophy of essences goes, any attempt to speak intelligibly of God and creation, in a way that does not ultimately dissolve into mythology, requires some such metaphysics. And, in fact, if we confine ourselves entirely to questions of the causality of created things, we must ultimately conclude that, speaking purely logically—purely metaphysically—there is no significant difference between the idea of creation and that of emanation (unless by the latter one means some ridiculously crude, intrinsically materialist concept of a divine substance that merely "expands" into universal space and time). The basic structure of *exitus* and *reditus*, *diastolē* and *systolē*—as, among many others, the Areopagite and Thomas both understood—is as inevitable for a doctrine of *creatio ex nihilo* as it is for a Plotinian metaphysics of the One. Moreover, I would go on to say that it is impossible to speak meaningfully of a God who is all Goodness and Truth, the source of all being and knowing, without acknowledging that our being and our knowing are sustained from within by a God who is for each of us *interior intimo meo*, and that at the level of *nous* or spirit (or whatever one would call the highest intellective principle within us) there is that place where the *Fünklein* or *scintilla* resides, where (as Augustine says) *nihil intersit*, where our ground is the divine ground, where Brahman and Atman are one, and in regard to which one may say of all things "*Tat tvam asi.*" Indeed, if we were simply to confine ourselves to purely *metaphysical* questions regarding the relation between the Absolute and the dependent, and never asked the still more fundamental *ontological* questions regarding the difference between divine and human being or the difference between God as God and each of us as *this* particular being, we would never have to venture speculatively beyond the conceptual law of *methexis*, within which both absolute dialectic and absolute identity have their parts to play, as the two mutually sustaining poles of a single philosophical grammar. For both are equally true, in their distinct ways, of the unmoving ground of being: we are wholly other than God ("He is in heaven and thou art on earth," he is all and we are nothing, he is absolute and we are contingent), and, at the same time, the highest level of our being abides in God (in the eternal act of God being and knowing God). And, indeed, if we were never to concern ourselves with anything other than the unmoving ground—if we were to regard the givenness, fortuity, transience, and irreducible particularities of our being as utterly subordinate and even subphilosophical matter for thought—we would never be obliged to consider many subtler, more disturbing questions of difference or identity, or of what real divine transcendence ultimately entails. We could remain ever thus, at the level of a purely natural metaphysics. But the *analogia entis* is not a principle native to any purely natural metaphysics.

Again, this is the wonderful—and, in a sense, liberating—novelty of the ontology Przywara finds within the Christian philosophical tradition. Any metaphysics can discern some order of participation uniting the here below to the there beyond, but not every metaphysics can grasp the analogical interval that disrupts the continuity of being within that order of participation. And this is a distinction of the greatest spiritual import. To the degree that any metaphysics remains confined to the oscillation between total otherness and total identity, it can conceive of no "resolution" of the difference between the absolute and the contingent that is not in some sense tragic; for—as both Western and Eastern philosophies attest—such a metaphysics must affirm either the "necessary" violences of historical dialectic, or the final nothingness of perfect identity or the perfect void. Without the interval of ontological analogy, the only alternative to the interminable and pointless disruptions of multiplicity is the final repose of simple unity. The ascent from unlikeness and finitude is necessarily a retreat not only from all transient attachments, but also from the disposable chrysalis of one's empirical self; within the terms of such a metaphysics, to find identity there is to negate it here. The *nous* must leave soul and body behind to enter into a bliss beyond self, in the journey of the alone to the alone. Atman must pass beyond the veil of *maya* and the boundless play of Isvara in order to return to its deep and dreamless sleep in Brahman, and so pass from self to Self. Or, if not this, the force of becoming—the ceaseless phenomenal succession of mental and physical states—must finally be extinguished in the *nibbana* of the Hinayana. Whatever the case, the nearer the creature approaches that ultimate terminus, the less creaturely it becomes.

The *analogia entis*, however, introduces an unclosable ontological caesura into what mere metaphysics treats (quite unconsciously) as a seamless ontological continuum. And this is the interval of being that lets us *be* as the creatures we are, that sets us free from our "own" ground; for, without it, all we are—insofar as any one of us is "this" rather than "that"—are deficient, remote, but ultimately recuperable moments within the eternal odyssey of the One's alienation from and return to itself, and our "redemption" in God is our annihilation as beings. This disruption—this infinite qualitative distinction between God and creatures—is one that, within the *ordo cognoscendi*, we must call "analogy," but only in order that we may see it properly as, within the *ordo essendi*, the mystery of the perfect gift: the gift of real difference whose "proportion" is that of infinite charity. For if there is no simple, uninterrupted ontological continuum as such between God and creation, and no sense in which the divine is diminished in the created, then creation is a needless act of freely imparted love, and so can be understood as an act not of alienation from God, but of divine expression. In this utter ontological difference from God—this merely analogous relation of our being to the God who is his own being—our identity is given to us as the creatures we are, who precisely as such give glory to and manifest God. The other language of identity—of simple unity or simple negation—belongs (again) to the unmoving ground of being. But, in truth—so says the analogy—the ceaseless dynamism of our existence is not something accidental to what we "more truly" are, dissembling a more essential changelessness within; we *are* that dynamism, liberated in every instant from nothingness. Our "return" to God is nothing other than our emergence into our own end, and our difference from God is the very revelation of the God who infinitely transcends us and who freely gives us to ourselves.

All of which, in the abstract, seems as if it ought to be quite inoffensive to those who persist in their distrust of the "invention of antichrist"; but I suspect that, as yet, this would still not be enough to calm their fears. So it would probably not go amiss to note that, for Przywara, the *analogia entis* is not a principle simply consistent with Christian thought, but is in fact a principle uniquely Christian, one that follows from the entire Christian story of creation, incarnation, and salvation; and, as such, it describes a vision of being that is not merely an option for Christian thought, but an ineluctable destiny.

II. The Analogy as the Destiny of Christian Thought

I think it fairly uncontroversial to say that, in the intellectual world of the first three centuries before Nicaea, especially in the eastern half of the empire, something like a "Logos metaphysics" was a crucial part of the philosophical *lingua franca* of almost the entire educated class, pagan, Jewish, Christian, and even Gnostic (even though the term generally preferred was rarely "logos"). Certainly this was case in Alexandria: the idea of a "derivative" or "secondary" divine principle was an indispensable premise in the city's native schools of Trinitarian reflection, and in the thought of either "Hellenized" Jews like Philo or of the Platonists, middle or late. And one could describe all these systems, without any significant exception, pagan and Jewish no less than Christian, as "subordinationist" in structure. All of them attempted, with greater or lesser complexity, and with more or less vivid mythical adornments, to connect the world here below to its highest principle by populating the interval between them with various intermediate degrees of spiritual reality. All of them, that is, were shaped by the same basic metaphysical impulse, one sometimes described as the "pleonastic fallacy": the notion that, in order to overcome the infinite disproportion between the immanent and the transcendent, it is enough to conceive of some sort of *tertium quid*—or of a number of successively more accommodating quiddities—between, on the one hand, the One or the Father or *ho theos* and, on the other, the world of finite and mutable things. In all such systems, the second "moment" of the real—that which proceeds directly from the supreme principle of all things: logos, or *nous*, or what have you—was understood as a kind of economic limitation of its source, so reduced in "scale" and nature as to be capable of entering into contact with the realm of discrete beings, of translating the power of the supreme principle into various finite effects, and of uniting this world to the wellspring of all things. This derivative principle, therefore, may not as a rule properly be called *ho theos*, but it definitely is *theos*: God with respect to all lower reality. And this inevitably meant that this secondary moment of the real was understood as mediating this supreme principle in only a partial and distorted way; for such a Logos (let us settle upon this as our term) can appear within the totality of things that are only a restriction and diffusion of—even perhaps a deviation or alienation from—that which is "most real," the Father who, in the purity of his transcendence, can never directly touch this world. For Christians who thought in such terms, this almost inevitably implied that the Logos had been, in some sense, generated *with respect to* the created order, as its most exalted expression, certainly, but as inseparably involved in its existence nonetheless. Thus it was natural for Christian apologists of the second century to speak of the Logos as having issued from the Father in eternity shortly before the creation of the world. And thus the essentially Alexandrian theology of Arius inevitably assumed the metaphysical—or religious—contours that it did: the divine Father is absolutely hidden from and inaccessible to all beings, unknowable even to the heavenly powers; and only through the mediation of an inferior Logos is anything of him revealed. What was fairly distinctive in Arianism was the absence of anything like a metaphysics of participation that might have allowed for some sort of real ontological continuity (however indeterminate) between the Father and his Logos; consequently the only revelation of the Father that

Arius's Logos would seem to be able to provide is a kind of adoring, hieratic gesture toward an abyss of infinitely incomprehensible power, the sheer majesty of omnipotent and mysterious otherness.[1] The God (*ho theos*) of Arius is a God revealed *only* as the hidden, of whom the Logos (*theos ho logos*) bears tidings, and to whom he offers up the liturgy of rational creation; but, as the revealer of the Father, his is the role only of a celestial high priest, the Angel of Mighty Counsel, the coryphaeus of the heavenly powers; he may be a kind of surrogate God to the rest of creation, but he too, logically speaking, cannot attain to an immediate knowledge of the divine essence.

Even, however, in late antique metaphysical systems less ontologically austere than Arius's, in which the economy of divine manifestation was understood as being embraced within a somewhat more generous order of *metochē* or *metousia*, the disproportion between the supreme principle of reality and this secondary principle of manifestation remains absolute. Hence all revelation, all disclosure of the divine, follows upon a more original veiling. The manifestation of that which is Most High—wrapped as it is in unapproachable darkness, up upon the summit of being—is only the paradoxical manifestation of a transcendence that can never become truly manifest: perhaps not even to itself, as it possesses no Logos immanent to itself. It does not "think"; it cannot be thought. This, at least, often seems to be the case with the most severely logical, and most luminously uncluttered, metaphysical system of the third century, that of Plotinus. For the One of Plotinus is not merely *a* unity, not merely solitary, but is oneness as such, that perfectly undifferentiated unity in which all unity and diversity here below subsist and by which they are sustained, as at once identity and difference. Plotinus recognized that the unity by which any particular thing is what it is, and is at once part of and distinct from the greater whole, is always logically prior to that thing; thus, within every composite reality, there must always also be a more eminent "act" of simplicity (so to speak) that makes its being possible. For this reason, the supreme principle of all things must be that One that requires no higher unity to account for its integrity, and that therefore admits of no duality whatsoever, no pollution of plurality, no distinction of any kind, even that between the knower and the known. This is not, for Plotinus, to deny that the One is in some special and transcendent sense possessed of an intellectual act of self-consciousness, a kind of "superintellection" entirely tran-

---

1. I am entirely persuaded by the portrait of Arius that Rowan Williams paints in his *Arius: Heresy and Tradition*, rev. ed. (Grand Rapids: Eerdmans, 2002).

scendent of subjective or objective knowledge.[2] But the first metaphysical moment of *theōria*—reflection and knowledge—is of its nature a second moment, a departure from unity, Nous's "prismatic" conversion of the simple light of the One into boundless multiplicity; the One itself, possessing no "specular" other within itself, infinitely exceeds all reflection. Nor did philosophy have to await the arrival of Hegel to grasp that there is something fundamentally incoherent in speaking of the existence of that which is intrinsically unthinkable, or in talking of "being" that possesses no proportionate intelligibility: For in what way is that which absolutely—even within itself—transcends intuition, conceptualization, and knowledge anything at all? Being *is* manifestation, and to the degree that anything is *wholly* beyond thought—to the degree, that is, that anything is not "rational"—to that very degree it does not exist. So it was perhaps with rigorous consistency that the Platonist tradition after Plotinus generally chose to place "being" second in the scale of emanation: for as that purely unmanifest, unthinkable, and yet transfinite unity that grants all things their unity, the One can admit of no distinctions within itself, no manifestation *to* itself, and so—in every meaningful sense—*is* not (though, obviously, neither is it not *not*).

In truth, of course, even to speak of an "ontology" in relation to these systems is somewhat misleading. Late Platonic metaphysics, in particular, is not so much ontological in its logic as it is "henological," and so naturally whatever concept of being it comprises tends toward the nebulous. "Being" in itself is not really distinct from entities, except in the manner of another entity; as part of the hierarchy of emanations, occupying a particular place within the structure of the whole, it remains one item within the inventory of things that are. Admittedly, it is an especially vital and "supereminent" causal liaison within the totality of beings; but a discrete principle among other discrete principles it remains. What a truly ontological metaphysics would view as being's proper act is, for this metaphysics, scattered among the various moments of the economy of beings. One glimpses its workings now here and now there: in the infinite fecundity of the One, in the One's power to grant everything its unity as the thing it is, in the principle of manifestation that emanates from the One, in the simple existence of things, even in that unnamed, in some sense *unnoticed*, medium in which the whole continuum of emanations univocally subsists. But, ultimately, the structure of reality within this vision of things is (to use the fashionable phrase) a "hierarchy within totality," held together at its

2. See Plotinus, *Enneads* 6.7.37.15–38.26; 9.6.50–55.

apex by a principle so exalted that it is also the negation of the whole, in all of the latter's finite particularities.[3] What has never come fully into consciousness in this tradition is (to risk a grave anachronism) the "ontological difference"—or, at any rate, the analogy of being. So long as being is discriminated from the transcendent principle of unity, and so long as both figure in some sense (however eminently) within a sort of continuum of metaphysical moments, what inevitably must result is a dialectic of identity and negation. Again, this is the special pathos of such a metaphysics: for if the truth of all things is a principle in which they are grounded and by which they are simultaneously negated, then one can draw near to the fullness of truth only through a certain annihilation of particularity, through a forgetfulness of the manifest, through a sort of benign desolation of the soul, progressively eliminating—as the surd of mere particularity—all that lies between the One and the noetic self. This is not for a moment to deny the reality, the ardor, or the grandeur of the mystical elations that Plotinus describes, or the fervency with which—in his thought and in the thought of the later Platonists—the liberated mind loves divine beauty.[4] The pathos to which I refer is a sadness residing not within Plotinus the man, but within any logically dialectical metaphysics of transcendence. For transcendence, so understood, must also be understood as a negation of the finite, and a kind of absence or positive exclusion from the scale of nature; the One is, in some sense, *there* rather than *here*. To fly thither one must fly hence, to undertake a journey of the alone to the alone, a sweetly melancholy departure from the anxiety of finitude, and even from being itself, in its concrete actuality: self, world, and neighbor. For so long as one dwells in the realm of finite vision, one dwells in untruth.

It is precisely here, however, that the advent of Nicene theology began to alter—altogether fundamentally—the conceptual structure of the ancient world. The doctrinal determinations of the fourth century, along with all their immediate theological ramifications, rendered many of the established metaphysical premises upon which Christians had long relied in order to understand the relation between God and the world increasingly irreconcilable with their faith, and at the same time suggested the need to conceive of that relation—perhaps for the first time in Western intellectual history—in a properly "ontological" way. With the gradual defeat of subordinationist theology, and with the definition of the Son

---

3. Plotinus, *Enneads* 6.7.17.39–43; 9.3.37–40; cf. 5.5.4.12–16; 11.1–6; κτλ.

4. There are rather too many passages on this mystical *erōs* in the *Enneads* to permit exhaustive citation; but see especially 6.7.21.9–22.32; 31.17–31; 34.1–39; 9.9.26–56.

and then the Spirit as coequal and coeternal with the Father, an entire metaphysical economy had implicitly been abandoned. These new theological usages—this new Christian philosophical grammar—did not entail a rejection of the old Logos metaphysics, perhaps, but they certainly did demand its revision, and at the most radical of levels. For not only is the Logos of Nicaea *not* generated with a view to creation, and *not* a lesser manifestation of a God who is simply beyond all manifestation; it is in fact the eternal reality whereby God is the God he is. There is a perfectly proportionate convertibility of God with his own manifestation of himself to himself; and, in fact, this convertibility is nothing less than God's own act of self-knowledge and self-love in the mystery of his transcendent life. His being, therefore, is an infinite intelligibility; his hiddenness—his transcendence—is always already manifestation; and it is this movement of infinite disclosure that is his "essence" as God. Thus it is that the divine persons can be characterized (as they are by Augustine) as "subsistent relations": for the relations of Father to Son or Spirit, and so on, are not extrinsic relations "in addition to" other, more original "personal" identities, or "in addition to" the divine essence, but are the very reality by which the persons subsist; thus the Father is eternally and essentially Father *because* he eternally has his Son, and so on.[5] God *is* Father, Son, and Spirit, and nothing in the Father "exceeds" the Son and Spirit. In God, to know and to love, to be known and to be loved are all one act, whereby he is God and wherein nothing remains unexpressed. And, if it is correct to understand "being" as in some sense necessarily synonymous with manifestation or intelligibility—and it is—then the God who is also always Logos is also eternal Being: not *a* being, that is, but transcendent Being, beyond all finite being.

Another way of saying this is that the dogmatic definitions of the fourth century ultimately forced Christian thought, even if only implicitly, toward a recognition of the full mystery—the full transcendence—of Being within beings. All at once the hierarchy of hypostases mediating between the world and its ultimate or absolute principle had disappeared. Herein lies the great "discovery" of the Christian metaphysical tradition: the true nature of transcendence, transcendence understood not as mere dialectical supremacy, and not as ontic absence, but as the truly transcendent and therefore utterly immediate act of God, in his own infinity, giving being to beings. In affirming the consubstantiality and equality of the

5. See Augustine, *De Trinitate* 7.1.2. Or, as John of Damascus puts it, the divine subsistences dwell and are established within one another (*De fide orthodoxa* 1.14).

persons of the Trinity, Christian thought had also affirmed that it is the transcendent God alone who makes creation to be, not through a necessary diminishment of his own presence, and not by way of an economic reduction of his power in lesser principles, but as the infinite God. He is at once *superior summo meo* and *interior intimo meo*: not merely the supreme being set atop the summit of beings, but the one who is transcendently present in all beings, the ever more inward act within each finite act. This does not, of course, mean that there can be no metaphysical structure of reality, through whose agencies God acts; but it does mean that, whatever that structure might be, God is not located within it, but creates it, and does not require its mechanisms to act upon lower things. As the immediate source of the being of the whole, he is nearer to every moment within the whole than it is to itself, and is at the same time infinitely beyond the reach of the whole, even in its most exalted principles. And it is precisely in learning that God is not situated within any kind of ontic continuum with creation, as some "other thing" mediated to the creature by his simultaneous absolute absence from and dialectical involvement in the totality of beings, that we discover him to be the *ontological* cause of creation. True divine transcendence, it turns out, transcends even the traditional metaphysical divisions between the transcendent and the immanent.

And, as I have said, this recognition of God's "transcendent immediacy" in all things was in many ways a liberation from that sad pathos native to metaphysics described above; for with this recognition came the realization that the particularity of the creature is not in its nature a form of tragic alienation from God, which must be overcome if the soul is again to ascend to her inmost truth. If God is himself the immediate actuality of the creature's emergence from nothingness, then it is precisely through becoming what it is—rather than through shedding the finite *idiōmata* that distinguish it from God—that the creature truly reflects the goodness and transcendent power of God. The supreme principle does not stand over against us (if secretly within each of us) across the distance of a hierarchy of lesser metaphysical principles, but is present within the very act of each moment of the particular. God is truly Logos, and creatures—created in and through the Logos—*are* insofar as they participate in the Logos's power to manifest God. God is not merely the "really real," of which beings are distant shadows; he is, as Maximus the Confessor says, the utterly simple, the very simplicity of the simple,[6] who is all in all things, wholly present in the totality of beings and in each particular being, indwelling

6. Maximus the Confessor, *Ambigua*, Patrologia Graeca 91:1232BC.

all things as the very source of their being, without ever abandoning that simplicity.[7] This he does not as a sublime unity absolved of all knowledge of the things he causes, but precisely *as* that one infinite intellectual action proper to his nature, wherein he knows the eternal "*logoi*" of all things in a single, simple act of knowledge.[8] God in himself is an infinite movement of disclosure, and in creation—rather than departing from his inmost nature—he discloses himself again by disclosing what is contained in his Logos, while still remaining hidden in the infinity and transcendence of his manifestation. When we become what we are, it is through entering ever more into the infinitely accomplished plenitude of his triune act of love and knowledge. And to understand the intimacy of God's immediate presence *as God* to his creatures in the abundant givenness of this disclosure is also—if only implicitly—to understand the true difference of Being from beings.

For Przywara, however, even this Trinitarian warrant for the *analogia entis* would be invisible to us were it not for the full revelation of God's transcendent immediacy to his creatures provided by the incarnation of the Son of God—understood in a truly Chalcedonian way. Balthasar's claim that Christ is in fact the "concrete *analogia entis*" is far more than a vague but pious nod in the direction of Scripture. Fully developed Christology is, when all is said and done, impossible to conceive apart from a proper understanding of the true difference between transcendent and immanent being. Of course, it is not entirely clear that Balthasar himself always grasped this, inasmuch as he did occasionally wonder whether a coherent Christology could be enucleated from Przywara's principle of the "*ever* greater difference" between God and creatures. In truth, it is precisely that word "ever" that lifts the doctrine of the incarnation out of the realm of myth, for it marks the difference between the divine and the human as an infinite qualitative distance, and as such makes intelligible the claim that there is no conflict or rivalry between Christ's divinity and his humanity, and that the latter participates in the former so naturally that the one person of the Son can be both fully divine and fully human at once. If the difference between God and man were a merely quantifiable difference between extrinsically related beings, the incarnation would be a real change in one or both natures, an amalgamation or synthesis; but then Christ would be not the God-man, but a monstrosity, a hybrid

---

7. Maximus the Confessor, *Ambigua*, Patrologia Graeca 91:1256B.

8. See Maximus the Confessor, *Centuries of Knowledge* 2.4; Patrologia Graeca 90:1125D–1128A.

of natures that, in themselves, would remain opposed and unreconciled. But, because the difference between the divine and human really is an infinite qualitative difference, the hypostatic union involves no contradiction, alienation, or change in the divine Son. Because the difference between God and creation is the difference between Being and created beings, Christ is not an irresoluble paradox fixed within the heart of faith, or an accommodation between two kinds of being; in his one person—both God and man—there is neither any diminishment of his divinity nor any violation of the integrity of his humanity. In a sense, in Christ one sees the analogy with utterly perspicuous brilliance: that is, one glimpses at once both the perfect ontological interval of divine transcendence and also the perfect fittingness of the divine image to its archetype. For the perfect man is also God of God: not a fabulous demigod, but human in the fullest sense because divine in the fullest sense. And it is here, ultimately, in the mystery of Christ the incarnate God, the irreducible *concretum* of infinite, self-outpouring charity, that the analogy of being finds its true and everlasting proportion.

SIX

The Mirror of the Infinite

Gregory of Nyssa and the *Vestigia Trinitatis*

I

The notion that, from the patristic period to the present, the Trinitarian theologies of the Eastern and Western catholic traditions have obeyed contrary logics and have in consequence arrived at conclusions inimical each to the other—a particularly tedious, persistent, and pernicious falsehood—will no doubt one day fade away from want of documentary evidence. At present, however, it serves too many interests for theological scholarship to dispense with it too casually: Eastern theologians find in it a weapon to wield against the West, which they believe has traditionally—so alleges, for instance, John Zizioulas—forgotten the biblical truth that the unity of the Trinity flows from the paternal *archē*, which is entirely "personal," and has come to believe instead "that that which constitutes the unity of God is the one divine substance, the one divinity";[1]

1. John Zizioulas, *Being as Communion: Studies in Personhood and the Church* (Crestwood, NY: St. Vladimir's Seminary Press, 1985), p. 40. It has become so lamentably common among my fellow Orthodox to treat the claim of Vladimir Lossky and others that Western theology in general posits some "impersonal" divine ground behind the Trinitarian hypostases, and so fails to see the Father as the "fountainhead of divinity," as a simple fact of theological history (and the secret logic of Latin "filioquism"), that it seems almost churlish to note that it is quite demonstrably untrue, from the patristic through the medieval periods, with a few insignificant exceptions; honesty, however, not to mention a modicum of shame, moves me to make the observation anyway. It would be comforting to think that only very incautious "scholars" fall prey to this error, but one can number some Orthodox theologians of genuine stature and brilliance, like Zizioulas and Dumitru Staniloae, among its victims.

113

THE HIDDEN AND THE MANIFEST

Western theologians of varying hues—quasi-Hegelian dialectical Trinitarians, social Trinitarians, "personalist" theologians—take it as a license
for their differing critiques of the "Platonism" or "Hellenism" of classical
Trinitarian metaphysics; and all of us who, in our weaker moments, prefer
synopsis to precision find in it a convenient implement for arranging our
accounts of doctrinal history into simple taxonomies, under tidily discrete
divisions. It was, learned opinion generally concurs, Théodore de Régnon
who probably first "discovered" the distinction between Western and Eastern styles of Trinitarian theology: the tendency, that is, of Latin thought
to proceed from general nature to concrete Person (the latter as a mode of
the former), so according priority to divine unity, and of Greek thought
to proceed from Person to nature (the latter as the content of the former),
so placing the emphasis first on the plurality of divine persons.[2] Régnon's
own aims, as it happens, were quite modest and irenic, and he certainly understood that, in whatever degree his analysis was correct, neither East nor
West enjoyed a manifestly better claim to dogmatic purity; but his distinction has served little purpose in recent years but to feed Eastern polemic
and Western insecurity, and to distort the tradition that both share. Now
we find ourselves in an age in which many of us have come to believe that
we must choose between "Greek" personalism and "Latin" essentialism,
or at least remain poised between them; and as a result we have become
insensible to the subtlety and richness of the sources that have thus been
subjected to these fairly arid categories.

The moment in ecclesial history at which the divergence between East
and West on these matters supposedly became acute, at least according
to the prevailing prejudices, was sometime in the late fourth century and
early fifth. This is supposedly especially obvious when one compares the
Trinitarian theology of the Cappadocian fathers (particularly Gregory of
Nyssa) to that of Augustine. Indeed, if one confines one's investigations
to a few select texts, one can make something of a case here: Did not Augustine, after all, refuse to draw an analogy of the Trinity from the relationship of husband, wife, and child,[3] favoring instead more elliptical
analogies drawn from the mind's inner complexity; and did not Gregory,
by contrast, go so far at one point as to defend Trinitarianism against the
accusation of tritheism by arguing not only that it is incorrect to speak of
three gods, but that it is only catachrestically that we speak even of three

2. Théodore de Régnon, *Études de théologie positive sur la Sainte Trinité*, 2 vols. (Paris,
1892), 1:433.

3. Augustine, *De Trinitate* 12.5.5–7.12.

men, insofar as human nature is one?[4] But the contrast is no sooner drawn than it begins to melt away: Augustine, certainly, evinces no less keen a sense of the distinct integrity of the divine persons as persons than does Gregory,[5] nor does Gregory actually argue that the unity of the Trinity is reducible to a common nature wherein the divine persons severally subsist (anyway—*vide infra*—Gregory's understanding of human "nature" is so splendidly peculiar as to make it impossible to draw any facile "social" conclusions from his argument); more to the point, in neither instance is either theologian actually attempting to provide a conceptual definition of the Trinity. We should perhaps do well to remember that it is one thing to move about in the realm of analogy, within which one merely seeks out locutions and similitudes by which creaturely language and thought can pass, however imperfectly, from created toward divine being; but it is another thing altogether to move in the far more mysterious realm of the *imago Dei*, where one must seek first not what we may say of God, but what God says of himself in fashioning us as the creatures we are, called from nothingness to participate in the being that flows from him, and to manifest his beauty in the depths of our nature. It is wise to keep this distinction constantly in view: for while Augustine and Gregory alike are quite willing to consider the many ways in which we may shape models of the Trinitarian relations in our words and reflections, both become rather more circumspect when attempting to identify precisely how the image of the triune God resides in us. It is precisely here, though—in contemplating where the image of God is impressed upon his creatures, and how—that Trinitarian reflection can achieve its fullest and supplest expression.

One should also note, at the outset, that for Gregory, no less than for Augustine, the divine image is first and foremost the possession of each individual soul, in the mystery of her simultaneous unity of essence and diversity of acts. For instance, Gregory, in *On the Making of Humanity*, explicitly rejects the suggestion that the most basic "form" of human sociality—the distinction between the sexes—is in any sense a feature of God's image in us: "for in Jesus Christ, according to the apostle, there is neither male nor female."[6] Rather, the image is more properly to be

---

4. Gregory, *Ad Ablabium: Quod non sint tres Dei*, Gregorii Nysseni Opera (hereinafter GNO), ed. Werner Jaeger et al. (Leiden: Brill, 1958–), 3/1:40–42.

5. See *De Trinitate* 15.5.7–8. I can do no better than recommend, on this matter, Rowan Williams's quite splendid essay "*Sapientia* and the Trinity: Reflections on the *De Trinitate*," in *Collectanea Augustiniana: Mélanges T. J. van Bavel*, ed. B. Bruning, M. Lamberigts, and J. van Houlm (Leuven: Leuven University Press, 1990), pp. 317–32.

6. Gregory, *De hominis opificio* 16; Patrologia Graeca (hereinafter PG) 44:181.

sought on the one hand in a variety of spiritual attributes inhering in the soul—reason, love, freedom—and on the other in the soul's simultaneous complexity and simplicity. Gregory is even willing to argue to the indivisibility of the Trinity from the indivisibility of the soul that is created in its image,[7] and then to argue back again, in the opposite direction, from the revealed nature of the Trinity to what constitutes God's image in us: God, Scripture tells us, is Mind and Word, and so we possess word and understanding in imitation of the true Word and Mind; God is love, God beholds and hearkens to and searches out all things, and hence we love, and hence we see and hear and seek understanding.[8] Even the mind's transcendence of itself—our inability to grasp how, again, an intelligible and simple unity can subsist in a dynamic and versatile plurality of movements and capacities—is an aspect of the divine image in us, reflecting God's own incomprehensibility and hiddenness.[9] Nor should one assume that the soul's singularity of personal identity is, for Gregory, simply and solely a defect in its likeness to the triune God, or any more of a limitation upon that likeness than is the social constitution of creaturely personality; certainly Gregory, insofar as he ventures any portrayal of the interior life of God, does not elevate divine triplicity over divine unity, any more than the reverse: "[T]he divine nature exceeds each [finite] good, and the good is wholly beloved by the good, and thus it follows that when it looks upon itself it desires what it possesses and possesses what it desires (*ho hexei, thelei, kai ho thelei, hexei*), and receives nothing from outside itself. . . . [T]he life of that transcendent nature is love, in that the beautiful is entirely lovable to those who know it (and the divine does know it), and so this knowledge becomes love (*hē de gnōsis agapē ginetai*), because the object of his recognition is in its nature beautiful."[10] It is all but impossible to read such a passage without discerning in it an essentially Trinitarian grammar. Surely this progression—from the divine nature's infinite source, through God's *gnōsis* of himself, to the "conversion" of that recognition into delighted love, into *agapē*—is a description of how the one God, even in his infinite simplicity, eternally conceives his equally infinite image, knowing himself perfectly in his Logos, and so eternally "wills" himself with an equally infinite love, so completing his Trinitarian life in the movement of the Spirit. This is, after all, entirely in keeping

7. Gregory, *De hominis opificio* 5; PG 44:137.
8. Gregory, *De hominis opificio* 5; PG 44:137.
9. Gregory, *De hominis opificio* 11; PG 44:153–56.
10. Gregory, *De anima et resurrectione*, PG 46:93–96.

with the venerable Cappadocian insight that in God—*ad extra* and so, necessarily, *ad intra*[11]—all is inaugurated in the Father, effected in the Son, and perfected in the Spirit.

Morphologically, at least, this account of the simplicity of God's nature as also an infinitely accomplished act of knowledge and love—or as the perfect coincidence of desire and possession—entirely follows the logic of Gregory's (and Basil's)[12] belief that the generation of the Son is directly from the Father, while the procession of the Spirit is from the Father only *per Filium* (*sed*, to borrow a phrase, *de Patre principaliter*). Admittedly, Gregory does not, in the passage just quoted, make an explicit connection between God's infinite immanent act of knowing and loving his own essence and the *taxis* of the Trinity; but Augustine does:

11. Since the time of Vladimir Lossky, various modern Orthodox theologians have, in their assault on "filioquism," adopted an exaggerated "Photianism," and argued that between God's acts in the economy of salvation and God's eternal life of generation and procession, there is not an exact correspondence of order. See especially Lossky, "The Procession of the Holy Spirit in Orthodox Trinitarian Doctrine," in Lossky, *In the Image and Likeness of God* (Crestwood, NY: St. Vladimir's Seminary Press, 1985), pp. 71–96. This, however, is a theologically disastrous course to tread, and one that leads away from the genuine Orthodox tradition altogether. One might note, to begin with, that were this claim sound, the arguments by which the Cappadocians defended full Trinitarian theology against Arian and Eunomian theology—in works like Basil's *De Spiritu Sancto* and Gregory's *Adversus Macedonianos*—would entirely fall apart. Just as terribly, however, behind such a severance of the *ordines* of the economic and immanent Trinities from one another lurks the specter of nominalism, the reduction of God to some finite being among beings, whose acts could be distinguishable from his nature, whose freedom would be mere arbitrary choice, who would preserve in his being some quantity of unrealized voluntative potential, and whose relation to the being of creation would be one not of self-disclosing revelation, but of mere power—all of which is quite repugnant to patristic tradition. All truth and goodness in creation are a participation in the eternal truth and goodness of God's Trinitarian act of knowledge and love of his own essence, and were any aspect of created reality—especially the economy of salvation—anything but a disclosure of this order of divine reality, it would be neither true nor good (nor, for that matter, real). Surely, if one is seeking a theological argument against the *filioque* clause (as opposed to the perfectly sufficient doctrinal argument that the creed should not have been altered without conciliar warrant), it would be better to point out that it fails adequately to account for other aspects of what is revealed in the economy of salvation: that the Son is begotten in and by the agency of the Spirit as much as the Spirit proceeds through the Son, inasmuch as the incarnation, unction, and even mission (Mark 1:12) of the Son are works of the Spirit, which must enter into our understanding of the Trinitarian *taxis*.

12. Concerning the latter, see Basil, *De Spiritu Sancto* 45–47; concerning the former, *vide infra*.

[T]he Son is from the Father, so as both to be and to be coeternal with the Father. For if the image perfectly fills the measure of him whose image it is, then it is coequal to its source. . . . He has, in regard to this image, employed the name "form" on account, I believe, of its beauty, wherein there is at once such harmony, and prime equality, and prime similitude, in no way discordant, in no measure unequal, and in no part dissimilar, but wholly answering to the identity of the one whose image it is. . . . Wherefore that ineffable conjunction of the Father and his image is never without fruition, without love, without rejoicing. Hence that love, delight, felicity or beatitude, if any human voice can worthily say it, is called by him, in brief, use, and is in the Trinity the Holy Spirit, not begotten, but of the begetter and begotten alike the very sweetness, filling all creatures, according to their capacities, with his bountiful superabundance and excessiveness. . . . In that Trinity is the highest origin of all things, and the most perfect beauty, and the most blessed delight. Therefore those three are seen to be mutually determined, and are in themselves infinite.[13]

Clearly, at any rate, for both theologians the simplicity of God's essence and the distinctness of his internal relations are to be held together, however imponderable the ultimate convertibility of these things must remain for the finite mind. This oscillation between the poles of the one and the three is constantly present in the thought of both. One sees it, to take an example almost at random, in Gregory's remark that "if the Father wills something, the Son, being in the Father, knows the Father's will—or, rather, the Son himself is the Father's will";[14] or in his statement that "just as a man's spirit within him and the man himself are one man, even so God's Spirit within him and God himself should truly be called the one, first, and sole God."[15] And both Gregory and Augustine resolve the aporia that theology must thus inevitably confront not by depicting the Trinity as a social "event" accomplished by three independent subjectivities, but in terms of the order of relations that distinguish the persons from one another "causally" within the absolute simplicity of the divine nature. Both even distinguish generation and procession within the Trinity in terms primarily of the order of cause—as one perhaps must, unless one wishes to compromise the simplicity of the Father's essence by positing within God two acts that are separate and *essentially* different, rather than distin-

---

13. Augustine, *De Trinitate* 6.10.11–12.
14. Gregory, *Ad Ablabium*, GNO 3/1:288.
15. Gregory, *Refutatio confessionis Eunomii*, GNO 2:403.

guished from one another by relation. As Gregory writes (in a passage that would fit very well in, say, book 5 of Augustine's *De Trinitate*),

> [W]hile confessing the immutability of the [divine] nature, we do not deny difference in regard to cause and that which is caused, by which alone we discern the difference of each Person from the other, in that we believe one to be the cause and another to be from the cause; and again we conceive of another difference within that which is from the cause: between the one who, on the one hand, comes directly from the principle and the one who, on the other, comes from the principle through the one who arises directly; thus it unquestionably remains peculiar to the Son to be the Only Begotten, while at the same time it is not to be doubted that the Spirit is of the Father, by virtue of the mediation of the Son that safeguards the Son's character as Only Begotten, and thus the Spirit is not excluded from his natural relation to the Father.[16]

None of which is to say that for Gregory there is no relationship between the image of God in us and our nature as creatures necessarily in communion with one another (in a very striking way, as will be seen, some such relationship lies at the heart of his understanding of creation and redemption); nor is it to say, in the narrow terms to which modern theology occasionally succumbs, that Gregory's Trinitarian theology is "psychologistic" rather than "social," or that he accords the unity of the divine essence priority over the distinction of the divine persons. Such oppositions are simply inapposite to classical Trinitarian theology, and are conceptually crude in any event. Surely, to indulge in something of an excursus, we must be acutely conscious of the analogical interval within those words—such as "person"—that we apply to both God and creatures, and always recall that the moral and ontological categories in which human personality is properly described are appropriate only to the finite and composite. The relationality of human persons, however essential it may be, remains a multiple reality, which must be described now in social terms, now in psychological, now in metaphysical; it is infinitely remote from that perfect indwelling, reciprocal "containment," transparency, recurrence, and absolute "giving way" that is the meaning of the word *perichōrēsis* or *circumincessio* (adopted by Trinitarian theology long after Gregory or Augustine, and yet so perfectly suited to the theology of both). For, if we forget this interval, we not only risk lapsing into either a collectivistic

16. Gregory, *Ad Ablabium*, GNO 3/1:55–56.

or a solipsistic reduction of human relationality—exclusively outward or inward—but we are likely to adopt either a tritheistic or a unitarian idiom when speaking of God. Our being is synthetic and bounded; just as (again to borrow later theological vocabulary) the dynamic inseparability but incommensurability in us of essence and existence is an ineffably distant analogy of the dynamic identity of essence and existence in God, the constant pendulation between inner and outer that constitutes our identities is an ineffably distant analogy of that boundless bright diaphaneity of coinherence, in which the exteriority of relations and interiority of identity in God are one, each person wholly reflecting and containing and indwelling each of the others. Because for us personality is synthetic, composite, successive, and finite, we are related always in some sense "over against," in a fragmentary way, and to be with others always involves for us a kind of death, the limit of our being. In God, though, given the simplicity of his essence, there is an absolute coincidence of relation and unity. For God, the "inwardness" of the other is each person's own inwardness, the "outwardness" of the other is each person's outwardness and manifestation.

It is precisely here that the artificial distinction between "Greek" and "Latin" theology has worked the most injurious mischief, by prompting many to rush to one end or the other of a scale that must be kept in balance. We must say, at once, that the divine simplicity is the "result" of the self-giving transparency and openness of infinite persons, but also that the distinction of the persons within the one God is the "result" of the infinite simplicity of the divine essence.[17] Otherwise, we will find ourselves trading in mythology: speaking of God as an infinite psychological subjectivity possessed of plural affects, or as a confederacy of three individual centers of consciousness; in either case reducing God, the transcendent source of all being, to a composite being, an ontic God, in whose "subjectivity" there would remain, even within the immanent divine life, some sort of unexpressed interiority (or interiorities), some surfeit of the indeterminate over the determinate, some reserve of self in which identity is constituted as the withheld. God is one because each divine person, in the circle of God's knowledge and love of his own goodness (which is both wisdom and charity), is a "face," a "capture," of the divine essence that is—as must be, given the infinite simplicity of God—always wholly God, in the full depth of his "personality." For any "mode of subsistence" of the infinite being of God must be an infinite mode, a way whereby God is entirely, "personally" God. God is never less than wholly God. Just as the Father is the pleni-

17. As Zizioulas cogently argues: *Being as Communion*, p. 89.

tude of divine goodness, in whom inhere both his Word (manifestation, form) and Gift (the life in which the Word goes forth, light in which he is seen, joy in which he is known, generosity wherewith he is bestowed); so in the Son, whom the Father generates, the depth of the paternal *archē* and the boundless spiritual light and delight of wisdom also inhere; and in the Spirit, whom the Father breathes forth, the plenitude of paternal being and filial form inhere in the "mode" of accomplished love. Each person is fully gathered and reflected in the mode of the other: as other, as community and unity at once. Here, in the mystery of divine infinity, one finds, necessarily, a perfect agreement with one another of the languages of "subsistent relations" and of "divine persons," and a warrant for seeing Trinitarian *vestigia* both in the multiplicit singularity of the soul, which subsists in memory, understanding, and will, and so forth, and in the communal implications of each of us in one another, in the threefold structure of love, within which circle we together, as the event of shared love, constitute (however poorly or sinfully) the human "essence." We waver between these two analogical orders at an infinite distance from their supereminent truth; and obviously the orders are not separate: knowledge and love of neighbor fulfill the soul's velleity toward the world, and so grant each of us that internally constituted "self" that exists only through an engagement with a world of others; but that engagement is possible only in that the structure of interiority is already "othered" and "othering," in distinct moments of consciousness' inherence in itself. In the interdependence of these two ways of analogy, enriching and chastening one another, it becomes possible to speak, with immeasurable inadequacy, of the Trinitarian God who is love.

Here, however, we have moved again from the question of the divine image in the soul, through the more ambiguous question of the Trinitarian *vestigia*, back to the question of analogy; but, again, analogical language about God is the effect of a prior divine language, an act of self-disclosure, in which the triune God declares himself "outside" the eternal utterance of himself in his immanent life, in a created likeness. Where I wish, therefore, to direct my gaze in what follows is toward Gregory's understanding of the relationship between the Trinitarian *taxis* and God's image in us, the better to show how, for Gregory, God's own internal life of perfect wisdom, charity, and bliss is (to use the most precise term) *reflected* in the human soul. I hope thus to demonstrate how God's life of light and joy is understood by Gregory as one of radiant "mirroring," to which the being of creation is joined by what might be called, for want of a better term, a "specular economy."

II

Certainly if one were to attempt to isolate the one motif that pervades Gregory's thought most thoroughly, and that might best capture in a single figure the rationality that unifies it throughout, it would be that of the mirror: the surface in which light is gathered, creating depths where none previously existed, and by which it is reflected back to the source of its radiance. One might say, to begin with, that for Gregory all knowledge consists in *theōria* of the reflected, and this is in some sense so even within the life of God: the Son is the eternal image in which the Father contemplates and loves his essence, and thus the Father can never be conceived of without his Son, for were he alone he would have no light, truth, wisdom, life, holiness, or power;[18] "if ever the brightness of the Father's glory did not shine forth, that glory would be dark and blind."[19] This "mirroring" is that one original act of knowledge in which each of the persons shares; the Only Begotten, says Gregory, who dwells in the Father, sees the Father in himself, while the Spirit searches out the deeps of God.[20] God himself is, one is tempted to say, an eternal play of the invisible and the visible, the hidden Father made luminously manifest in the infinite icon of his beauty, God "speculating" upon himself by way of his absolute self-giving in the other. And it is from this original "circle of glory"[21] that the "logic" of created being unfolds: a specular ontology, according to which creation is constituted as simply another inflection of an infinite light, receiving God's effulgence as that primordial gift that completes itself in summoning its own return into existence. Creation is only as the answer of light to light, a created participation in the self-donating movement of the Trinity, existing solely as the manifestation—the reflection—of the splendor of a God whose own being is manifestation: recognition and delight.

Even "material" nature, for Gregory, is entirely subsumed in this economy of reflectivity: the physical world, he says, in its interminable dialectic of constancy and change, stands on the one hand in absolute contrast to divine reality,[22] but, on the other hand, it mirrors within its extraordinary intricacy, magnitude, and inscrutability the incomprehensibility

18. Gregory, *Contra Eunomium* 3.1; GNO 2:32.
19. Gregory, *Refutatio confessionis Eunomii*, GNO 2:355.
20. Gregory, *Contra Eunomium* 2; GNO 1:340.
21. See Gregory, *Adversus Macedonianos: De Spiritu Sancto*, GNO 3/1:109; *Contra Eunomium* 1; GNO 1:217–18.
22. Gregory, *De hominis opificio* 1; PG 44:128–32.

and majesty of God.[23] And the beauty that perdures in the midst of the world's ceaseless becoming excites in the soul a longing for the infinite beauty that it reflects.[24] Indeed, it is not an exaggeration to say that, for Gregory, apart from that reflex of light that lies at creation's heart, there is no world to speak of at all; Gregory, like Basil before him,[25] in various places denies that the world possesses any material substrate apart from the intelligible acts that constitute its perceptible qualities: the world of bodies is a confluence of "thoughts," "bare concepts," "words," noetic "potentialities,"[26] proceeding from the divine nature; its *esse*, one might almost say, is *percipi*. The phenomenal realm is not, says Gregory, formed from any underlying matter at all, for "the divine will is the matter and substance of created things,"[27] the "matter, form (*kataskeuē*), and power (*dynamis*) of the world."[28] The here below, it seems, is like a mirror without tain, a depth that is pure surface, and a surface composed entirely of the light that it reflects. Otherwise said, the physical world is a "primordial, archetypal, and true music," a purely rhythmic and harmonious complication of movements—in which, adds Gregory, human nature can discover an image of itself.[29]

The intelligible creation, however, is an even more thoroughly specular reality. For one thing, all talk of human "nature" most properly refers, in Gregory's thought, not merely to some abstract set of properties instantiated in any given individual, but to the *plērōma* of all persons who come into existence throughout time, who together constitute, as in a single body, the one humanity that God first willed in fashioning a creature in his image,[30] the ideal *anthrōpos* who dwells eternally in the wisdom and foresight of God, comprehended "altogether in its own plenitude."[31] This alone is truly that "God-like thing"[32] in whom God has condescended to

23. Gregory, *Contra Eunomium* 2; GNO 1:245–54, 260–62.

24. Gregory, *De beatitudinibus* 4; GNO 7/2:121; *De hominis opificio* 12; PG 44:161–64.

25. Basil, *In Hexaemeron* 1.8; PG 29:21.

26. See Gregory, *In Hexaemeron*, PG 44:68–72; *De anima et resurrectione*, PG 46:124; *De hominis opificio* 24; PG 44:212–13. There are other places, one should note, where Gregory seems to speak of matter more "concretely"—in, for instance, *In Hexaemeron*, PG 44:77–80.

27. ὕλη καὶ οὐσία τῶν δημιουργημάτων; Gregory, *In illud: Tunc et ipse filius*, GNO 2/2:11.

28. Gregory, *De vita Gregorii Thaumaturgi*, GNO 10/1:24.

29. Gregory, *In inscriptiones Psalmorum* 1.3; GNO 5:30–33.

30. Gregory, *De hominis opificio* 16; PG 44:185.

31. Gregory, *De hominis opificio* 17; PG 44:189.

32. τὸ θεοείκελον χρῆμα; Gregory, *De hominis opificio* 22; PG 44:204.

impress his likeness. When, eschatologically, its temporal unfolding is complete and it is united to the Logos as his pure and glorious body, subjected to the Father, the form of Christ will be proclaimed,[33] made visible in a body stamped with his shape, in whose every part the divine image will shine with equal brightness.[34] Humanity, then, is nothing, either ideally or collectively, apart from its power to display in itself the "form and fashion" of its creator; and this final beauty—this unveiling of the divine likeness—can be glimpsed even now in the church, which Gregory describes as the mirror in which the face of the sun of righteousness, Christ, has become visible within creation, to the wonder and enlightenment even of the heavenly powers.[35] Nowhere, though, does the beauty of the divine image shine forth with a more pristine radiance than in the individual soul purged of sin; for while indeed there will come about, in the eschatological submission of all things to Christ, a coincidence of the beauty of the eternal Logos (who reflects in his depths the full splendor of the unseen Father, in the Spirit's light) and the form of his redeemed creation, still only God can possess that beauty as identical with his essence. Created nature, which is in its inmost essence nothing but change,[36] can manifest God's loveliness only insofar as it continues forever to "capture" it, and continues to preserve within its mutability a dynamism entirely oriented toward God, by which it can grow into an ever greater embrace of divine glory;[37] and this can occur only within the individual will. Rational creation will indeed ultimately come to mirror the splendor of the Logos "in the convergence upon the One Good of all united one to another,"[38] and divine beauty will spread throughout all the members of the body, and the grace of the Lord will radiate through all, making everyone of one mind, alike in loveliness, everyone rejoicing in the beauty that appears in one's neighbor;[39] but all this will come to pass only insofar as each "facet" of that

---

33. Gregory, *In illud*, GNO 2/2:20.

34. Gregory, *De mortuis oratio*, GNO 9:63.

35. Gregory, *In Canticum Canticorum* 7; GNO 6:255–57.

36. See Gregory, *De anima et resurrectione*, PG 46:141; *In Canticum Canticorum* 12; GNO 6:351.

37. The idea that the union of the soul—and so of all lower creation—to God consists in a perpetual progress, an *epektasis*, into God's infinity is so utterly characteristic of Gregory's thought that there is little purpose in citing particular passages from his work; I will note, however, that it is the governing theme of the greatest of his spiritual treatises: *In Canticum Canticorum*, *De vita Moysis* (GNO 7/1), and *De perfectione* (GNO 8/1).

38. Gregory, *In Canticum Canticorum* 15; GNO 6:466.

39. Gregory, *De mortuis oratio*, GNO 9:66. Cf. Augustine, *De civitate Dei* 22.29–30.

perfect creation will have been purified and made bright within itself with the beauty of holiness.

Hence it is here that the enchantment of the mirror, and its sway over Gregory's theology, reaches its profoundest and most paradoxical intensity: such is the soul's "glassy essence" that it cannot help but assume the aspect of that toward which it is turned, and thus its intrinsic mutability and plasticity make of it also a "stable" surface in which anything—however noble or debased—can be made manifest. Human nature, says Gregory, is a mirror that takes on any appearance, bears the impression of any form, and is molded solely by the determinations of free will.[40] In its most proper nature, the human mind is in fact that uniquely privileged surface in which the beauty of the divine archetype is reflected and thereby mediated to the entirety of material creation, which is "a mirror of the mirror." Indeed, the lower creation, able to reflect only what humanity reflects, was subjected to the deformity that human nature conceived in itself when it turned toward sin[41] and forsook those endowments— impassibility, beatitude, incorruption—by which the divine image was originally impressed upon it.[42] And we, when humanity languished in the chill of idolatry, assumed in our nature the lifeless coldness of what we worshiped; but, when the sun of righteousness arose, our nature grew warm and lustrous again in his radiance.[43] Now, when our nature draws near to Christ, it becomes beautiful with the reflection of his beauty.[44] Gregory calls the soul a "free and living mirror" that, in gazing upon the face of its lover the Word, is adorned with his comeliness;[45] by looking at him, says Gregory, one becomes what he is.[46] The Word is the bridegroom who tells his bride, the soul, that she has become beautiful by approaching his light and communing with his eternal beauty;[47] and he is also the blinding sun that cannot be looked at directly, but can be glimpsed only in its image: the soul that mirrors his beauty in her own purity.[48] So entirely is the soul's relation to God a matter of this play of light within light, of

40. Gregory, *In Canticum Canticorum* 4; GNO 6:104.
41. Gregory, *De hominis opificio* 12; PG 44:161–64.
42. Gregory, *De mortuis oratio*, GNO 9:53.
43. Gregory, *In Canticum Canticorum* 5; GNO 6:147.
44. Gregory, *In Canticum Canticorum* 5; GNO 6:150.
45. Gregory, *In Canticum Canticorum* 15; GNO 6:440.
46. Gregory, *In Canticum Canticorum* 2; GNO 6:68.
47. Gregory, *In Canticum Canticorum* 4; GNO 6:104.
48. Gregory, *In Canticum Canticorum* 3; GNO 6:90–91; *De virginitate* 11; GNO 8/1:294–97; *De beatitudinibus* 6; GNO 7/2:148.

radiance and reflex, that Gregory can even reverse (or, at any rate, complicate) his specular imagery: just as the bodily eyes cannot see themselves, or perceive their own act of perception, but must find their image outside themselves, in a likeness reflected elsewhere, so the soul that mirrors her divine archetype and his beauty knows herself only in contemplating this reflection, finding in the figure of her archetype the mirror of her own nature.[49]

Obviously, though, in the case of God and the soul, what is reflected immeasurably exceeds the surface in which it appears: the infinite cannot dwell in the finite as a fixed and secure possession (the finite, being nothing but change, cannot even contain itself); God's nature, like a flowing fountain, is inexhaustible and ever new in our sight;[50] but so long as the soul continues to follow after the shining form of the Word, "stretching out" into his infinity, being transformed throughout eternity into an ever more incandescent—ever more divine—vessel of divine glory,[51] she can preserve within her very changeableness a changeless beauty,[52] and display it with an ever fuller splendor. In a sense, the infinity of God's glory is reflected in the insatiable *erōs* it awakens: as the soul always bears the impress of what she mirrors, one glimpse of the divine loveliness leaves an ecstasy ever unexpressed in the depths of the mind, like a longing for the ocean deeps or for the sun, inspired by the lingering taste—mere drops and glimmers—of its beauty.[53] And, no matter how far the soul ventures into the infinity of God, she will continue always to yearn for more of God's beauty, to hunger for his sweetness, nor will she ever find any end to the reality in which she moves[54]—and herein lies the ultimate truth of the soul's similitude to God. Gregory does not distinguish, as other fathers do, between God's image and God's likeness in us (between our created "similarity" to the divine and our ultimate assimilation to God in Christ), for such a distinction could have little meaning in his theology. Granted, he often speaks of those proper possessions of rational nature that constitute our aboriginal conformity

49. Gregory, *De mortuis oratio*, GNO 9:41; see Gregory, *In ecclesiasten* 7; GNO 5:411.

50. Gregory, *In Canticum Canticorum* 11; GNO 6:321.

51. Gregory, *In Canticum Canticorum* 6, GNO 6:173–79; 8, GNO 6:246, 253; *De virginitate*, GNO 8/1:280–81; *De perfectione*, GNO 8/1:212–14; *Contra Eunomium* 1; GNO 1:112, 285–87; *De mortuis oratio*, GNO 9:34–39; *In inscriptiones Psalmorum* 1.5; GNO 5:39–40; *De vita Moysis* 2; GNO 7/1:41–42, 114–18; *et multa cetera*.

52. Gregory, *De vita Moysis* 1; GNO 7/1:32–33.

53. Gregory, *De virginitate* 10; GNO 8/1:289.

54. Gregory, *De vita Moysis* 1, GNO 7/1:4–5; 2, GNO 7/1:114–18; *De anima et resurrectione*, PG 46:105.

to the divine, but all of them—including even freedom—exist in us only as reflections of the one good,[55] and only to the degree that we are turned toward it; and this likeness to God is destined to increase in purity, intensity, and resplendency through all eternity. Thus the soul, which is finite but infinitely motile, both is and yet is still called to become the moving mirror of the infinite, in which the glory of God that nothing can comprise and no one see expresses and manifests itself as beauty within change, eternity within movement; and this Gregory calls the *theoria tōn atheōrētōn*: the contemplation of the inconceivable, the vision of the invisible.[56]

Here, however, we seem not to have advanced beyond paradox, which (despite its often mysterious and even thrilling allure) is, in itself, invariably fruitless and, if left to itself, not a little banal. One could nevertheless bring one's reading of Gregory here to a very plausible close, and be content to see in the "dialectic" between God's infinity and created finitude (between hiddenness and revelation, the invisible and the visible, divine darkness and created light) the entire mystery of the divine image in us; but in doing so one would fail to take account of the deeper truth that allows such a relation—such a proportion between incommensurables—to be a real event both of divine self-disclosure and of creaturely participation in God's goodness. After all, were the relation between God and humanity simply that between the infinitely hidden and the finitely manifest, it would be no relation at all, but only an impossible interval, posed between the ontological and the ontic, the actual and the possible, the absolute and the contingent; its only true proportion would be an infinite otherness, and its only true expression the creature's eternal frustration. There must then already be in God, for Gregory's "dynamist" theology of the image to be meaningful, the ground of possibility that would allow the hiddenness of God at once to remain inviolable and yet to unveil itself in a created icon; there must be a Trinitarian "economy" (to use an entirely inappropriate word, given the infinite self-donation of the Father in the Son and Spirit) of invisibility and disclosure, and the created image of God must participate at once in this invisibility and this disclosure: it must acquire its brightness "within" the Trinitarian order of relations, according to an economy (the word being here appropriately employed) that, in keeping with Gregory's language, might best be called the economy of glory. And, for Gregory, glory means more than an "attribute" of God: it is his light, his splendor, and—most importantly—his Son and Spirit.

---

55. Gregory, *Oratio catechetica*, GNO 3/4:15–20.
56. Gregory, *In Canticum Canticorum* 11; GNO 6:326. See 10; GNO 6:307–11.

III

There are two distinct, though consequent, senses in which it is correct to speak of the invisibility of God: there is, on the one hand, the sheer infinity of the divine nature, which—flowing from the Father—is the common *proprium* of the divine persons, who as one forever exceed and excite our souls' most extravagant ecstasies; and there is, on the other hand, that invisibility of the Father within the Trinitarian *taxis* that is altogether convertible with (or, rather, "converted in") the "visibility" or manifestation of the Logos to the Father and the "visibility" or illumination of the Spirit for the Father.[57] The infinity, and so inaccessibility, of God is known to us in both aspects, and it is only because the former invisibility (divine transcendence) proceeds from the latter (the plenitude of the paternal *archē* within the Trinitarian structure of manifestation, of self-outpouring love and self-knowing wisdom) that the restless mutability of our nature can become, by grace, a way of mediation between the infinite and the finite. We can mirror the infinite because the infinite, within itself, is entirely mirroring of itself, the Father's incomprehensible majesty being eternally united to the coequal "splendor of his glory," his "form" and "impress," in seeing whom one has seen the Father.[58] We can become images of God that shine with his beauty because the Father always has his image in his Son, bright with the light of his Spirit, and so is never without form and loveliness.[59] And (most importantly) the motion of our soul can reflect the eternal peace of God because it can be assimilated to, and made to share in, that one eternal act whereby God is God, by the advent of that act in us under the form of sanctification. Thus, in the surface of the soul, the nature of the Trinitarian life, while always eluding our understanding, somehow appears to us; in his light we see light.

Or, to phrase it differently, God's light is always Trinitarian; his glory is inseparable from his triune being. Moreover, glory, the one indivisible splendor of the Trinity, often figures in Gregory's vocabulary as a special name for the Holy Spirit. This is not to say that divine glory is not a possession of the Father for Gregory, or that Gregory does not, following Scripture, call the Son glory, or the splendor of glory, or the seal of glory, who is as inseparable from the Father as is radiance from light.[60] There is,

---

57. See Gregory, *De perfectione*, GNO 8/1:188–89.
58. Gregory, *De perfectione*, GNO 8/1:189.
59. Gregory, *De perfectione*, GNO 8/1:189.
60. Gregory, *Ad Simplicium: De fide*, GNO 3/1:63–64.

though, a very particular sense in which the light of the Spirit, for Gregory, is that "perfecting" radiance, that fullness of glory, that "completes" the unity of the Godhead:[61] when Christ prays, in John 17, according to Gregory, that his followers might be one even as he and his Father are one and indwell one another, and says that the glory that the Father has given him he has given them, he is speaking of the gift of the Holy Spirit; indeed, that glory *is* the Spirit, the glory that the Son had with the Father before the world was made,[62] the "bond of peace" or "bond of unity" (so like the Augustinian *vinculum caritatis*) by which Father and Son dwell in one another, and by which we dwell in God when the Son breathes the Spirit forth upon us.[63] The Spirit, who forever searches the depths of God, and who forever receives from and is sent by the Son, has also always himself possessed his glory, and so has the power to glorify, from everlasting and in infinite superabundance—and "how can any grant the grace of light unless he be himself light?"[64]

> Thus the Spirit glorifies the Father and the Son. Nor does he speak falsely who says, "I glorify them that glorify me." "I have glorified you," the Lord says to his Father. And again: "Glorify me with that glory I had with you before the world existed." The divine voice answers: "I have glorified and will glorify." Do you see the revolving circle of glory, from like to like (*enkyklion tēs doxēs dia tōn homoiōn periphoran*)? The Son is glorified by the Spirit. The Father is glorified by the Son. Again, the Son has his glory from the Father, and so the Only Begotten becomes the glory of the Spirit. For by what will the Father be glorified if not by the true glory of his Only Begotten? And, again, in what will the Son be glorified if not in the majesty of the Spirit? So, again, our confession and praise, circling back again (*anakykloumenos ho logos*) glorifies the Son through the Spirit, and through the Son the Father.[65]

This last sentence is of the essence, for it shows that it is this very circle of glory into which the Spirit draws us,[66] and that it is by being refashioned after and in the Trinitarian ordering of self-outpouring light that we are made like God. Thus the "course" of glory in the Godhead—the

61. See Gregory, *Adversus Macedonianos*, GNO 3/1:109.
62. Gregory, *In illud*, GNO 2/2:21–22; *In Canticum Canticorum* 15; GNO 6:466–68.
63. Gregory, *In illud*, GNO 2/2:22; *In Canticum Canticorum* 15; GNO 6:466–67.
64. Gregory, *Adversus Macedonianos*, GNO 3/1:108.
65. Gregory, *Adversus Macedonianos*, GNO 3/1:109.
66. See Gregory, *Contra Eunomium* 1; GNO 1:216–18.

taxis of the divine being—impresses its own reflex in our specular natures, almost under the form of an inversion of the light (as is proper
for a mirror), so that God's own loving "return" to himself is our integration into him. Everything—being, power, creation,[67] holiness, love,
truth, faith[68]—flows from the Father, through the Son, to the Spirit, and
is restored by the Spirit, through the Son, to the Father; and this order
of relations, and its doxological dynamism, is the very order of the economy of salvation, which is therefore nothing less than the Trinitarian life
gathering us into itself.

In the Song of Songs, says Gregory, when the bride (the soul) cries
out that she has been wounded with love, we should see the Father as the
archer, sending forth the arrow of his Son, whose "three-pointed arrowhead" has been "dipped in the Spirit of life"; the arrowhead is faith, by
which the bolt is fixed deep in the bride's heart; and then (as Gregory as-
tutely observes) the imagery of archery is replaced by that of nuptial delight.[69] That is: as the light of the Spirit appears in the mirror of the soul,
the Trinitarian mystery of love becomes manifest; "in this light [human
nature] assumes the beautiful form of the dove: that is, the dove that sym-
bolizes the presence of the Holy Spirit."[70] The eyes of the bride are lovely
because the dove is reflected in them, and hence they receive the impression of the spiritual life within themselves, so that—thus purified—they
are now able to contemplate the beauty of the bridegroom.[71] It is impossible to say Jesus is Lord, or mount in thought to the Son or, through him,
to the Father, except in the Holy Spirit.[72] "[T]here is no means whereby
to look upon the Father's *hypostasis* save by gazing at it through its stamp
(*charaktēr*), and the stamp of the Father's *hypostasis* is the Only Begotten,
to whom, again, none can approach whose mind has not been illuminated
by the Holy Spirit."[73] The light of the Father, proceeding in the Holy Spirit,
makes the Father's Only Begotten light visible, and so the Spirit's glory
makes Father and Son perceptible to our intelligence. Thus, though in one
sense it is true that "none has ever seen God," still the grace of the Spirit
elevates human nature to the contemplation of God, for "where the Spirit

67. Gregory, *Adversus Macedonianos*, GNO 3/1:99–100.
68. Gregory, *Epistula* 24; GNO 8/2:77.
69. Gregory, *In Canticum Canticorum* 4; GNO 6:127–28.
70. Gregory, *In Canticum Canticorum* 5; GNO 6:150–51.
71. Gregory, *In Canticum Canticorum* 4; GNO 6:105–6.
72. Gregory, *In Canticum Canticorum* 4; GNO 6:106; *Adversus Macedonianos*, GNO 3/1:98–99.
73. Gregory, *Ad Eustathium: De Sancta Trinitate*, GNO 3/1:13.

is, there the Son is seen and the Father's glory is grasped."[74] Here, then, in the fused light of holiness—of the Spirit's radiance purifying the soul of every stain and filling her with every splendor—the Trinitarian relations "declare" or "express" themselves, as at once the threefold "community" of glory and also the perfect unity of divine being's structure of infinite self-manifestation: the absolute inseparability of the paternal "depth" from its "image" and "glory."

Moreover, as one considers the sequence of the soul's movements, as the Spirit works upon her, it becomes even clearer that the Trinitarian image appears in us at once as "nature" and as "grace," and appears in each soul as both the ground of "interior" identity and the effect of a transforming act of relation; for the mystery of God's life is reflected not only in the purity of the soul's surface, nor only in the limpid display of the economy of divine revelation there, but also in the "inward" structure of the soul's assimilation to the triune God. Where the light of the Spirit touches the mirror of the soul, one might say, it achieves a chiastic shape; a mirror, after all, not only inverts the light that strikes it, returning it to its source, but also reproduces in itself, under the form of that inversion, the figure of what it faces, thus gathering into itself what it is gathered into. The mirror of the soul is that ideal surface where two depths are reconciled, or where one depth creates another: the infinite light of God, flowing from the Father, through the Son, to the Spirit, and the "spectacle" of its created likeness, rising up from the more "exterior" to the more "interior" aspects of the soul, repeating in the realm of created finitude the infinite's play of hiddenness and manifestation. The three marks of the Christian life, says Gregory, appear in practice, word (*logos*), and thought (*enthymion*); the principle (*archikōteron*) of all three is thought, for mind (*dianoia*) is that original source (*archē*) that then manifests itself in speech, while practice comes third and puts mind and word into action. It is within this threefold constitution of our essential act of being and manifesting ourselves that we either conceive the image of sin or of Christ, and so we must strive within the circumvolving mutability of our souls to fashion ourselves after the latter; and, when our life is shaped by a mind whose movements are in conformity to Christ, "there is a harmony of the hidden man with the manifest."[75] It is not fanciful, obviously, given the classically "linear" nature of Cappadocian Trinitarianism, to discern

---

74. Gregory, *In Sanctum Stephanum* 1; GNO 10/1:90–91.

75. συμφωνίαν εἶναι τοῦ κρυπτοῦ ἀνθρώπου πρὸς τὸν φαινόμενον; Gregory, *De Perfectione*, GNO 8/1:210–12.

a Trinitarian shape in this account of the human soul (of, that is, mind and body); nor is it excessive to speak of a kind of pneumatological chiasm brought about by the purifying work of sanctification in the soul: inasmuch as the soul's principle, the mind, expresses itself in word and act, moving from full hiddenness to open disclosure, just so the Spirit, meeting us in our fleshly acts and words, conducts the Trinitarian glory "upward" into our thought, refashioning us so that our "depths" are ever more conformed to the brightening "surface" of our natures, making our "return" to ourselves at once a reflex of God's return to himself within his circle of glory and also our ascent out of ourselves—out of our creaturely insubstantiality—into his infinity.

This becomes especially clear in a passage from the *Adversus Macedonianos*: the Spirit, Gregory notes, comes to us first in the life-giving power of baptism, in our flesh, as the power of sanctification; but this requires also a prior act of faith in Christ; but, again, this grace proceeds through the Son from the ingenerate source, the Father, and so faith in the Father somehow comes first. Thus divine life and grace stream down to us from the Father, through the Son, in the perfecting action of the Spirit, and either our praise or our blasphemies return again to the beneficent wellspring of deity, in the Spirit and through the Son; and thus "the pious worshipper of the Spirit sees in him the glory of the Only Begotten and in the Son beholds the image of the infinite [invisible] one,[76] and by this image stamps the archetype upon the mind. . . . [B]ut such is this power that whosoever exalts the Spirit in speech (*tō logō*) exalts him prior to speech in thought: for speech is not able to ascend alongside thought. When one will have attained to the uttermost extent of human power, to the most exalted thoughts within reach of the human mind, one must still think it inferior to his grandeur."[77] Doxology becomes *theōria*, as the words that respond to the Spirit's act within our acts ascend to thought, and thought transcends itself toward God; and, again, the *taxis* of the Trinity shapes the *taxis* of the soul, as the ascent of glory from the Spirit and Son back to its paternal source is mirrored in the soul as an ascent from expression to mind. In this way, says Gregory, all duality is overcome, even that between

---

76. The word Gregory uses here is ἀόριστος ("τοῦ ἀορίστου"); as infinity is something Gregory ascribes to all three persons of the Trinity, as the "measure" of their coequality, it seems somewhat odd to see the Father described as "the infinite"; but Gregory may mean simply that the infinity of the divine essence, flowing from the paternal source, is paradoxically seen in the Father's coequal image; or it could be that ἀόριστος here carries the force (or may even be a faulty transcription) of ἀόρατος.

77. Gregory, *Adversus Macedonianos*, GNO 3/1:105–7.

body and soul, so that "the manifest exterior is found in the hidden interior, and the hidden interior in the manifest exterior."[78]

One should note here, however, that this is not simply some barely baptized form of Neoplatonism, according to which the absolute principle emanates itself in diminishing degrees of divinity—from the One, through Nous, to Psyche—and returns to itself in the finite soul's ascent to its own inward and noetic simplicity. Gregory's is not a metaphysics of identity that would dissolve the divine and human into a bare unity of essence, but a metaphysics of "analogy": of, that is, divine self-sufficiency and its entirely gratuitous reflection in a created likeness. Between God and soul the proportion of the analogy remains infinite. The Father is not a sublime abyss of undifferentiated light; nor is the Son the prism or cymophane in which that light acquires color through its refraction, fragmentation, or distortion; nor is the Spirit that light's delicate and diffuse opalescence here below, waiting to be gathered up again in the soul's contemplative intellect. Gregory's thought is, in a way more radical than any "identitarian" idealism could ever be, utterly "speculative." The disproportion between word and thought in us does not reflect any inequality within the simplicity of the divine nature; there is no subordination within God's circle of glory. Moreover, we are drawn into God not by a nisus of the alone to the alone—the reduction of the soul's motion to the austerely featureless light of some "substantial" identity—but by way of ecstasy, of the dynamism of change within a soul that is itself pure change, with no "principle" or "past" to return to or remember. The soul is an absolute futurity,[79] rising up from nothingness into the infinite, forever. We are music moved to music, light born within light, but God dwells in the fullness of his own glory and fellowship, while we reflect that plenitude and love across the infinite distance of imparted glory, in the ever more luminous surface of our mutable nature, both like and unlike the beauty that gives us being and shape, revealing that beauty both in what we are becoming and in the infinity with which it always exceeds the changing mirrors of our souls. Yet, even so, it is here, to this miraculous incommensurability within union between the infinite and the finite, in the dual action (which is really one and the same act) of creation and redemption, that we must look for our images, however insufficient, of God's triune nature.

---

78. Gregory, *De beatitudinibus* 7; GNO 7/2:160–61.

79. Gregory, *Contra Eunomium* 1; GNO 1:136; *De anima et resurrectione*, PG 46:93; *In Canticum Canticorum* 12; GNO 6:366.

IV

To return, then, to this essay's beginning: if it is so that this is how the divine image is constituted in us—as the play of God's glory gathering in the mirror of our nature—and that it is a Trinitarian image, then, in considering how God reveals himself in the economy of creation and salvation, we must ultimately find ourselves far beyond all simple oppositions between "social" and "psychological" Trinitarianism, or between "personalism" and "essentialism," or—most certainly—between Greeks and Latins. Just as we must resist every temptation toward those twin reductions of the human essence to either simply society or simply ego (which are vapid as abstractions and vicious as ideologies), we must surely avoid reducing our understanding of God to rudimentary images of either confederacy or subjectivity. In our own souls, in their absolute implication within one another of the exterior and the interior, we discover—without grasping—an icon of that infinite transparency of the divine persons within and to one another that is also the infinite depth of each divine person's distinctness. On the one hand, it seems we must understand this infinite coincidence in God of relation and identity by reflecting upon the unity of the soul's motion outward toward expression and inward toward thought (however we may wish to employ "social" models, in themselves they can offer only pictures of extrinsic accommodations between monads, or perhaps of the "transparency" of collective identity, but in neither case can such models account for the mysterious complexity and amphibology of personality, or for the reality of the soul's unity within difference); but, on the other hand, for Gregory no less than for Augustine, the turn inward proves to be, in a still more radical sense, a turn outward: I am an openness whose depth does not belong to me, but to the boundless light that creates me, and whose identity is then given me as other. And as the otherness of God is the soul's true depth, she can possess no identity apart from the otherness of the neighbor; and both the soul's otherness from God and the otherness of each soul from every other reflect the mystery of God's act of "othering" himself within his infinite unity.

It is thus not strange that we find, at the end of Gregory's commentary on the Song, that the bride—who is the figure of the soul joined to Christ the bridegroom—represents also the unity of all souls united to one another in the dove: in the Spirit of glory.[80] The Trinitarian image appears in each soul as she is purified by grace, and then integrally in the body of the

---

80. Gregory, *In Canticum Canticorum* 15; GNO 6:466–69.

Logos, which consists in all of humanity bound with the bond of peace, the very Spirit who is the bond of God's unity. This is an "analogical ontology" in the truest sense: our participation in the being that flows from God is an imparted splendor, always seizing us from nothingness, drawing us into the infinite depth of God's essential simplicity and Trinitarian diversity, into his knowledge and love of his own beauty, but always only insofar as we comprise within our "essence" an interval of incommensurability that is the created likeness of the infinite ontological interval between God and us. That is to say, perhaps more obscurely, that our likeness to God, posed between the pure ontic ecstasy of our being *ex nihilo* and the infinite ontological plenitude of his being *in se* (between, one might say, our intrinsic nothingness and his supereminent "no-thing-ness"), cannot simply take the form of a homonymy of "attributes" applied to two discrete substances, but must consist, radically, in the rhythm of our difference from him, our likeness to his unlikeness, under the form of a dynamic synthesis of distinct moments of being that, in God, coincide in simple and infinite identity. The distance within us between what we are and that we are, as between our movements *intus* and *foro*, is the necessary expression within the ontic of the distance between God and contingent reality, which distance has as its ontological possibility and *actus* the "distance" that is opened by the eternal act of the hypostatic distinctions within God's unity. I am slipping rather too easily into scholastic terminology. In something more like Gregory's own terms, I should say this: that we are in every way mirrors set among mirrors, within the infinite movement of a light that is always already its own reflection; and in all the complexity of our existence—in moments of interior *theōria* and of exterior communion—we can come to shine with his loveliness, both in the fullness of our nature and in each soul's glorious and ardent thirst for the whole of God's beauty, because in God difference is identity and distinction is unity. Somehow, in this mystery of the moving and finite image of the eternal and infinite God, we are vouchsafed a glimpse of how God knows and loves himself, and is entire in every moment of that act, and receives his glory completely in utterly pouring it forth in another.

Which yields, finally, only this reflection: that a simple, and almost entirely misguided, critical distinction between differing styles of Trinitarianism should have become, over the last century, not only a petrified and petrifying formula in theological scholarship, and not only a justification for pursuing any number of narrower and narrower dogmatic projects, but yet another weapon (and another myth) in the interminable war of recrimination between East and West, is an almost excruciating irony. That the language of God's Trinity—of God's perfect unity within the "diversifying" act of his knowing love—should become the grammar of a dispute that seems always to harbor yet greater dimensions of suspicion and misunderstanding is an offense not only against reason, but also against love. It may well be that the truest Trinitarian theology of which the Eastern and Western catholic traditions are now capable would consist in the resolution to turn in charity each to the other, in the hope of each finding mirrored in the other those hidden depths that neither is competent to recognize in itself; for the glory of the Spirit is never visible to us apart from our willingness to receive its light from without. Such observations quickly become either saccharine or sanctimonious; so suffice it to remark that no theologian has ever been more adamant than Gregory in insisting that all we are and should be lies outside our grasp, ahead of us, and that we who insist on clinging to our own particular "substances," rather than seeking our proper being in our ecstatic openness to the light that is beyond us, in fact cling to nothing, embrace phantoms, chase shadows and *ignes fatui*, and subjugate ourselves to the transient and empty; and so long as either East or West refuses the glory that appears in the other, it refuses the Holy Spirit—the bond of peace, of unity, and of love—and all our worlds grow dark.

SEVEN

The Hidden and the Manifest

Metaphysics after Nicaea

I

This essay, I must confess, is intended only as a tentative approach to what I take to be an inherently elusive critical object; and so the investigations it comprises are necessarily somewhat hesitant and incomplete, and may ultimately prove no more than suggestive of inquiries that might be taken up in the future. My principal interest lies in what I want to call "Nicene ontology," but I am aware not only of the invincible vagueness of such a concept, but of the impatience I am likely to provoke from scholars who would argue that no general ontology can be extracted from Nicene dogma, or from the theology of the Nicene party, and that theologians like the Cappadocian fathers, Hilary of Poitiers, and Augustine never aspired to be what we call "thinkers of Being." Even so, it seems undeniable to me that the development of the Christian understanding of God implicitly involved a metaphysical revision of certain prevailing understandings of Being; and that, as the Trinitarian debates of the fourth century unfolded, and as dogmatic definitions took shape, and as those debates and definitions were clarified in the next century, inevitably certain elements of a Christian "narrative of Being"—or narrative of the relation between the being of the world and the being of God[1]—also became clear for the first

1. In phrasing the matter thus, I hope I indicate how my concerns differ from those of Jean-Luc Marion (in the volume from which this essay was taken), and why my argument is not related to his. The question that concerns me is not how the fathers came to "denominate" God "within the horizon of being" or "within the metaphysics of being *qua* being." Rather, my interest is in the question of how "being" had to be reconceived by

137

time, and received either explicit or implicit expression in the thought of the first few generations of Nicene theologians. This I find fascinating for a number of reasons, but most particularly because, as one considers how this new, Christian vision of reality announced itself in the thought of the greatest earliest champions of Nicene theology, one begins to see that many of them were responding to the same conceptual revolution, not always consciously, and yet almost inevitably in the same way. And this, in a broad sense, is the guiding theme of my argument.

Before proceeding, however, I should note that the immediate context of this essay is a conference on the Eastern Orthodox understanding of Augustine's theology, conducted by Eastern and Western Christian scholars together, and convoked in the hope that their shared efforts might help to dispel certain of the misunderstandings haunting relations between the "Greek" and "Latin" traditions. This is a project admirable in its ambition, obviously, but also one that innumerable obstacles conspire to thwart. In any modern engagement between Christian East and Christian West, we begin from the long history of an often militant refusal—on both sides—of intellectual reconciliation; more to the point, we begin from very different theological grammars, and with terminologies that can achieve only proximate correspondences, and from within conceptual worlds whose atmospheres are not perfectly congenial to one another's flora, and from a settled tradition of mutual (and frequently willful) incomprehension. All too often, moreover, this incomprehension takes the depressing form of a simple and deplorable failure of imagination: an inability to appreciate that, in order to understand another intellectual tradition, rooted in a different primary language, it is not enough to translate its terms into one's own dialect and then proceed to interpret them according to the rules of one's own tradition. And the consequence of this is that, as often as not, "ecumenism" between East and West consists in little more than a relentless syncope of category errors: the drearily predictable alarm and indignation with which traditional Thomists find that Gregory Palamas, transposed into Thomas's Latin, is not a Thomist; the deep and slightly macabre delight with which earnest Palamites discover that Thomas, read through Palamite lenses, proves to be no Palamite; arch dismissals of Eastern understandings of grace as "semi-Pelagian" by doctrinaire Augustinians; the

Christian thinkers within the horizon of the relation between the transcendent God and creation; and my conviction is that the development of Christian thought led inevitably to the dissolution of the idea of "being" as a metaphysical "object" within the economy of beings, and rendered the very idea of "being" analogical between God and creatures, and so impotent to comprise the difference dividing them.

reckless intensity with which a particular kind of Orthodox polemicist fixes upon some single principle found somewhere in Latin theological tradition—like "subsistent relations" or "created grace"—violently misinterprets it, and then uses it to diagnose a fundamental deformity in Western theology that must estrange it forever from the wellsprings of Orthodox truth; and so on. Perhaps this kind of thing is inevitable when a conversation arises between two traditions that claim to possess the sole, incontrovertible truth of things. It would be humbling indeed to discover that many of our most finely wrought systems of thought possess many accidental elements, peculiar to our particular cultural sensibilities or native tongues, or that perhaps our ways of depicting the truth to ourselves might be only partial and corrigible approximations to a truth that others, under extremely different forms, have approached with equal or better success. More terrible yet is the possibility that many of our differences will prove to be *only* differences of sensibility and language, and not of substance at all, thus reducing our systems to relative expressions of the truth, rather than the pristine vehicles of truth we wish them to be.

Whatever the case, an honest consideration of Augustine in relation to the Eastern fathers *should* be able to provide a fairly powerful solvent, either of false distinctions or of false accords. For, whatever else may be true about Augustine, it is certainly the case that the profoundest differences between Eastern and Western tradition are to a very great degree the result not only of differences of language, but of the uniquely pervasive influence of Augustine's theology in the Latin West, and of the almost complete absence of its influence in the Greek and Syrian East. And, of course, on some matters these differences are quite real, substantial, and irreconcilable. The theology of grace of the late Augustine, his increasingly intransigent extremism regarding the creature's "merit," his hideous theology of predestination and original guilt, his conviction that genuine trust in the purity and priority of grace obliged him to affirm the eternal damnation of infants who died unbaptized—in short, the entire range of his catastrophic misreading of Paul's theology (attributable only in part to bad Latin translations)—all of this is very far from what an Orthodox Christian today would in all likelihood be willing to recognize as the Christian faith. It imbues the works of Augustine's senescence with an inexpungible tincture of tragic moral idiocy, one that he bequeathed to broad streams of Catholic and Protestant tradition. This, however, is not really very important, since that aspect of Augustine's thought has fewer defenders than once it did; and, really, charity dictates that it should probably be disregarded as the product of intellectual fatigue. Rather, the issues that truly demand our attention are of another kind altogether, and concern areas of Augustine's thought where, in various times and places, scholars both Western and Eastern have believed they perceived vast and ultimately unbridgeable fissures between "Greek" and Augustinian thought—of a kind that make rapprochement between our traditions, theological or dogmatic, quite impossible—regarding the very nature of God as Trinity, the relation of created being to divine being, and the limits of what we can know of either. These, at any rate, are the topics that concern me here. I wish to speak of "Being" and of God, of the Trinity and of our ability to know God, in the theology of Augustine and of the Greek fathers, Gregory of Nyssa in particular. But I wish to pursue these topics very much at the margins of the debates that have often preoccupied both Catholic and Orthodox theologians in recent years, for the simple reason that I believe that very many of the large and now standard claims often advanced regarding the divergence of our traditions on these matters, in form, content, or intent, are unsustainable, in light either of history or of reason; and that our debates all too often concern only differing and frequently tendentious reconstructions of the Christian past.

Most obviously, I suppose, I shall ignore altogether the venerable notion (first advanced by Théodore de Régnon)[2] that the general tendency of Latin Trinitarian reflection has always been to accord priority to the unity of God's nature or essence rather than to the plurality of the divine persons, while that of Greek Trinitarian reflection has been the reverse. Not only do I find the sheer vastness of this assertion dauntingly imprecise, but I also find it utterly impossible to defend from the actual textual evidence of either East or West, ancient, medieval, or modern. More importantly, I think it clearly the case that the assertion made by a number of Orthodox theologians—from Vladimir Lossky to John Zizioulas—that Latin theology views not God the Father, but rather the divine "essence," in its "impersonal" primacy, as the *archē* or *principium* of the Trinitarian *taxis*, is simply impossible to reconcile with the writings of the major figures of Western theological tradition, and can be corroborated only by extremely forced readings of a few isolated texts. In both East and West, at least as far as the main currents of theological speculation are concerned, the *monarchia* of the Father—the *fons deitatis*—remains a governing premise within all serious Trinitarian reflection, whatever differences in idiom there may be between Greek and Latin affirmations

2. Théodore de Régnon, *Études de théologie positive sur la Sainte Trinité*, 2 vols. (Paris, 1892), 1:433.

of the principle.[3] Even if this were not so, however, in the case of Augustine there can be no doubt that, in its basic shape, his account of the order of intra-Trinitarian relations is all but indistinguishable from that of the Cappadocians: the Son is begotten directly of the Father, while the Spirit proceeds from the Father through the Son.[4] Indeed, Gregory of Nyssa, like Augustine after him—though, in fact, far less hesitantly than Augustine—delineates generation from procession chiefly by reference to this order of relations, arguing that, inasmuch as the divine nature remains immutably the same in each of the divine persons, we discern the persons as distinct only by distinguishing between that which causes and that which is caused, and then further distinguishing between "the one who arises immediately from the principle and the one who arises from this principle only *through* the one who arises immediately."[5] As for the accusation that Augustine's "filioquism" logically entails a belief on his part in some sort of divine essence prior to the Trinitarian relations, or more original than the Father, neither in *De Trinitate* nor in any other of his works can one find a single sentence to justify it.

I also find quite incredible the notion (which one associates with the thought of, among others, Christos Yannaras) that the Latin and Greek traditions are set radically at odds by the former's willingness to speak of God as Being and the latter's insistence that God is, properly speaking, entirely beyond being. For one thing, as a purely historical claim, this is clearly false, since both locutions are common to both traditions, and with precisely the same meanings in either case. More fundamentally, though, it is simply a false opposition, inasmuch as the word "being" is certainly not univocal between the two usages; in fact, the word "being" does scant justice to the full spectrum of terms it is often called upon to represent: *ens, esse, essentia, existentia, [actus] essendi, on, ōn, ousia, einai*, and so forth. When the Greek fathers spoke of God as Being—as, that is, *to ontōs on* or *ho ōn* (etc.)—or when Latin theologians, patristic or medieval, spoke of God as *ens, actus essendi subsistens*, or *esse* (etc.), they were speaking of God as the transcendent source and end of all things, whose being is not merely the opposite of nonbeing, and in whom there is no unrealized potential,

3. I have addressed this matter at greater length in "The Mirror of the Infinite: Gregory of Nyssa and the *Vestigia Trinitatis*," *Modern Theology* (Fall 2002): 541–61; reprinted in *Re-Thinking Gregory of Nyssa*, ed. Sarah Coakley (Oxford: Blackwell, 2003), pp. 111–31, and as chapter 6 in the present volume.

4. See, for instance, Basil, *De Spiritu Sancto* 45–57.

5. Gregory of Nyssa, *Ad Ablabium: Quod non sint tres Dei*, Gregorii Nysseni Opera (hereinafter GNO), ed. Werner Jaeger et al. (Leiden: Brill, 1958–), 3/1:55–56.

deficiency, or change. But it is precisely in this sense that God is also (to use the venerable Platonic phrase) *epekeina tēs ousias*: "superessential," "supersubstantial," "beyond being." That is, he wholly transcends "beings," and discrete "substances," and the "totality of substances," and the created being in which all beings share; and no concept we possess of beings or of being makes it possible for us to comprehend him. Thus, as Maximus the Confessor says, both names, "Being" and "not-being," at once properly apply and properly do not apply to God: the one denotes that he is the cause of the being of all things, and the latter that he is infinitely beyond all caused being; but neither should be mistaken for a "description" of what he is.[6] In this, Maximus is following the Pseudo-Dionysius, who says that Being is a proper divine name insofar as God is "He Who Is," *Egō eimi ho ōn*, the source of all that exists, present within all things, around and within whom all being abides, in whom all things participate, and within whom the exemplars of all things eternally preexist as a simple unity; but he is not in any sense *a* being: he is not contained by—but rather contains— being, and so, with regard to his own essence, should properly be called not-being.[7] In Augustine's terms, God is the plenitude of Being, without which nothing is,[8] but such is his transcendence as the One Who Is that, by comparison to him, those things that are, *are* not[9] (which is obviously a semantic, but not a conceptual, shift). It may be momentarily—but *only* momentarily—arresting to note that Thomas, in deference to God's own pronouncement out of the burning bush,[10] prefers to identify "Being" (or, rather, "to be," or the subsistent act "to be") as the more proper "name" of God; but, again, "being" has many acceptations and, as Thomas's metaphysical designation for God, it signifies that same perfect transcendence of and supremacy over created being that, say, Palamas describes in his remarks upon Exodus 3:14.[11] In either case, there is no *conceptum univocum entis* to span the divide between divine and created being, and thus the true distinction to be drawn is not one between two incompatible ways of naming God, peculiar respectively to West and East, but between two forms of the same name, corresponding to two distinct moments within what I would be content to call the "analogy of being" (though that is a term that frequently excites controversy).

6. Maximus the Confessor, *Mystagogia*, Patrologia Graeca (hereinafter PG) 91:664AC.

7. Ps.-Dionysius, *De divinis nominibus* 5.1–8; PG 3:816B–824C.

8. Augustine, *Soliloquiae* 1.1.3–4.

9. Augustine, *Enarrationes in Psalmos* 134.4.

10. Thomas is also, of course, following John of Damascus: *De fide orthodoxa* 1.9.

11. Gregory Palamas, *Triads* 3.2.12.

II

In the intellectual world of the first three centuries before Nicaea, especially in the East, something like a "Logos metaphysics" was a crucial part of the philosophical *lingua franca* of almost the entire educated class, pagan, Jewish, Christian, and even Gnostic (even though the term generally preferred was rarely "logos"). Certainly in Alexandria the idea of a "derivative" or "secondary" divine principle was a common premise in the city's native schools of Trinitarian reflection, and in the thought of either "Hellenized" Jews like Philo or of the Platonists, middle or late. And one could describe all these systems, pagan and Jewish no less than Christian, as "subordinationist" in structure. All of them attempted, with greater or lesser complexity, and with more or less elaborate mythic detail, to connect the world here below to its highest principle by populating the interval between them with various intermediate degrees of spiritual reality. All of them were shaped by the same basic metaphysical impulse, one sometimes described as the "pleonastic fallacy": the notion that, in order to overcome the infinite disproportion between the immanent and the transcendent, it is enough to conceive of some sort of scale of successively more accommodating hypostases or emanations or abstract causes between, on the one hand, the One or the Father or *ho theos* and, on the other, the world of finite and changing things. In all such systems, the second moment of the real—that which proceeds directly from the supreme principle of all things: *logos*, or *nous*, or what have you—was understood as a kind of economic limitation of its source, so reduced in nature as to be capable of entering into contact with the realm of discrete beings, of translating the power of the supreme principle into various finite effects, and of uniting this world to the wellspring of all things. This derivative principle may not as a rule properly be called *ho theos*, but it definitely is *theos*: God with respect to all lower reality.[12] And this meant that this secondary moment of the real was understood as mediating this supreme principle in only a partial and distorted way; for such a principle can appear within the totality of things that exist only as a restriction and diffusion of—even perhaps a deviation or alienation from—that which is "really real," the Father who, in the purity of his transcendence, can never directly touch this world. For Christians who thought in such

12. This, of course, is why Augustine, in *Confessions* 7.9, quite properly credits the Platonists with having taught him the truths revealed in John 1:1–3 (though, of course, a modern scholar would prefer to say that the prologue of John is a "Middle Platonic" text).

terms, this almost inevitably implied that the Logos had been, in some sense, generated *with respect to* the created order, as its most exalted expression, certainly, but also somehow contingent upon it. Thus Christian apologists of the second century often spoke of the Logos as having issued from the Father in eternity shortly before the creation of the world. And thus the irreducibly Alexandrian theology of Arius inevitably assumed the metaphysical contours that it did: the divine Father is absolutely hidden from and inaccessible to all beings, unknowable even to the heavenly powers; and only through the mediation of an inferior Logos is anything of him revealed. What was fairly distinctive in Arianism was the absence of anything like a metaphysics of participation that might have allowed for some sort of real ontological continuity (however indeterminate) between the Father and his Logos; consequently the only revelation of the Father that Arius's Logos would seem to be able to provide is a kind of adoring, hieratic gesture toward an abyss of infinitely incomprehensible power, the sheer majesty of omnipotent and mysterious otherness. The God (*ho theos*) of Arius is a God revealed *only* as the hidden, of whom the Logos (*theos ho logos*) bears tidings, and to whom he offers up the liturgy of rational creation; but, as the ambassador of the Father, his is the role only of a celestial high priest, the Angel of Mighty Counsel, the coryphaeus of the heavenly powers; he may be a kind of surrogate God to the rest of creation, but he too, logically speaking, cannot attain to an immediate knowledge of the divine essence.

Even, however, in late antique metaphysical systems less ontologically austere than Arius's, which saw the order of divine manifestation as revealing also an order of *metochē* or *metousia*, the disproportion between the supreme principle of reality and this secondary principle of manifestation remained absolute. Hence all revelation, all disclosure of the divine, follows upon a more original veiling. The manifestation of that which is Most High—wrapped as it is in unapproachable darkness, up upon the summit of being—is only the paradoxical manifestation of a transcendence that can never become truly manifest: perhaps not even to itself, as it possesses no Logos immanent to itself. It does not "think"; it cannot be thought. This, at least, often seems to be the case with the most severely logical, and most luminously uncluttered, metaphysical system of the third century, that of Plotinus. The One of Plotinus is not merely *a* unity, not merely solitary, but is oneness as such, that perfectly undifferentiated unity in which all unity and diversity here below subsist and are sustained, as at once identity and difference. Plotinus recognized that the unity by which any particular thing is what it is, and is at once part of and distinct from the greater whole, is always logically prior to that thing; thus, within every composite reality, there must always also be a more eminent "act" of simplicity (so to speak) that makes its being possible. For this reason, the supreme principle of all things must be that One that requires no higher unity to account for its integrity, and that therefore admits of no duality whatsoever, no pollution of plurality, no distinction of any kind, even that between the knower and the known. Admittedly, the One is in some transcendent sense possessed of an intellectual act of self-consciousness, a "superintellection" entirely transcendent of subjective or objective knowledge.[13] But the first metaphysical moment of *theōria*—reflection and knowledge—is of its nature a second moment, a departure from unity, Nous's "prismatic" conversion of the simple light of the One into boundless multiplicity; the One itself, possessing no "specular" other within itself, infinitely exceeds all reflection. And, of course, there is something fundamentally incoherent in speaking of the existence of that which is intrinsically unthinkable, or of "being" in the absence of any proportionate intelligibility: For in what way is that which absolutely transcends intuition, conceptualization, and knowledge, even within itself, anything at all? Being *is* manifestation, and to the degree that anything is *wholly* beyond thought—to the degree, that is, that anything is not "rational"—to that very degree it does not exist. Hence the Platonist tradition after Plotinus generally chose to place "being" second in the scale of emanation: for as that purely unmanifest, unthinkable, and yet transfinite unity that grants all things their identities and singularities, the One can admit of no distinctions within itself, no manifestation *to* itself, and so—in every meaningful sense—*is* not (though, obviously, neither is it not *not*).

To be honest, even to speak of an "ontology" in relation to these systems is somewhat misleading. Late Platonic metaphysics, in particular, is not so much ontological in its logic as "henological," and so naturally whatever concept of being it comprises tends toward the nebulous. "Being" in itself is not really distinct from entities, except in the manner of another entity; as part of the hierarchy of emanations, occupying a particular place within the structure of the whole, it remains one item within the inventory of existing things. True, it is an especially vital and "supereminent" causal liaison within the totality of beings, but it remains a discrete principle among other discrete principles. What a truly ontological metaphysics would view as being's proper act is, for this meta-

---

13. See Plotinus, *Enneads* 6.7.37.15–38.26; 9.6.50–55.

physics, scattered among the various moments of the economy of beings. One glimpses its workings now here and now there: in the infinite
fecundity of the One, in the One's power to grant everything its unity as
the thing it is, in the principle of manifestation that emanates from the
One, in the simple existence of things, even in that unnamed, in some
sense *unnoticed*, medium in which the whole continuum of emanations
univocally subsists. But, ultimately, the structure of reality within this
vision of things is (to use the fashionable phrase) a "hierarchy within totality," held together at its apex by a principle so exalted that it is also the
negation of the whole, in all the latter's finite particularities.[14] What has
never come fully into consciousness in this tradition is (anachronistically
speaking) the "ontological difference"—or, at any rate, the *analogy* of
being. So long as being is discriminated from the transcendent principle
of unity, and so long as both are situated (however eminently) within
a continuum of metaphysical moments, what inevitably must result is
a dialectic of identity and negation. This is the special pathos of such a
metaphysics: for if the truth of all things is a principle in which they are
grounded and by which they are simultaneously negated, then one can
draw near to the fullness of truth only through a certain annihilation
of particularity, through a forgetfulness of the manifest, through a sort
of benign desolation of the soul, progressively eliminating—as the surd
of mere particularity—all that lies between the One and the noetic self.
This is not for a moment to deny the reality, the ardor, or the grandeur
of the mystical elations that Plotinus describes, or the fervency with
which—in his thought and in the thought of the later Platonists—the
liberated mind loves divine beauty.[15] The pathos to which I refer is a
sadness residing not within Plotinus the man, but within any logically
dialectical metaphysics of transcendence. For transcendence, so understood, must also be understood as a negation of the finite, and a kind
of absence or positive exclusion from the scale of nature; the One is, in
some sense, *there* rather than *here*. To fly thither one must fly hence,
to undertake a journey of the alone to the alone, a sweetly melancholy
departure from the anxiety of finitude, and even from being itself, in its
concrete actuality: self, world, and neighbor. For so long as one dwells
in the realm of finite vision, one dwells in untruth.

---

14. Plotinus, *Enneads* 6.7.17.39–43; 9.3.37–40; cf. 5.5.4.12–16; 11.1–6; ktl.

15. There are rather too many passages on this mystical *erōs* in the *Enneads* to permit
exhaustive citation; but see especially 6.7.21.9–22.32; 31.17–31; 34.1–39; 9.9.26–56.

III

What exactly, one might justly ask, does any of this have to do with Nicene theology? The answer, simply enough, is that the doctrinal determinations of the fourth century, along with all their immediate theological ramifications, rendered many of the established metaphysical premises upon which Christians had long relied in order to understand the relation between God and the world increasingly irreconcilable with their faith, and at the same time suggested the need to conceive of that relation—perhaps for the first time in Western intellectual history—in a properly "ontological" way. With the gradual defeat of subordinationist theology, and with the definition of the Son and then the Spirit as coequal and coeternal with the Father, an entire metaphysical economy had implicitly been abandoned. These new theological usages—this new Christian philosophical grammar—did not entail a rejection of the old Logos metaphysics, but they certainly did demand its revision, and at the most radical of levels. For not only is the Logos of Nicaea *not* generated with a view to creation, and *not* a lesser manifestation of a God who is simply beyond all manifestation; it is in fact the eternal reality whereby God is the God he is. There is a perfectly proportionate convertibility of God with his own manifestation of himself to himself; and, in fact, this convertibility is nothing less than God's own act of self-knowledge and self-love in the mystery of his transcendent life. His being, therefore, is an infinite intelligibility; his hiddenness—his transcendence—is always already manifestation; and it is this movement of infinite disclosure that is his "essence" as God. Thus it is that the divine persons can be characterized (as they are by Augustine) as "subsistent relations": meaning not that, as certain critics of the phrase hastily assume, the persons are nothing but abstract correspondences floating in the infinite simplicity of a logically prior divine essence, but that the relations of Father to Son or Spirit, and so on, are not extrinsic relations "in addition to" other, more original "personal" identities, or "in addition to" the divine essence, but are the very reality by which the persons subsist; thus the Father is eternally and essentially Father *because* he eternally has his Son, and so on.[16] God *is* Father, Son, and Spirit; and nothing in the Father "exceeds" the Son and Spirit. In God, to know and to love, to be known and to be loved are all one act, whereby he is God and wherein nothing remains unexpressed. And, if it is correct to understand "being" as in some sense necessarily synonymous with mani-

---

16. See Augustine, *De Trinitate* 7.1.2. Or, as John of Damascus puts it, the divine subsistences dwell and are established within one another (*De fide orthodoxa* 1.14).

festation or intelligibility—and it is—then the God who is also always Logos is also eternal Being: not *a* being, that is, but transcendent Being, beyond all finite being.

Another way of saying this is that the dogmatic definitions of the fourth century ultimately forced Christian thought, even if only tacitly, toward a recognition of the full mystery—the full transcendence—of Being within beings. All at once the hierarchy of hypostases mediating between the world and its ultimate or absolute principle had disappeared. Herein lies the great "discovery" of the Christian metaphysical tradition: the true nature of transcendence, transcendence understood not as mere dialectical supremacy, and not as ontic absence, but as the truly transcendent and therefore utterly immediate act of God, in his own infinity, giving being to beings. In affirming the consubstantiality and equality of the persons of the Trinity, Christian thought had also affirmed that it is the transcendent God alone who makes creation to be, not through a necessary diminishment of his own presence, and not by way of an economic reduction of his power in lesser principles, but as the infinite God. In this way, he is revealed as at once *superior summo meo* and *interior intimo meo*: not merely the supreme being set atop the summit of beings, but the one who is transcendently present in all beings, the ever more inward act within each finite act. This does not, of course, mean that there can be no metaphysical structure of reality, through whose agencies God acts; but it does mean that, whatever that structure might be, God is not located within it, but creates it, and does not require its mechanisms to act upon lower things. As the immediate source of the being of the whole, he is nearer to every moment within the whole than it is to itself, and is at the same time infinitely beyond the reach of the whole, even in its most exalted principles. And it is precisely in learning that God is not situated within any kind of ontic continuum with creation, as some "other thing" mediated to the creature by his simultaneous absolute absence from and dialectical involvement in the totality of beings, that we discover him to be the *ontological* cause of creation. True divine transcendence, it turns out, transcends even the traditional metaphysical divisions between the transcendent and the immanent.

This recognition of God's "transcendent immediacy" in all things, it should also be said, was in many ways a liberation from a certain sad pathos native to metaphysics; for with it came the realization that the particularity of the creature is not in its nature a form of tragic alienation from God, which must be overcome if the soul is again to ascend to her inmost truth. If God is himself the immediate actuality of the creature's emergence from nothingness, then it is precisely through becoming what it is—rather than through shedding the finite *"idiōmata"* that distinguish it from God—that the creature truly reflects the goodness and transcendent power of God. The supreme principle does not stand over against us (if secretly within each of us) across the distance of a hierarchy of lesser metaphysical principles, but is present within the very act of each moment of the particular. God is truly Logos, and creatures—created in and through the Logos—*are* insofar as they participate in the Logos's power to manifest God. God is not merely the "really real," of which beings are distant shadows; he is, as Maximus the Confessor says, the utterly simple, the very simplicity of the simple,[17] who is all in all things, wholly present in the totality of beings and in each particular being, indwelling all things as the very source of their being, without ever abandoning that simplicity.[18] This he does not as a sublime unity absolved of all knowledge of the things he causes, but precisely *as* that one infinite intellectual action proper to his nature, wherein he knows the eternal *"logoi"* of all things in a single, simple act of knowledge.[19] God in himself is an infinite movement of disclosure, and in creation—rather than departing from his inmost nature—he discloses himself again by disclosing what is contained in his Logos, while still remaining hidden in the infinity and transcendence of his manifestation. And to understand the intimacy of God's immediate presence *as God* to his creatures in the abundant givenness of this disclosure is also—if only implicitly—to understand the true difference of Being from beings.

One consequence of all this for the first generations of Nicene theologians was that a new conceptual language had to be formed, one that could do justice not only to the Trinitarian mystery, nor even only to the relation between this mystery and finite creation, but also to our knowledge of the God thus revealed. For the God described by the dogmas of Nicaea and Constantinople was at once more radically immanent within and more radically transcendent of creation than the God of the old subordinationist metaphysics had ever been. He was immediately active in all things; but he occupied no station within the hierarchy of the real. As Augustine says, he is manifest in all things and hidden in all things, and none can know him as he is.[20] He was not the Most High God of Arius, immune to all contact with the finite, for the Logos in whom he revealed himself as

17. Maximus the Confessor, *Ambigua*, PG 91:1232BC.
18. Maximus the Confessor, *Ambigua*, PG 91:1256B.
19. See Maximus the Confessor, *Centuries of Knowledge* 2.4; PG 90:1125D–1128A.
20. Augustine, *Enarrationes in Psalmos* 74.9.

creator and redeemer was his own, interior Logos, his own perfect image, his own self-knowledge and disclosure; nor certainly was his anything like the paradoxical transcendence of the One of Plotinus, "revealed" only as a kind of infinite contrariety. In fact, the God who is at once the Being of all things and beyond all beings, and who is at once revealed in a Logos who is his coequal likeness and at the same time hidden in the infinity of his transcendence, is immeasurably *more* incomprehensible than the One, which is simply the Wholly Other, and which is consequently susceptible of a fairly secure kind of *dialectical* comprehension (albeit, admittedly, a comprehension consisting entirely in negations). The Christian God, by contrast, requires us to resort to the far severer, far more uncontrollable, and far more mysterious language of analogy—to indulge in a slight terminological anachronism—in the sense enunciated in Roman Catholic tradition by the Fourth Lateran Council: a likeness always embraced within and exceeded by a greater unlikeness. In the terms of Gregory of Nyssa, however much of God is revealed to the soul, God still remains infinitely greater, with a perfect transcendence toward which the soul must remain forever "outstretched." Or, as Maximus says, Christian language about God is a happy blending of affirmation and negation, each conditioning the other, telling us what God is not while also telling us what he is, but in either case showing us only *that* God is what he is, while never allowing us to imagine we comprehend *what* it is we have said.[21]

That said, in a very significant way, the fully developed Trinitarianism of the fourth century allowed theologians to make real sense of some of those extravagant scriptural claims that, within the confines of a subordinationist theology, could be read only as pious hyperbole: "we shall see face-to-face," for instance, and "I shall know fully, even as I am fully known" (1 Cor. 13:12); or "we shall see him as he is" (1 John 3:2); or "who has seen me has seen the Father" (John 14:9); or "the Son . . . is the exact likeness of his substance" (Heb. 1:3); or even "blessed are the pure of heart, for they shall see God" (Matt. 5:8)—*makarioi hoi katharoi tē kardia, hoti autoi ton theon genēsontai* (note that last definite article). In considering the God of Nicene theology, we discover that the knowledge of the Father granted in Christ is not an external apprehension of an unknown cause, not the remote epiphenomenon of something infinitely greater than the medium of its revelation, and not merely a glimpse into the "antechamber of the essence"; rather, it is a mysterious knowledge of the Father himself within the very limitlessness of his unknowability. But, then again, the

21. Maximus the Confessor, *Ambigua*, PG 91:1288C.

God who is the infinite source of all cannot be an object of knowledge contained within the whole; and, if the Logos is equal to the Father, how can he truly reveal the Father to finite minds? And if—as became clear following the resolution of the Eunomian controversy—the Spirit too is not the economically limited medium of God's self-disclosure, but is also coequal with the Father and the Son, and is indeed the very Spirit by which God's life is made complete as knowledge and love, power and life, how can he reveal to us the Father in the Son?

These questions are made all the more acute, obviously, by the quite pronounced apophatic strictures that all post-Nicene theologians—Augustine no less than his Greek counterparts—were anxious to impose upon their language. As Augustine repeatedly affirms, every kind of vision of God in himself is impossible for finite creatures;[22] none can ever know him as he is;[23] nothing the mind can possibly comprehend is God;[24] God is incomprehensible to anyone except himself;[25] we are impotent even to conceive of God;[26] and so when speaking of God we are really able to do so properly only through negation.[27] And yet he also wants to say that, even in failing to comprehend God in himself, we are led by the Spirit truly to see and know and touch God. Similarly, Gregory of Nyssa denies that any creature is capable of any *theōria* of the divine essence, and yet wants also to say that, in stretching out in desire toward God, the soul somehow sees God[28] and attains to a *theōria tōn atheōrētōn*, a vision of the invisible.[29] Gregory even speaks of David as going out of himself really to *see* the divine reality that no creature *can* see, and remaining ever thereafter unable to say how he has done this.[30] Maximus, who raises the "Greek" delight in extravagant declarations of apophatic ignorance to its most theatrical pitch, nonetheless makes it clear that his is an apophaticism of intimacy, born not from the poverty of the soul's knowledge of God, but from the overwhelming and superconceptual immediacy of that knowledge. The mind rises to God, he says, by negating its knowledge of what lies below, in

---

22. See, for example, Augustine, *De Trinitate* 2.16.27; *In Ioannis Evangelium tractatus* 124.3.17; *Contra Maximinum Arianorum episcopum* 2.12.2.

23. Augustine, *Enarrationes in Psalmos* 74.9.

24. Augustine, *Sermon* 52.6; *Sermon* 117.5.

25. Augustine, *Epistle* 232.6.

26. Augustine, *Sermon* 117.5.

27. Augustine, *Enarrationes in Psalmos* 80.12.

28. Gregory of Nyssa, *De vita Moysis* 2; GNO 7/1:87.

29. Gregory of Nyssa, *In Canticum Canticorum* 11; GNO 6:326.

30. Gregory of Nyssa, *In Canticum Canticorum* 11; GNO 6:307–11.

order to receive true knowledge of God as a gift, and to come ultimately—beyond all finite negations—to rest in the inconceivable and ineffable reality of God.[31] When the mind has thus passed beyond cognition, reflection, cogitation, and imagination, and discovers that God is not an object of human comprehension, it is able to know him directly, through union, and so rushes into that embrace in which God shares himself as a gift with the creature,[32] and in which no separation can be introduced between the mind and its first cause in God.[33]

If this language of knowing God in a condition of insuperable unknowing seems at times little more than paradox, or to promise nothing more than a (logically impossible) affective experience of God totally devoid of concepts, what we must at all cost avoid doing is allow ourselves—solely for the sake of convenience—to impose later medieval systems of thought on the patristic texts, in the hope of thereby dispelling the difficulties with which they present us: either, as was once common among Catholic scholars, to read Augustine unreflectively through Thomism or, as is now too often the case among Orthodox scholars, to read the Eastern fathers unreflectively through Palamism. For one thing, especially in the context of a discussion between communions, if we retreat to the medieval syntheses, we will immediately find ourselves drawn into the tedious and irresoluble "disagreement" between the two traditions concerning the eschatological knowledge of God: between, that is, the Thomistic affirmation of an ultimate vision of the divine essence by souls elevated by grace and the Palamite denial of any vision of God's *ousia*, or of any encounter with God except through his "energies." This is a sublimely pointless argument at the end of the day. For one thing, inasmuch as Thomas explicitly denies that the mind that enjoys such a "vision" can ever *comprehend* the divine essence, and even states that the mind does not actually possess an immediate intuition of the essence, but sees God only through a certain created glory instilled in the intellect by the operations of grace;[34] and inasmuch as Palamas, however much he denies that any intellect can penetrate the divine essence, also wants to affirm that God's operations communicate the real presence of God to the mind; it is not entirely clear that the two positions are divided by anything much more profound than the acceptations of their preferred metaphors ("essence," after all, is only slightly more uni-

31. Maximus the Confessor, *Ambigua*, PG 91:1240C–1241A.
32. Maximus the Confessor, *Ambigua*, PG 91:1220BC.
33. Maximus the Confessor, *Ambigua*, PG 91:1260D.
34. Thomas Aquinas, *Summa theologiae* I.7.7.

vocal a term than "being"). Even if the two traditions should prove finally irreconcilable, neither should be trusted as an unproblematic précis of the theologies of the patristic period. In the case of Thomistic interpretations of Augustine, Jean-Luc Marion's essay gives sufficient evidence of the precipitous misreadings toward which such interpretations can lead. As for Palamite readings of the Eastern fathers, they frequently prove no less procrustean and no less deceptive. As David Bradshaw correctly notes in his essay,[35] whatever distinction may be drawn in the thought of, say, Gregory or Maximus between, on the one hand, the divine essence and, on the other, the divine energies or processions or "things around God" (assuming these are nearly equivalent terms), it is not a fixed distinction, but a kind of receding horizon, because God, in his operations toward creatures, reveals ever more of himself and yet always infinitely exceeds what he reveals. Whether, however, this is how Palamas understood the distinction between the divine essence and the divine energies is more than a little debatable.[36] What is beyond debate is that, for many contemporary Palamites—I have in mind especially Vladimir Lossky—the distinction is something altogether more (for want of a better term) dialectical, and altogether more inviolable. Even all of this, however, is rather beside the point, for the simple reason that both traditions, when they talk about the knowability or unknowability of the divine *ousia* or *essentia*, are for the most part talking pious nonsense. There is no such "thing" as the divine essence; there is no such discrete object, whether of knowledge or of ignorance. It is ultimately immaterial whether we prefer to use the term *ousia* to indicate the transcendence and incomprehensibility of God in himself or to use the term "incomprehensibility of the essence" instead. God is *essentially* Father, Son, and Spirit, and (as modern Orthodox theologians never tire of insisting) there is no other reality prior to, apart from, or more original than the paternal *archē*, which perfectly reveals itself in an eternal and coequal Logos and communicates itself by the Spirit who searches the deep things of God and makes Christ known to us. There is no divine essence understood as a discrete object unto itself, then, into the vision of which the souls of the saved will ultimately be admitted, nor

---

35. Marion's and Bradshaw's essays both appear in the same volume in which this essay originally appeared.

36. And, in fact, a question impossible to settle. If the texts attributed to Palamas are indeed all the work of his hand, then it is quite likely that no one will ever be able convincingly to explain what Palamas meant by the distinction of essence and energies in God, for the simple reason that it is not clear that Palamas himself ever decided exactly what he meant.

even from the knowledge of which human minds are eternally excluded, and any language that suggests otherwise—whether patristic, Thomist, or Palamite—is an empty reification. The question of the knowledge of God, properly conceived—conceived, that is, in the terms provided by Scripture and the best of patristic dogmatic reflection—is the question of how we know the Father in the Son through the Spirit, even as the Father infinitely exceeds our knowledge; it is, that is to say, an intrinsically Trinitarian question, to which none but a truly Trinitarian answer is adequate.

IV

The single passage from the New Testament that perhaps most perfectly expresses the answer toward which Nicene theology, East and West, was inexorably driven is Paul's comparison, in 2 Corinthians 3:12–18, between the veiled face of Moses and the unveiled faces of those being transformed, from glory to glory, into the likeness of Christ; and perhaps no word in that passage more perfectly captures the essence of this answer than the single, somewhat amphibolous participle *katoptrizomenoi*: either "beholding in a mirror" or "mirroring" or both—"speculating," "reflecting," "reflecting upon." At the risk of reducing an immense diversity of theological impulses and tendencies to a small set of abstract principles, I think it possible to identify two distinct but inseparable moments within Nicene thought regarding our knowledge of the Trinitarian God: first, the recognition that the interior life of this God is one of infinite and "reflective" intelligibility—from everlasting, a life that is always already Logos and Spirit—and, second, the affirmation that we know God by being admitted to a finite participation in that intelligibility, through our transformation by the Spirit into ever purer reflections of the Logos in whom the depths of the Father shine forth. That is to say, we know God by being drawn into the mystery of his own Trinitarian act of self-knowledge, which yet remains ever infinitely beyond us. The medium of God's revelation, therefore, is God himself; and the site—the matter—of that revelation is the living soul. As Augustine says, what we know of God we know through an image directly impressed upon our nature.[37] Or, as Gregory of Nyssa says, human nature is a mirror, capable of bearing the impress of whatever it is turned toward,[38] created to reflect its divine archetype within itself and

---

37. Augustine, *De Trinitate* 14.15.21; *Enarrationes in Psalmos* 4.8.
38. Gregory of Nyssa, *In Canticum Canticorum* 4; GNO 6:104.

to communicate that beauty to the whole of creation; and the soul comes to know God only insofar as it looks to Christ and thereby becomes what he is,[39] adorned with his beauty.[40] Revelation is sanctification, and the mind knows the Father in the Son by becoming itself an ever truer image of that Image.

The indiscerptibility of these two principles, in the theologies of both East and West, can be illustrated quite vividly by a fairly straightforward comparison between the thought of Gregory of Nyssa and that of Augustine, one that comes into focus for me principally around a (so to speak) matched set of quotations to which I often find myself returning. The first is from Gregory's *On the Soul and Resurrection*:

[T]he divine nature exceeds each [finite] good, and the good is wholly beloved by the good, and thus it follows that when it looks upon itself it desires what it possesses and possesses what it desires, and receives nothing from outside itself.[41]

And this line of reflection that Gregory takes up again a few lines below:

[T]he life of that transcendent nature is love, in that the beautiful is entirely lovable to those who recognize it (and the divine does recognize it), and so this recognition becomes love, because the object of his recognition is in its nature beautiful.[42]

The second, much longer quotation is from book 6 of Augustine's *De Trinitate*:

[T]he Son is from the Father, so as both to be and to be coeternal with the Father. For if the image perfectly fills the measure of him whose image it is, then it is coequal to its source.... [Hilary of Poitiers] has, in regard to this image, employed the name "form" on account, I believe, of its beauty, wherein there is at once such harmony, and prime equality, and prime

39. Gregory of Nyssa, *In Canticum Canticorum* 2; GNO 6:68.
40. Gregory of Nyssa, *In Canticum Canticorum* 15; GNO 6:440.
41. Gregory of Nyssa, *De anima et resurrectione*, PG 46: 93.[Ἐπεὶ δὲ οὖν παντὸς ἀγαθοῦ ἐπέκεινα ἡ θεία φύσις, τὸ δὲ ἀγαθὸν ἀγαθῷ φίλον πάντως διὰ τοῦτο ἑαυτὴν βλέπουσα καὶ ὃ ἔχει, θέλει καὶ ὃ θέλει, ἔχει, οὐδὲν τῶν ἔξωθεν εἰς ἑαυτὴν δεχομένη.]
42. Gregory of Nyssa, *De anima et resurrectione*, PG 46:96. [ἥ τε γὰρ ζωὴ τῆς ἄνω φύσεως ἀγάπη ἐστίν, ἐπειδὴ τὸ καλὸν ἀγαπητὸν πάντως ἐστὶ τοῖς γινώσκουσι (γινώσκει δὲ ἑαυτὸ τὸ θεῖον), ἡ δὲ γνῶσις ἀγάπη γίνεται, διότι καλόν ἐστι φύσει τὸ γινωσκόμενον.]

similitude, in no way discordant, in no measure unequal, and in no part dissimilar, but wholly answering to the identity of the one whose image it is. . . . Wherefore that ineffable conjunction of the Father and his image is never without fruition, without love, without rejoicing. Hence that love, delight, felicity or beatitude, if any human voice can worthily say it, is called by him, in brief, use, and is in the Trinity the Holy Spirit, not begotten, but of the begetter and begotten alike the very sweetness, filling all creatures, according to their capacities, with his bountiful superabundance and excessiveness.[43]

And this, according to Augustine, leads us to say, "In that Trinity is the highest origin of all things, and the most perfect beauty, and the most blessed delight. Therefore those three are seen to be mutually determined, and are in themselves infinite."[44] Admittedly, Augustine is speaking here directly about the Trinity, while Gregory is merely speaking with a Trinitarian grammar (to appreciate the full profundity of which one must seek supplementary arguments from his other works). But what these passages reveal is that, for both theologians, God's one act of being God is also that one, eternal, "speculative" act by which he knows and loves the fullness of his own essence. As Augustine takes such pains to argue, it is not the case that the Father merely begets his image, wisdom, and being in the Son, while remaining something apart; he already is wisdom and being—he already knows and is—and begets his image not by reduction or alienation, but as the perfect expression of his essence: and hence he eternally begets, of his nature.[45] Or, as Gregory argues—from the opposite direction, as it were, but with the same end in view—the Son is the eternal image in which the Father contemplates and loves his essence, and thus the Father can never be conceived of without his Son, for "if ever the brightness of the Fa-

43. Augustine, *De Trinitate* 6.10.11. [Imago enim si perfecte implet illud cuius imago est, ipsa coaequatur ei, non illud imagini suae. In qua imagine speciem nominavit, credo, propter pulchritudinem, ubi iam est tanta congruentia, et prima aequalitas, et prima similitudo, nulla in re dissidens, et nullo modo inaequalis, et nulla ex parte dissimilis, sed ad identidem respondens ei cuius imago est. . . . Ille igitur ineffabilis quidam complexus patris et imaginis non est sine perfruitione, sine charitate, sine gaudio. Illa ergo dilectio, delectatio, felicitas vel beatitudo, si tamen aliqua humana voce digne dicitur, usus ab illo appellatus est breviter, et est in trinitate spiritus sanctus, non genitus, sed genitoris genitique suavitas, ingenti largitate atque ubertate perfundens omnes creaturas pro captu earum.]

44. Augustine, *De Trinitate* 6.10.12. [In illa enim trinitate summa origo est rerum omnium, et perfectissima pulchritudo, et beatissima delectatio. Itaque illa tria, et ad se invicem determinari videntur, et in se infinita sunt.]

45. Augustine, *De Trinitate* 7.1.2.

ther's glory did not shine forth, that glory would be dark and blind."[46] And this "infinite speculation," if one may phrase it that way, is for Gregory that one original act of knowledge in which each of the divine persons shares: the Only Begotten who dwells in the Father, sees the Father in himself, while the Spirit searches out the deeps of God.[47] God himself is, as it were, an eternal play of the invisible and the visible, the inaccessible depths and heights of the Father made radiantly manifest in the infinite impress of his beauty, God "mirroring" himself and so knowing himself by pouring himself out wholly in the Son and Spirit. And it is from the Trinity's own eternal "circle of glory"[48] that the logic of created being unfolds: creation, one could say, is another inflection of an infinite light, receiving that light as the very gift of its being. There are not, then, discrete moments of being's dispensation within a scale of which God is somehow "part": he does not lie beyond the economy of manifestation as the essentially unmanifest mystery whose solitude is inverted and so distorted in all that lies below him. Rather, God himself is the immediate source of every moment of finite reality: its hidden depths, its manifest surface, its rational structure, its beauty. Creation *is* only as the answer of light to light, a gracious "overflow" of the self-donating movement of the Trinity, existing solely as the manifestation—the reflection—of the splendor of a God whose own being is manifestation, recognition, and delight.

For Augustine, this understanding of God bears especially plentiful fruit when he (as famously he does) employs metaphors such as memory, understanding, and will, or mind, love, and knowledge, in order to understand the way in which the three persons of the Trinity are each wholly God and yet distinct within the single act of God's being. When, for instance, the mind knows and loves itself, each moment of that single act is in itself what it is, and yet each entirely indwells and reveals and is the life of each of the other two. "But when the mind knows itself in these three, and loves itself, there remains a trinity: mind, love, knowledge; nor are they confused with one another by any sort of intermingling, even though each is single in itself and entire in the totality, either each one in the other two or the other two in each, but in any case *all in all*."[49] Which is to say, with a somewhat infuriating precision, that

46. Gregory of Nyssa, *Refutatio confessionis Eunomii*, GNO 2:355.

47. Gregory of Nyssa, *Contra Eunomium* 2; GNO 1:340.

48. See Gregory of Nyssa, *Adversus Macedonianos: De Spiritu Sancto*, GNO 3/1:109; *Contra Eunomium* 1; GNO 1:217–18.

49. Augustine, *De Trinitate* 9.5.8. [At in illis tribus cum se novit mens et amat se, manet trinitas, mens, amor, notitia; et nulla commixtione confunditur quamvis et singula

They are, moreover, within one another, for the loving mind is within love, and love is within the knowledge of the lover, and knowledge is within the knowing mind. Thus each is in the other two, because the mind that knows and loves itself is within its own love and knowledge, and the love of the mind that loves and knows itself is within the mind and its knowledge, and the knowledge of the mind that knows and loves itself is in the mind and its love, because it loves itself as knowing and knows itself loving. And thus also each pair of these is within the third of them, for the mind that knows and loves itself is within love always along with its knowledge, and within knowledge always along with its love, and love and knowledge are simultaneously present within the mind that loves and knows itself.[50]

And these images acquire richer hues as Augustine attempts to form remote analogies by which to think of the Trinitarian processions from the life of the mind. When the mind knows and approves itself, he says, this knowledge is its "word," because it is a knowledge exactly adequate to and identical with what it knows ("ut ei sit par omnino et aequale atque identidem") and thus constitutes a perfect and equal likeness, for the begotten is equal to the begetter ("et est gignenti aequale quod genitum est").[51] And when the mind knows and loves itself, the object of that love and knowledge—which, like every object known or loved, "cogenerates" that knowledge or love[52]—is one with the source from which that knowledge or love flows: "And this is a certain image of the Trinity, the mind itself and its knowledge, which is its offspring and its word concerning itself, and love then being the third, and these three are one and are one substance."[53] Similarly, we say that memory, understanding, and will—while distinct

sint in se ipsis et invicem tota in totis, sive singula in binis sive bina in singulis, itaque omnia in omnibus.]

50. Augustine, *De Trinitate* 9.5.8. [In alternis autem ita sunt quia et mens amans in amore est et amor in amantis notitia at notitia in mente noscente. Singula in binis ita sunt quia mens quae se novit et amat in amore et notitia sua est, et amor amantis mentis seseque scientis in mente notitiaque eius est, et notitia mentis se scientis et amantis in mente atque in amore eius est quia scientem se amat et amantem se novit. Ac per hoc et bina in singulis quia mens quae se novit et amat cum sua notitia est in amore et cum suo amore in notitia, amorque ipse et notitia simul sunt in mente quae se amat et novit.]

51. Augustine, *De Trinitate* 9.11.16.

52. Augustine, *De Trinitate* 9.12.18 [. . . omnis res quamcumque cognoscimus congenerat in nobis notitiam sui; ab utroque enim notitia paritur, a cognoscente et cognito].

53. Augustine, *De Trinitate* 9.12.18. [Et est quaedam imago trinitatis, ipsa mens et notitia eius, et amor tertius, et haec tria unam atque una substantia.]

and complete in themselves—must still be called one mind, one life, and one being. Each contains the other two entirely: I remember my memory, understanding, and will; I understand that I remember, understand, and will; I will that I remember, understand, and will; and so on; and I understand all three of these in their totality together; and what I do not understand, I do not will or remember; and what I do not remember, I do not understand or will; and what I do not will I cannot remember or understand. . . .[54] This is, of course, exquisitely correct (if exasperatingly repetitive). And yet—it seems worth noting—Augustine's analogies, however schematically exact they may be, never cease to function as metaphors; these elements of the inner self as such do not yet, for him, constitute the true image of God within us. In that sense, in fact, Augustine's position is actually more cautious than Gregory's (conceptually vaguer) suggestion that, because God is Mind and Word, so we—in imitation of him—possess words and understanding, and that, because God is love and beholds and hearkens to and searches out all things, so we love and see and hear and seek to understand.[55] That said, Gregory no more than Augustine means to suggest that the divine image in us can be reduced to some particular set of attributes, or even to the structure of consciousness as a whole.

I should also note that Augustine's profound sense of the simplicity of the one "diversified" act of God's being is in no way weakened by his insistence that names like "Wisdom" are accorded to the Son only through appropriation—that, for instance, the Son is called Wisdom because he always reveals the Father to us. It would be absurd, after all, to imagine that the Father is wise only through the Son, in the sense of the Son being "that part" of God, apart from which the Father would be devoid of Wisdom; for "if the Father who begot Wisdom is thereby made wise, and if to him it is not the same thing to be and to be wise, then the Son is one of his qualities, not his offspring, and then he will no longer be absolute in his simplicity."[56] And for Augustine it is not merely the simplicity of the divine nature, but the paternal *monarchia*, that is at stake: "[I]f . . . it is the Son who makes the Father wise [and] if in God it is the same thing both to be and to be wise, and in him essence is Wisdom, then it would not be the Son who has his essence from the Father, which is the true state of things, but rather the Father who has his essence from the Son, which is

54. Augustine, *De Trinitate* 10.10.13–12.19.
55. Gregory of Nyssa, *De hominis opificio* 16; PG 44:181.
56. Augustine, *De Trinitate* 7.1.2. [. . . si et pater qui genuit sapientiam ex ea fit sapiens neque hoc est illi esse quod sapere, qualitas eius est filius, non proles eius, et non ibi erit iam summa simplicitas.]

both supremely absurd and supremely false."[57] Gregory, admittedly, does at one point appear to argue the opposite—that the Father can never be conceived of without his Son, for were he alone he would have no light, truth, wisdom, life, holiness, or power[58]—but, read in context, this claim has nothing to do with the sort of crudely mechanical concept of the Trinity that Augustine is attacking; indeed, it is precisely such a concept that Gregory is rejecting. More importantly, Augustine is not in any way denying that there is a distinct paternal or filial or spiritual modality or idiom; Augustine is not a tritheist, who believes God to be a confederation of three individual consciousnesses, any more than Gregory imagines God to be a composite of separable functions. Both, however, find themselves on this point running up against the limits of language with particular force.[59]

In any event, for both theologians the hiddenness of God the Father—unlike the inviolable singularity of the One—is always already also a fully commensurate disclosure of the Father in the Son and Spirit. God the infinitely hidden is also God the infinitely manifest. Creation, moreover, belongs entirely to this mystery: not as the immeasurably remote consequence of a departure from the One, a final negation of an original negation, but as a peaceful emergence into the light of God of that which in itself is nothing, and a finite expression of and moment within God's eternal act of love and knowledge.[60] And for both Gregory and Augustine, the relationship of creatures to God—inasmuch as neither thinks in terms of some secret ground of identity along a continuum of substances, or thinks of God as some ineffably remote substance at the other end of that continuum—lies in the immediate and simple relation of the image to that which it reflects. Nor, then, are creatures images simply in the sense that they constitute mere signs of the power of God to cause finite effects. If they were, no created image would be more a likeness of God than a dissemblance, no more a participation than an alienation; creatures then would be mere univocal instances of a single creative event, and no "image" would constitute a nearer or more appropriate analogy of God's na-

---

57. Augustine, *De Trinitate* 15.7.12. [si . . . filius patren sapientem facit. . . . Et si hoc est deo esse quod sapere et ea illi essentia est quae sapientia, non filius a patre, quod verum est, sed a filio potius habet pater essentiam, quod absurdissimum atque falsissimum est.]

58. Gregory of Nyssa, *Contra Eunomium* 3/1; GNO 2:32.

59. One should perhaps, however, note that, if either of these positions can be said to be more reminiscent of the Palamite position (if only obliquely), it is Augustine's.

60. See Gregory of Nyssa, *De perfectione*, GNO 8/1:188–89. No theologian rang more magnificent changes on this theme, of course, than Maximus the Confessor, but that is a topic for another time.

ture than another. The image of God in creation—and in rational natures in particular—must be an actual communication of the light of God's own inward life, his own eternal Image of himself within the Trinitarian mystery. It is, so to speak, a created reprise of the movement of God's being as God, coming to pass within beings who have no existence apart from their capacity to reflect his presence.

It is possible, then, to affirm both that the Father infinitely exceeds all finite knowledge and that, in mirroring Christ within ourselves, we are somehow being conformed to the Father's coequal manifestation of himself to himself: the very "splendor of his glory," his "form" and "impress," in seeing whom we truly see the Father. We can become images of God because God is always already, in himself, Image.[61] When either Gregory or Augustine speaks of divinization—which neither tends to do as frequently as do other fathers—it is typically understood as a greater and more perfect fulfillment of the divine image within us. For, in the infinite intelligibility of God's life, in that eternal act whereby God knows and loves himself, we *are* as known and loved by God; and so we become truly what we are the more perfectly we show forth God's beauty in ourselves—the more purely the soul reflects God's knowledge of himself, by coming to know even as it is known. As Augustine says, our enlightenment is participation in the Word who, "being made a partaker in our mortality, made us partakers in his divinity";[62] and the image of God in us will achieve true likeness to God only as it achieves the vision of God: we shall be like God only when, as Scripture promises, we shall see him face-to-face, and shall look with face unveiled at the glory of the Lord "in a mirror," precisely by being transformed into that same image from glory to glory, and becoming like him, and thus seeing him as he is.[63] Gregory, of course, develops this theme of our transformation "from glory to glory" as no other theologian ever did: as we venture into God, we find the divine nature to be inexhaustible,[64] but so long as the soul follows after the Logos, it is continuously transformed, throughout eternity, into an ever more radiant vessel of divine glory,[65]

61. Gregory of Nyssa, *De perfectione*, GNO 8/1:188–89.

62. Augustine, *De Trinitate* 4.2.4 [. . . factus particeps mortalitatis nostrae fecit partcipes divinitatis suae].

63. Augustine, *De Trinitate* 14.17.23.

64. Gregory of Nyssa, *In Canticum Canticorum* 11; GNO 6:321.

65. Gregory of Nyssa, *In Canticum Canticorum* 6, GNO 6:173–79; 8, GNO 6:246, 253; *De virginitate*, GNO 8/1:280–81; *De perfectione*, GNO 8/1:212–14; *Contra Eunomium* 1, GNO 1:112, 285–87; *De mortuis oratio*, GNO 9:34–39; *In inscriptiones Psalmorum* 1.5, GNO 5:39–40; *De vita Moysis* 2, GNO 7/1:41–42, 114–18; etc.

while never ceasing joyously to yearn for yet more of God's beauty[66] (and so on). By comparison, Augustine's imagery seems rather homely: Christ is for us both the way to God and also the eternal abode within the divine, and so "by walking in him we draw near to him."[67]

What both theologians have in common, however, is their obvious certainty that this awakening within us of the image—and thus the knowledge—of God is a fully Trinitarian event, in two senses: it is both a real entry into the life of the Trinity, by the grace of the Spirit, and also a refashioning of the soul into an ever more faithful likeness of the Trinitarian *taxis*. Insofar, says Augustine, as we know God, we are made like him, however remotely; and when we know God, and properly love this knowledge, we are made better than we were, and this knowledge becomes a word for us, and a kind of likeness to God within us.[68] And it is only thus that the coinherence within us of memory, understanding, and will is raised to the dignity of the divine likeness; the mind is the image of God not simply when it remembers and understands and loves itself, but only when it is able to remember and understand and love him by whom it was made; and in this way, says Augustine, the mind participates in the supreme light.[69] And it is the Spirit who makes the Son visible in and to us, and through the Son reveals the Father. As Gregory writes, "[T]here is no means whereby to look upon the Father's *hypostasis* save by gazing at it through its stamp (*charaktēr*), and the stamp of the Father's *hypostasis* is the Only Begotten, to whom, again, none can approach whose mind has not been illuminated by the Holy Spirit."[70] As Augustine says, we are images of the Word who became flesh, created through him, and as we become ever more resplendent likenesses of him, he reveals to us who the Father is; he is light, born of a Father who is light, and in becoming a man he established that perfect "exemplum" that refashions us after the divine image; and the Spirit, as the supreme charity conjoining Father and Son, is that love that subjoins us to the Son and Father.[71] Gregory speaks in nearly identical terms: when, he says, Christ prays that his followers might be one even as he and his Father are one and coinhere in one another, and says

66. Gregory of Nyssa, *De virginitate* 10; GNO 8/1:289.

67. Augustine, *De Trinitate* 7.3.4–6.

68. Augustine, *De Trinitate* 9.11.16.

69. Augustine, *De Trinitate* 14.13.15. [Haec igitur trinitas mentis non propterea dei est imago quia sui meminit mens et intelligit ac diligit se, sed quia potest etiam meminisse et intellegere et amare a quo facta est.]

70. Gregory of Nyssa, *Ad Eustathium: De Sancta Trinitate*, GNO 3/1:13.

71. Augustine, *De Trinitate* 7.3.4–6.

that he has given his followers the same glory his Father has given him, he is speaking of the gift of the Holy Spirit; indeed, that glory *is* the Spirit, the glory that the Son had with the Father before the world was made,[72] the "bond of peace" or "bond of unity" (so like the Augustinian *vinculum pacis* or *vinculum caritatis*) by which Father and Son dwell in one another, and by which we dwell in God when the Son breathes the Spirit forth upon us.[73] And, for Gregory, this process of sanctification is one in which a kind of "trinitarian" structure intrinsic to human existence becomes an ever purer mirror of the Trinity. The Spirit meets us, successively, in our practice, word (*logos*), and thought (*enthymion*), the last of these being the principle (*archikōteron*) of all three; for mind (*dianoia*) is the original source (*archē*) that becomes manifest in speech, while practice comes third and puts mind and word into action. Thus the Spirit transforms us, until "there is a harmony of the hidden man with the manifest";[74] and thus, one might say, the Spirit conducts the Trinitarian glory upward into our thought, making our own internal life an ever fuller reflection of God's own "circle of glory."

Here, however, I shall draw to a close. As I announced at the beginning of this essay, my ambition has been only to make a tentative initial move in the direction of investigations that require more searching attention than I can grant them here. I can, though, offer a summary of the themes upon which such investigations, it seems to me, might proceed. First, that Christian Trinitarianism as developed in the fourth century did most definitely involve, however implicitly, a new kind of metaphysics, one that was—perhaps for the first time in Western thought—fully "ontological" in its structure. Second, that with this revision of prevailing models of reality came also a new understanding of the nature of divine transcendence, one that finally liberated the thought of God (and of his hiddenness) from the metaphysics of mere ontic supremacy. Third, that with the idea of God's life as truly Trinitarian—in which Logos and Spirit are not secondary or lesser moments within a divine economy, but the actual being of God as God—came a new, more mysterious, but far richer understanding of the relation between God in himself and the way the image of God is reflected in created being. Fourth, that this relation, so understood, at once prom-

72. Gregory of Nyssa, *In illud: Tunc et ipse filius*, GNO 2/2:21–22; *In Canticum Canticorum* 15; GNO 6:466–68.

73. Gregory of Nyssa, *In illud*, GNO 2/2:22; *In Canticum Canticorum* 15; GNO 6:466–67.

74. Gregory of Nyssa, *De Perfectione*, GNO 8/1:210–12 [συμφωνίαν εἶναι τοῦ κρυπτοῦ ἀνθρώπου πρὸς τὸν φαινόμενον]. Cf. *Adversus Macedonianos*, GNO 3/1:98–99.

ises us a far more intimate knowledge of God than previously conceivable and also apprises us of a depth of mystery within God far greater than previously imaginable. And, fifth, that our union with God comes not through the reduction of the soul to a featureless identity more real than any image, or an asymptotic approach to such an identity, but as an ever greater fullness of the Trinitarian image within us, and in the ever more expressive beauty, and splendor, and holiness by which the infinity of God—that pure, incomprehensible depth of limitless intelligibility—is reflected in the mirrors of creation and in the awakening splendor of the sanctified soul. And the reason that these investigations seem to me particularly germane to the discussions that have prompted this essay is that, taken together, these themes appear to indicate the ground of a deep and astonishingly rich unity between our traditions, a unity too easily forgotten or obscured when we devote ourselves to interpreting the past in the light of our later separation, and to inventing ever more abstract principles by which not only to explain the real differences that do exist between us, but also to justify to ourselves divisions that are really, in essence, little more than historical accidents.

EIGHT

From "Notes on the Concept of the Infinite in the History of Western Metaphysics"

Part II

1. Nicholas of Cusa understood, perhaps better than any other Christian philosopher, the remarkable consequences of imagining the infinite's freedom from the *principium contradictionis* as a positive good in the realm of act. For him, God is the *coincidentia oppositorum*, but not in the sense of a coincidence of opposed possibilities such as one could ascribe to the realm of pure potential. Rather, God—as infinite actuality—is the one in whom the supereminent fullness of being *simply* comprises the totality of what is, such that even the polarities of finite existence are present in his essence as a single act. The fetching images he uses to illustrate his insight—such as the actual identity of an "infinite circle" and a straight line—are wonderfully evocative; more powerful and more illuminating, however, are the various names he applies to God in an attempt to unfold the ontological implications of his vision of the divine: God as the absolute maximum who is also (by virtue of comprising nothing in a composite way or as a series) the absolute minimum; God as the infinite "complication" of all things who is at once implicated and explicated in all things; God as the *non aliud* who, as the transcendent act of the infinite, is not any thing over against other things, but is the ever more inward act of every act of being.

2. In Christian thought, then, the difference between the infinite and the finite is the difference between Being and beings. In Thomistic terms, it is the difference between an infinite actuality, in which essence and existence are one and the same, and that condition of absolute contingency in which there is a constant dynamic synthesis of essence and existence, and in which the act of existence is limited by essence and essence is actualized by existence, and in which both essence and existence are imparted

to the finite being from a transcendent wellspring of being. Whether one uses Thomistic language or not, however, is unimportant. For Christian philosophy, the thought of the utter qualitative difference between infinite and finite is one with the thought of what Heidegger (rather rebarbatively) calls "the ontico-ontological difference."

3. The story of the infinite as a metaphysical concept can be brought to an end here. More could be said, but it is perhaps enough to make two final observations. The first is that, speaking in the broadest and most impressionistic terms, the course of this history could be described almost as a kind of palindrome: both beginning and ending with an unresolved dialectic (or opposition) between indeterminacy and totality, the interval between beginning and end spanned by the rise and fall of a fully onto-logical metaphysics of the infinite. The second is that, once the thought of the infinite has been thought—and with it a fully coherent concept of the difference between being and beings—it cannot be conjured away again. As that devoutly Christian philosopher Leibniz asked, "Why is there any-thing at all, and not—much rather—nothing?" This question having ap-peared upon the philosophical horizon, we can never cease to recognize it as an enigma that cannot be reduced to an "analytic" collapse of being into beings, or to a "finitist" dialectic of the "nothing nothinging" (to use the Heideggerean term). It is a question that renders all philosophy henceforth questionable. It is, so to speak, an infinite question.

NINE

Impassibility as Transcendence

On the Infinite Innocence of God

I

I shall begin (provocatively, perhaps) with a quote from Heidegger at his most, if not oracular, at least plangently ominous:

> So kann, wo alles Anwesende sich im Lichte des Ursache-Wirkung-Zusammenhangs darstellt, sogar Gott für das Vorstellen alles Heilige und Hohe, das Geheimnisvolle seiner Ferne verlieren. Gott kann im Lichte der Kausalität zu einer Ursache, zur causa efficiens, herabsinken. Er wird dann sogar innerhalb der Theologie zum Gott der Philosophen, jener nämlich, die das Unverborgene und Verborgene nach der Kausalität des Machens bestimmen, ohne dabei jemals die Wesensherkunft dieser Kausalität zu bedenken.[1]

> [Thus, when all that comes to presence presents itself in the light of the connection between cause and effect, even God—as far as representation is concerned—can lose all that is high and holy, the very mysteriousness of his distance. God, seen in the light of causality, can sink to the level of a cause, to the level of the *causa efficiens*. Even in theology, then, he is thus transformed into the God of the philosophers, which is to say, of those who define the unhidden and the hidden according to the causality of making, without ever also considering the essential origin of this causality.]

1. Martin Heidegger, "Die Frage nach der Technik," in *Die Technik und die Kehre*, 7th ed. (Stuttgart: Verlag Günther Neske, 1988), p. 26.

There is a profound and disturbing truth in these lines, one in fact of almost inexhaustible relevance for the theologian, but one of which far too few theologians typically take heed. This is hardly surprising, really. Perhaps the most difficult discipline the Christian metaphysical tradition requires of its students is the preservation of a consistent and adequate sense of the difference between primary and secondary causality: between, that is, the transcendent and the contingent, or between—to abuse Heidegger's idiom—the ontological and the ontic. It is a distinction so elementary to any metaphysics of creation that no philosophical theologian consciously ignores it; and yet its full implications often elude even the most scrupulous among us. This is no small matter; for the theological consequences of failing to observe the proper logic of divine transcendence are invariably unhappy, and in some cases even disastrous.

Consider, for instance, one of Reginald Garrigou-Lagrange's more cherished axioms: "God determining or determined: there is no other alternative."[2] This is a logical error whose gravity it would be difficult to exaggerate. It is a venerable error, admittedly, adumbrated or explicit in the arguments of even some of the greatest theologians of the Western Church; but an error it remains. Applied to two terms within any shared frame of causal operation, between which some reciprocal real relation obtains, such a formula is perfectly cogent; but as soon as "God" is introduced as one of its terms, the formula is immediately rendered vacuous. If divine transcendence is an intelligible concept, it must be understood according to a rule enunciated by Maximus the Confessor: whereas the being of finite things has nonbeing as its opposite, God's being is entirely beyond any such opposition.[3] God's being is necessary, that is, not simply because it is inextinguishable or eternally immune to nothingness, but because it transcends the dialectic of existence and nonexistence altogether; it is simple and infinite actuality, utterly pure of ontic determination, the "is" both of the "it is" and of the "it is not." It transcends, that is to say, even the distinction between finite act and finite potency, since both exist by virtue of their participation in God's infinite actuality, in which all that might be always supereminently *is*. God is absolute, that is to say, in the most proper sense: he is eternally "absolved" of finite causality, so much

2. This is far and away the most tiresome refrain in his "classic" work on predestination (a book that often seems to consist almost exclusively in tiresome refrains); in fact, it is the phrase with which the text closes—at least, if one reads through to the end of the appendices. See Reginald Garrigou-Lagrange, *Predestination: The Meaning of Predestination in Scripture and the Church*, trans. Dom Bede Rose (St. Louis: B. Harder Book Co., 1939).

3. Maximus the Confessor, *Chapters on Love* 3.65.

so that he need not—in any simple univocal sense—determine in order to avoid being determined. His transcendence is not something achieved by the negation of its "opposite."

This logic should always govern our talk of divine *apatheia*. Though the theologian certainly must affirm that God is by nature beyond every pathos—in the purely technical sense of a change or modification of his nature or essence, passively received *ab extra*—this is not merely to say that he is impervious to external shock. If it were, it would mean only that he enjoys to a perfect degree the same affective poverty as a granite escarpment. He would not really be *beyond* suffering at all, but simply incapable of it; to call him impassible would be then to say no more than that, in the order of the mutable, he is immutable;[4] or that, in the order of the contingent, he is rescued from contingency simply by virtue of being that force that is supreme among all other forces. This would, in a very real sense, place God in rivalry to finite things, though a rivalry that—through the sheer mathematics of omnipotence—he has always already won. But this is folly. Divine *apatheia* is not merely the opposite of possibility; it is God's transcendence of the very distinction between the responsive and the unresponsive, between receptivity and resistance. It is the Trinity's infinite fullness of perfected love, which gives all and receives all in a single movement, and which does not require the supplement of any external force in order to know and to love creation in its uttermost depths. Whereas we—finite, composite, and changing beings that we are—cannot know, love, or act save through a relation to that which affects us and which we affect, God's impassibility is the infinitely active and eternally prior love in which our experience of love—in both its active and its passive dimensions—lives, moves, and has its being. God's *apatheia* is his perfect liberty to be present in both our passions and our actions, but in either case as a free, creative, and pure act.

This is, after all, the great "discovery" of the Christian metaphysical tradition: the true nature of transcendence. When, in the fourth century, theology took its final leave of all subordinationist schemes of Trinitarian reflection, it thereby broke irrevocably with all those older metaphysical systems that had attempted to connect this world to its highest principle by populating the interval between them with various intermediate degrees of spiritual reality. In affirming that the persons of the Trinity are coequal and of one essence, Christian thought was led also to the recognition that it is the transcendent God alone who gives being to creation; that

---

4. I am grateful to Andrew Peach for this formulation.

he is able to be at once both *superior summo meo* and *interior intimo meo*; and that he is not merely the supreme being set atop the summit of beings, but is instead the one who is transcendently present in all beings, the ever more inward act within each finite act. And it is precisely *because* God is not situated within any kind of ontic continuum with the creature that we can recognize him as the ontological cause of the creature, who freely gives being to beings. True divine transcendence, it turns out, is a transcendence of even the traditional metaphysical demarcations between the transcendent and the immanent. At the same time, the realization that the creature is not, simply by virtue of its finitude and mutability, alienated from God— at a tragic distance from God that the creature can traverse only to the degree that everything distinctively creaturely within it is negated—was also a realization of the true ontological liberty of created nature. If God himself is the immediate actuality of the creature's emergence from nothingness, and of both the essence and the existence of the creature, then it is precisely through becoming what it is—rather than through overcoming those finite *idiōmata* that distinguish it from God—that the creature truly reflects the goodness and transcendent power of God.

Now, in all likelihood, very little of what I have said to this point would surprise or offend anyone sympathetically inclined toward the traditional Christian teaching of divine impassibility. And in the past, when I have written on these matters,[5] it has never occurred to me to defend this understanding of divine transcendence against any theologies but those that explicitly reject that teaching. I have come to believe, however, that in many cases it is those who adhere most fiercely to the traditional language of impassibility who often prove most oblivious to the true logic of transcendence, and that their maladroit devotion to a principle they only partially understand frequently leads them to conclusions that cannot help but bring that principle into disrepute. This may have been an especially prevalent tendency in the theology of the sixteenth and seventeenth centuries, a period when metaphysical subtlety seems to have been at its lowest ebb throughout the Christian world. It was certainly pronounced in the Baroque "commentary Thomism" of Domingo Bañez, Diego Alvarez, John of St. Thomas, and others, as it was in the theology of their disciples, such as—in the twentieth century—Garrigou-Lagrange and Jean-Hervé Nicolas, and as it is in the thought of a small number of

---

5. David Bentley Hart, "No Shadow of Turning: On Divine Impassibility," *Pro Ecclesia* 11, no. 2 (Spring 2002): 184–206; Hart, *The Beauty of the Infinite: The Aesthetics of Christian Truth* (Grand Rapids: Eerdmans, 2003), pp. 155–67, 354–60.

marginal contemporary Thomists. And nowhere was this tendency more resplendently obvious than in the "Bañezian" concept of the *praemotio physica*: an irresistible divine movement of the creature's will that in no way violates the creature's own freedom.

There may be, of course, something inherently absurd in my presuming to weigh in on the "*de auxiliis*" controversy (especially since, from the Eastern Christian perspective, the principal issue of debate—the idea of predilective predestination to salvation—is an ancient exegetical error, abetted by an unfortunate Latin translation of the Epistle to the Romans, and so without any real theological legitimacy to begin with). Nor is there really an urgent need for anyone to address a school of thought that so obviously has no significant future within its own church. And arguments regarding which kind of Thomism is truest to Thomas do not much concern me.[6] My interest in this issue is bloodlessly clinical. To me, the *praemotio* is a perfect specimen of a deformation of theological reason that seems especially characteristic of the modern age, both early and late: not necessarily a conscious denial of any of classical Christianity's claims regarding God's nature, but rather a far more general and destructive forgetfulness of the true meaning of those claims—one that renders either their denial or their affirmation largely irrelevant.

II

The concept of physical premotion is not terribly difficult to grasp.[7] It is a device intended, in principle, to safeguard a proper understanding of divine

6. Being merely a selective reader of Thomas, whose interest in Thomas's thought begins and ends with his metaphysics of *esse* and of *actus*, I lack the authority necessary to pronounce upon the degree to which Bañez or the larger Baroque commentary tradition "got Thomas right" on this matter. I tend to think that it was a vanishingly small degree, however, and find the expositions of a number of scholars of Thomas entirely persuasive on this score. The now classic "refutation" of the older reading of Thomas on divine causality is, of course, Bernard Lonergan's *Grace and Freedom: Operative Grace in the Thought of St. Thomas Aquinas* (Toronto: University of Toronto Press, 2000). See also, Brian J. Shanley, OP, "Divine Causation and Human Freedom in Aquinas," *American Catholic Philosophical Quarterly* 72, no. 1 (1998): 99–122.

7. In fact, most of what one needs to know about the concept—if one is not interested in its precise history—can be extracted from certain recent attempts to rehabilitate the Baroque Thomist position. Two articles that appeared in 2006, side by side in a single issue of the English language version of *Nova et Vetera*, are particularly convenient in this regard: Thomas M. Osborne Jr., "Thomist Premotion and Contemporary Philosophy of

transcendence and omnipotence (though, in fact, it accomplishes precisely the opposite). It is called "physical" in order to make clear that it is not merely a moral premotion, which would act only as a final cause upon the rational will; it is a work of real efficient agency on God's part.[8] As a *premotion*, its priority is one not of time, but only of causal order. As God is the primary cause of all causing—so the argument goes—he must be the first efficient cause of all actions, even those that are sinful;[9] and yet, as he operates in a mode radically transcendent of the mode of the creature's actions, he can do this without violating the creature's freedom. From eternity, God has infallibly decreed which actions will occur in time, and he brings them to pass either by directly willing them or by directly permitting them. Nor is divine permission in any way indeterminate, such that God would have to "wait upon" the creature's decisions, for then God's power would be susceptible of a moral or epistemic pathos;[10] rather, his is an eternal and irresistible "permissive decree," which predetermines even the evil actions of creatures.[11] God, however, is not the cause of evil; such is the natural defectibility—the inherent nothingness—of finite spirits that they cannot help but err if not upheld in the good by an extraordinary grace, and so if God withholds this grace, they will, of their own nature, infallibly gravitate toward sin; and the

---

Religion," *Nova et Vetera* 4, no. 3 (2006): 607–31; Steven A. Long, "Providence, Freedom, and Natural Law," *Nova et Vetera* 4, no. 3 (2006): 557–605. Both essays are quite accurate as regards the fundamental ideas and concerns of the tradition they defend, as far as I can tell from my sporadic readings in classical Thomism, and whatever defects in their arguments I might fancy I see are directly attributable to that tradition. Bañez himself—for all his considerable limitations as a theologian or philosopher—was an exceedingly clear and careful writer and is, in that respect, preferable to many of his later expositors; but I—in my admittedly limited survey of his works—have failed to find a single comprehensive summary of his understanding of the *praemotio physica* that is easily extractable from its context. Perhaps the best treatment of the theme in the Dominican literature written during the early disputes with the Molinists is that of Diego Alvarez in his *De auxiliis gratiae et humani arbitrii viribus* (Rome, 1610); see especially *disputationes* 28 and 83. The most thorough later defense of the position can be found in A. M. Dummermuth, *Defensio doctrinae S. Thomae Aq. de praemotione physica* (Paris, 1895)—a title that somewhat obscures the not insignificant point that Thomas himself never anywhere enunciates a doctrine of *praemotio physica*. See also Dummermuth's *S. Thomas et doctrina praemotionis physicae* (Paris, 1886).

8. See Thomas de Lemos, *Acta omnia congregationum et disputationum . . . de auxiliis divinae gratiae* (Louvain, 1702), p. 1065.

9. Domingo Bañez, *Commentaria in Summa Th. S. Thomae*, first part (Salamanca, 1584), I, q. 14, art. 13.

10. See Alvarez, *De auxiliis*, disp. 24:15.

11. Alvarez, *De auxiliis*, disp. 83:9.

will toward evil must, then, be ascribed entirely to the creature.[12] There is no injustice in this, moreover, inasmuch as God is not obliged to supply the creature with any grace at all; and so God remains innocent of any implication in the creature's sin, even though he has irresistibly predetermined in every instance that the creature will commit *this* sin.[13]

As for human freedom, the argument continues, it is in no wise abrogated by the *praemotio*. The proper definition of a free act is one that is not *contingently* determined, for an effect is deemed necessary or contingent only in regard to its proximate cause; hence, even if an act is determinately present in its primary cause, so long as it is contingent as regards its antecedent secondary causes, it is by definition free. Logically the creature could act otherwise, though in fact this possibility will never—can never—be realized; for though the creature's act is contingent in its own mode, it is necessary as eternally decreed by God. That is, it is not necessary in a "divided sense" (which would be the case only if the creature's potentiality for doing otherwise simply did not exist), but is necessary only in a "composed sense" (which is to say, necessary only in the sense that the creature cannot actually do otherwise than it is doing—which God has irresistibly predetermined).[14] It is not a physical necessity, therefore, but a necessity of "supposition"; for it lies within God's omnipotence irresistibly to predetermine an effect *as a* contingent effect. In the case of the rational creature, God infallibly causes him to act through his own intellect and will.[15] Nor are God and the creature competing causes within the act; so radically different are their proper modes of causality, and so radically distinct the orders to which they belong, that each can be said entirely to cause the act, though as superior and inferior agents.[16] Indeed, God does not even really *determine* the will; this he could do only by way of secondary causes, which would make the creature's act logically necessary; rather he directly and, so to speak, vertically *predetermines* the will, creating its power to choose and then efficiently causing the entire act he intends:[17] thus the will remains free.[18]

12. Charles René Billuart, *Summa summae S. Thomae sive compendium theologiae* (Liège, 1754), *Tractatus de Deo et eius attributis*, dissertatio 8, art. 5.

13. Alvarez, *De auxiliis*, disp. 19:7. See Osborne, "Thomist Premotion," pp. 608–13, and Long, "Providence, Freedom, and Natural Law," pp. 569, 572, 584, 588, 594, 595, etc.

14. Billuart, *Summa summae: de Deo*, dissertatio 8, art. 4.

15. See Alvarez, *De auxiliis*, disp. 22:19.

16. Alvarez, *De auxiliis*, disp. 22:39.

17. See Alvarez, *De auxiliis*, disp. 28; see also Jean Baptiste Gonet, *Clypeus theologiae thomisticae contra novos eius impugnatores* (Bordeaux, 1659–1669), disp. 11:5.

18. See Osborne, "Thomist Premotion," pp. 611–19, 623–29, 630; see especially 625:

Thomists of this persuasion sometimes argue that one cannot deny the reality of the *praemotio* without simultaneously denying the omnipotence and primary causality of God. To suggest that human beings are free to resist God's grace, or even to act at all without God directly "applying" them to their actions, is both morally and metaphysically incoherent. To suggest that God's "permissive will" might actually liberate the creature to an indeterminate diversity of possible free acts would be to imply that human liberty escapes divine providence and that the human will enjoys an absolute libertarian autonomy that places it beyond divine causality.[19] God then could know the creature only by way of a pathos, to which he would then reactively respond.[20] But, as Bañez says, "God knows sin by an intuitive cognition, insofar as the will of God is the cause of the entity of the sinful act *(causa entitatis actus peccati)*"—though, he adds, God *permits* free will to fail to observe the proper law of action, and thus to "concur with this act *(ad eundem actum concurrat)*."[21] Moreover, these Thomists contend, every act of the will is a movement from potency to act, a new actuality, which can be supplied only by the first cause of all being;[22] creatures are not able to bring about a new effect *ex nihilo*, but must be "applied" to action by a divine act; thus, in addition to his act of creation, God must always supply an additional movement of the will, directing it toward one end or another.[23]

That God elects to predetermine good acts in some and evil acts in others belongs, of course, to his predilective predestination of a few to salvation and his reprobation of the rest to damnation. As for the scriptural assurance that God wills that all men be saved, it would impugn God's causal omnipotence to suggest that what he "efficaciously" wills could possibly fail to occur;[24] thus his "universal will to salvation" applies only to the order of grace, where he supplies what is "sufficient" for the redemption

---

"If God physically predetermined the will through intermediate causes, then in Thomist language such motion would not be predetermination but determination, and consequently incompatible with free choice."

19. Alvarez, *De auxiliis*, disp. 122:16. Long, "Providence, Freedom, and Natural Law," is especially insistent upon this point: pp. 558, 559, 562, 564, 591, 601, 603, etc. See also Osborne, "Thomist Premotion," pp. 611, 627.

20. John Paul Nazarius, *Commentaria et controversiae in Summa Th. S. Thomae*, first part (Bologna, 1620), I, q. 22, art. 4.

21. Bañez, *Commentaria in Summa Th.*, I, q. 23, art. 3, d. 2, c. 2.

22. See de Lemos, *Acta*, p. 1065.

23. Gonet, *Clypeus*, disp. 9:5; Osborne, "Thomist Premotion," pp. 612, 626; Long, "Providence, Freedom, and Natural Law," pp. 559, 562–63, 567, 569, 573, etc.

24. Alvarez, *De auxiliis*, disp. 92:6.

of all; in the order of nature, however, he generally declines to provide the *praemotio* of the creature's will necessary to make that grace "efficacious." And God's purpose in infallibly permissively decreeing the evil that men do is to make both his mercy and his justice known: through the gratuitous rescue of the elect and the condign damnation of the derelict. After all, any world that God might create would still be composed of finite beings, inherently prone to defect, moved by competing and contrary goods, and every possible world falls infinitely short of the goodness of God; thus the permission of evil is intrinsic to the act of creation. But—by God's providence—evil will always serve a greater good: the final knowledge of God's goodness in the variety of its effects.[25]

III

The immediate and vulgar response of most Christians to this style of theology is to dismiss it as absurd and repellent. The more considered and sophisticated response, however—by one of those delightful coincidences that are all too rare—is usually the same. The difference is one of detail. One must concede, though, that the God of this obviously rather degenerate theology is indeed impassible—if only in a trivial sense. But he is certainly not truly transcendent. It is one thing for a theologian simply to assert that God's "mode of causality" is utterly different from that of the creature, and that therefore God may act within the act of the creature without despoiling the latter of his liberty; but such an assertion is meaningful only if all the conclusions that follow from it genuinely obey the logic of transcendence. As primary cause of all things, after all, God is first and foremost their *ontological* cause. He imparts being to what, in itself, is nothing at all; out of the infinite plenitude of his actuality, he gives being to both potency and act; and yet what he creates, as the effect of a truly transcendent causality, possesses its own being, and truly exists as other than God (though God is not some "other thing" set alongside it). This donation of being is so utterly beyond any species of causality we can conceive that the very word "cause" has only the most remotely analogous value in regard to it. And, whatever warrant Thomists might find in Thomas for speaking of God as the first efficient cause of creation (which I believe to be in principle wrong), such language is misleading unless the analogical scope of the concept of efficiency has been extended almost to the point of apophasis.

25. See Long, "Providence, Freedom, and Natural Law," pp. 572–77.

Easily the weakest traditional argument in favor of the idea of the *prae-motio* is that God must supply the "effect of being" for each movement of the will from potency to act. For one thing, this line of reasoning simply assumes the identity of ontological causation and efficient predetermination, which is the very issue in dispute. More to the point, it divides primary causality into two distinct moments: creation and an "additional" predetermining impulse of the will. This is simply banal. Obviously the act of creation is not simply the act of giving bare existence to static essences, which then must be further animated by some other kind of act. As the transcendent cause of being, God imparts to the creature its own dependent actuality, while also creating the potentialities to which that actuality is adequate; and, inasmuch as both act and potency are ontologically reducible to, and sustained by, their primary cause, and inasmuch as the will is always moved by its primordial inclination toward the good, it is silly to speak of the need for something in addition to creation to "cause" the movement of the spiritual will. What God gives in creation is the entire actuality of the world, in all its secondary causes; and, as those causes possess actual being, they are able to impart actuality to potentialities proportionate to their powers. It certainly, at any rate, makes no sense to say that every particular act is a unique creation *ex nihilo*, of which the distinction between act and potency in creation is a purely formal condition. This would be no better than a straightforward occasionalism—which is surely not what it means to say that all causes are reducible to the first cause.[26]

All of this, however, merely points to the more pervasive problem bedeviling physical premotion. Champions of the concept clearly believe that it serves to protect a proper understanding of the qualitative difference between divine and human action; and yet this is precisely what it can never do. For, if the *praemotio* works as its defenders say it does, as the direct and infallible efficient predetermination of *this* rather than *that* act, then God and the creature most definitely operate within the same order; and, though the neo-Bañezian may claim otherwise, God acts as a rival— indeed, even in a kind of "negative real relation"—to the creature (though this is, again, a rivalry God has always already won). The God of physical premotion is not fully transcendent, but merely supreme; he is not a fully primary cause, but merely a kind of "infinite" secondary cause; he is not

---

26. For an especially enlightening treatment of the issue of God's causation of freedom as occurring within the act of creation, see David B. Burrell, *Freedom and Creation in Three Traditions* (Notre Dame: University of Notre Dame Press, 1993); see especially pp. 95–139.

fully the *causa in esse* of all things, but merely the *causa in fieri* that reigns over all other motive forces. Rather than causing all causes as causes, he is that absolute immanent power that all other immanent causes at once dissemble and express. Thus, when the "classical Thomist" attempts to explain how God can create dependent freedom, the best he seems able to manage is to talk of a direct and irresistible predetermination of the will, and then—to avoid the contradiction this entails—to attempt to reduce the question of freedom to one of mere logical contingency. But freedom lies not simply in an action's logical conditions, but in the action itself; and if an action is causally necessitated or infallibly predetermined, its indeterminacy with regard to its proximate cause in no way makes it free.

Of course, it may well have been that, in the late sixteenth century— due to certain drastic changes within the idea of causality—the very concept of a created freedom had become all but unintelligible. It is, at least, tempting to see the notion of physical premotion as a kind of invasion of theology by the mechanical philosophy. Certainly at this point in intellectual history, any concept of ontological causality could not help but seem rather vague and fabulous; and to speak of the infinite plenitude and transcendence of God's creative act somehow no longer seemed an adequate way of affirming his omnipotence. In the age of mechanism, the only fully credible kind of causality—the cause par excellence—was efficient causality. Whereas once it might have sufficed to assert that, within the fourfold causality of finite reality, there dwelled another, mysterious, and transcendent cause, acting in an entirely different manner, it now became necessary to ground God's transcendence in a more respectable kind of causality: efficient supremacy. And even spiritual freedom was reduced to the physical effect of a prior external force.

One unavoidable result of this general impoverishment of metaphysics was that God had to be conceived as the author of evil—whether directly and explicitly, as with the Calvinists, or elliptically and self-deludingly, as with the Bañezians. And the "classical Thomist" evasion of this conclusion scarcely rises to the level of the risible. Neither the theologically dubious notion that the "natural" tendency of any defectible rational creature not upheld by extraordinary grace is toward sin, nor the related claim that when God permits evil he does no more than abandon the creature to its own inevitable operations, exculpates the creator of complicity in the creature's sins. To begin with, if God's relation to creation really is efficiently causal in the way Bañezian thought suggests, then the very distinction between nature and grace within God's creative act is largely specious; the question becomes simply at what stage of gratuitously imparted blessings—being, will, reason, adherence in the good—he elects to halt in his creative activity toward the creature. And if he has elected to relinquish his gracious "restraint" of the creature's "naturally defectible" will while yet sustaining the creature in being; and if he has eternally, infallibly, irresistibly, "permissively" decreed that the creature will commit *this* sin and suffer *this* damnation, not on account of any prevision of the creature's sins, but solely on account of his own predetermining act of reprobation; and if this irresistible "antecedent permissive decree" applies even to the creature's intention of evil (as logically it must); and if the creature is incapable of availing himself of "sufficient" grace—or indeed incapable of any motion of the will at all—without being applied to its act by God's physical premotion; then moral evil is as much God's work as is any other act of the will.[27] Only if providence is as transcendent as the ontological cause it manifests—if, that is, it is the way in which God, to whom all time is present, permits and fully "accounts for" and "answers" acts that he does not directly determine, but that also cannot determine him—is God's permission of evil indeed *permission*. But if instead it is an irresistible predetermination of every action, then it neither preserves creaturely freedom nor wrests good from evil, but merely accomplishes the only action within creation that is truly undetermined: God's positive intention—for the purpose of a "greater good"—toward evil.

In fact, it can plausibly be argued that, in a very real sense, the Bañezian God does not create a world at all, and that this species of "classical" Thomism amounts only to what the greatest Catholic philosopher of the twentieth century, Erich Przywara, called "theopanism."[28] After all, the *praemotio* is not a qualitatively different act on God's part within the creature's act, but merely a quantitatively more coercive variety of the same kind of act. To speak of a superior and inferior agent within a single free

27. See Jacques Maritain, *God and the Permission of Evil*, trans. Joseph W. Evans (Milwaukee: Bruce Publishing Co., 1966), pp. 30–31: "In the theory of the antecedent permissive decrees, God, under the relation of efficiency, is not the cause, not even (that which I do not concede) the indirect cause, of moral evil. But He is the one primarily responsible for its presence here on earth. It is He who has invented it in the drama or novel of which He is the author. He refuses His efficacious grace to a creature because it has already failed culpably, but this culpable failure occurred only in virtue of the permissive decree which preceded it. God manages to be nowise the cause of evil, while seeing to it that evil occurs infallibly. The antecedent permissive decrees, be they presented by the most saintly of theologians—I cannot see in them, taken in themselves, anything but an insult to the *absolute innocence of God*."

28. See Erich Przywara, *Analogia Entis: Metaphysik; Ur-Struktur und All-Rhythmus* (Einsiedeln: Johannes-Verlag, 1962), pp. 70–78, 128–35, 247–301.

operation is perfectly coherent, so long as the infinite analogical interval between ontological and ontic causality is observed; but to speak of a superior and inferior determining efficient cause within a single free operation is gibberish. If there were such a physical premotion, all created actions would be merely diverse modalities of God's will. And inasmuch as God is not some distinct object or physical force set over against the world, but is the supereminent source of all being, then—apart from some kind of *effective* divine indetermination of the creature's freedom in regard to specific goods—there is no ontological distinction between God and the world worth noting. It is true that *agere sequitur esse*, but also true that each essence *is* only insofar as it discloses itself in its act; and if all acts are expressions of the divine predetermination of *these* particular acts, then all essences are merely modes—or phenomenal masks—of the divine will.

What is, of course, absent from this picture of divine causality is that ancient metaphysical vision that Przywara chose to call the *analogia entis*. In this "analogical ontology," the infinite dependency of created being upon divine being is understood strictly in terms of the ever greater difference between them; and, under the rule of this ontology, it is possible to affirm the real participation of the creature's freedom in God's free creative act without asserting any ontic continuity of kind between created and divine acts. When, however, the rule of analogy declines—as it did at the threshold of modernity—then invariably the words we attempt to apply both to creatures and to God ("goodness," "justice," "mercy," "love," "freedom") dissolve into equivocity, and theology can recover its coherence only by choosing a single "attribute" to treat as univocal, in order that God and world might be united again. In the early modern period, the attribute most generally preferred was "power" or "sovereignty"—or, more abstractly, "cause."

IV

Can God really create freedom? Is his so transcendent an act that he can—without suffering any pathos—create wills capable of resisting him? Certainly no answer can be provided in the terms of the early modern debates between Bañezians and Molinists. Anyway, the two positions are effectively the same. The logic of Molina's position, after all, was that God—in knowing all possible worlds and states of affairs—chooses one reality to make actual and thereby infallibly destines all real actions. This implied— oddly enough—that it is secondary causes that determine free choices, and consequently that God's election of one world out of an infinity of incompossible alternatives is an act of divine predetermination, however it may be portrayed as a divine "response" to the creature. Bañez, being more rigorous, denied that there was any such response; but for him, still, God's "vertical" predetermination of the creature's "free" act nevertheless aborts all other possible courses of action. In either case, God elects this world out of an infinity of possibilities and thereby infallibly decrees what shall be. Molina was perhaps the more amiable figure of the two, insofar as he hoped to preserve some sense of the innocence of God; but that was an impossible ambition given the narrowly mechanistic concepts available in his time. And, on either side of the debate, theologians were attempting to remedy the ontological deficiency of their theory by way of an ontic supplement: either *praemotio physica* (a solution conceived from the perspective of act) or *scientia media* (a solution conceived from the perspective of potency).

Of course, the very notion of God choosing among possible worlds— especially if, as the classical Thomist position unfortunately holds, there is by definition no "best" world among them—is already haunted by the specter of a kind of divine voluntarism, an arbitrariness that would make God that much more complicit in each particular evil within creation. But, more importantly, it is a view of creation utterly uninformed by revelation. At the very least, one must start from the knowledge that this world—as the world that belongs to the event of Christ—is the world (fallen or unfallen) in which God most fully reveals himself; and, unless one thinks Christ was merely an avatar of God, and that his human identity was somehow accidental to his divine identity, one must then also grant that the world to which the human identity of Christ naturally belongs is one uniquely and eternally fitted to that revelation. Creation is not simply a multifarious demonstration of God's power and goodness, which might equally well be expressed by some other contingent cosmic order, but is the event within God's Logos of beings uniquely—and appropriately— called to union with him. And within this world—within God's manifestation of himself in the Son—freedom necessarily exists, as the way by which created being can be assumed into the eternal love of the Trinity.

To say, moreover, that this freedom is not causally predetermined by God does not imply that it is somehow "absolute" or that it occupies a region independent of God's power (as one strain of neo-Bañezian apologetics contends). It is in his power to create such autonomy that God's omnipotence is most abundantly revealed, for everything therein comes from him: the real being of agent, act, and potency; the primordial movement of the soul toward the good;[29] the natural law inscribed in the creature's intellect and will; the sustained permission of finite autonomy; even the indetermination of the creature's freedom is an utterly dependent and unmerited participation in the mystery of God's infinite freedom. And, in his eternal presence to all of time, God never ceases to exercise his providential care or to make all free acts the occasions of the greater good he intends in creating. The purpose of created autonomy is, as Maximus the Confessor says, its ultimate surrender in love to God, whereby alone rational nature finds its true fulfillment.[30] But, whereas in God perfect freedom and "theonomy" coincide in the infinite simplicity of his essence, in us the free movement of the will toward God is one that passes from potency to act, and as such is dynamic and synthetic in form. Thus God works within the participated autonomy of the creature as an act of boundless freedom, a sort of immanent transcendence, an echo within the soul of that divine abyss of love that calls all things to itself, ever setting the soul free to work out her salvation in fear and trembling.

In the end, it is no more contradictory to say that God can create—out of the infinite wellspring of his own freedom—dependent freedoms that he does not determine, than it is to say that he can create—out of the infinite wellspring of his being—dependent beings that are genuinely somehow other than God. In neither case, however, is it possible to describe the "mechanism" by which he does this. This aporia is simply inseparable from the doctrine of *creatio ex nihilo*—which, no matter how we may attempt to translate it into causal terms we can understand, remains forever incomprehensible to us. There is no process by which creation happens, no intermediate operation or *tertium quid* between God and what he calls into being. As for those who fear that, in knowing actions he does not predetermine, God proves susceptible of pathos, one can only exhort them always to consider the logic of transcendence. God knows in creating, which is an action simply *beyond* the realm of the determined and the determining. Nothing the creature does exceeds those potentialities God has created, or draws upon any actuality but that which God imparts, or escapes God's eternal knowledge of the world of Christ. Just as—according to Thomas— God can know evil by way of his positive act of the good, as a privation thereof,[31] even so can he know the free transgressions of his creatures by

29. See Shanley, "Divine Causation," pp. 112–14.

30. See Maximus the Confessor, *Ambigua* 7; Patrologia Graeca (hereinafter PG) 91:107B.

31. Thomas Aquinas, *Summa theologiae* I.14.10.

way of the good acts he positively wills through the freedom of the rational souls he creates. Just as the incarnate Logos really suffers torment and death not through a passive modification of his nature, imposed by some exterior force, but by a free act, so God can "suffer" the perfect knowledge of the free acts of his creatures not as a passive reaction to some objective force set over against himself, but as the free, transcendent act of giving being to the world of Christ—an act to whose sufficiency there need attach no mediating "premotion" to assure its omnipotence. And that eternal act of knowledge is entirely convertible with God's free intention to reveal himself in Christ.

V

The issue of God's epistemic passibility, of course, is far less pressing if one does not presume real differentiations within God's intention toward his creatures. For, surely, Scripture is quite explicit on this point: God positively "wills" the salvation of "all human beings" (1 Tim. 2:4). "Paul" does not say that God merely generically desires that salvation, or that he simply formally allows it as a logical possibility, or that he wills it antecedently but not consequently, or that (most ridiculous of all) he enables it "sufficiently" but not "efficaciously." If God were really to supply saving grace sufficient for all, but to refuse to supply most persons with the *necessary* natural means of attaining that grace, it would mean that God does *not* will the salvation of all.

Certainly, a far better account of the relation of God to the free acts of his creatures would be that of, for instance, Maximus the Confessor. For Maximus, I think it fair to assert, one could never truly say that God causes some to rise while permitting others to fall; rather, one would have to say that he causes all to rise, and permits all to fall, and imparts to all—out of his own abyssal freedom—the ability to consent to or to resist the grace he extends, while providentially ordering all things according to his universal will to salvation. Or, rather, perhaps one should say that God causes all to rise, but the nature of that cause necessarily involves a permission of the will. God's good will and his permission of evil, then, are simply two aspects of a single creative act, one that does not differ in intention from soul to soul: God's one vocation of all rational creation to a free union in love with himself; his one gracious permission that spiritual freedom in some way determine itself in relation to the eternal good toward which it is irresistibly drawn; his one gift of sufficient aid, both in conferring saving grace on all and in sustaining human nature in its power to respond; his one refusal to coerce the will as some kind of determining cause; his one providence; his one upholding of all in being. Indeed, in this sense it almost makes sense to speak of God's infallible permissive decree for his creatures *ante praevisa merita*: in God's one act of self-outpouring love, he decrees that the creature will always be moved by its primordial impulse toward the good, and will always act under permission toward various ends; and that permission infallibly sets the creature free—within its irresistible natural impulse toward the good—to whatever end the creature elects. God and the creature do indeed act within utterly different orders.

This double movement of the will Maximus defines as the distinction between the "natural" and "gnomic" wills within us[32] (a distinction, incidentally, absolutely central to orthodox Christology, East and West). The former is that dynamic orientation toward the infinite goodness of God that is the source of all rational life and of all desire within us; the latter is that deliberative power by which we obey or defy the deep promptings of our nature and the rule of the final good beyond us. It is the movement of the natural will toward God, moreover, whose primordial motion allows the gnomic will its liberty and its power of assent to or rejection of God. In the interval between these two movements—both of which are rational—the rational soul becomes who God intends her to be or, through apostasy from her own nature, fabricates a distance between herself and God that is nothing less than the distance of dereliction. For, whatever we do, the desire of our natural will for God will be consummated; it will return to God, whether the gnomic will consents or not, and will be glorified with that glory the Son shares with the Father from eternity. And, if the gnomic will within us has not surrendered to its natural supernatural end, our own glorified nature becomes hell to us, that holy thing we cannot touch. Rejection of God becomes estrangement from ourselves, the kingdom of God within us becomes our exile, and the transfiguring glory of God within us—through our refusal to submit to love—becomes the unnatural experience of dereliction[33] (for as long as it persists). God fashions all rational natures for free union with himself, and all of creation as the deathless vessel of his eternal glory. To this end, he wills that the dependent freedom of the creature be joined to his absolute freedom; but an indispensable condition of what he wills is the real power of the creature's deliberative will to resist the irresistible work of grace. And God

---

32. See, for instance, Maximus the Confessor, *Opusculum* 14; PG 91:153A–B.
33. See Maximus the Confessor, *Quaestiones ad Thalassium* 59; PG 90:609A–B.

both wills the ultimate good of all things and accomplishes that good, and knows the good and evil acts of his creatures, and *reacts* to neither. This is the true sublimity of divine *apatheia*: an infinite innocence that wills to the last the glorification of the creature, in the depths of its nature, and that never ceases to sustain the rational will in its power to seek its end either in God or in itself.

VI

One reason, I would think, for preferring this vision of God's will for the creature to the Bañezian—quite apart from its closer conformity to revelation—is the not insignificant concern that the God described by the latter happens to be evil. This seems as if it should be a problem. I hasten to add, moreover, that I do not think I am guilty, in using this word, of the querulous vessel's impertinent reproaches of its maker. The use of the word "evil" here is nothing more than an exercise in sober precision. In the "manual Thomist" or "second scholastic Thomist" understanding of God, the word "good" has been rendered utterly equivocal between creatures and God; it has become simply a metaphysical name for the divine essence, to which no moral analogy attaches, and so—as far as common usage is concerned—has been rendered vacuous. If, though, God acts as the Bañezian position claims, and if indeed his "justice" is expressed in his arbitrary decision to inflict eternal torment on creatures whom he has purposely crafted to be vessels of his eternal wrath, then it is possible to construct an *analogia mali* between human cruelty and God's magnificent "transcendence" of the difference between good and evil, without doing the least violence to language or reason. And, as for the ancient argument that such actions constitute no injustice on God's part, because the creature cannot *merit* grace, this should be dismissed as the non sequitur it has always been. The issue has never been one of merit, for indeed the creature "merits" nothing at all, not even its existence; the issue is, rather, the moral nature of God, as revealed in his acts toward those he creates. And the God of this theology is merely an infinite engine of pure, self-expressive, amoral power, who creates untold multitudes for everlasting misery, and whom—were he really to exist—it would be an act of supreme condescension on our parts to view with contempt. This sort of "Christianity" enjoys no conspicuous moral superiority over satanism—indeed, it makes the latter seem somehow morally pardonable. (I hope no one would accuse me of rhetorical excess on this point.)

No less distasteful—but even less intellectually respectable—is the equally ancient argument that God requires the dereliction of the reprobate in order to make his "goodness" more fully known, through a display of both his justice and his mercy.[34] If ever there were a purely ad hoc attempt to justify a morally incoherent position, this is it. For one thing, it is sheer nonsense to suggest that anything meaningfully called "goodness" could be revealed in God's willful, eternal, and predetermining reprobation of souls to endless suffering, simply as "demonstration cases," so to speak. For another, the full nature of God's justice was revealed on the cross, where God took the penalty of sin upon himself so that he might offer forgiveness freely to all. Moreover, the image this entire line of reasoning summons up is at best coarsely mythological. Nothing could be cruder than the notion that final knowledge of God is like knowledge of some external object set before the intellect, which needs to be grasped by an extrinsic, calculative cognition of its "attributes," and by an accumulation of "information" about the divine essence, and by edifying displays of God's power to torture and destroy. The beauty and variety of creation declare God's glory, but God, being infinite, could never be an extrinsic "object" for the finite mind. True knowledge of God comes, rather, through an immediate and deifying communication of divine goodness to the created intellect, by which the created soul is in some way admitted into a finite, created participation in God's knowledge of himself. And that goodness—since all real possibility is supereminently present in it—is sufficient to communicate itself without the

34. The passage from Paul typically adduced to support this argument (Rom. 9:22–23) proves no support at all if it is read in the context of the argument that unfolds from chapter 9 through chapter 11. For one thing, the issue of election in these verses has no obvious or even logical connection to the idea of the predestination of individual souls to salvation or damnation; rather, it concerns solely the election of either Israel or the church as the people of God within history, as bearers of the covenant. More importantly, when Paul reaches the conclusion of his argument, he proclaims that in fact the purpose behind the mystery of election is not an eschatological demonstration of divine power in the destruction of vessels of wrath and preservation of vessels of mercy; rather, it turns out, it is for the sake of a reconciliation between the two peoples, church and Israel, whereby a blessing will be bestowed on all; for, as Paul says, God binds all in disobedience in order to show mercy toward all—and all of Israel shall be saved; hence there is no division between vessels of wrath and vessels of mercy after all. This is, after all, the pattern of election as one finds it displayed in Hebrew Scripture, especially in Genesis: division of the elect from the reprobate, but for the sake of a final reconciliation that enfolds both in God's providential mercy (hence Paul's typology of Jacob and Esau, for instance). The tragic tradition of selective reading within, and misprision of, these chapters is of course irreversible; but that does not make it somehow theologically legitimate. An error, however ancient, is still only an error.

"clarifying" supplement of evil; even if the finite mind cannot grasp God's goodness in its infinite simplicity, the infinite diversity of goods of which the divine essence is capable nowhere requires the shadow of evil to make the lineaments of those goods more evident.[35] And created reason, if it is indeed naturally fitted to the good, would suffer no deficiency of knowledge in being "deprived" of the vision of damnation—which, as I have argued above, is nothing but an internal and utterly invisible absurdity, the "impossible" experience of exile in the very midst of an infinite glory.

Simply said, if God required evil to accomplish his good ends—the revelation of his nature to finite minds—then not only would evil possess a real existence over against the good, but God himself would be dependent upon evil: to the point of it constituting a dimension of his identity (even if only as a "contrast"). And one cannot circumvent this difficulty by saying that the necessity involved applies only to finite creatures and not to God in himself; for if God needs the supplement of evil to accomplish any good he intends—even a contingent good—then he is dependent upon evil in an absolute sense. There would be goods of which the good as such is impotent apart from evil's "contribution." And, if in any way evil is necessary to define or increase knowledge of the good, then the good is not ontological—is not, that is, convertible with real being itself—but is at most an evaluation. What must be emphasized here, however, is that the defects within the Bañezian position are the result not of too strict a fidelity to the principle of divine impassibility, but of an absolute betrayal of that principle: one that robs it of its true meaning, and thereby reduces God to a being among lesser beings, a force among lesser forces, whose infinite greatness is rendered possible only by the absolute passivity of finite reality before his absolute supremacy. It is the failure to understand omnipotence as transcendence that renders every attempt to speak coherently of God's innocence futile. It is the failure to place divine causality altogether beyond the finite economy of created causes that produces a God who is merely beyond good and evil.

---

35. Thomas's notorious argument to the contrary, in *Summa theologiae* I.23.5, ad 3, is unobjectionable in suggesting that it is through the variety of created goods that finite minds conceive some knowledge of the plenitude of God's goodness; but, in trying to integrate the theology of predilective predestination *ante praevisa merita* into this vision of things, he attempts to import an impossible alloy into his reasoning. Indeed, the entirety of I.23, inasmuch as it merely attempts to justify an Augustinian reading of Paul that is objectively wrong (that is, a hermeneutical error, based upon bad translations and broad misconstruals of Paul's concerns), can largely be ignored as a set of forced answers to false questions.

VII

The great irony of the enthusiasm that a few reactionary Catholic scholars harbor for Bañezian or "classical" Thomism is their curious belief
that such a theology offers a solution to the pathologies of modernity—
voluntarism, antinomianism, atheism, disregard of natural law, nihilism. Nothing could be further from the truth. Far from constituting an
alternative to modernity, Baroque Thomism is the most quintessentially
modern theology imaginable. To think that one could defeat the patho-
gens of human voluntarism by retreating to what is in effect a limitless
divine voluntarism is rather like thinking one could cure bronchitis with
tuberculosis. And the mere formal assertion by the Bañezian party that,
in their system, God's will follows his intellect—which is the very opposite
of the voluntarist view—simply bears no scrutiny. No less than in any of
his other variants—Lutheran or Calvinist, for example—the modern God
of the Bañezians is one whose will is defined by an ultimate spontaneity,
and a quite insidious arbitrariness. A God whose predestining and repro-
bative determinations are both utterly pure of prevision and irresistible,
who creates a world that bears no more proper relation to his nature than
any among an infinite number of other possible worlds (one, say, in which
little Suzy is damned rather than saved, or where she dies of cancer rather
than lives to a happy old age), who requires a justice of his creatures that he
himself does not exhibit, who condemns whom he chooses to condemn,
and who is himself an efficient cause of the sinful actions he punishes, is
a God whose will is sheer power, not love, and certainly not governed by
reason. This is the God of early modernity in his full majesty: the God who
either determines or is determined, and who therefore must absolutely
determine all things—a pure abyss of sovereignty justifying itself through
its own exercise. He may be a God of eternal law, but behind his legislations
lies a more original lawlessness. He is, in every way, the God of nihilism.

Voluntarism, after all, began as a doctrine regarding God, and only
gradually (if inevitably) migrated to the human subject. The God of absolute will who was born in the late Middle Ages had by the late sixteenth
century so successfully usurped the place of the true God that few theologians could recognize him for the imposter that he was. And the piety
he inspired was, in some measure, a kind of blasphemous piety: a servile
and fatalistic adoration of boundless power masquerading as a love of
righteousness. More importantly, this theology—through the miraculous technology of the printing press—entered into common Christian
consciousness as the theology of previous ages never could, and in so

doing provided Western humanity at once both with a new model of freedom and with a God whom it would be morally and psychologically necessary, in the fullness of time, to kill. It was from this God that we first learned to think of freedom as a perfect spontaneity of the will, and from him we learned the irreducible prerogatives that accrue to all sovereign power, whether that of the absolute monarch, or that of the nation-state, or that of the individual. But, if this is indeed what freedom is, and God's is the supreme instance of such freedom, then he is not—as he was in ages past—the transcendent good who sets the created will free to realize its nature in its ultimate end, but is merely the one intolerable rival to every other freedom, who therefore invites creatures to rebel against him and to attempt to steal fire from heaven. If this is God, then Feuerbach and Nietzsche were both perfectly correct to see his exaltation as an impoverishment and abasement of the human at the hands of a celestial despot. For such freedom—such pure *arbitrium*—must always enter into a contest of wills; it could never exist within a peaceful order of analogical participation, in which one freedom could draw its being from a higher freedom. Freedom of this sort is one and indivisible, and has no source but itself.

More importantly, perhaps, so terrible was the burden that this cruel predestining God laid upon the conscience of believers that it could not be borne indefinitely. It was this God who, having first deprived us of any true knowledge of the transcendent good, died for modern culture, and left us to believe that the true God had perished. The explicit nihilism of late modernity is not even really a rejection of the modern God; it is merely the inevitable result of his presence in history, and of the implicit nihilism of the theology that invented him. Indeed, worship of this god is the first and most inexcusable nihilism, for it can have no real motives other than craven obsequiousness or sadistic delight. Modern atheism is merely the consummation of the forgetfulness of the transcendent God that this theology made perfect. Moreover, it may be that, in an age in which the only choice available to human thought was between faith in the modern god of pure sovereignty and simple unbelief, the latter was the holier—indeed, the more Christian—path. For, at some level, faith in the god of absolute will always required a certain extirpation of conscience from the soul, or at least its pacification; and so perhaps it is better that the natural longing of each soul for God—even if only in the reduced form of moral alarm, or an inchoate impulse toward natural goodness, or of a longing for a *deus ignotus*—refuses to make obeisance before this idol. Perhaps it was the last living trace of Christian conscience that moved Western humanity—like the Christian "atheists" of the first few centuries of the church—to reject any God but a God of infinite love. Late modernity might even be thought of as a time of purgatorial probation, a harsh but necessary hygiene of the spirit, by enduring which we might once again be made able to lift up our minds to the truly transcendent and impassible God, eternally absolved of all evil, in whom there is no darkness at all.

I began this essay with a quotation from Heidegger, and shall draw to a close with another. Speaking at one point of how God enters into philosophy—specifically, modern metaphysics, which understands "being" solely as the causal ground of beings—Heidegger writes:

[Der] Grund selbst aus dem von ihm Begründeten her der ihm gemäßen Begründung, d.h. der Verursachung durch die ursprünglichste Sache bedarf. Dies ist die Ursache als die Causa sui. So lautet der sachgerechte Name für den Gott in der Philosophie. Zu diesem Gott kann der Mensch weder beten, noch kann er ihm opfern. Vor der Causa sui kann der Mensch weder aus Scheu ins Knie fallen, noch kann er vor diesem Gott musizieren und tanzen.

Demgemäß ist das gott-lose Denken, das den Gott der Philosophie, den Gott als Causa sui preisgeben muß, dem göttlichen Gott vielleicht näher. Dies sagt hier: Es ist freier für ihn, als es die Onto-Theo-Logik wahrheben möchte.[36]

[(The) ground itself must in due measure be grounded: that is, must be caused by the most primordially causative thing. This is the cause understood as *causa sui*. This is how the name of God appropriate to philosophy is inscribed. To this god can man neither pray nor make offering. Neither can man fall to his knees in awe before the *causa sui*, nor before this god can he make music and dance.

Perhaps, then, that god-less thinking that must abandon the god of philosophy—God, that is, understood as *causa sui*—is nearer to the divine God. That is to say, it is freer for him than onto-theo-logy would wish to grant.]

Such, at least, is Heidegger's verdict upon the god of "onto-theo-logy," the god of the metaphysics of the "double founding"—the grounding of beings in being and of being in a supreme being—which reduces all of reality

36. Martin Heidegger, "Die Onto-Theo-Logische Verfassung der Metaphysik," in *Identität und Differenz*, 10th ed. (Stuttgart: Verlag Günther Neske, 1996), pp. 64–65.

(including divine reality) to a closed totality, an economy of causal power, from which the mystery of being has been fully exorcised.

I confess that, in twenty years of reading Heidegger, I have never before allowed myself to feel the full force of these words: *freier für ihn*. . . . There are some things that I simply have not cared to be told by Heidegger—whereof I here repent. One need not accept Heidegger's monolithic history of metaphysics, or despair as he did of the possibility of speaking analogically of God, or embrace his ontology, to value his thought as a solvent of the decadent traditions of early modern metaphysics. When all that is high and holy in God has been forgotten, and God has been reduced to sheer irresistible causal power, the old names for God have lost their true meaning, and the death of God has already been accomplished, even if we have not yet consciously ceased to believe. When atheism becomes explicit, however, it also becomes possible to recognize the logic that informs it, to trace it back to its remoter origins, perhaps even to begin to reverse its effects. It may be that a certain grace operates through disbelief: perhaps we shall be ready again to receive the truly "divine God" (as Heidegger phrases it) only when certain gods of our own making have vanished. This is the moment (as Heidegger also says) of highest risk, a moment in which an absolute nihilism threatens; but it is also then a moment in which it may become possible once again to recall the God who is beyond every nihilism. It is certainly not a moment for lamentation or misguided nostalgias. Better to fix before our minds the piercing words of Meister Eckhart: "I pray that God deliver me from god."[37] It is principally the god of modernity—the god of pure sovereignty, the voluntarist god of "permissive decrees" and the *praemotio physica*—who has died for modern humanity, and perhaps theology has no nobler calling for now than to see that he remains dead, and that every attempt to revive him is thwarted: in the hope that, in becoming willing accomplices in his death, Christians may help to prepare their world for the return of the true God revealed in Christ, in all the mystery of his transcendent and impassible love.

---

37. Meister Eckhart, sermon 52: "Beati pauperes spiritu."

TEN

Thine Own of Thine Own

The Orthodox Understanding of Eucharistic Sacrifice

I

I should say, before all else, that a single essay can in no way adequately address the issue of the Eastern Orthodox understanding of the Eucharist in its relation to Christ's sacrifice, as either a historical or a theological topic. I trust, therefore, that I will be forgiven if my treatment of the matter is occasionally somewhat broadly synoptic, as well as slightly licentious in its approach to questions chronological. And I hope that my attempt to draw together various strands of Orthodox tradition in a single, internally consistent theological reflection will be seen as at most synthetic, and not in any sense procrustean. I want to argue that, whatever variations in terms and emphases have marked the evolution of Eastern eucharistic theology, from the patristic to the high Byzantine to the modern age, there has persisted all along a more or less unified vision of what is accomplished in every celebration of the Divine Liturgy, what its relation is to the saving life, death, and resurrection of the incarnate God, and what light it casts upon our understanding of how God acts in Christ to draw all things together to himself. Byzantine Christianity cannot boast quite as intricate and elaborate a history of scholastic and dogmatic interrogations of eucharistic doctrine as can the Western Church (which makes my task slightly easier, perhaps, than a Roman Catholic theologian's would be), but I hope to show that its vision of the eucharistic oblation—its understanding of how it is an oblation—is one not only of considerable theological coherency, but also of exceeding profundity and beauty.

First, though, it would be well to determine in what sense that almost infinitely plastic term "sacrifice" is to be used. Perhaps no word serves better to capture the intuition that governs the Orthodox tradition's reflections on sacrifice (whether in relation to the self-offering of Christ or the offering of bread and wine in the Liturgy) than the Hebrew *qurban*, with its connotation of "drawing nigh," or "coming into the Presence." I say this not only because of the prominence the book of Hebrews has traditionally enjoyed in Orthodox texts as a heuristic of the eucharistic oblation, and the consequently frequent resort of Orthodox theologians to the language of Israel's Day of Atonement offering as part of their sacramental grammar, but because the word *qurban* (or *qurbana*, as Christians who worship in Syriac call the Eucharist) points to an understanding of sacrifice as not, obviously, a simple propitiation of the divine (crudely conceived) or an attempt to importune God under the shelter of an ingratiating tribute, but as a miraculous reconciliation between God, who is the wellspring of all life, and his people, who are dead in sin. Sacrifice, in this sense, means a marvelous reparation of a shattered covenant, and an act wherein is accomplished, again and again, that divine indwelling, within the body of his people, that is God's purpose in shaping for himself a people to bear his glory. If it is indeed always the will of God to "tabernacle" upon the earth, indeed ultimately to make the whole earth his temple, then the atonement sacrifice is that moment when God restores to himself the body he has chosen to dwell within and so also makes of himself an abode for his creatures. When the blood of the people, so to speak, which is its life, now forfeit through sin, is brought into the ambit of the *Shekhinah*, before the mercy seat, an exchange occurs in which the life's blood of those who were perishing is made pure again, infused with the life that flows from God, and the nuptial bond of this mutual indwelling—God in his creatures and they in him—is repaired.

Another way of saying this is that the entire question of eucharistic sacrifice, at least for Orthodox tradition, might most plausibly be answered in terms of the theme of *theōsis*. That is to say, what occurs in the incarnation of the Word is the consummation of that "drawing nigh" for which all of creation is intended: its glorification in the light of God, its transformation into a vessel of the Glory of the Presence, and our transfiguration into partakers in the divine nature. As Christ is himself our *hilasmos* and *hilastērion*, our atonement and place of atonement, he accomplishes that perfect sacrifice in his person that unites us to God, by emptying himself out into our nature and so filling us up with his; and the Eucharist, in Orthodox tradition, is almost always understood as the place where our offering of ourselves to God is opened up and brought to fruition within Christ's offering of himself, and it comes to pass that we dwell in him and he in us. This is, in large part, why I have chosen as the title of this essay, a phrase from a part of the Byzantine anaphora that the celebrant speaks between the words of institution and the epiclesis: "Thine own of thine own, we offer unto thee, on behalf of all, and for all." God's body is what we are graciously given to offer, within which we ourselves are both offered up and made alive. Stated simply, as Christ's resurrected body is now the eternal temple where the divine glory inhabits created nature, and as it is in the bread and wine of communion that we eat his flesh and drink his blood and so have life in him, it is in the Eucharist that we enter into the miraculous exchange—the reconciling sacrifice—by which we too are being made bearers of God's glory.

To unfold that claim, however, I shall have to proceed by steps, not all in obviously the same direction.

II

In its developed form, Byzantine mystagogy tends to view the Eucharist as being a sacrifice in a threefold sense: it is at once an offering of bread and wine and so of ourselves (our substance), the one all-sufficing sacrifice made by Christ on our behalf in the economy of his earthly mission, and the abiding presence of his offered humanity upon the heavenly altar, before the throne of God, where he, as our Great High Priest, makes everlasting intercession for us. All these sacrificial themes had a substantial, if somewhat diffuse, existence in Eastern Christian theology at least as early as the homilies of John Chrysostom, and they already constituted a profound allegorical and theological unity in the majestic eucharistic commentary of Patriarch Germanos I of Constantinople (d. 733), the *Mystic Contemplation*,[1] with its lovely interweaving of the imagery of Levitical

1. The authorship of Germanos's Ἱστορία Ἐκκλησιαστικὴ καὶ μυστικὴ θεωρία was, until recently, a subject of some debate, and the text has appeared in so many variants (including the irredeemably corrupt version found in Patrologia Graeca [hereinafter PG] 98:384–53) that precise dating has often proved quite elusive; it has even been ascribed to the thirteenth-century Constantinopolitan patriarchs Germanos II and Germanos III. The traditional attribution has now, though, been sufficiently well established; see Robert F. Taft, "The Liturgy of the Great Church: An Initial Synthesis of Structure and Interpretation on the Eve of Iconoclasm," *Dumbarton Oaks Papers* 34–5 (Washington, DC: DO, 1980–1981). The original text has been very plausibly reconstructed by Nilo Borgia, in *Il commentario liturgico di S. Germano patriarca Constantinopolitano, Studi Liturgici* 1

sacrifice; Isaiah's vision in the temple; the liturgy of the heavenly court; the whole motion of Christ's *kenōsis*, life, death, resurrection, and ascension; and the liturgy of the Great Church. For instance: "The holy table corresponds to the spot in the tomb where Christ was placed. On it lies the true and heavenly bread, the mystical and unbloody sacrifice. Christ sacrifices His flesh and blood and offers it to the faithful as food for eternal life. The holy table is the throne of God, on which, borne by the Cherubim, He rested in the body."[2] And:

> The altar corresponds to the holy tomb of Christ. On it Christ brought Himself as a sacrifice to [His] God and father through the offering of His body as a sacrificial lamb, and as highpriest and Son of Man, offering and being offered as a mystical bloodless sacrifice, and appointing for the faithful reasonable worship, through which we have become sharers in eternal and immortal life....
>
> The altar is and is called the heavenly and spiritual altar, where the earthly and material priests who always assist and serve the Lord represent the spiritual, serving, and hierarchical powers of the immaterial and celestial Powers, for they also must be as a burning fire.[3]

By the early Middle Ages, the threefold scheme had assumed a certain systematic form. The great archbishop of Bulgaria, Theophylact of Ochrida (ca. 1050–ca. 1108), for instance, certainly employed it in his commentary on Hebrews,[4] as did the Constantinopolitan monk Euthymios Zigabenos

---

(Grottaferrata, 1912), and has been translated into English, with Borgia's text facing, as St. Germanus of Constantinople, *On the Divine Liturgy*, trans. Paul Meyendorff (Crestwood, NY: St. Vladimir's Seminary Press, 1984).

2. St. Germanus of Constantinople, *On the Divine Liturgy*, trans. Meyendorff, p. 59.

3. St. Germanus of Constantinople, *On the Divine Liturgy*, trans. Meyendorff, p. 61. The first sentences of this passage ("Θυσιαστήριόν ἐστι κατὰ τὸ ἅγιον μνῆμα τοῦ Χριστοῦ. ἐν ᾧ ἑαυτὸν προσήγαγε...") appear in the PG text as "Θυσιαστήριόν ἐστιν ἱλαστήριον, ἐν ᾧ προσφέρετο περὶ τῆς ἁμαρτίας κατὰ τὸ ἅγιον μνῆμα τοῦ Χριστοῦ..." (PG 98:389). The latter rendering has the virtue of teasing out one of those multivalent series of biblical associations from which Byzantine mystagogy proceeds: that is, the equation of the tomb of Christ with the heavenly altar, far from reflecting mere ungoverned poetic fancy, is surely a reflection upon the Johannine Easter narrative, which depicts the angels in the empty tomb as seated one at the head and one at the foot of Christ's catafalque—which itself certainly echoes iconically the two cherubim whose wings overshadowed the ark of the covenant's mercy seat.

4. Theophylactus of Bulgaria, *Epistolae divi Pauli ad Hebraeos expositio*, PG 125:185–404. See especially 265Cff.

(d. 1118) in his commentary on the same book,[5] and both were clearly anxious to show that, even in its triplicity, there is but one atoning sacrifice in the Eucharist, present under several aspects: the already accomplished historical mission of Christ, the eternal efficacy of this mission in the presence of God, and the real availability in the present of the reconciliation it effects (in both its creaturely and divine dimensions) in the tangible—and frangible—form of Christ's body and blood. Nicholas of Methone, writing in 1157,[6] produced two brief treatments of the eucharistic sacrifice that simply presume the threefold scheme: there is one offering, made once in the past, made everlastingly in heaven, and made continually present to us in time, in the liturgy.[7] And the greatest Orthodox sacramental theologian, Nicholas Cabasilas, whose work constitutes a grand synthesis of the entire Eastern tradition on these matters, frames his account of the Eucharist's salvific efficacy, for the church as a body and for every baptized Christian, precisely in terms of this triple sacrificial economy:

> [T]he Lord was not satisfied with sending the Holy Spirit to abide with us; he has himself promised to be with us, even unto the end of the world. The Paraclete is present unseen because he has not taken a human form, but by means of the great and holy mysteries the Lord submits himself to our sight and touch and through the dread and holy mysteries, because he has taken our nature upon him and bears it eternally.
>
> Such is the power of the priesthood, such is the Priest. For after once offering himself, and being made a sacrifice he did not end his priesthood, but is continually offering the sacrifice for us (*leitourgei tēn leitourgian hēmin*), by virtue of which he is our advocate before God for ever.[8]

---

5. Euthymios's commentaries on Paul's epistles were published in Athens in 1887, edited by Archbishop Kalogeras. The text of his Hebrews commentary was made available to me, in scanned form, over the Internet, by P. Konstantinides, devoid (alas) of pagination.

6. Nicholas, among other things a distinguished commentator on Proclos's *Elements*, was writing in support of a council called the previous year in Constantinople, by Emperor Manuel Comnenos, to condemn the teaching of Soterichos Panteugenos that we must say that Christ's offering was and is made only to the Father and not to the whole Trinity (lest, like the "Nestorians," we erect a partition between his humanity and his divinity).

7. The two treatises were published in Leipzig in 1865, edited by Andronikos Demetrakopoulos; for their contents, however, I am in part trusting the report of Darwell Stone, who in his *A History of the Doctrine of the Holy Eucharist*, 2 vols. (New York: Longmans, Green, and Co., 1909) gives a much fuller account of this entire aspect of Byzantine eucharistic theology: see 1:143–73, among other sources.

8. Nicholas Cabasilas, *A Commentary on the Divine Liturgy*, trans. J. M. Hussey and P. A. McNulty (Crestwood, NY: St. Vladimir's Seminary Press, 1977), 28.3–4, p. 71. I take

In one sense, then, this may be said to be what Orthodox tradition understands by talk of the Eucharist as "sacrifice": our perpetual entry, through the mediation of Christ's priesthood, into that atonement—that way of return given by God first to Israel—that Christ has everlastingly accomplished for us. But in another sense, this is to tell only half the tale.

One has not yet arrived at the heart of Byzantine eucharistic theology until one appreciates the radically ontological nature of the Eastern Christian understanding of "atonement" and of the "drawing nigh" of God in Christ that Christ's sacrifice achieves for us. As, typically, the Orthodox tradition's eucharistic discourse is determined by the logic of its Christology (and, indeed, not infrequently the reverse), its understanding of eucharistic sacrifice will remain largely unintelligible if not viewed in light of that wondrous exchange of natures, that *commercium mirabile* between the divine and the human, that occurs in Christ. It is the absolute reconciliation of God and humanity in the person of the incarnate Word—the divinization of human nature in its assumption by God the Son—that is, in fact, the final place of atonement, to which we gain entry in the mystery of the holy table. "Sacrifice" here means a reconciling *transitus* whose proper form is the very *communicatio idiomatum* of Christ's divinity and humanity; as Cyril of Alexandria argues, when Christ says, in John 20:17, "I am going to my Father and your Father, to my God and your God," he is describing the very essence of redemption, showing it to be so intimate an interchange of natures and prerogatives that his Father by nature is now ours through our exaltation in him, and our God by nature is his by condescension.[9] (Of course, as scarcely needs be said, Cyril's certitude regarding the unity of Christ is always, throughout his work, secured by his belief that in the Eucharist we are experiencing nothing less than the deification of our humanity.) Christ is, so to speak, the chiasmus of the created and the divine, the tabernacle *and* the Glory of the Presence, and in the bread and wine of communion that everlasting reconciliation of natures, and all its transfiguring grace, is sprinkled upon his people. If Christ is himself our access to the mercy seat, our *hilastērion*, he is also the one in whom the veil between us and God's glory has been "rent in twain," so that that glory comes forth to make its habitation immediately

---

the Greek, and the paragraph numbers, from the text in Nicolas Cabasilas, *Explication de la Divine Liturgie*, trans. Séverien Salaville, Greek text editors René Bornert, Jean Gouillard, and Pierre Périchon (Paris: Les Éditions du Cerf, 1967), p. 178.

9. Cyril of Alexandria, *Quod unus sit Christus*, PG 75:1272-73.

within our souls and bodies, and to shed its splendor upon all flesh. This is why Nicholas of Methone says that the supernatural *metabolē* of the elements in the eucharistic consecration is as miraculous and incomprehensible as the incarnation, resurrection, and ascension of Christ, and has as its whole purpose and end the participation in Christ by those who receive from him eternal life and divinization (*ektheōsis*);[10] and why Theophylact, commenting on John 6:56–58, says that he who eats Christ is transformed—elementally—into Christ, and it is thus that God comes to dwell in us and we in him.[11] As Sergius Bulgakov says, in the ascension of Christ's glorified body, "that which is of the world . . . already belongs to the divine life, manifesting both a perfect deification of human nature and a perfect inhumanization of the divine nature"; and, he adds, "here we find the foundation of the eucharistic dogma."[12]

Behind all such language, of course, stands that venerable patristic narrative of salvation that at one time (in the dark days of theology's intellectual and spiritual captivity to foreign gods with names like Ritschl and Harnack) was often dismissed as the "physical theory" of the atonement, a coarse mythology of "salvation" rather than a sophisticated moral narrative of justification (narrowly construed): to wit, the belief that we are saved because in the Word's *kenōsis*, a new and deified humanity was created, one that has now triumphed over death and the devil and ascended into the very Trinitarian life of God, into which nature we are incorporated first through the very definitely corporeal mediations of the sacraments. It is the story of redemption through God's indwelling of our nature, which is beautifully likened by Athanasius to a king coming to dwell in a city that, as a consequence, is ennobled in its every quarter;[13] and by the same author, in more vividly material terms, as the banishment of corruption from our flesh by the Word, whose divinity saturates our nature like asbestos soaking stubble, so that fire can no longer consume it.[14] The fathers, certainly, felt no squeamishness—especially when explicitly linking this soteriology to the "medicine of immortality" that the Eucharist is for us—

10. Nicholas of Methone, *Ad eos qui haesitant, aiuntque consecratum panem et vinum non esse corpus et sanguinem domini nostri Jesu Christi*, PG 135:509–18.

11. He understands Christ to be saying "ὁ τρώγων με ζήσεται δι' ἐμὲ ἀνακιρνώμενος, ὥσπερ καὶ *μεταστοιχειούμενος* εἰς ἐμὲ τὸν ζωογονεῖν ἰσχύοντα." Theophylactus, *Enarratio in Evangelium Joannis*, PG 123:1309–12.

12. From "The Eucharistic Dogma," in Sergius Bulgakov, *The Holy Grail and the Eucharist*, trans. and ed. Boris Jakim (New York: Lindisfarne Books, 1997), p. 104.

13. Athanasius, *De incarnatione verbi Dei*, PG 25:112–13.

14. Athanasius, *De incarnatione verbi Dei*, PG 25:173–76.

about describing our salvation in the most frankly physiological fashion. Gregory of Nyssa, for instance, in one of the more restrained passages in his *Catechetical Oration*, puts the matter thus:

> As, therefore, that God-bearing flesh took its substance and sustenance from this [food and drink], and as the God who made himself manifest thus mingled himself with the mortal nature of men in order that by communion with divinity the human might be made divine, through the economy of grace he disseminates himself in the faithful by means of that same flesh, which is nourished by wine and bread, blending himself with the bodies of the faithful, so that, by union with the immortal, man too may come to be a partaker in incorruptibility. These things he vouchsafes to us through the power of that blessing whereby he transforms (*metastoicheiōsas*) the nature of visible things into the incorruptible.[15]

Or, as John Chrysostom says, with his customary rhetorical aplomb:

> We become one body and, [as the apostle] says, members of his flesh and of his bones [Eph. 5:30]. Let the initiated follow my words. In order that we might become such not only according to love, but in actual fact, let us be blended into that flesh. For this happens through the food he has graciously given us, wishing to reveal to us the desire he has for us; thus he has mixed himself together with us, and has kneaded his body into us. . . . Those who long for him he has allowed not only to see him, but also to touch him, and to devour him, and to fix their teeth in his flesh, and to embrace him, and to satisfy all their desire.[16]

15. Gregory of Nyssa, *Oratio catechetica* 37, ed. James Herbert Srawley (Cambridge: Cambridge University Press, 1956), pp. 151–52. ['Ἐπεὶ οὖν καὶ τοῦτο μέρος ἡ Θεοδόχος ἐκείνη σὰρξ πρὸς τὴν σύστασιν ἑαυτῆς παρεδέξατο, ὁ δὲ φανερωθεὶς θεὸς διὰ τοῦτο κατέμιξεν ἑαυτὸν τῇ ἐπικήρῳ τῶν ἀνθρώπων φύσει, ἵνα τῇ τῆς Θεότητος κοινωνίᾳ συναποθεωθῇ τὸ ἀνθρώπινον, τούτου χάριν πᾶσι τοῖς πεπιστευκόσι τῇ οἰκονομίᾳ τῆς χάριτος ἑαυτὸν ἐνσπείρει διὰ τῆς σαρκός, ἧς ἡ σύστασις ἐξ οἴνου τε καὶ ἄρτου ἐστί, τοῖς σώμασι τῶν πεπιστευκότων κατακιρνάμενος, ὡς ἂν τῇ πρὸς τὸ ἀθάνατον ἑνώσει καὶ ἄνθρωπος τῆς ἀφθαρσίας μέτοχος γένοιτο. Ταῦτα δὲ δίδωσι, τῇ τῆς εὐλογίας δυνάμει πρὸς ἐκεῖνο μεταστοιχειώσας τῶν φαινομένων τὴν φύσιν.]

16. John Chrysostom, *In Sanctum Joannem apostolum et evangelistam*, Homilia 46; PG 59:260. ["Ἓν σῶμα γινόμεθα, μέλη, φησὶν, τῆς σαρκὸς Αὐτοῦ. Οἱ δὲ μεμυημένοι παρακολοθείτωσαν τοῖς λεγομένοις. Ἵν' οὖ μὴ μόνον κατὰ τὴν ἀγάπην γενώμεθα, ἀλλὰ καὶ κατ' αὐτὸ τὸ πρᾶγμα, εἰ ἐκείνην ἀνακερασθῶμεν τὴν σάρκα. Διὰ τῆς τροφῆς γὰρ γίνεται ὡς ἐχαρίσατο, βουλόμενος ἡμῖν δεῖξαι τὸν πόθον, ὃν ἔχει περὶ ἡμᾶς, διὰ τοῦτο ἀνέμιξεν Ἑαυτὸν ἡμῖν, καὶ ἀνέφυρε τὸ σῶμα Αὐτοῦ εἰς ἡμᾶς . . . οὐκ ἰδεῖν Αὐτὸν μόνον

Indeed, as Cyril of Alexandria says, while we may well say of the flesh of Paul or Peter that "the flesh profiteth nothing," we must say just the opposite of the flesh "of our savior Christ, in whom dwelt all the fullness of the Godhead bodily, for it would be very odd indeed that honey should infuse its own quality into things that are naturally devoid of sweetness, and should transform the qualities (*metaskeuazein*) of those things with which it is mixed into its own, but that we should not think that the life-creating nature of God the Word should elevate into its own goodness that wherein his body dwelt."[17] And John of Damascus's explanation of the Eucharist in *On the Orthodox Faith* is, predictably, the most systematically thorough treatment of the matter among patristic texts:

> The bread and wine are not a figure of the body and blood of Christ—God forbid!—but the actual deified body of the Lord (*to sōma tou Kyriou teth-eōmenon*). . . . With eyes, lips, and faces turned toward it let us receive the divine burning coal, so that the fire of the coal may be added to the desire within us to consume our sins and enlighten our hearts, and so that by this communion of the divine fire we may be set afire and deified (*tē metousia tou Theiou pyros pyrōthōmen kai theōthōmen*). Isaias saw a live coal, and this coal was not plain wood but wood joined with fire. Thus also, the bread of communion is not plain bread, but bread joined with the Godhead.[18]

Perhaps such language is somewhat unrefined by certain later standards, but only because those standards reflect a lamentable failure to grasp what it means to worship an incarnate God. It requires imagination, granted, but also some considerable breadth of theological vision to see how common bread and wine can become the site where God's self-outpouring and our exaltation occur for us, the substance of our reconciliation with God, and the evidence of God's utter condescension for our sakes. As Gregory Palamas remarks, the union of humanity with Christ that this

---

παρέσχε τοῖς ἐπιθυμοῦσιν, ἀλλὰ καὶ ἅψασθαι, καὶ φαγεῖν, καὶ ἐμπῆξαι τοὺς ὀδόντας τῇ σαρκὶ, καὶ συμπλακῆναι, καὶ τὸν πόθον ἐμπλῆσαι πάντα.]

17. Cyril of Alexandria, *In Joannis Evangelium* 4; PG 73:601–4. [Σωτῆρος ἡμῶν Χριστοῦ, ἐν ᾧ κατώκησε πᾶν τὸ πλήρωμα τῆς Θεότητος σωματικῶς. Καὶ γὰρ ἂν εἴη τῶν ἀτοπωτάτων τὸ μὲν μέλι τοῖς οὐκ ἔχουσι κατὰ φύσιν τὸ γλυκὺ τὴν ἰδίαν ἐπιτιθέναι ποιότητα, καὶ εἰς ἑαυτὸ μετασκευάζειν τὸ, ᾧπερ ἂν ἀνμίσγηται. τὴν δὲ τοῦ Θεοῦ Λόγου ζωοποιὸν μὴ ἀνακομίζειν οἴεσθαι πρὸς τὸ ἴδιον ἀγαθὸν τὸ, ἐν ᾧπερ ἐνῴκησε σῶμα.]

18. The translation is that of Frederic H. Chase Jr., in St. John of Damascus, *Writings* (Washington, DC: CUAP, 1958), pp. 358–59. The Greek is taken from the text in PG 94:1148–49.

sacrament accomplishes constitutes the highest expression of God's love for us;[19] and he goes on to observe, with all the physiological literalism not only of the early fathers but also of Symeon the New Theologian, and with absolutely no trace of liberal Protestant pudency: "O many-sided and ineffable communion! Christ has become our brother, for He has fellowship with us in flesh and blood. . . . He has bound us to Himself and united us, as the bridegroom unites the bride to himself, through the communion of this His blood, becoming one flesh with us. He has also become our father through divine baptism in Himself, and He feeds us at His own breast, as a loving mother feeds her child."[20]

In any event, this is the crux of the matter: the Eucharist is the *site* where that same indissoluble bond between God and humanity accomplished in Christ becomes our food and drink, substance and sustenance for us, and where, as Gregory the Theologian says, through a bloodless sacrifice we partake of Christ, in regard to both his sufferings and his Godhead.[21] And in that sacrificial partaking, there is a real exchange of substance for substance, an exhaustion of our poverty, so to speak, to make way for the riches he pours into us. If there is any value to the ancient dispute over the use of azymes in the Eucharist (which for the most part there is not), it is the light it casts upon Eastern understandings of the connection between eucharistic theology and both Christology and soteriology; behind the Byzantine suspicion that churches that use unleavened bread are perhaps guilty of that more or less mythical heresy called "monophysitism" (and so feel free to leave unrepresented the "earthly leaven" of Christ's humanity), lies a fairly pervasive prejudice to the effect that, no less than Christ's flesh was common flesh, so the bread of communion should be our ordinary, daily bread, our *artos epiousios*, which truly nourishes our bodies. John Meyendorff is simply conventionally Byzantine when he asserts the importance of the fact that the *prosphora* and *antidōron* consumed during and after the Divine Liturgy is true, consubstantial bread, rather than ethereal (and nutriently vapid) azymes; God has truly become our sustenance, the wine and bread that feeds our humanity, and has transfigured it into glory in his death

19. Gregory Palamas, Ὁμιλίαι, ed. S. Oikonomos (Athens, 1861), 56.6, p. 207.

20. Gregory Palamas, Ὁμιλίαι, 56.7, pp. 207–8. I have borrowed the translation found in Georgios I. Mantzarides, *The Deification of Man: St. Gregory Palamas and the Orthodox Tradition*, trans. Liadain Sherrard (Crestwood, NY: St. Vladimir's Seminary Press, 1984), pp. 52–53.

21. Gregory of Nazianzus, *Oratio* 4.52 (*Contra Julianum* 1); PG 35:575.

and resurrection.[22] For Nicholas Cabasilas, food is the firstfruit of our nature, and bread and wine are not random specimens of the viands that we gather from the world, but uniquely human nourishments, and so in offering them we are handing over the firstfruits of our substance to God.[23] So the oblation of this our substance is assumed into his offering of our humanity, as himself the firstfruits of the human race and the firstborn under the Law.[24] "It is he who commands us to offer bread and wine," writes Cabasilas; "it is he who gives us in return the Living Bread, the chalice of everlasting life. . . . He commands those to whom he would give eternal life (that is, his life-giving Body and Blood) to offer the food of our fleeting mortal life: so that we may receive life for life, eternity for temporality; so that what is grace may seem to be an exchange, so that infinite generosity may have the appearance of justice."[25] Christ is, then, both the Way for us and the waybread that sustains us.

It is very much the same prejudice that has moved most modern Orthodox theologians to regret that the Eastern Church, in the late Middle Ages and early modern period, adopted the language of "transubstantiation" from Western theology. One cannot quite agree with John Meyendorff that this borrowing was extremely rare and in general jarring to Byzantine sensibilities.[26] Of course, we attribute it primarily to "Latinophrones" like George Gennadios (Scholarios), who, prior to the fall of Constantinople and his elevation to the patriarchate by Mehmet II, was an avid student of Western theology. His most famous text on eucharistic theology, a homily from 1453, is in fact simply a Greek summary of Latin thought: what occurs in the consecration of the elements is a *metousiōsis*, wherein the substance (*ousia*) of the bread and wine is displaced by the substance of Christ's body and blood, though their accidents (*symbebēkota*) are preserved.[27] But Gennadios's language is scarcely an anomaly, at least not from the perspective of later church teaching: the *Orthodox Confession* of the metropolitan of Kiev Peter Mogila, written in 1640, uses the same terminology,[28] which document was subsequently approved by the

22. John Meyendorff, *Byzantine Theology* (New York: Fordham University Press, 1974), pp. 204–5.

23. Cabasilas, *Explication* 3.2–4, pp. 72–74; *Commentary*, pp. 31–32.

24. Cabasilas, *Explication* 2.3–4, pp. 70–72; *Commentary*, p. 31.

25. Cabasilas, *Explication* 4.2, p. 76; *Commentary*, pp. 32–33.

26. Meyendorff, *Byzantine Theology*, p. 205.

27. Patriarch Gennadius, *De sacramentale corpore Jesu Christi*, PG 160:351–73.

28. See Ernst Julius Kimmel, *Monumenta fidei ecclesiae Orientalis* (Jena: F. Mauke, 1850), 1:125–26, 180–84; in the latter passage, the confession affirms that after the words

Council of Jassy in 1642; and by the patriarchs of Constantinople, Antioch, Alexandria, and Jerusalem in 1643; and by the Council of Jerusalem of 1672—at which was also adopted the *Confession* of Dositheos, patriarch of Jerusalem, which affirms that in the consecration of the elements, the natural substance is entirely banished, so that we can partake of Christ's body and blood under the *eidos* and *typos* of bread and wine.[29] And a council held in Constantinople in 1727 declared the doctrine of *metousiōsis* to be the ancient teaching of the whole catholic church.[30] Notwithstanding which, Meyendorff is essentially correct when he says that, generally speaking, "the Byzantines did not see the substance of the bread somehow changed in the Eucharistic mystery into another substance . . . but viewed this bread as the 'type' of the humanity: our humanity changed into the transfigured humanity of Christ."[31]

Among modern Orthodox theologians, none has been more adamant in his rejection of the language of transubstantiation than Sergius Bulgakov; for one thing, he regards it as a philosophically inane concept in an era in which the idea of intransitive "substance" has disappeared from empirical science and speculative philosophy alike, displaced by talk of quantifiable process, or dialectical determination, or linguistic contingency; or by the language of transcendental philosophy, in which context substance can mean either the purely posited but inaccessible *Ding an sich* behind any particular appearance, or the coherence of phenomenal experience achieved by the *cogito*'s transcendental unity of apperception—neither of which can bear the weight of the traditional dogma. But, more to the point, he thinks it reflects a deficient sense of the way in which the Eucharist grants us access to the deified humanity of Christ. No more than the incarnation expels the true substantial humanity of Jesus does the divine presence expel the natural substance of the eucharistic elements; just as Christ's assumed humanity, while retaining its creaturely integrity, is transformed into his glorified and heavenly body, so our bodies, and indeed the whole world, have the potential of becoming divine within their proper substances, not in spite of them.[32]

---

of institution and the epiclesis, when the μετουσίωσις occurs, only the species (εἴδη) of bread and wine remains.

29. Jean Hardouin, *Conciliorum collectio regia maxima* (17??), 11:249–56. The relevant passages from the confession are translated in Stone, *Doctrine of the Holy Eucharist*, 1:180–82, which volume contains a fuller account of this aspect of late Byzantine theology, pp. 172–92.

30. Stone, *Doctrine of the Holy Eucharist*, 1:184–85.

31. Meyendorff, *Byzantine Theology*, p. 205.

32. See Bulgakov, "The Eucharistic Dogma," especially pp. 137–38.

Of course, whether Bulgakov has quite done justice to the theology of transubstantiation is debatable (one obvious rejoinder would be that the Roman Catholic position does not posit that in the Eucharist the divine displaces the creaturely, but rather that the presence of the incarnate Christ, in both his divinity and humanity, is made radically available), but he definitely marks a trend. Typically, now, the touchstones to which Orthodox theologians are wont to resort, in regard to the sacrament, are such things as a letter from the latter half of the fifth century, traditionally ascribed to John Chrysostom, which argues that when the bread of communion really becomes the body of Christ, it still retains its nature as bread, just as, when the divine nature took to itself a body, two natures were made one Son;[33] or the sixth-century christological formula of Leontius of Byzantium (which will hardly strike Western ears as unfamiliar) that the supernatural does not destroy the natural, but elevates it above its "natural" capacity, educing and animating its potential so that it becomes capable of more than itself.[34]

In any event, I call attention to this matter not because I think it a particularly fruitful debate, but because, again, it demonstrates how thoroughly the Eastern view of the Eucharist is determined by its theology of incarnation and *theōsis, kenōsis,* and *plērōsis,* abasement and exaltation; and by the certainty that we who are called to become partakers of the divine nature do so now, already, in the degree to which we are able, under the real material form of bread and wine. What we offer in the eucharistic oblation is our entire being, and what we receive is the transformation of our being in Christ, soul, mind, and body. This food is nothing less than our re-creation in Christ as sons and daughters of God, coheirs of the kingdom, and vessels of God's glory.

III

One of the more peculiar aspects of the Divine Liturgy is the graduality with which it unfolds its sacrificial motion—by which I mean the numerous ways in which it adumbrates or indeed enacts a sacrifice of the gifts, well before the actual anaphora. Obvious examples are the piercing and dividing of the *prosphora* with a small spear-shaped instrument during the *prothesis* or *proskomidē* (the preparation of the elements before the liturgy begins), which is accompanied by such phrases as "Sacrificed is the Lamb

33. John Chrysostom, *Ad Caesarium monachum*, PG 52:758.
34. Leontius of Byzantium, *Contra Nestorium et Eutychem* 2; PG 86:1333.

of God, who takes away the sin of the world, for the life of the world and its salvation"; or the extraordinary reverence of the procession of the elements into the altar during the Great Entrance, and the veneration they receive from the congregation, and the great Cherubic Hymn the choir sings (which speaks of the arrival of the "King of All, who comes invisibly upborne by the angelic hosts"), and the prayers the celebrant then quietly recites over them (which speak of them as the slain body of Christ lying in the tomb while Christ accomplishes our salvation in hell, on earth, and in heaven, making his tomb the fountain of our salvation). In truth, the "sacrifice" as such is often rather difficult to locate; it is somehow shrouded in its own ubiquity. And the history of Eastern Christian mystagogy reflects this: the tendency of Byzantine commentaries on the liturgy to expand into ever richer and more fulsome allegories, as they strain to show how the entire economy of Christ's incarnation, death, resurrection, and ascension into the heavenly place is dramaturgically represented in the celebration of the mystery, comes of a deep desire to rationalize the sheer prodigality with which the Byzantine liturgy announces the presence of Christ in the gifts and the eventuation of his sacrifice in the people's midst. Indeed, it is in large part the result of the liturgical hypertrophy of the Great Entrance—to which, for instance, the emperor Justin II in 573–574 added the Cherubic Hymn and which soon came to be accompanied, at Easter, by the hymn "Let all mortal flesh . . ." from the Liturgy of Saint James, which seems to describe the elements as the "King of kings and Lord of lords" entering to be slain. So exuberantly profligate a display of (apparently premature) reverence simply *necessitated* the development of Byzantine theology's long tradition of the composition of ingenious mystagogical *fantasias* upon the various actions of the rite.[35] Nicholas Cabasilas feels moved to defend the congregation's veneration of the gifts at the Entrance by arguing that in fact the people are actually prostrating themselves before the priest, entreating him to remember them in his prayers in the altar;[36] and Gabriel Severus[37] feels he must isolate three distinct phases in the veneration of the bread and wine in the liturgy: they are honored first *physikōs*, insofar as they are good creatures of God; then *metochikōs*, when they are set apart as gifts consecrated to become Christ's body and blood; and finally *metousiaskikōs*, when they have been

35. See Hans-Joachim Schulz, *The Byzantine Liturgy*, trans. Matthew J. O'Connell (New York: Pueblo Publishing Co., 1986), pp. 139–96.

36. Cabasilas, *Explication*, pp. 162–64; *Commentary*, pp. 65–66.

37. Severus was made bishop of Philadelphia in 1577, but spent most of his episcopacy as bishop to the Orthodox diaspora in the Venetian states.

consecrated and have become worthy of full worship (*latreia*).[38] In general, however, Orthodox mystagogues, greatly to their credit, have felt no need for such apologetics.

There are two distinct tendencies in the Eastern tradition of liturgical allegory: one that elects a symbolic interpretation of the rite in conscious or unconscious preference to the radical eucharistic realism of earlier patristic theology, and another in which that realism has become so intense that it becomes positively necessary to see the whole sacrificial movement of Christ, from his *kenōsis* to his session at the right hand of the Father, written—however forcibly—into the sacramental action. The two most notable representatives of the former tendency are the Pseudo-Dionysius and Maximus the Confessor, both of whom tend to subordinate sacramental *koinōnia* to mystical *theōria*. The Pseudo-Dionysius sees in the eucharistic bread and wine beautiful symbols of our peaceful participation in Christ's divinity, but he also longs for the veil of symbolism to be drawn aside so that we might contemplate the intelligible reality;[39] and Maximus's *Mystagōgia* never actually discusses the anaphora or the transformation of the elements, and it presents the rest of the liturgy as principally a succession of soteriological *tableaux*: our reception of the "life-giving elements," he says, *denotes* a communion and identity with Christ according to that participation through likeness (*kata methexin endechomenēn di' homoiotēs*) whereby man becomes God, but what we await now in faith and receive in the Spirit we will really partake of in the world to come, when we will truly see Christ translating us into himself (*metapoiountas hēmas pros heauton*) and granting us those "archetypal mysteries" that are here represented by "perceptible symbols."[40] In either case, some part of the realism of Gregory of Nyssa or John Chrysostom is absent, and some small but inviolate interval appears to have been introduced between the truth of our dwelling in the temple of Christ's body and the palpable actuality of the Eucharist's fleshly economies. Still, even these more "theoretic" approaches to the Eucharist are colored by a profound certainty that the mystery is a revelation to us of the exchange that occurs between us and Christ, and so between our humanity and his divinity, in his saving action for and in us. For the Pseudo-Dionysius, the eucharistic celebration concerns the descent of God in Christ and our total incorporation in him through con-

---

38. *Fides Ecclesiae Orientalis seu Gabrielis Metropolitae Philadelphiensis Opuscula*, Latin trans. and ed. Richard Simon (Paris, 1671), pp. 3–4.

39. Dionysius the Areopagite, *Ecclesiastica hierarchia* 3.3.1–2; PG 3:428.

40. Maximus the Confessor, *Mystagogia* 24; PG 91:704–5.

tinuous participation. And Maximus's allegory in every instance points toward the truth of this saving commerce, which allows us to offer ourselves in the self-oblation of Christ: the first entry of the bishop into the church and ascent into the altar, he says, is a representation of Christ's whole mission in the flesh, from his incarnation to his ascension, whereby he freed our nature from slavery to sin and death, gave us in exchange for our destructive passions his healing and life-giving passion, and entered in for us before the heavenly throne;[41] and the entry of the people into the church represents their conversion from ignorance and vice to knowledge and virtue, as they enter with Christ into God's goodness;[42] and in the sealing of the doors, and reading of the Gospel, and the mysteries that ensue, Christ leads the faithful, who have received the Spirit of adoption, and have been divinized by love and made like him through participation, up to the Father.[43]

By far, however, it is the other tendency that predominates in Byzantine mystagogy: a profound sense that Christ is really present in all that we see, hear, and taste in the liturgy, so totally so that every aspect of his divine and human life is being shared with us in everything that occurs, transforming us by drawing us, at every juncture, more deeply into the saving history of the incarnation. Germanos's commentary already obeys this logic, and Cabasilas is an inheritor of this tradition (though he is able to give it greater theological stability than his predecessors). It reaches its most elaborate expression in the eleventh-century *Protheōria* of Nicholas of Andida, which Theodore of Andida revised in the eleventh or twelfth century.[44] In this work, images of Christ's mission are found everywhere in the liturgy: lying on the paten, the *prosphora* is the Christ child, and the asterisk placed above it the star of Bethlehem; the *prothesis* represents the first thirty years of Jesus's life; the priest who performs the first part of the liturgy is John the Baptist; the reading of the Gospel is the beginning of Christ's ministry; and so on. Nor are these aspects simply of an edifying ecclesial pageant: what one sees are not simply symbols, but manifestations, of the incarnate Christ, making his sacrifice present in our midst. And as, in the East, commendably, the church never actually forgot that for the church fathers it is the entirety of Christ's mission—from his sacrificial descent into our nature to his sacrificial ascent with our nature into

41. Maximus the Confessor, *Mystagogia* 8; PG 91:688.
42. Maximus the Confessor, *Mystagogia* 9; PG 91:688-89.
43. Maximus the Confessor, *Mystagogia* 13; PG 91:692.
44. Nicholas of Andida, *Brevis commentatio de divinae liturgiae symbolis ac mysteriis*, PG 140:417-68.

the heavenly holy of holies—that constitutes his reconciling oblation for us,[45] even the most implausible allegorical readings of the rite have the great virtue of imparting a clear sense of the totality of Christ's action on behalf of the world; the whole course of Christ's life, as he recapitulates the human in himself and then makes it a pure offering of atonement, is his sacrifice, and the whole course of the liturgy is a progressive integration of worshipers into the journey of his life, into that wondrous exchange he brings about within the temple of his body, so that when at last the consecrated elements "scatter" him among his worshipers, his life has become theirs. As Theodore the Studite remarks, the Eucharist is the mystery that recapitulates the entire dispensation of salvation; nor is it an image only, but the very reality of what it portrays.[46]

I am tempted to speak here of Orthodox mystagogy's "allegorical realism," by which I mean its adoption of a sacramental narrative dependent upon the *reality* of our divinizing union with God in Christ: in the Eucharist we see and are ever more drawn into the simultaneity of the incarnation's double motion, wherein (to employ a figure from a rather remote source) the journey of the Son of God into the far country is also, at the same time, the homecoming of the Son of Man; and because it is the Eucharist where we know this, we do not see this reconciliation simply as a redemptive rupture of our experience of the world, a sheer interruption that invades but does not inhabit our earthly time, leaving us to drift about in the ontic aftermath, but as a real presence here and now, with a real temporal axis and palpable form, a true time and place where we partake—in every sense—of the Godhead Christ has brought near. The Eucharist is that same place of atonement (*hilastērion*), then, that Christ is: the chiasmus where eternity and time are poured out into one another, where eternity empties itself and time is raised into the eternal, and where we lose ourselves in the abyss of divine beauty to find ourselves restored in the utterly humble abandon of divine love. The mystical spectacle that Byzantine commentators see in the Divine Liturgy is like the hidden language of the Logos that Origen sees written everywhere in Scripture; and the deeply rational imagination with which it is abstracted from its "text" is no less an achievement of theological vision than his luxuriant exegeses. The great Eastern liturgical allegories point to the same dogmatic

45. Indeed, to cite one example at random, Patriarch Eutychius of Constantinople (ca. 512–582) could call the last supper Christ's self-sacrifice and state that it was on rising from the dead that Christ offered himself to the Father for humanity's salvation: *Sermo de Paschate et de Sacrosancta Eucharistia*, PG 86:2396–97.

46. Theodore the Studite, *Antirrheticus* 1; PG 99:340–41.

intuitions that inform the language of the threefold sacrificial economy discussed above: they find in the celebration of the mystery a divine dramaturgy, unfolding for us, with inexhaustible vividness, the single reality of Christ's sacrifice in becoming a man, dying, rising, and ascending; the abiding presence of his offering upon the heavenly altar and in his body, where he accomplishes our everlasting *Yom Kippur*, so to speak; and the ever immediate availability for us of what he accomplishes on our behalf, the impartation of the *Shekhinah*, our transformation in him. More simply, they display, with wonderful embroideries and brightly illuminated margins, the truth that he, our God, is now food and drink for us, and so he dwells in us and we in him.

IV

This brings me to my final theme: that of indwelling. After all, Christian talk of divinization is essentially the christological radicalization of the language of indwelling that lies at the heart of the biblical account of God's election of Israel, and indeed of God's election of creation, for himself, from nothingness. God fashions the world to be the theater of his glory and intends to transfigure it, so Paul says, in the manifestation of "the glorious liberty of the children of God" (Rom. 8:19–21).[47] And God has dwelt in the flesh of Israel, in the midst of the nation, though he is the boundless God: "Will God indeed dwell on the earth? behold, the heaven and heaven of heavens cannot contain thee; how much less this house that I have builded?" (1 Kings 8:27); and yet he *does* bring his glory to rest within the temple—"So that the priests could not stand to minister because of the cloud: for the glory of the LORD had filled the house of the LORD" (1 Kings 8:11)—just as he did within the tent of meeting's tabernacle: "And Moses was not able to enter into the tent of the congregation, because the cloud abode thereon, and the glory of the LORD filled the tabernacle" (Exod. 40:35). It is this same glory that then tabernacles in the body of the Mother of God: "The Holy Ghost shall come upon thee, and the power of the Highest shall overshadow thee: therefore also that holy thing which shall be born of thee shall be called the Son of God" (Luke 1:35). And in Christ, whose death rends the veil of the holy of holies, and who is himself the temple that, once torn down, is built again in three days, the inner tabernacle and the hidden glory are made manifest, as the light of the transfiguration and the light of the

---

47. Biblical quotations in this paragraph are from the King James Version.

resurrection, which enters into us precisely because "the cup of blessing which we bless is . . . the communion of the blood of Christ [and] the bread which we break [is] . . . the communion of the body of Christ" (1 Cor. 10:16). Thus we are heirs to the promise—which Christ himself confirms in John 10:34—adumbrated in Psalm 82:6: "Ye are gods; and all of you are children of the most High." I recite all these pericopes because it is only within this web of associations, I want very emphatically to urge, that one can grasp the Orthodox understanding of Eucharist, and of the Eucharist as a sacrifice, and of how the mystery conducts us ever more deeply into the salvation Christ has wrought for us and the whole cosmos. When I speak of indwelling, I mean only this: that all of Scripture testifies to the fact that, throughout the history of God's mighty and saving acts, in creation, the election of Israel, and the calling of the nations, God has been preparing for himself a habitation; and in the incarnation, death, resurrection, and ascension of God the Son, he has brought to completion that *qurban*, that reconciling "drawing nigh" of and to the "exceeding glory," which is his plan for creation from before the foundations of the world. And as nature groans in anticipation of the day when all flesh will see that glory (Rom. 8:22), and all that Christ has accomplished will be consummated for creation, and God will be all and all (1 Cor. 15:28), we now enter, physically and spiritually, into that reconciling union in the Eucharist, and in the whole Christian life that it sustains. As Palamas writes,

[T]he Son of God, in his incomparable love for humanity, not only united his divine hypostasis to our nature, assuming both an animated body and rational soul so as "to appear upon the earth and live among men" (Baruch 3:38), but unites himself—O miracle of such incomparable superabundance!—even with human hypostases, mingling himself with each of the faithful through communion in his holy body, and becomes one body with us and transforms us into the temple of the whole Godhead—for in the body of Christ itself "dwelt all the fullness of the Godhead bodily" (Col. 2:9).[48]

48. Grégoire Palamas, *Défense des saints hésychastes*, French trans. and ed. Jean Meyendorff, critical edition, Spicilegium Sacrum Lovaniense, fasc. 30–1 (Louvain, 1959), p. 193. [. . . μὴ μόνον τὴν ἑαυτοῦ θεϊκὴν ὑπόστασιν ὁ τοῦ Θεοῦ Υἱός, βαβαὶ τῆς ἀνεικάστου φιλανθρωπίας, ἥνωσε τῇ καθ᾽ ἡμᾶς φύσει, καὶ σῶμα λαβὼν ἔμψυχον καὶ ψυχὴν ἔννουν "ἐπὶ γῆς ὤφθη καὶ τοῖς ἀνθρώποις συνανεστράφη," ἀλλ᾽ ὦ θαύματος οὐδεμίαν ἀπολείποντος ὑπερβολήν, καὶ αὐταῖς ἀνθρωπίναις ὑποστάσεσιν ἑνοῦται, τῶν πιστευόντων ἑκάστῳ συνανακιρνῶν ἑαυτὸν διὰ τῆς τοῦ ἁγίου σώματος αὐτοῦ μεταλήψεως, καὶ σύσσωμος

The theme of divine indwelling, as the proper grammar for understanding the Eucharist and the way it reveals to us the *liaison* of the divine and human in Christ's eternal priesthood, everywhere pervades—and achieves its richest and most developed expression in—what, to my mind, is one of the finest texts of sacramental theology that Christian thought, East or West, can boast: Nicholas Cabasilas's *The Life in Christ*. In this book (to which I should like briefly to surrender my prerogatives as this essay's voice) the sacraments—baptism, chrismation, and Eucharist, to be precise—are treated as moments of divine advent that reconstitute us as vessels of divine glory, even as they draw us into the shelter of Christ, who now embraces all of creation in his incarnate presence. The Lord promised, says Cabasilas, not only to be present with his saints, but, more, to make his abode in them: a union Scripture portrays in terms of inhabitant and dwelling, or of vine and branch, or of a marriage, or of members and head (though, of course, none of these images is adequate to the reality).[49] To dwell in Christ is to find in him all that suffices for us, and more:

> There is nothing of which the saints are in need which He is not Himself. He gives them birth, growth, and nourishment; He is life and breath. By means of Himself He forms an eye for them and, in addition, gives them light and enables them to see Himself. He is the one who feeds and is Himself the Food; it is He who provides the Bread of life and who is Himself what He provides. He is life for those who live, the sweet odour for those who breathe, the garment for those who would be clothed. Indeed, He is the one who enables us to walk; He Himself is the way (Jn. 14:6), and in addition He is the lodging on the way and its destination.[50]

It is through the sacraments, says Cabasilas, that he thus dwells in us and we in him.[51] "This is the way we draw this life into our souls—by being initiated into the mysteries, being washed and anointed and partaking of the holy table. When we do these things, Christ comes and dwells in us, He is united to us and grows into one with us. He stifles sin in us and infuses

ἡμῖν γίνεται καὶ ναὸν τῆς ὅλης θεότητος ἡμᾶς ἀπεργάζεται, καὶ γὰρ ἐν αὐτῷ τοῦ Χριστοῦ σώματι "κατοικεῖ πᾶν τὸ πλήρωμα τῆς θεότητος σωματικῶς."]

49. Nicholas Cabasilas, *The Life in Christ*, 1.6–8, trans. Carmino J. deCantanzaro (Crestwood, NY: St. Vladimir's Seminary Press, 1998), pp. 45–46; the Greek text, and the paragraph numbers, are taken from Nicolas Cabasilas, *La Vie en Christ*, French trans. and ed. Marie-Hélène Congourdeau, 2 vols. (Paris: Les Éditions du Cerf, 1989), 1:80–82.

50. Cabasilas, *Vie* 1.13, vol. 1, pp. 86–88; *Life*, pp. 47–48.

51. Cabasilas, *Vie* 1.19–20, vol. 1, pp. 94–96; *Life*, pp. 49–50.

into us His own life and merit and makes us to share in His victory."[52] Here is where, indeed, we are given power to become children of God: just as he "united our nature to Himself through the flesh which He assumed," so he "also united each of us to His own flesh by the power of the Mysteries."[53] And of the mysteries, the Eucharist is the most perfect, because it consummates all others; while baptism and chrism, respectively, cleanse and enliven us, the holy table transforms us entirely into Christ's own state: "The clay is no longer clay when it has received the royal likeness but is already the Body of the King."[54] In this final sanctifying encounter with Christ's real presence, "[t]hat of which we partake is not something of Him, but Himself. It is not some ray and light which we receive in our souls, but the very orb of the sun. So we dwell in Him and are indwelt and become one spirit with Him. The soul and the body and all their faculties forthwith become spiritual, for our souls, our bodies and blood, are united with His."[55] "O how great are the Mysteries!" expostulates Cabasilas. "What a thing it is for Christ's mind to be mingled with ours, our will to be blended with His, our body with His Body and our blood with His Blood!"[56] The Eucharist leads us to the summit of all goodness, the final aim of all human effort: "in it we obtain God Himself, and God is united with us in the most perfect union."[57] And, again, the Eucharist is the *site* where the exchange of natures that in Christ is one life and person becomes for us a real exchange of our natural substance for his.

> He did not merely clothe Himself in a body, but He also assumed a soul, mind, and will and everything else that is human, in order to be united to the whole of our nature and completely penetrate us and resolve us into Himself by totally joining what is His to that which is ours.
>
> . . . So perfectly has He coalesced with that which He has taken that He imparts Himself to us by giving us what He has assumed from us. As we partake of His human Body and Blood we receive God Himself into our souls. It is thus God's Body and Blood which we receive, His soul, mind, and will, no less than those of His humanity.[58]

52. Cabasilas, *Vie* 1.54, vol. 1, p. 124; *Life*, p. 60.
53. Cabasilas, *Vie* 1.32, vol. 1, p. 106; *Life*, p. 53.
54. Cabasilas, *Vie* 4.2, vol. 1, pp. 262–64; *Life*, pp. 113–14.
55. Cabasilas, *Vie* 4.8, vol. 1, p. 268; *Life*, pp. 115–16.
56. Cabasilas, *Vie* 4.9, vol. 1, p. 270; *Life*, p. 116.
57. Cabasilas, *Vie* 4.10, vol. 1, p. 270; *Life*, p. 116.
58. Cabasilas, *Vie* 4.26, vol. 1, pp. 286–88; *Life*, p. 122.

We are so penetrated then by Christ's presence, says Cabasilas, employing a venerable analogy common to Christology and mysticism alike, that we are like iron penetrated by fire, assuming the properties of the fire into itself; and "Christ infuses Himself into us and mingles Himself with us," says Cabasilas. "He changes and transforms us into Himself, as a small drop of water is changed by being poured into an immense sea of ointment."[59] Thus Christ liberates all who were slaves: "He makes them to share in His body, blood, spirit, and everything that is His. It is thus that He recreated us and set us free and deified us as He, the healthful, free, and true God mingled Himself with us."[60]

I should add that, for Cabasilas, this talk of divine indwelling and human deification does not concern simply the personal experience of individual Christians. As for the fathers, but with perhaps a keener emphasis, divinization for Cabasilas is an experience of the church as a whole, and it is within the mystical body of Christ, indeed by becoming that mystical body, that Christians have access to the immediate presence of the divinized humanity made available in the bread and wine of communion. The advent of Christ in us is the work of the sanctifying grace of the Holy Spirit, which is first and foremost a Pentecostal reality; it is only in the outpouring of the Spirit upon the entire church that God comes to tabernacle in the flesh of those who have been made members of his body. This is especially clear in Cabasilas's *Commentary on the Divine Liturgy*, not only in his defense of the Orthodox belief that only in the epiclesis is the consecration of the elements complete, but also in his explanation of the eucharistic *zeon* (the addition of warm water to the chalice of consecrated wine, which the deacon quietly announces as "The fervency of faith, full of the Holy Spirit"): after reminding us, in good Byzantine mystagogical fashion, that in the holy bread we have seen a symbolic representation of the whole pattern of Christ's work on our behalf—the infant Christ, Christ led to his death, his crucifixion and the piercing of his side—and that we have also seen the bread genuinely transformed into the body that suffered for us, rose from the dead, ascended, and is now seated at the right hand of the Father, Cabasilas argues that it is fitting that there should in addition be a proper symbol of the later fulfillment of these great works, a representation of the ultimate effects of salvation, in order that the liturgy might be complete; hence the *zeon*: "What is the effect and the result of the sufferings and works and teaching of Christ? Considered in relation to

59. Cabasilas, *Vie* 4.28, vol. 1, p. 290; *Life*, p. 123.
60. Cabasilas, *Vie* 4.83, vol. 1, pp. 334–36; *Life*, p. 140.

ourselves, it is nothing other than the descent of the Holy Spirit upon the Church."[61] And it is the Spirit's descent upon the church, which is what always makes Christ present to us in the sacraments, that *is* our divinization: our being made one body in the one bread we share, and that body the body of Christ:

> For the holy mysteries are the Body and Blood of Christ, which are to the Church true food and drink. When she partakes of them, she does not transform them into the human body, as we do with ordinary food, but she is changed into them, for the higher and divine element overcomes the earthly one. When iron is placed in the fire, it becomes fire; it does not, however, give the fire the properties of iron; and just as when we see white-hot iron it seems to be fire and not metal, since all the characteristics of the iron have been destroyed by the action of the fire, so, if one could see the church of Christ, insofar as she is united to him and shares in his sacred Body, one would see nothing other than the Body of the Lord. Because of this, Paul wrote: "Ye are the body of Christ, and members in particular."[62]

I should also add that for Cabasilas the reality of the Eucharist, of course, must possess a fairly radically eschatological significance; for the end of all things will be the glorification of all of creation in Christ, when the divine indwelling will become perfect and God, in Christ, will be all in all. This is the end for which creation was shaped, for which God became a man and joined created nature to his, and for which we have been redeemed. And so the Eucharist, in its very physicality, insofar as it is both food and God's presence for us, is a proleptic foretaste of that ultimate reality when—to employ an image favored by many a modern Orthodox theologian—the world will be like the burning bush, entirely permeated with divine fire, but unconsumed. The bread we eat, says Cabasilas, is no less than the dazzlingly radiant flesh of Christ that, in coming again, will make all things to shine with its own brilliance;[63] this bread is as much now as we can bear of that final reality, but it prepares us by supplying us with gifts to bear with us to the wedding feast of the kingdom: those who have eaten of it "have enjoyed the . . . delight of the banquet though they do not obtain it fully yet; but when Christ has been manifested they will perceive more clearly

61. Cabasilas, *Explication* 37.3, pp. 226–28; *Commentary*, pp. 90–91.
62. Cabasilas, *Explication* 38.2, p. 230; *Commentary*, pp. 91–92.
63. Cabasilas, *Vie* 4.102, vol. 1, p. 350; *Life*, p. 146.

what it is they have brought with them." And this, adds Cabasilas, is "how the kingdom of heaven is within us (Luke 17:21)."[64]

V

I shall conclude by observing first that, in the light of these reflections, the language of the threefold economy of sacrifice from which I began my account of Orthodox eucharistic theology more fully discloses its intrinsic logic, and shows itself to be not simply a loose but evocative aggregation of motifs, pointing toward a splendid mystery, but an exceedingly lucid explication of the way in which the biblical understanding of sacrifice and atonement is summed up and recapitulated in the indissoluble unity between Christ's saving action and the celebration of the sacrament. If the sacrificial *transitus* that Christ perfects is that same reconciling approach to the divine glory that God commands of Israel, which restores the peaceful economy of that glory's approach to and indwelling of his creatures, and if this act of atonement is oriented, as Hebrew prophecy and Christian *kērygma* proclaim, toward the eschatological reign of God's glory in the peace of all creation, then the Eucharist can have no fuller meaning. The bread and wine of communion, the body and blood of Christ: this is our surety that creation has indeed been reconciled to God, within its humblest and most material dailiness, and that God henceforth truly indwells and transfigures creation, and will transfigure it fully in himself. *Theōsis*, in both its human and cosmic aspects, is the truth of Israel's *qurban*; and the Eucharist, as our *qurbana*, is our perpetual entry into that union of creation with its God that occurs forever in the unity of the God-man.

Perhaps this is the obvious conclusion of my argument; but I wish to add to it another observation. Above, when I cited a passage from Maximus the Confessor's *Mystagōgia*,[65] I neglected to call attention to a fairly salient feature of its argument: that Maximus sees in the Eucharist, in the sanctifying power of our sacramental entry into Christ's body, the full Trinitarian economy of salvation. In the mystery, we receive the Spirit of adoption, who unites us to Christ, who deifies us in himself and leads us up to the Father. This is of course completely right: in keeping with the dogmatically and philosophically absolutely necessary prem-

---

64. Cabasilas, *Vie* 4.108–9, vol. 1, p. 356; *Life*, pp. 147–48.
65. Maximus the Confessor, *Mystagōgia* 13; PG 91:692.

ise that the *taxis* of the economic Trinity is the *taxis* of the immanent Trinity, and that therefore the order of salvation is a revelation, quite actually, of how God is God, one must say that the Eucharist is in some essential way a Trinitarian event of divine disclosure. Moreover, this is not only apposite to the theme of sacrifice, but provides us with its inmost truth and ultimate rationale. For if it is the sacramental grace that the advent of the Spirit accomplishes that saves us by joining us to Christ, so that we are united *by* God, *in* God, *to* God, then the bread and wine we eat in the Eucharist make concrete that most extreme extent of a Trinitarian outpouring and tabernacling that do nothing less than seize us up into God's triune life. This, after all, is the truth of sacrifice: that behind the mystery of Christ's offering up of himself lies the infinite truth of a God whose life is always already one of self-outpouring in another, as well as the response of love that that outpouring allows; it is because God, as God, is already thus somehow sacrificial in this biblical sense—that is, a God who goes forth from himself, and in so doing also "draws nigh"—that it is explicable that God should go forth from himself again in creating, shaping for himself a habitation in that which is not God; that he should pour forth in creatures his presence— as their glory and their sanctification—though they can add nothing to him, because he loves them from the sheer superabundance of his self-emptying love; that he should go forth to dwell in the body of Israel; and that he should go forth yet again in the sublime self-outpouring of *kenōsis* for the salvation of his creatures, thus showing that no matter how far we venture from him, he has already, in his eternal life of love, ventured infinitely farther than we can ever reach. Because God is Trinity, Christ's self-oblation for us is a naturally divine act; and the divinization of creation that it brings about is the perfect revelation of the *qurban* of God's Trinitarian being; and we see this in the Eucharist. We, in some real sense, taste and are nourished by the whole mystery of our redemption, our "sacrificial" entry into the Trinity's life, and so in the drama of offering up and receiving, we gain some slight but true glimpse of the Trinity's infinite beauty.

To sum the matter up with a brevity that to this point has eluded me: in eucharistic communion, to the degree that the eyes of faith are illuminated by the wisdom that only the Spirit can impart, we see the truth of our divinization in Christ, taste the deep mystery that underlies the creation of the world, discover the hidden depths of our own nature, anticipate in our flesh the glory to which all the world has been called from eternity, and distantly, finitely experience, in the passing moment, the infinite life of

God—all under the unsurpassably ordinary form of bread and wine. And so, again, the shape of Christology is the shape of sacramental sacrifice: in this radical availability of the infinite in a condition of absolute inanition, and our transformation thereby into creatures capable of participating in the infinite's absolute plenitude, every offering of ourselves is made possible—and every offering is made complete.

ELEVEN

Matter, Monism, and Narrative

An Essay on the Metaphysics of *Paradise Lost*

I

It would be in keeping with at least one strand of conventional critical wisdom to assign John Milton a place in the long Western tradition of philosophical "monism," in either of two senses: that of a simple material monism, a "panhylism," that denies any ultimate distinction between "matter" and "mind"; or that of a genuinely metaphysical monism that (in venerable Neoplatonic fashion) regards all Being as somehow one, from the divine source of existence down to the realm of inanimate matter. Certainly, in the case of the former sense of "monism," it may safely be affirmed that Milton did indeed regard all created beings, whether "physical" or "spiritual," as subsisting in a single *materia prima*, and so understood intellect to be merely a more highly refined manifestation—a more ethereal impress—of creation's one underlying substance than, say, flesh; but this is a view tremendously complicated by Milton's convictions regarding the freedom of the spiritual will and the autonomy of spiritual identity (as I shall argue below). As for the second species of monism, the belief that the hierarchy of Being is a system of divine emanation and return, or at least that the created order is ontologically continuous with the divine, it is altogether more uncertain in what sense this position can be ascribed to Milton without serious qualifications, despite a seeming abundance of evidence favoring such a move.

In the fifth book of *Paradise Lost*, Adam says to the angel Raphael:

Well hast thou taught the way that might direct
Our knowledge, and the scale of nature set
From centre to circumference, whereon
In contemplation of created things
By steps we may ascend to God. (ll. 508–512)[1]

If one examines the dialogue between Adam and Raphael from which these lines are drawn in the light of the seventh chapter of Milton's *De doctrina Christiana* (which rather notoriously contains his explicit rejection of the Christian orthodoxy of a *creatio ex nihilo* in favor of his own peculiar doctrine of a creation *de Deo*), it is quite tempting to suppose that Milton's particular form of monism had the shape of the *scala naturae* to which Adam adverts in this passage; but I wish to argue that to regard this "ladder" as the guiding metaphor of Milton's metaphysics of creation would be a mistake. In point of fact, the idea of the cosmos as ordered in a *scala naturae* is only a monist principle when it is taken to imply a *vinculum entis*: that is, when it is employed to describe not merely the notional hierarchy of the discrete levels of creation, but the order of ontic mediations whereby all things enjoy a real participation in the first good, the one real Being. And it is just this conception of creation that is absent from Milton's theology; the scale of nature Raphael describes to Adam is an image of the universal striving of creation upward toward God, and of the way in which the various orders of creation reflect more of the divine nature as they approach the heavenly realm, but it does not describe the metaphysical unity of God and creation.

Two questions, therefore, motivate this essay: First, in what sense was Milton a metaphysical monist, and second, what appeal could such monism have held for Milton the epic poet? I have not, therefore, undertaken a strictly critical task, but one that might loosely be described as philological: I am interested in the origins, nature, and significance of the kind of language Milton used concerning the relation of God and his creatures.

II

J. H. Adamson, in an impressive (and influential) attempt to exonerate Milton's cosmology of the charge of heterodoxy, has argued that there exists a venerable Christian tradition of theologians who have espoused

---

1. This and all subsequent quotations from *Paradise Lost* are taken from Alastair Fowler's edition (New York: Longman, 1971).

a doctrine of *creatio ex Deo*, in whose company Milton belongs.[2] It is an asseveration at once attractive and perhaps seemingly plausible, but also quite demonstrably false; the tradition of which Adamson speaks is more a phantom than a fact of Christian history, and even the tenuous reality it does possess sets it quite apart from the kind of speculations in which Milton indulged; but Adamson's argument is at least instructively false.

During the early centuries of Christian history, the theology of the church was influenced decisively by only two traditions of pagan philosophy whose premises could be called "monist": that of the Stoa and that of Neoplatonism. The panhylism and "pantheistic materialism"[3] of Stoicism arose from the simple conviction that a thing must possess a body in order to be—that existence is extension, so to speak—and that, therefore, all things are united in a common materiality. This became a metaphysical monism properly speaking where Stoicism distinguished between the passive, plastic principle of unformed matter and the *logos* or *pneuma* (conceived of as a rarefied, vaporous, and omnipervasive fire that organizes, animates, and preserves all things): this divine and rational fire is at once, according to the Stoics, the primordial unity from which all things have emerged, the spirit of which all individual spirits—all immanent *logoi*—are emanations, and the undifferentiated singularity into which all existing things will be dissolved at the end of time in the universal ecpyrosis. Neoplatonic monism, on the other hand, the monism of Plotinus, Porphyry, Proclus, and the rest of the tradition as it evolved from the third through the sixth centuries, proved ultimately more of a temptation to Christian theology; though the metaphysical terminology of Stoicism was employed loosely by several of the third-century Christian apologists, almost with a perverse indifference to the philosophy from which it originated, only the ethics and eschatology of Stoicism had any influence over the theology of the church during the golden age of patristic literature. More appealing to the minds of men such as the Cappadocian fathers, Ambrose, or Augustine were the vast cosmic harmonies that one found in the emanationist systems of Neoplatonism. This tradition's disdain for the aesthetic world in the light of the noetic (which caused it to relegate matter to that place in the hier-

2. J. H. Adamson, "The Creation," in W. B. Hunter, C. A. Patrides, and J. H. Adamson, *Bright Essence* (Salt Lake City: University of Utah Press, 1971), p. 81. This essay still provides the most thoroughgoing attempt to "place" Milton within a genealogy of "orthodox" Christian monism.

3. J. N. D. Kelly, *Early Christian Doctrines*, 5th ed. (London: A. & C. Black, 1977), pp. 17–18.

archy of emanations from the One where reality, at its far periphery, is exhausted and verges on unbeing, on evil and darkness),[4] the conviction that the intellectual soul possesses a natural affinity with the divine and that the mind becomes a reflection of the divine in the exact degree to which it is able to prescind itself from the mutable world of things and events, the tendency to view God as wholly beyond the realm of space and time—all these things engaged the imaginations of the Christian philosophers of the Greco-Roman world.

And yet, for all of its philosophical awkwardness, the doctrine of *creatio ex nihilo*, according to which God formed the world from neither any preexistent and independent matter (as had the demiurge of the *Timaeus* and the *Philebus*), nor from any aspect of himself discharged for the purpose (which to pious ears could sound scarcely less depraved than the divine dégringolade into materiality of certain gnostic systems), but solely through the exercise of his sovereign will, was stridently affirmed both by such sober characters as Justin Martyr and Athanasius and by such unintentionally exotic thinkers as Clement of Alexandria and Origen. And this was so quite simply because no other doctrine could be reconciled with the patristic understanding of the austere monotheism of the Scriptures that the church inherited from Judaism.

In his eagerness to find Milton a place in the succession of a forgotten strand of Christian orthodoxy, Adamson somewhat indiscriminately combines, and somewhat misconstrues, the theologies of a number of Christian philosophers. For instance, he describes Gregory of Nyssa (d. ca. 395) as an *ex Deo* theologian,[5] and then likens Gregory's theology to Milton's on the rather insubstantial grounds that for both thinkers God is a spirit able to produce bodies by a kind of external efficiency.[6] It would perhaps be well to linger over this point for a short time, because it brings into relief a number of themes that will prove crucial below. Adamson's argument is based on the fact that Gregory chose to resolve the conundrum of how spirit can cause material things by redefining material bodies as no more than convergences of intelligible qualities (such as extension, weight, color, duration), which, if they could be decorticated from the material substrate, would leave nothing at all behind. In creation, Gregory argued, God first established the thoughts and concepts (*ennoiai* and

---

4. W. R. Inge, *The Philosophy of Plotinus*, 2 vols. (London: Longmans, Green, & Co., 1918), p. 130.

5. Adamson, "The Creation," p. 84.

6. Adamson, "The Creation," p. 90.

noēmata) whereof matter is composed,[7] and it is these ideas (*logoi*) that, taken together, form bodies;[8] thus material reality is only a concourse of intelligible potentialities (*dynameis*) proceeding from a noetic nature.[9] Obviously, what concerned Gregory was the need to explain how the origins of the sensible world could lie in the intelligible without falling back on Platonic dualism or a certain kind of Neoplatonic emanationism. In fact, to call this a doctrine of *creatio ex Deo* in even the broadest sense would be to ignore the real nature and purpose of Gregory's argument. Richard Sorabji, for example, suggests that Gregory's view was in fact a precursor of Berkeleyan idealism, and so chooses to translate Gregory's terms *ennoiai* and *noēmata* as "thoughts" *tout court*, asserting that were these words taken to mean "things thought," Gregory could not be said to have solved the causal problem.[10] This is true enough, but Gregory was at no time concerned with the question of where the world had come from—he had no doubt that it came from nothing—but was concerned only with how *such* a world should have been created; hence "things thought" (signifying distinct "intelligible elements") works just as well. Gregory, after all, subscribed to the presupposition of his age that between a cause and its effect there must be some real likeness or affinity, and so he was somewhat hard pressed to say how the composite, mutable fabric of the sensible world should have been the creation of a simple, changeless, and incorporeal God. Adamson seems to be under the influence of an exceedingly poor (though influential) article by H. A. Wolfson from 1970,[11] according to which Gregory's real intention was to describe a gross emanation of matter directly from the divine *ousia*. In reality, the confluence of intelligible qualities Gregory describes is no more than a plausible account of *creatio ex nihilo*: the world is composed of elements that one can conceive of as being caused by a wholly noetic nature, while all that mediates between God and the world is the divine will, of which creation is an energy.[12]

7. Gregory of Nyssa, *In Hexaemeron*, in Patrologia Graeca (hereinafter PG) 44:68D–72C.

8. Gregory of Nyssa, *De anima et resurrectione*, PG 46:124B–D.

9. Gregory of Nyssa, *De hominis opificio* 24; PG 44:212D–213C.

10. Richard Sorabji, *Time, Creation, and the Continuum* (London: Duckworth, 1983), p. 291.

11. H. A. Wolfson, "The Identification of *Ex Nihilo* with Emanation in Gregory of Nyssa," *Harvard Theological Review* 63 (1970): 53–60.

12. Gregory of Nyssa, *De hominis opificio* 33; PG 44:212B–C; cf. Gregory of Nyssa, *Oratio catechetica*, ed. James Herbert Srawley (Cambridge: Cambridge University Press, 1903), ch. 24, p. 91; Gregory of Nyssa, *In illud: Tunc et ipse filius*, PG 44:1312A.

The significance of the case of Gregory here lies in just how clearly it illustrates the divergence of the strategies pursued by Milton on the one hand and by the classical tradition of Neoplatonism (and Neoplatonic Christianity) on the other. Gregory, like Plotinus, and like various other pagan and Christian philosophers, wished to reconcile the material order with the spiritual source of all things by, so to speak, deconstructing the very concept of matter; and, in fact, Gregory was more successful than Plotinus; but it is just this that Milton does not care to do. For Milton, matter is as real as God himself, and the ascent to God is an escape from neither materiality nor time. It is true that Adamson can point to Pseudo-Dionysius the Areopagite,[13] according to whom all the principles and causes of creation, including even the material cause, come from God, and who ascribed to God both unity and multiplicity;[14] or to John Scotus Eriugena, who regarded not only the ideas, but also the primal causes of all things, as residing in God, who furthermore regarded creation as being God himself through and through,[15] and who interpreted the phrase *creatio ex nihilo* by construing this *nihil* as a reference to the divine essence itself (so designated by virtue of its absolute transcendence of *things*);[16] and so on. But none of these figures make out materiality as such to be continuous with the divine (which Milton did); and even the most unarguably monist of these figures, John Scotus Eriugena, adopted Gregory of Nyssa's account of matter in order to exorcise its irksome presence from his system.

Of course, the Neoplatonism of western Europe from the fifteenth to the seventeenth century (that of the Florentine academy or of the Cambridge Platonists) was colored by kabbalistic speculations, by the Florentine fascination with the *Corpus Hermeticum*, and by various aspects of the fashionable occult. Adamson could more plausibly have argued that Milton's theology was in many ways a product of its time and that his monism has more in common with Renaissance esotericism than with classical Christianity; but here as well, though this is a sounder course to follow, one can still be distracted too easily from consideration of what distinguishes Milton's *de Deo* account of creation as original and peculiar to him. But, then again, Adamson is far too concerned to place Milton

13. Adamson, "The Creation," p. 84.

14. Stephen Gersch, *From Iamblichus to Eriugena* (Leiden: Brill, 1978), p. 141.

15. Dermot Moran, *The Philosophy of John Scottus Eriugena* (Cambridge: Cambridge University Press, 1989), pp. 233–34.

16. Jaroslav Pelikan, *The Christian Tradition*, vol. 3, *The Growth of Medieval Christianity* (Chicago: University of Chicago Press, 1978), p. 102.

in some tradition of "metaphysical monism" to notice what it is that sets Milton apart.

> Thinkers in this tradition assert that we are not in a dualistic universe of body and spirit, matter and form, but rather in a monistic universe where everything that exists is a gradation of one prime matter. At the lower end of the scale are what a dualist would call material things: rocks, earth, flesh and money. At the other end of the scale are the immaterial things such as soul, spirit, and pure intelligence. God is neither one nor the other; he is beyond both, above any concept that may be formed of him. But the higher end of the scale is nearer God, in a sense more like him, than the lower end.[17]

Actually, it would be difficult to make quite this account correspond with the thought of the great majority of the thinkers Adamson treats as metaphysical monists; it is however a good description of what one does find in Milton's thought: a particular kind of mingling of the scholastic category of *materia prima* or *materia universalis* with a *scala naturae* cosmology. But when Adamson subjoins to these lines the remark that "Materiality is that in the universe which has emanated farthest from its source; it is the thing most unlike God," he goes too far: Milton was not a Neoplatonist (at least, not in any classical sense), and his concept of divine transcendence, like his concept of materiality, is far more ambiguous and far more subversive of orthodox Christian theology than his able apologist would have it.

III

Here it would perhaps be wise to consider what Milton's writings actually say about the nature and origin of material reality. The creation narrative of the seventh book of *Paradise Lost*, which recounts the divine Son's labors to effect his Father's will, by organizing the primordial chaos into a world, follows a pattern familiar from other contemporary accounts, such as Du Bartas's *La Sepmaine* of 1587 or Hugo Grotius's *Adamus Exul* of 1601.[18] Where, however, Milton is anything but conventional is in his

---

17. Adamson, "The Creation," pp. 88–89.

18. Watson Kirkconnell, *The Celestial Cycle* (New York: Gordian Press, 1967), pp. 47–49.

account of how the primal stuff of creation came into being. "O Adam,"
expostulates Raphael,

> one almighty is, from whom
> All things proceed, and up to him return,
> If not depraved from good, created all
> Such to perfection, one first matter all
> Indued with various forms, various degrees
> Of substance, and in things that live, of life. (5.469–474)

There is nothing exceptional in the idea of prime matter; it was a commonplace of ancient, medieval, and Renaissance philosophy. And the concept
of matter as a real, tractable, and universal "substance," passively susceptible to form, but constituting an almost organic unity of all things, was
known to Milton from any number of sources, such as John Weemes's
Potraiture of the Image of God in Man.[19] But the idea takes on a special significance in Milton's theology. In *De doctrina Christiana* Milton asserts
that before matter was embellished by the accession of forms, it arose as
an "efflux of deity."[20]

> [I]t is an argument of supreme power and goodness, that such diversified,
> multiform, and inexhaustible virtue should exist and be *substantially* in-
> herent in God (for that virtue cannot be *accidental* which admits of de-
> grees, and of augmentation or remission, according to his pleasure) and
> that this diversified and substantial virtue should not remain dormant
> within the Deity, but should be diffused and propagated and extended as
> far and in such manner as he himself may will. For the original matter of
> which we speak, is not to be looked upon as an evil or trivial thing, but
> as intrinsically good, and the chief productive stock of every subsequent
> good. It was a substance, and derivable from no other source than from
> the fountain of every substance, though at first confused and formless,
> being afterwards adorned and digested into order by the hand of God.[21]

19. Three editions, 1627–1636.

20. John Milton, *A Treatise on Christian Doctrine*, the translation of *De doctrina* by
Bishop Charles R. Sumner, in *The Prose Works of John Milton*, vols. 4–5 (London: Henry G.
Bohn, 1853), p. 180. The use of this, the standard English translation, must always be
a cautious one, as Bishop Sumner was not always as scrupulous in his terminological
distinctions as was Milton (especially in Milton's demarcation of the terms *essentia* and
substantia).

21. Milton, *Christian Doctrine*, p. 179.

This, then, is how Milton resolves the classical problem of how body can arise from a spiritual cause: by imagining an original material nature that is (at least *in potentia*) an eternal aspect of God.

Certain critics have striven to dispel the impression that Milton departed so far from the traditional metaphysics of Christian theology as to expound the theory of a gross emanation of matter from the divine. Walter Clyde Curry, for instance, makes much of the fact that in the passage just quoted Milton speaks only of a *vis corporea* in the divine *substantia*,[22] a power inherent in God that produces matter when it is actualized. Milton himself expands on his assertions regarding this corporeal power by observing that "spirit being the more excellent substance, virtually and eminently contains within itself the inferior one; as the spiritual and rational faculty contains the corporeal, that is, the sentient and vegetative faculty."[23] Adamson hears here an echo of scholastic nomenclature; he points out that the words "virtually" and "eminently" were "scholastic terms used to indicate that a thing possessed or contained another thing in a more perfect or higher manner than was required for formal possession of it."[24] He notes also that Aquinas saw God as "virtually" containing all things, just as effects virtually inhere in their causes in a fashion appropriate to the nature of those causes; he explains that in Duns Scotus's system of eminence and dependence, God is the "final cause" of all things, and so contains all actuality and perfection; and he thus concludes that it is in this manner that one may (and Milton did) speak of spirit containing material reality while remaining itself entirely uncontained.[25]

Certainly Curry and Adamson are justified in making these claims, and much of Milton's language affords them ample encouragement. But one should be wary of drawing too facile an analogy between Milton's terminology and that of scholastic theology: whether the scholastic language be Thomist or Scotist or other, it is meant to describe a purely causal relationship, either aetiological or teleological. Milton is not concerned to show how spirit causally *contains* matter, but how the divine is the original source of material substance; the "diversified and substantial virtue" of which Milton speaks is one that can be "diffused and propagated and extended," which is scarcely the kind of language that would be congenial to Thomist or Scotist metaphysics. Of course, Milton was at times an awkward logician, and some

---

22. Walter Clyde Curry, *Milton's Ontology, Cosmogony, and Physics* (Lexington: University of Kentucky Press, 1966), p. 181.
23. Milton, *Christian Doctrine*, p. 181.
24. Adamson, "The Creation," p. 89.
25. Adamson, "The Creation," p. 89.

confusion attends any reading of such passages as these, but if one examines other aspects of the arguments they present, one suspects that Curry and Adamson have missed a fairly crucial tendency in Milton's reasoning. In defense of his thesis, Milton adduces those verses of Scripture (Rom. 11:36; 1 Cor. 8:6; and—at something of a stretch—Heb. 2:11) that state that all things have their origin in God, taking these handy pericopes to mean that God, as prime cause, embraces all four of the Aristotelian orders of causality, including the material.[26] By itself, this already seems an extraordinary line of argument, but as it proceeds it becomes even more unusual. In its essence, Milton continues, matter is incorruptible;[27] and this he deduces not from the inherent simplicity of *materia universalis*, but from the incorruptibility of the divine nature from which it proceeds. It would seem that for Milton the substance of matter is not entirely divorced from the substance of God. This much is evident where, in defense of his contention that body emanates from spirit, he writes: "Nor, lastly, can it be understood in what sense God can properly be called infinite if he be capable of receiving any accession whatever; which would be the case if anything could exist in the nature of things, which had not first been of God and in God."[28] Rather than reasoning that the divine infinity is transcendent of all such categories as accession and change, he implicitly accepts the premise that the substance of creation has implications for one's understanding of the divine substance.

Similar conclusions might be drawn from certain lines in *Paradise Lost*. When Adam says to God,

> No need that thou
> Shouldst propagate, already infinite;
> And through all numbers absolute, though one . . . (8.419–421),

or when Michael tells Adam that God's

> omnipresence fills
> Land, sea, and air, and every kind that lives,
> Fomented by his virtual power and warmed . . . (11.336–338),

one can read either passage as no more than a pious affirmation of divine ubiquity. When, however, God the Father is portrayed as saying to the Son,

26. Milton, *Christian Doctrine*, pp. 178–79.
27. Milton, *Christian Doctrine*, p. 180.
28. Milton, *Christian Doctrine*, p. 181.

Boundless the deep, because I am who fill
Infinitude, nor vacuous the space ... (7.168–169),

one should be struck by the strangeness of the logic. Just as Milton conceived of the divine immutability as implying the necessary incorruptibility of matter, so the poet here seems to suggest that the infinity of God is the basis of the infinity and limitless plenitude of physical space: that is, that divine infinity is one with the boundlessness of the universe God pervades. The peculiarity of such language is the conflation it effects between the two quite distinct concepts of divine infinity and divine omnipresence. In the traditional semantics of Christian theology, God may be called infinite in regard to his wisdom and power, or the absolute simplicity of his essence and his freedom from all contradiction, or the unboundedness with which he is what he is, or his perfect transcendence of all the categories of sensible and temporal existence, but never as an assertion of his spatial infinitude; and while it is considered a dogmatic necessity to ascribe to God omnipresence *in* space, it would be regarded as merely nonsensical to construe this as meaning anything like infinite extension.

By none of which I mean to suggest that I suspect Milton of attributing to God some kind of corporeity; certainly his God ineffably transcends those created natures he comprehends. But, in designating the divine substance as the fountain of all substance, Milton is doing more than simply positing an abstract causal relation between God and creation; spirit contains inferior substance within itself, according to Milton, not only "virtually," but "essentially."[29] God may transcend material reality, but he is not finally "wholly other" than matter. Thus, while it would be misguided to conclude that Milton's God is somehow material, one cannot say Milton would reject the idea that the material cosmos is in some sense an aspect of God's being. One should not overlook how thoroughly for Milton the material realm is implicated in the divine life, nor should one ignore his apparent conviction that the material cosmos is a substantial ramification of the divine presence.

IV

How then, at the last, can Milton be called a metaphysical monist?

29. Milton, *Christian Doctrine*, p. 181.

>   ... one almighty is, from whom
> All things proceed, and up to him return,
> If not depraved from good, created all
> Such to perfection, one first matter all,
> Indued with various forms, various degrees
> Of substance, and in things that live, of life;
> But more refined, more spirituous, and pure,
> As nearer to him placed or nearer tending
> Each in their several active spheres assigned,
> Till body up to spirit work, in bounds
> Proportioned to each kind. So from the root
> Springs lighter the green stalk, from thence the leaves
> More airy, last the bright consummate flower
> Spirits odorous breathes: flowers and their fruit
> Man's nourishment, by gradual scale sublimed
> To vital spirits aspire, to animal,
> To intellectual, give both life and sense,
> Fancy and understanding, whence the soul
> Reason receives, and reason is her being. . . .
>   . . . time may come when men
> With angels may participate, and find
> No inconvenient diet, nor too light fare:
> And from these corporal nutriments perhaps
> Your bodies may at last turn all to spirit. (5.469–487, 493–497)

The temptation is powerful to view this as some variation of the Neoplatonic narrative: one sees the divine diastole and systole, the striving of all reality upward toward God, the ordered hierarchy of being and becoming, and the superiority of spirit over matter. But while Milton's philosophy may possess something of Neoplatonism's form, it retains virtually nothing of the substance. Raphael tells Adam that the spiritual is more proximate to God than the corporeal, but by this he means not that spirit is radically different from flesh, not that spirit is an entirely noetic reality aware of itself as emanating from and ultimately identical with the wholly noetic Godhead, but simply that spirit is the more refined organization of universal matter. In rising up to a higher spiritual nature, humanity would be no nearer the kind of unity with God—the kind of identity—that Neoplatonic tradition regards as the final truth of all reality; there is no point in this scale of nature where the soul, liberated from the multiplicity and finitude of material existence, would discover itself to be indistinguishable from the first source of all things. Indeed, the free, irreducibly autonomous, and individual character of the soul (which is to say, of the rational, sentient person) is never questioned in Milton's theology. In whatever sense one could call Milton a monist, it would not involve a continuity between God and the soul considered as an intelligent individuality; in terms derived from Milton's trinitarian theology (to be touched on below), one's substance may emerge from God's substance, but one's essence is—though creaturely—one's own; in the Neoplatonic argot, one's *psychē* is not a lower manifestation of *nous*.

What does unite all things, however, with one another and even with God, is that primal matter, that ubiquitous stuff, which has its origin in the divine.

> . . . food alike those pure
> Intelligential substances require,
> As doth your rational; and both contain
> Within them every lower faculty
> Of sense, whereby they hear, see, smell, touch, taste,
> Tasting concoct, digest, assimilate,
> And corporeal to incorporeal turn.
> For know, whatever was created, needs
> To be sustained and fed; of elements
> The grosser feeds the purer. (5.407–416)

This fragment of Raphael's discourse to Adam contains a concise depiction of Milton's account of the great *regressus* of creation up to its creator: corporeal existence is not merely an emanation of the spiritual, but is sublated in it; and spiritual reality is nearer to God because it is more like materiality as it exists in the divine substance under the form of a *vis corporea*. Thus what for Neoplatonic thought constitutes the lowest emanation, the periphery, the dark outward of Being, is for Milton the foundation of metaphysical unity between God and all the realms of created existence. When, in lines quoted above, Milton employs an alchemical metaphor to describe the ascent of creation to God, he does not do so allegorically; he is merely explaining one material process by reference to another.

This, then, is Miltonic "monism" (a term that, for want of any better, one must still employ): the oneness of the primary matter underlying the diversity of all of its secondary manifestations constitutes also a continuity of substance between things and God, such that all substances are contained by the divine substance. In some ways, it is nearer Stoic than Neoplatonic monism. God, one might almost say, is present in the very fabric of things; for it is matter that is the ground of all unity, and matter—whether crass or ethereal—that participates in the eternal and immutable substantiality of God.

V

In attributing to Milton this species of "panhylism" (so to speak), I have still not indicated all the ways in which he distinguished himself as an original thinker. It is remarkable not only how far he was willing to exalt every aspect of the earthly realm into the heavenly, but also how near to earthly life he allowed his depiction of heavenly life to approach. For instance, Milton clearly entertained notions peculiar to himself regarding the question of angelic corporeity. It is true that Milton was hardly unique in imagining angels to be material beings; it was quite a prevalent feature of much of the Protestant angelology of his time; but the idea for Milton had implications that for most angelologists would have been more than a little distasteful. Though Milton's language concerning angelic materiality is often as ambiguous as that of many of his contemporaries (such as Robert Fludd, Archbishop Ussher, or Richard Baxter), he, as did they, ascribed to angels bodies that are aery and subtle.[30] Numerous passages in *Paradise Lost* portray angels as requiring time to traverse space, as encountering physical opposition, as shaping objects from elemental matter, and so forth. At the same time,

> spirits that live throughout
> Vital in every part, not as frail man
> In entrails, heart or head, liver or reins,
> Cannot but by annihilating die;
> Nor in their liquid texture mortal wound
> Receive, no more than can the fluid air:
> All heart they live, all head, all eye, all ear,
> All intellect, all sense, and as they please,
> They limb themselves, and colour, shape or size
> Assume, as likes them best, condense or rare. (6.344–354)

30. Robert H. West, *Milton and the Angels* (Athens: University of Georgia Press, 1955), p. 137.

The simplicity and protean plasticity of Milton's angels suggest that he subscribed to the then widespread theory that angelic bodies are constituted from "quintessential" or "ethereal" matter—that is, the celestial fire of the highest heaven—and indeed his language regarding angelic matter in *Paradise Lost* incorporates such terms as "empyreal substance" (1.118), "ethereal substance" (6.330), "empyreal forme" (6.433), and "ethereal mould" (2.139). In this respect, Milton was quite conventional. Even in ascribing erotic embraces to spiritual beings (8.620–629), Milton was not entirely alone (Henry More allowed the angels their carnal revels). But Milton clearly departs from just about all traditional angelology when he describes the meal shared by Adam and Raphael:

> So down they sat,
> And to their viands fell, nor seemingly
> The angel, nor in mist, the common gloss
> Of theologians, but with keen despatch
> Of real hunger, and concoctive heat
> To transubstantiate; what redounds, transpires
> Through spirits with ease; nor wonder; if by fire
> Of sooty coal the empiric alchemist
> Can turn, or hold it possible to turn
> Metals of drossiest ore to perfect gold
> As from the mine. (5.433–443)

He dismisses out of hand the Thomistic doctrine that angels appear to men in bodies gathered from mist and the attendant assertion that, even though angels may seem to eat (as in the case of the three who visited Abraham), it is an illusion; and he goes well beyond the Scotist claim that in fact angels do in such cases manage to ingest food but, having no use for it, cannot digest it. Milton's angels consume human fare, are nourished by it, and expel its residue; and this is quite remarkable: even theorists of Milton's time willing to entertain the notion of angelic edacity, such as Henry More or Joseph Glanvill, imagined only that angels are sustained by heavenly victuals, and certainly would not have approved of the idea that an ethereal body could assimilate the gross earthly diet of mortals.[31] But Milton does not hesitate to follow the logic of his beliefs to even its most ungainly conclusions: if all creation consists in various interconnected grades of one prime matter, and if the properties of the lower grades are possessed in a

---

31. West, *Milton and the Angels*, p. 167.

more perfect way by the higher, then spiritual beings must be capable of assuming inferior forms of materiality into their own substances. Spirit and flesh are not to be regarded as different realities altogether, but as different manifestations of one reality. It is for this reason that Milton, when touching upon the question of human nature, declines to treat body and soul as separate economies. "The whole man is soul, and the soul man, that is to say, a body, or substance individual, animated, sensitive, and rational; and . . . the breath of life was neither a part of the divine essence, nor the soul itself, but as it were an inspiration of some divine virtue fitted for the exercise of life and reason, and infused into the organic body; for man himself, the whole man, when finally created, is called in express terms 'a living soul.'"[32] Nowhere, in Milton's view, does any aspect of created being (save that of the abstract category of individuality, essence) fall outside of the consubstantiality of material existence.

Again, I should say, when I exclude what I vaguely describe as "essence" from so otherwise sweeping a declaration, I am making slightly illicit use of a term proper to Milton's Trinitarian theology. I refer specifically to the fifth chapter of *De doctrina Christiana*, book 1 (the chapter that has won Milton the reputation of being a latter-day Arian). It is here that he chooses, despite the etymological impropriety of the move, to translate the Greek *hypostasis* not as *substantia*, but as *essentia*, and to treat both as synonymous with *ousia*,[33] the consequence of which is Milton's conviction that he is justified in rejecting the traditional ascription to God of three *hypostaseis*, as in his eyes it is tantamount to tritheism, to a doctrine of three *ousiai* or essences. Moreover, he sharply distinguishes between the terms "essence" and "substance," meaning by the former the unique and incommunicable Godhead of the Father and by the latter that which the Father is able to impart to the Son in limited measure. God's essence, that is to say, is that whereby he is himself, in his abstractly considered "whoness." By "substance," I suspect, Milton means something akin to the Greek *hypokeimenon*, or substrate, or concrete nature; which, in his metaphysics, would be that which is capable of *apospasma* (impartation) and *apaugasma* (effulgence or efflux). Thus W. B. Hunter can speak of "the substratum or stuff of God the Father which underlies the Son."[34] No less is it God's own substance that is the source of every substance. One might

32. Milton, *Christian Doctrine*, p. 190.
33. Milton, *Christian Doctrine*, p. 190.
34. W. B. Hunter, "Further Definitions: Milton's Theological Vocabulary," in Hunter, Patrides, and Adamson, *Bright Essence*, p. 15.

argue that one reason for Milton's defiance of orthodox Trinitarian theology, his insistence on the creatureliness and subordinate status of the
divine Son, is that were the eternal and essential Godhead communicable,
were it capable of being imparted to that which shares in or is derived from
the divine substance, it would draw a theologian of Milton's inclinations
perilously close to the position of one who is unable to affirm an absolute
distinction between God and his creation.

Which leads one to remark that it is not true of Milton only that in
his cosmology spiritual existence is near to earthly life, or contains it, but
also that in his system God is himself immediately involved in the created
universe: so much so in fact that, on the one hand, the divine Creator who
directly shares the divine substance is present to the cosmos as the highest
of creatures and that, on the other hand, the same divine substance is implicated in all the finite substances of which it is the real source. But Milton
should still not be called a Neoplatonist; strictly speaking, it is neither
human beings nor angels that emanate from God, but only the substratum
from which flesh and spirit alike are formed; abstract essence—"whoness"
—is not dissoluble into a higher kind of identity; there is no such thing as
coessentiality. Still, it remains proper to ascribe to the Son a consubstantiality with the divine, and even perhaps to say (though certainly one departs considerably from Milton's language in so phrasing it) that creation
is too, in its fashion, somehow consubstantial with the divine. It is, at least,
not separate from the life of God.

VI

The question that remains is what appeal this kind of metaphysical monism might have had for Milton not as a theologian, but as an epic poet;
and it is this thoroughly speculative question for which the rest of this
essay has been the pretext. It would, of course, be an unprofitable task to
attempt to discover whether it was the poetic or the theological imagination that was dominant in Milton, but I suspect (if only out of a charitable
desire to pay more attention to the thing he did with genius than to the
thing at which he was so mediocre) it was the former.

In speaking of what I have called Milton's "panhylism," I have failed
to mention one fairly notable contemporary of Milton's whose thought
in many ways resembles his on this topic—that is, Thomas Hobbes. Mo-
tivated in part by an annoying tendency to demand complete univocity
of whatever kind of predication he used, Hobbes was almost a Stoic in his

disdain for the pious fiction of an immaterial reality; all substance, he contended, must possess quantity, spirit no less than flesh or stones.[35] I raise the point now because closely akin to this assumption was the refusal on the part of Hobbes to tolerate the notion of an eternity that is a fixed, unitary, and nonsuccessive *now*, to which all time is fully present;[36] to him, eternity without duration or succession was as risible an idea as infinity without extension. And, in point of fact, Milton too seems to have been uninterested in the orthodox image of God as untouched by the flow of time, as entirely transcendent of event and progression. If nothing else, Milton regarded God's ontological superiority over creation as involving of necessity a temporal anteriority. Thus, in Milton's depiction of creation, the divine Son is begotten in time, the effluence of matter occurs at some particular moment, the making of the heavens and all below them is an episode in the divine life. More than that, even in the depths of his eternity, the God of Milton has a hidden history: "As to the actions of God before the foundation of the world, it would be the height of folly to inquire into them, and almost equally so to attempt a solution of the question."[37] So writes Milton, and indeed most Christian theologians throughout history would be inclined to agree; but for these latter the folly would reside in the sheer meaninglessness of the question. With rare exception, and with virtually none since Augustine, Christian theologians have regarded time as a creature; the transcendent and immutable God in his unapproachable stillness has no before or after. But Milton's thinking tends another way: "[I]t is not imaginable that God should have been wholly occupied from eternity in decreeing that which was to be created in a period of six days, and which, after having been governed in divers manner for a few thousand years, was finally to be received into an immutable state with himself, or to be rejected from his presence for all eternity."[38] Thus, just as he could supplant the idea of divine omnipresence in space with one of infinite extension, so Milton replaces the concept of omnipresence in time with one of infinite duration. Successiveness is part of God from eternity. Surely it is this notion that lies behind the description of the celestial sequence of days and nights with which the sixth book of *Paradise Lost* commences (ll. 4–12). Milton's God is the God of event, action, story, presence; and so space and time—the theater of these things—are part of divine existence.

35. Thomas Hobbes, *Leviathan* (Chicago: Encyclopaedia Britannica, 1952), pp. 174–76, 258–60.
36. Milton, *Christian Doctrine*, p. 271.
37. Milton, *Christian Doctrine*, pp. 169–70.
38. Milton, *Christian Doctrine*, p. 170.

In one sense, then, Milton was an eminently traditional Christian: in good patristic fashion, when dealing with an outwardly Neoplatonic scheme (that of a hierarchically ordered universe rising from gross matter up to pure spirit), he was obliged to transform what was originally an ontological description into a historical narrative. The static morphology of Being became the course of events; what for Neoplatonism was the shape of things became for Christianity the story of things. That is to say, in the Christian imagination Being is also history, and so ultimate meaning resides not only in the simultaneous relation of God to the individual soul within every moment, but also in the historical horizon. Thus the *egressus* from and *regressus* to God of Neoplatonism is for the Christian that which transpires between creation and the eschaton; the hierarchy of ontic mediations becomes the story of redemption, of the Mediator. In this respect, at least, Milton was pursuing the same end as Gregory of Nyssa: both wished to reconcile the beautiful harmonies of Neoplatonism with the radical historicality of Christianity, and so reconcile Being to existence. Beyond that, though, Milton and Gregory (the *ex nihilo* theologian, whose thought retained the absolute demarcation between eternity and time) went separate ways. For the poet, there was nothing, not even God, that was not somehow historical, and so therefore potentially story. Even those aspects of the Christian doctrine that the church had declared to be "not story"—such as the begetting of the Son before the ages—Milton made into narrative again. More than that, in positing a real continuity between God and creation, Milton made all history in some sense part of the one story of God; he was even willing to entertain the heterodox notion of a successively eternal God, infinitely extended into the past and anticipating a future that somehow he does not yet possess, rather than allow any part of Being to lie absolutely beyond the possibility of theological or epic narrative, beyond story. It is true that the God of *Paradise Lost* maintains "his holy rest / Through all eternity." It is also true that Milton resolved the diastema between the temporal and the eternal not by imagining a nisus of the alone to the alone, to the undifferentiated silence of the One, but by, so to speak, drawing God down into eventuality. One finds in *Paradise Lost* (though on a much vaster scale) something like what one finds in Homer (for example), for whom the gods do not occupy a proper place *in illo tempore*, but always belong to the contrariety and momentariness of history—so that, say, a goddess can be wounded by a mortal on the field of battle to which she has descended. In Milton's poetic vision, Being becomes epic.

Paradise Lost ends in the somber glow of a tender pathos, a sense both of hope and of a tragedy whose finality God has mercifully averted.

The world was all before them, where to choose
Their place of rest, and providence their guide:
They hand in hand with wandering steps and slow,
Through Eden took their solitary way. (12.646–649)

When Adam and Eve leave the garden, they leave the realm in which the story of God and man was to be told and enter into the profane realm of history, the exile of profane space, but it is a historical prospect bounded by eschatological promises of a redemption from the threat of meaninglessness and final destruction. Milton does not write of a human history fixed in the gaze of God in his eternal stillness, but of a divine story in which the subversive histories of the fallen are involved. But evil cannot ultimately subvert the narrative, as that narrative is one with the life of God, and so evil is always set finally in the context of God's design; nothing escapes the circle of God's determinations. The promise with which the parents of humanity leave paradise is that the divine narrative will yet triumph over the inanity, the chaos, of history, through restoration and a final act of inclusion and exclusion. The perfect God of beginning and end, the alpha and omega, is not merely immutably the same God, but is the God who is who he is at creation and who will establish himself again when he becomes all in all. One might even say that the divine story virtually and eminently contains human history.

As I have said, it would be vain to speculate as to whether the poet or the theologian predominated in Milton, but it is obvious what appeal his theology might have for the writer of epic verse, or how it might arise from a fundamentally narrative imagination: if the material universe is part of God's infinity, if the history of creation is an event in the life of the eternal, an episode in the endless successiveness of the divine narrative, then every aspect of Being is joined in one great story, one epic, which—though no created mind can comprehend it—lies open to the advances of the poet. It is in this regard that one should most emphatically reject the definition of Milton as a Neoplatonist, because the highest good of Neoplatonism rested in the flight from story, upward into the silence and plenitude of the One; but in the Miltonic scheme of things, all is story, all may be told. Perhaps then the first question asked by this essay—in what sense one may call Milton a monist—can be answered in these terms: he was not simply a "metaphysical," nor even a "material," but a *narrative* monist. This, I suspect, is more important for an understanding of Milton's philosophical tendencies than such subordinate considerations as where he might fit in the tradition of Christian metaphysics. It is, moreover, the most elegant conclusion that I can draw from the argument of these pages.

TWELVE

The Whole Humanity

Gregory of Nyssa's Critique of Slavery in Light of His Eschatology

I

Nowhere in the literary remains of antiquity is there another document quite comparable to Gregory of Nyssa's fourth homily on the book of Ecclesiastes:[1] certainly no other ancient text still known to us—Christian, Jewish, or pagan—contains so fierce, unequivocal, and indignant a condemnation of the institution of slavery.[2] Not that it constitutes a particularly lengthy treatise: it is only a part of the sermon itself, a brief exegetical excursus on Ecclesiastes 2:7 ("I got me male and female slaves, and had my home-born slaves as well"), but it is a passage of remarkable rhetorical intensity. In it Gregory treats slavery not as a luxury that should be indulged in only temperately (as might an Epicurean), nor as a necessary domestic economy too often abused by arrogant or brutal slave owners (as might a Stoic like Seneca or a Christian like John Chrysostom), but as intrinsically sinful, opposed to God's actions in creation, salvation, and the church, and essentially incompatible with the gospel. Of course, in an age when an economy sustained otherwise than by bonded servitude was

---

1. Gregory, *In Ecclesiasten homiliae*, in Gregorii Nysseni Opera (hereinafter GNO), ed. Werner Jaeger et al. (Leiden: Brill, 1958–), 5:334–52.

2. Unless one includes in this consideration other texts by Gregory himself, where remarks regarding slavery (of a more diffuse and occasional nature) are also found. See especially, *Contra Eunomium* 1, GNO 1:178; *De oratione dominica* 5, GNO 7/2:70–71; and *De beatitudinis* 3, GNO 7/2:105–6, 126–27. For a fuller treatment of the broader scope of Gregory's remarks on slavery and freedom, see Daniel F. Stramara Jr., "Gregory of Nyssa: An Ardent Abolitionist?" *St. Vladimir's Theological Quarterly* 41, no. 1 (1997): 37–60.

all but unimaginable, the question of abolition was simply never raised, and so the apparent uniqueness of Gregory's sermon is, in one sense, entirely unsurprising. Gregory lived at a time, after all, when the response of Christian theologians to slavery ranged from—at best—resigned acceptance to—at worst—vigorous advocacy.[3] But, then, this makes all the more perplexing the question of how one is to account for Gregory's eccentricity. Various influences on his thinking could of course be cited—most notably, perhaps, that of his revered teacher and sister Macrina, who had prevailed upon Gregory's mother to live a common life with her servants—but this could at best help to explain only Gregory's general distaste for the institution; it would still not account for the sheer uncompromising vehemence of his denunciations.

Of course, the Ecclesiastes homilies were preached during the Great Lent of 379, when Gregory's moral authority had no doubt been considerably fortified by his recent triumphant return to Nyssa from two years of banishment under the Arian emperor Valens; it is appropriate that they should sternly admonish, reprove, and summon to repentance, in order to prepare his congregation for Easter, and explicable that they should be marked by a certain confidence of tone. Moreover, ever since Constantine had granted churches the power of *manumissio in ecclesia* in 321, propertied Christians had often made Easter an occasion for emancipating slaves, and Gregory was obviously encouraging his parishioners to adopt an established custom.[4] Even so, he could, in all likelihood, have quite effectively recommended manumission—simply as a salutary spiritual hygiene, or as a gesture of benevolence—in terms calculated better to persuade than to offend. But Gregory's sermon goes well beyond any mere exhortation to the exercise of charity; he leaves no quarter for pious slave owners to console themselves that they, at any rate, are merciful masters, not tyrants, but stewards of souls, generous enough to liberate the occasional worthy servant, but responsible enough to govern others justly. Gregory's language is neither mild nor politic: for anyone to presume mastery over another, he says, is the grossest arrogance, a challenge to and robbery of God, to whom alone we all belong;[5] to deprive a person of the freedom granted all of us by God is to overturn divine law, which gives us no prerogatives one over another (5:355); at what price, asks Gregory, can

---

3. Examples of the latter can be found in the work of Theodoret (*De providentia divina* 7) or in that of Gregory's elder brother Basil (*De Spiritu Sancto* 20).

4. See Gregory, *In sanctam ecclesiam*, GNO 9:250–51.

5. Gregory, *In Ecclesiasten homiliae*, GNO 5:344. Parenthetical page references in the following text are to this work.

one purchase the image of God—God alone possesses the resources, but as divine gifts are irrevocable, and God's greatest gift to us is the liberty restored to us in salvation, it lies *not even in God's power* to enslave humanity (5:336); when a slave is bought, so are his or her possessions, but each person is set up by God as governor of the entire world, and no sum can purchase so vast an estate (5:336); the exchange of coin and receipt of deed may deceive you that you possess some superiority over another, but all are equal, prey to the same frailties, capable of the same joys, beneficiaries of the same salvation, and subject to the same judgment (5:337); we are equal in every respect (5:338) but—as Gregory phrases it—"You have divided human nature between slavery and mastery and have made it at once slave to itself and master over itself" (5:335).

Gregory's rhetoric, in short, presses well beyond the issue of mere manumission and adumbrates that of abolition; the logic seems as irresistible as it does anachronistic—and therein lies its mystery. If any part of Gregory's sermon perhaps provides a clue to the deeper currents of his thought, and to the stridency with which he expresses himself, it is this last phrase: "You have divided human nature. . . ." Perhaps it is only a rhetorical flourish, but it is an odd phrase in itself (in what sense, precisely, is a "nature" divisible?), and if one reads it according to the theological grammar established by Gregory's eschatology (particularly as developed in two treatises of 380, *On the Soul and Resurrection* and, most especially, *On the Making of Humanity*), it takes on a meaning at once unexpectedly literal and daringly speculative. This, at least, is my argument: the unique ferocity of Gregory's critique of slavery is understandable only in light of his eschatology; or, otherwise stated, Gregory's enmity toward the institution was the result of his habit of viewing all things (and especially human "nature") in an eschatological light.

II

Before proceeding, though, I should state an axiom that will govern the argument to follow: Christian eschatology, properly understood, is not only different from, but frequently inimical to, every worldly teleology. The eschatological concerns not the fulfillment of the immanent designs of "nature," history, consciousness, or destiny, but concerns rather a judgment that falls across all of these from beyond the totality—the cosmos—they describe, and that rescues creation from everything within them that obeys the logic of violence and death.

When, for instance, Aristotle distinguishes between those who are free by nature and "natural slaves," he does so teleologically, according to a science of the human essence and the end toward which it properly tends, and to a clear notion of what constitutes a degenerate or aberrant expression of the common nature.[6] Knowing the ends of humanity, he knows as well who is capable of them and who, deficient in nature, must serve as "a living tool."[7] The Aristotelian world is, to resort to a fashionable phrase, a hierarchy erected within totality, a closed order of immanence, within which every distinction is a difference in rank and natural prerogative: in such a world, nothing could be more obvious than the superiority of city over nature, reason over appetite, Greek over barbarian, man over woman, master over slave. The "violence of metaphysics" (another fashionable phrase)[8] always functions thus: the securing of first principles or foundations by which one may discern the essences of things, recognize the order of noble and base or good and bad, construct taxonomies, determine the difference between the ideal and its distorted reflection, know what ends are right and what measures expedient, decide how to govern and whom to rule, and understand the shape of destiny. This is perhaps no more true of Aristotle's discourse concerning nature than of Hegel's concerning history: and within either, instructively enough, slavery plays some necessary part, as belonging either to the just deployment of persons of varying capacity (in one case) or to the probationary maieutic of the master-slave dialectic (in the other). To describe the hierarchy of substances or the grand narrative of history is usually to justify one or another regime, or at least to describe its "necessity."

But eschatology, for Christian thought, concerns neither "nature" nor history, but the kingdom of God, which is, as the Gospels assert, adventitious to both: it comes suddenly, like a thief in the night, and so fulfills no immanent process, consummates none of our grand projects, reaps no harvest from history's "dialectic." Only thus will it complete all things. At the same time, the kingdom has already, at Easter, been made visible

---

6. See Aristotle, *Politics* 1254a–b, 1260a, 1280a.

7. Aristotle, *Nicomachean Ethics* 1160b; *Eudemian Ethics* 1241b.

8. Consider, for example, the words of Gianni Vattimo: "When Nietzsche speaks of metaphysics as an attempt to master the real by force, he does not describe a marginal characteristic of metaphysics but indicates its essence as it is delineated right from the first pages of Aristotle's *Metaphysics*, where knowledge is defined in relation to the possession of first principles" ("Towards an Ontology of Decline," in *Recoding Metaphysics: The New Italian Philosophy*, ed. Giovanni Borradori [Evanston, IL: Northwestern University Press, 1988], p. 64).

within history and now impends upon each moment, a word of judgment falling across all our immanent truths of power, privilege, or destiny. None of the founding gestures of a metaphysics suffice to secure reflection against this disruption. In the paschal light of the kingdom, the household, the city, the entire epic of civilization and culture are all denuded of the glamour of "necessity"; thought is deprived equally of the Platonic myth of *anamnēsis*, the recollection of immutable truths by eternal selves, and of the Hegelian myth of *Geist*, the totalization of history that abandons transient selves to a "spiritual" logic; and "human nature" is expelled from the stable regime of the Aristotelian *polis*. From the securer vantage of a fixed metaphysics, the eschatological must seem at best an insane act of speculative expenditure, one that casts aside all the hard-won profits of history's turmoils and tragedies at the prompting of an impossible hope; but eschatology opens the future as a horizon of hope only in taking leave of every idealism, indeed of every attempt to disclose a continuity between the stories humanity tells of its metaphysical pedigrees and the ultimate order of things, so as to resituate humanity in a narrative that places both origins and ends in the hands of the transcendent God. As a discourse entirely of the divine future, it reaffirms the sheer gratuity of creation, over against myths that would root the world in a divine or cosmic past, a theogony or primordial struggle, and so interrupts every self-aggrandizing saga of origins, of autochthony, and every taxonomy that sets persons in their proper places. Phrased simply, Christian eschatology, correctly grasped, should always constitute a provocation of the powers that prevail within, or the institutions that compose, a social world. The light of this absolute futurity should unsettle every present.

But, even if all of this is axiomatic, at least for the argument at hand, what sense does it make of Gregory's complaint against the slaveholder, "You have divided human nature"? Talk of "nature" scarcely seems to venture beyond the limits of a metaphysically determined world, with its immanent essentialisms. But this phrase may actually mark a profound inversion of categories: "human nature," understood as a worldly telos, however imagined, can at most confirm the orders and prudential necessities of a world; lifted up, however, into the eschatological consummation of creation that opens in Christ, as it is for Gregory, it can perhaps expose those orders and necessities as mere sinful conventions—but only if it is indeed so lifted up, rendered eschatological without reserve. This requires an altogether radical act of reconceptualization, and this is what Gregory's treatises from the year following the Ecclesiastes homilies provide.

III

On the face of it, admittedly, Gregory's own eschatology might well seem indistinguishable from one or another species of metaphysical closure, an idealist recuperation of history's vagaries into rational meaning, at once a barely regenerate Platonism and a foreshadowing of German idealism. One could view Gregory as the first metaphysician of history, the first to allow the Greek *logos* to be shaken by the historicality of Scripture, even a brilliant precursor of Hegel, but an idealist for all that. For him, the making and redemption of the world belong to a single great "process," by which is brought to pass a perfect creation, conceived and willed by God before the ages and residing eternally in his will; the entirety of time is an *akolouthia*, a gradual unfolding of God's eternal design, in time and by way of change. Creation is twofold, so to speak; or, in a sense, there are two creations, a prior (or eternal) creation that abides in God, as the end toward which all things are directed, for the sake of which all things are brought about; and a posterior creation, the temporal and cosmic exposition of this divine model, which from the creature's vantage precedes the ideal, but which is in fact guided by it. The idealist cast of such a scheme is scarcely difficult to see; and it is made especially obvious by Gregory's description of the fashioning of humanity in the divine will: from eternity, he says, God has conceived of humanity under the form of the ideal Human Being (*Anthrōpos*), the archetype and perfection of the human, a creature shaped entirely after the divine likeness, neither male nor female, possessed of divine virtues, deathless and entirely beautiful.[9] By all appearances, this is merely wholesome Christian Platonism. And yet this apparent idealization of humanity becomes at once unstable, and begins to divest itself of its ideality, where Gregory goes on to describe the first Human Person as comprising (as indeed being) the entire plenitude—*plērōma*—of all human beings, throughout all the ages, from first to last. In his reading of Genesis 1:26–27, Gregory takes the creation of humanity according to the divine image to refer not principally to Adam, but to this fullness of humankind, comprehended by God's "foresight" as "in a single body."[10] Adam and Eve, however superlatively endowed with the gifts of grace at their origin, constitute in Gregory's eyes only the first increments (so to speak) of that concrete community that, as a whole, reflects the beauty

---

9. See C. N. Tsirpanlis, "The Concept of Universal Salvation in Saint Gregory of Nyssa," in *Studia Patristica* XVII (Leuven: Peeters, 1982), 3:1132.

10. Gregory, *De hominis opificio* 16; Patrologia Graeca (hereinafter PG) 44:185C.

of its creator and that, in the fullness of its beauty, will come into being only at the end of its temporal *akolouthia*, when it will be recapitulated in Christ. The entirety of "the human" exists, until then, only in the purity of the divine wisdom, where it is comprehended "altogether" in its own fullness,[11] and here alone—in the coinherence of the "whole humanity"—has God fashioned a creature in the divine likeness: "Thus the 'Human Being according to the image' came into being, *the whole nature*, the God-like thing. And what thus came into being was, through omnipotent wisdom, not part of the whole, but *the entire plenitude of the nature* altogether."[12] It is this peculiar coincidence in Gregory's thought of the idea of *physis* with that of *plērōma* that marks an irreversible break from classic Platonism and that (more relevant to the matter at hand) makes somewhat unexpected sense of the use to which the word *physis* is put in the fourth sermon on Ecclesiastes.

Of course, whatever its novelty, Gregory's account of creation still seems to bear the semblance of an idealist metaphysics of some kind, a "rescue" of the doctrine of creation from its ungovernable arbitrariness by way of an ultimate ideality. Gregory's exegesis of Genesis bears more than a passing resemblance to Philo of Alexandria's, which also distinguishes the first account of humanity's creation from the second: the former, Philo (like Gregory) claims, concerns an ideal, divine humanity, shaped in God's eternal counsels before the beginning of the world, while the latter concerns the actual race of finite men and women who live and die in time.[13] But, for Philo, this primordial *Anthrōpos* is still a Platonic form: an interval remains between the two creations, a *chōrismos* between eternity and history, idea and image. In Gregory's account, however, the primal person is neither in any real sense preexistent, nor finally transcendent, of the plenitude of persons who come into being throughout time; persons are neither shadows of, nor separated participants in, human "nature," but are in fact its very substance.[14] Gregory's reading certainly resembles Philo's, but finally differs from it radically: Gregory submerges the ideal in the historical (rather than the reverse), while still allowing the "ideal" (which now should really be read as the "eschatological") to prevent the

---

11. Gregory, *De hominis opificio* 17; PG 44:189C.

12. Gregory, *De hominis opificio* 22; PG 44:204D.

13. See Philo of Alexandria, *De mundi opificio*, in *Opera quae supersunt*, ed. Leopoldus Cohn and Paulus Wendland, 7 vols. (Berlin: Reimeri, 1896–1930; reprint in 8 facsimiles, Berlin: W. de Gruyter, 1962–1963), 1:38.

14. See G. B. Ladner, "The Philosophical Anthropology of Saint Gregory of Nyssa," *Dumbarton Oaks Papers* 12 (1958): 82.

historical from assuming the aspect of an enclosed order oriented toward an immanent end. The first creation stands over against—in judgment— any attempt to wrest a meaning, natural privilege, or "destiny" from the prudent arrangements and sinful ambitions of history by sacrificing the good of particular persons, because it is precisely the full community of persons throughout time that God elects as the divine image, truth, and glory. At the same time, the very openness of history, thus liberated from its worldly end, also stands over against any ideality that might serve to reduce this perfect and primordial creation to an abstraction. If the ideal and the actual constitute not two realities, but only two sides of what ultimately stands as a single reality, a kind of reciprocal critique must pass continually between them, such that neither ever suffices to explain or "found" itself.

Which is to say, perhaps, that "the eschatological" names that species of thought in which history's truth and the truth of history's disruption uniquely coincide. Still, within this very indistinction of ideal from actual, inasmuch as the reconciliation of its terms occurs under the form of an *akolouthia*, a certain division remains, between the innocence of time and the violence of history, between the good creation God wills and the destructive fictions of a fallen world. This is the ironic power of the eschatological, which makes every moment within time one of discrimination, a *critical* moment. Gregory's sense of this division is probably most vividly expressed in the form of a speculative mythology he devises concerning what might have been had we not fallen: but for sin, he opines, humanity would have propagated itself in a more angelic fashion; only God's foresight separated the race into distinct sexes, so that even when deprived of the properties necessary for celestial procreation (whatever those might be), humanity could bring the race to its foreordained plenitude.[15] Gregory's prudery aside, the important idea here is that God brings the good creation he wills to pass in spite of sin, both in and against human history, and never ceases to tell the story he intends for creation, despite our apostasy from that story. But for sin, says Gregory, God's design would have still *unfolded*, but peacefully, continuously, from potentialities established in creation at the beginning, according to an innate dynamism,[16] and everything would have come without obstruction to partake of divine glory.[17] Sin, though, inaugurates its own sequence, an *akolouthia* of priva-

---

15. Gregory, *De hominis opificio* 17; PG 44:189D.
16. Gregory, *De mortuis*, PG 46:517D.
17. Gregory, *De anima et resurrectione*, PG 46:105A.

tion and violence, spreading throughout time from its own principles;[18] and so God's gracious purpose appears in time always now as a counterhistory, the story of the church enmeshed in stories of power.[19] Humanity, as the *plērōma* of God's election, still possesses that deathless beauty that humanity, as a historical being, has lost; and God, seeing that beauty, draws all things on toward the glory originally intended for them,[20] by drawing persons into the body of Christ. In the incarnation, Christ enters into this human plenitude, into the midst of its temporal *akolouthia*, and orients it again toward its transcendent end. And because it is a living unity, the incarnation of the Logos must be of effect for the whole: Christ has, one might say, assumed the *plērōma*, in its history of fallenness, to restore to it the unity of his body—to which all persons properly always already belong[21]—and so his glory enters into all that is human.[22]

This is, of course, one of the points at which Gregory's theology opens out onto his notorious universalism: in the incarnation, Christ implicates the entire human plenitude in the pattern he establishes; such, says Gregory, is the indivisible solidarity of humanity that the *entire* body must ultimately be in unity with its head, either the first or the last Adam.[23] This is the meaning Gregory finds in John 20:17: when Christ goes to his God and Father, to the God and Father of his disciples, he presents all of humanity to God in himself;[24] and so Christ's obedience to the Father even unto death will be made complete only eschatologically, when humanity, gathered together in him, will be yielded up as one body to the Father in the Son's act of obedience, and God will be all in all.[25] Until then, the resurrection of Christ has already inaugurated an *akolouthia* of resurrection, so to speak, in humanity's one body:[26] an unfolding that cannot now cease (given the solidarity of human nature) until the last residue of sin—the last shadow of death—

18. Gregory, *De virginitate*, GNO 8/1:299.

19. See A. J. Philippou, "The Doctrine of Evil in St. Gregory of Nyssa," *Studia Patristica* 9 (1966): 252.

20. See Gregory, *Contra Eunomium* 3.2; GNO 2:74; *De infantibus qui praemature abripiuntur*, PG 46:177D–180D.

21. J. Laplace, "Introduction," in *Gregory of Nyssa, la création de l'homme*, Sources Chretiennes 6 (Paris: Éditions du Cert, 1943), p. 28.

22. Gregory, *In illud: Tunc et ipse filius*, PG 44:1313B.

23. See Jean Daniélou, "L'apocatastase chez Saint Grégoire de Nysse," *Recherches de science religieuse* 30 (1940): 345.

24. Gregory, *Refutatio confessione Eunomii*, GNO 2:346–47.

25. Gregory, *In illud*, PG 44:1316A–B.

26. Gregory, *Refutatio confessione Eunomii*, GNO 2:387.

has vanished.[27] But Easter will be complete only in the raising up of the whole humanity, in the final restoration of creation.

For now, in the between times, the mystical body of Christ, the church, is the only visible form of that redeemed nature; but the visible manifests the as yet invisible. As Hans Urs von Balthasar observes, "the theological unity of the Mystical Body of Christ is entirely based on this philosophical unity. The total Christ is none other than total humanity."[28] And, ultimately, there can be no true human unity, nor even any real unity between God and humanity, except in terms of the concrete solidarity of all persons in that complete community that is, alone, God's true image. Obviously, Gregory's thought must admit of a certain tension here, between free historical contingency and God's eternal will. Humanity is one, as God first fashioned and eternally wills it, and cannot finally be divided; nor can any soul be redeemed outside of this human *plērōma*. But while each person is "objectively" implicated in the salvation Christ has wrought in human nature before any "subjective" appropriation of it,[29] it is in each person, as he or she takes on the lineaments of Christ's form, that the likeness of God also dwells in its fullness and is expressed.[30] Gregory's eschatological subversion of Platonic categories would otherwise be unintelligible. God will be all in all, according to Gregory, not by comprising humanity within himself according to a metaphysical premise that comprehends the "idea" of the human, but by way of each particular person, in each unique inflection of the *plērōma*'s beauty;[31] and yet this assumption of the human unfolds only within human freedom, within our capacity to venture away. Of course, for Gregory, sin is always only accidental to human nature, a privation, a disease that corrupts the will, the opposite of real human freedom, ultimately to be purged from human nature, even if needs be by hell (which is, according to Gregory—as is most clearly stated in *De anima et resurrectione*—a period of purgation, not an eternal perdition).[32]

27. Gregory, *In illud*, PG 44:1313D–1316A.

28. Hans Urs von Balthasar, *Presence and Thought: An Essay on the Religious Philosophy of Gregory of Nyssa* (San Francisco: Ignatius, 1995); see also, A. H. Armstrong, "Platonic Elements in St. Gregory of Nyssa's Doctrine of Man," *Dominican Studies* 1 (1948): 115.

29. Gregory, *Oratio catechetica* 32, ed. James Herbert Srawley (Cambridge: Cambridge University Press, 1956), pp. 114–22.

30. Gregory, *Contra Eunomium* 1; GNO 1:78–79.

31. Gregory, *De infantibus qui praemature abripiuntur*, PG 46:181B.

32. It is only to the less clever that the fire of hell is presented as a terrible punishment; to the wise, it is recognizable as a saving therapy (*Oratio catechetica* 7, pp. 46–49). Which is not to say that, for either class of souls, the chastisements of that fire will not exceed everything one can imagine (*Oratio catechetica* 15, pp. 163–64). The logic of hell is

The power of evil is inherently finite and must, sooner or later, exhaust itself, and relinquish its grip upon every soul, as each is drawn into the infinity of God's splendor and peace.[33] Evil, after all, builds only toward an end; it is a history with an immanent telos: in the light, however, of the God who gives himself as an infinite future, from beyond all immanent ends, evil's "end" (its "consummation") proves to be nothing but its own disappearance.[34]

By framing his account of the birth of humanity "according to the image" in terms of a temporal unfolding, which makes the "ideal" and the actual each the "cause" of the other, Gregory distinguishes himself as one of a very few theologians capable of viewing worldly time in the light of salvation without resorting to some notion of sacral history set like an island in a sea of otherwise meaningless temporality (much as he does not think in terms of a particular saved humanity extracted from the mass of the reprobate): the story of Christ is also quite literally the story of all time, the story of the lordship of the Logos over the body of

explained at greatest length in *De anima et resurrectione*, PG 46:97B–105A, by Makrina, on her deathbed, to Gregory. At 101B–104A, incidentally, Gregory provides—implicitly—his interpretation of the *aiōnios kolasis* of Matt. 25:46: a punishment so terrible that it persists for "an entire age."

33. Gregory, *De hominis opificio* 21; PG 44:201B–204A.

34. See Jean Daniélou, "Comble du mal et eschatologie chez Grégoire de Nysse," in *Festgabe Joseph Lortz* II (Baden-Baden, 1958), and M. Canévet, "Nature du mal et économie du salut chez Grégoire de Nysse," *Recherches de science religieuse* 56 (1968). Gregory even suggests that the Logos awaited a day when every manifestation of evil (which, apparently, is capable of only a finite number of forms) had made its appearance upon the earth before entering into human history, so that the divine cure might touch every extremity of our illness (*Oratio catechetica* 29, pp. 107–9). And Makrina, in *De anima et resurrectione* (PG 46:104A–105A), explains to Gregory that when evil is finally abolished, by being purged from every individual will, then every soul, having regained its proper freedom, will turn freely to God and be joined to him, the fountainhead of all virtue, and God will be "all in all" both in the sense of "instead of all" (God becoming the sole "element" in which our life will subsist) and in the sense of "in all" (God entering into each of us and so abolishing evil in the depths of our nature). See Gregory, *In illud*, PG 44:1313A–16A; *In Christi resurrectionem*, PG 46:661C–D; and *In Canticum Canticorum* 8, GNO 6:247–49; 11, GNO 6:335–36; 14, GNO 6:421. The image that most perfectly expresses Gregory's sense of the intrinsic nothingness of evil's "consummation," and its necessary limitation, is found in *De hominis opificio* 21 (PG 44:201B–204A), where Gregory likens evil to night, which (according to the geocentric cosmology of late antiquity) is nothing but a cone of shadow cast weakly by the earth, out into a universe of light. This is another reason, incidentally, for Gregory's denial of hell's eternity: there can be no endless godlessness posed over against the endlessness of God; he is the sole infinite, and the infinitely good (see *In inscriptiones Psalmorum* 2; GNO 5:100–101).

humanity.[35] Seen from the perspective of the kingdom, time is redeemed from our sinful histories, the story that every secular dispensation fails to tell is told at last, and the distinction between the ideal person and the multiplicity of contingent persons throughout time disappears upon the horizon of God's good creation. The inevitability of Gregory's universalism is obvious here: each person, as God elects him or her from eternity,[36] is indispensable, because the humanity God eternally wills could never come to fruition in the absence of any member of that body, any inflection of that beauty. Apart from the one who is lost, humanity as God wills it could never be entire, nor even exist as the creature fashioned after the divine image; the loss of even this one would leave the body of the Logos incomplete and God's purpose in creation unrealized. Gregory's anthropology sometimes seems like Philo's, caught in the same penumbral interval between idealism and the biblical story, but it is this eschatological collapse of the distinction of ideal from actual that sets his formulation apart. The kingdom, as he imagines it, will be achieved only in the harmonious play of all created differences: "Then will be found only that single saved one, in the convergence upon the One Good of everyone united one with another."[37] The old idealism dissolves in the narrative of creation, and in the light of this eschatology. At the same time, another idealism is resisted in advance, that of the dialectical recuperation that rescues (or sublates) spiritual truth from the provisionality of *mere* historical particularity. Platonic beauty suffers defatigation in its transposition from the ideal to the phenomenal realm, Hegelian truth emerges from and rises above the interminable, tragic welter of the particular; but for Gregory, the only site of the beautiful or the true is in the entirety of creation's living body. Human history is embraced from beyond itself, receives its only true meaning from an end transcendent of it, and so is justified not through any sacrificial rationality or prudential logic of its own, but by grace.

And if the "essence" of the human is none other than the plenitude

---

35. One might note here that Gregory in a sense offers a Christian answer to Hegel's understanding of universal history different from a more "Barthian" approach: he allows all history its place as the theater of God's ordination neither by making the violence of history a necessary negative probation nor by subordinating the merely particular to the synthetic; and he clearly marks the difference of God's true story from the stories of sinful humanity without making it seem as if the true story told in Christ is simply an intrusion upon worldly time, a radical rupture.

36. Gregory, *De hominis opificio* 22; PG 44:207C–208B.

37. Gregory, *In Canticum Canticorum* 15; GNO 6:466.

of all men and women, every essentialism is rendered empty: all persons express and unfold the human not as shadows of an undifferentiated idea, but in their concrete multiplicity and hence in all the intervals and transitions belonging to their differentiation; and so human "essence" can be only an "effect" of the whole. Every unlikeness, in the harmonious unity of the body of the Logos, expresses in an unrepeatable way the beauty of God's likeness. The human "original," no longer a paradigm, is the gift and fruit of every peaceful difference and divergence; and only as this differentiating dynamism is the unity of the human "essence" imaginable at all, as the peaceful unity of all persons in the Spirit, who is bringing creation to pass and ushering in the kingdom. And even in the kingdom, that essence will not be available to us as a fixed *proprium*. According to Gregory, the final state of the saved will be one of endless motion forward, continuous growth into God's eternity, *epektasis*; salvation will not be an achieved repose, but an endless pilgrimage into God's infinity, a perpetual "stretching out" into an identity always infinitely exceeding what has already been achieved;[38] there will always be the eschatological within the eschaton, a continuous liberation of the creature, subsuming all that has gone before into an ever greater fullness of God's presence to the soul, so that the creature will simply be freed of all memory, all recollection,[39] and so all anamnetic grounding in the absolute. The eschaton, thus conceived, brings nothing to a halt, returns nothing to its pure or innocent origin; it repeats the gracious liberation of difference that creation always is, endlessly, but it never secures beings within being, or fixes them in their proper places, or discriminates the noble from the base; it is, rather, a perpetual venturing away from our world, our totality.

And, most importantly, it has appeared already, in our midst, at Easter; the verdict of the resurrection now breaks upon every instant, disrupts every representable essence, every serene proportion. All our discourses

38. The doctrine of perpetual progress, of the soul's *epektasis* into God, so thoroughly pervades Gregory's developed thought that there is little purpose in citing particular passages from his work; the theme is, however, developed most fully (and most beautifully) in the two great "spiritual" treatises *De vita Moysis* and *In Canticum Canticorum*.

39. Gregory, *In Canticum Canticorum* 6; GNO 6:174. This abandonment of anamnesis, in favor of a pure "towardness," rapt up into an infinite divine future, marks one of Gregory's most striking departures from the atmosphere of Platonism. Worldly memory's tragic anxiety and philosophical recollection's otherworldly pretensions alike are displaced by the force of his eschatological vision. One might also recall Gregory's reproaches of Arians and Pneumatomachoi for thinking of God only as the unshaken origin, the absolute and beginningless past, and not as the endless future—for thinking, that is, in terms of memory rather than of hope (*Contra Eunomium* 1; GNO 1:666–72).

of power and privilege belong to the language of death, which has already been conquered in our one shared, indivisible nature. Even the finality of death has now been deprived of its authority, its power of consummative completeness, and so now no refuge is left for our "essence": except there, in God, where we dwell "altogether."

IV

The first conclusion to be drawn from these considerations is that, whatever metaphysical grammar it may borrow, Christian eschatology must inevitably subvert the discourses by which (in every age) we rationalize creaturely differences in hierarchies of high and low, noble and base, great and nameless. The verdict of God is on the side of the particular person, and so neither justice nor truth can ever stand against the other who confronts us as the stranger, the enemy, or the "slave." Ultimately, for Christian thought, the eschatological light that breaks upon reflection not merely as a promise, but as the paschal event that constitutes all Christian memory, exposes the falsehood of our worldly teleologies: for there is no good end immanent to a nature we each privately possess, to which some may attain and of which others fall short. Our only just and permissible end is given us all, as one, from beyond the world we fabricate to accommodate our violences. We own neither essence nor prerogative, but belong to Christ; this is a freedom exceeding any power we exert over one another, because it is freedom from death. But it is also one we have rejected so long as we continue to "divide human nature between slavery and mastery." The precise meaning and peculiar power of this phrase become clear at last: for Gregory, no accusation could be more terrible, nor any more precise. Every violence or coercion that divides us quite literally divides the one body—the only true identity—that we can ever possess. Moreover, as even this "whole humanity" belongs not to us, but to Christ, as his body, all divisions between free and slave, privilege and poverty, eminence and abasement are wounds that we, in our arrogance and faithlessness, inflict upon him. Writes Gregory, in his fifth homily on the Lord's Prayer, nature never so divided us—only power has done so—nor did God ever ordain slavery, not even on account of sin.[40] Which brings me to my final observations.

First, given the extreme concreteness and essential sociality of Greg-

---

40. Gregory, *De oratione dominica* 5; GNO 7/2:70.

ory's language concerning human nature, it would have been impossible for him to draw any specious distinction between slavery to sin and death and slavery to political or social power; if God acts to liberate us from the one, God condemns and overthrows the other. As Gregory says, all freedom is essentially one and the same thing: it is to be without master.[41] So long, then, as human power continues to exercise mastery, violence, or coercion over souls and bodies, God's saving purpose is resisted. And there is inevitably a social provocation in Gregory's eschatology; if Christ has assumed to himself the human *plērōma*, the eschatological fulfillment of our shared nature has entered our history, and left us no time any longer for the provisional employment of unjust but "necessary" arrangements of political or social order. We are already condemned and raised up together, in him in whom there is neither Jew nor Greek, free nor slave, man nor woman;[42] and so our nature's redemption is neither an abstraction nor even only a promise, but is even now a practice, a church, a newness of life in which we participate only insofar as we really enact a redeemed society. If, says Gregory, Christians indeed practiced the mercy Christ commands of them in the Beatitudes, humanity would no longer admit of division within itself between slavery and mastery, poverty and wealth, shame and honor, infirmity and strength; all things would be held in common, and all would be equal one with another.[43] Gregory's Easter vigil sermon of 379 (*On the Holy Pascha*), which would have followed upon the Ecclesiastes homilies, celebrates every form of emancipation, seamlessly joining the theme of liberation from death to that of the manumission of slaves, while again urging the latter.[44]

And my last observation is this: if this eschatological light indeed deprives us of every essentialism, and pierces the metaphysical canopy under which we shelter ourselves and construct hierarchies within totality to legitimate our prejudices, ambitions, and violences, and promises us no homeland but Christ, then in a sense the slave is the one always nearest God, and always most human: for the slave truly owns no essence, no *ousia* (which is, in Greek, also to say "wealth"), has no clan or homeland, can boast neither autochthony nor telos, has no grasp of first principles. Amid the divisions—the slaveries—we are always forging—political,

---

41. And so virtue is the highest and most invincible freedom. Gregory, *De anima et resurrectione*, PG 46:101D.

42. See Dumitru Staniloae, "L'image de Dieu et la déification de l'homme," *Communio Viatorum* 19 (1976): 109–19.

43. Gregory, *De beatitudinis* 5; GNO 7/2:126–27.

44. Gregory, *In sanctum pascha*, GNO 9:248–50.

social, economic—the one who is dispossessed, homeless, nameless, with neither power nor privilege to call upon, is the one whose humanity has been verified for us in the body of the slave who was raised from the dead. All myths of eminence and power are overturned at Easter. And no theologian has ever evinced a profounder sense of this than Gregory. Late in the course of his *Contra Eunomium* of 382, he addresses Eunomius's argument that Christ could not really be God because Paul describes him as bearing the form of a slave, and no one could be both slave and Lord of all things. Gregory's answer is as various as it is indignant, but one point he makes with special force is that God assumes the slavery in which we all languish precisely in order to purge slavery—along with every other ill—from our shared nature: "And as," writes Gregory, "in the life we hope for, there shall be neither sickness nor curse nor sin nor death, so also slavery will vanish along with these things. And to the truth of what I say, I summon the Truth himself as witness, who tells his disciples, 'I call you no longer slaves, but friends.'"[45] For Gregory, clearly, this truth has reoriented all our "truths"; this verdict has fallen upon all our romances of power, irrevocably. Often it is as if, in Gregory's thought, one is confronted by the tableau, from the Fourth Gospel, of Christ standing before Pilate, scourged and mocked, while Pilate demands of him that he produce his pedigrees—"Whence art thou?"—and then pronounces the only truth that he himself knows—"I have power to crucify thee." By every worldly wisdom, Christ—beaten, derided, crowned with thorns—is an absurd figure, madly prating of an otherworldly kingdom, oblivious to the powers into whose hands he has been delivered; but Easter reverses the ordering of this scene, vindicates Christ over against the power that crucifies, locates truth there where he stands, in the place of the victim and the captive. And if this judgment has already come upon us, and liberated us from death, we can do no other now than desire and advance the release of all who lie in bondage. This cannot be gainsaid. And Gregory seems often to have seen with a clarity rare not only for his time, but perhaps for every age of the church, the magnitude of this truth: we can never again deceive ourselves that we can call justly upon any power but that which sets others free if, in the resurrection of Christ—much to our consternation and embarrassment, no doubt, even to our condemnation, but ultimately for our redemption—the form of God and the form of humanity have both been given to us, completely, now and henceforth always, in the form of a slave.

---

45. Gregory, *Contra Eunomium* 3.8; GNO 2:259.

THIRTEEN

Death, Final Judgment, and the Meaning of Life

The ancient injunction *memento mori*—whispered by a slave into the ear of a victorious general in his triumphal chariot or by a monk to his own heart in the solitude of his cell—has frequently been translated as "Remember that thou art mortal," which may be faithful to the phrase's special hortatory force; but, of course, the literal meaning of the injunction is "Remember to die." This is not, one would think, something we generally need to be told; at least, as a purely practical counsel, it would seem to lack any genuine urgency, given that most of us really have very little to say in the matter and all of us will certainly prove equal to the task when the occasion presents itself. And yet, in point of fact, though we may be unique among animals in our awareness of our own mortality and in our ability to anticipate and reflect upon our own deaths, to die is something we do, in some sense, need to be reminded to do—and not merely because our deaths belong to the future (which is notoriously difficult to remember), nor merely because in moments of great elation we are liable (like the general at his triumph) to forget that all glory is fleeting, that all joy is transient, and that Fortune's wheel never ceases turning. We cannot easily remember to die because death runs contrary to the whole orientation of human consciousness—or, rather, cuts entirely across its grain. And this is true even for those far advanced in years, for whom the prospect of death lies quite near at hand.

I

In his *La mentalité primitive* of 1922,[1] Lucien Lévy-Bruhl notes that one of the distinctive traits of the "primitive mind" is its inability to conceive of death as natural. And, indeed, the field researches of anthropologists confirm that, in many tribal societies throughout the world, it is assumed that death is always *unnatural*: the effect of poison, evil spirits, magic, or some other adventitious agency, some enemy, seen or unseen. In such societies, every death is in some sense murder, the violent interruption of a life that would otherwise have continued indefinitely. Most of us, of course, would tend to attribute some of the more peculiar characteristics of tribal culture to a simple lack of intellectual sophistication, and assume that the failure to recognize death as something natural and inevitable must be the result mostly of simple ignorance, of the sort that might be remedied by a comprehensive education in the principles of organic chemistry. But we might do well to ask ourselves whether, in fact, we—absorbed as we are most of the time in watching television, visiting shopping malls, and watching more television—necessarily possess a subtler understanding of the ambiguities that haunt the human experience of death than do the inhabitants of tribal cultures. At some very profound level, the "primitive" intuition is surely correct, and it is one we might share if we were more attentive to the conditions of experience than we generally are. Simply said, death can never be wholly and unequivocally "natural" for us, precisely because we are conscious of it; hence—quite unnaturally—it has a meaning for us, even if we think that meaning to be no more than the end of all meaning. As organisms, we are subject—like all animals—to the inescapable circularity of natural existence: "birth and copulation and death," to use T. S. Eliot's phrase; the pitiless regularity with which one generation succeeds another; the survival of some, the defeat of others, the ultimate extinction of all. But, as rational beings, blessed and burdened with reflective consciousness, our existence is not simply "circular" or organic, but prospective and creative. The horizon of human awareness is one of indeterminate futurity, an openness that aims *naturally* beyond nature; we have projects, plans, expectations, ambitions, ideas that cannot be contained within the close confines of the present, designs that can be only incrementally embodied, desires that can be only progressively pursued; we are capable of novelty, we understand time as a realm of possibilities, and we know that there will be an end to all our striving. To be human is

---

1. In English, Lucien Lévy-Bruhl, *Primitive Mentality* (London: Macmillan, 1923).

to possess—consciously, that is—a future, and to be able to turn one's will and imagination toward it. Death, therefore, must always come as an interruption for us, a guest anticipated but never properly prepared for and always arriving out of season. Before any death's advent, a particular *story* was being told, one that has now been brought to an abrupt conclusion; and because our orientation toward the future is part of the very essence of our humanity, even a death long awaited and arriving late in the day is a kind of negation of human "nature"—a kind of ultimate meaninglessness.

Obviously, of course, one could just as well say that, in another sense, death "belongs" to our nature in a way that it cannot for any other animal: that only our consciousness of our finitude makes us capable of having "stories" to interrupt; that we alone enjoy the "privilege" of approaching our deaths with wills reconciled to its inevitability and expectations shaped by the limit it sets; that the terror, anxiety, or resignation with which we regard our own deaths gives shape, purpose, and some degree of exigency to how we conduct our lives; and that, consequently, death is part of us. Heidegger, famously, defined the uniquely human way of being ("being there," *Dasein*) as "being towards death" (*Sein bis Tod*): the existential comportment of each of us toward our ultimate "possibility," the power of each of us to take his death upon himself and thereby to act with resolve.[2] Even this, however, is merely to say, again, that humanity's relation to death constitutes something very like an absolute alienation of human consciousness from the rest of the natural world. Death provokes, torments, and threatens us with the possibility of nothingness, the futility of all enterprises, the overthrow of all hopes, the impossibility of indemnification for our miseries or recompense for our disappointments; it awaits us as a final crisis that makes all life questionable. But for this futurity that both makes us conscious of our deaths and makes death an interruption of our lives—but for our exile, that is, from the circle of natural life and natural death—we would suffer neither hope nor despair; we would not be strangers in the world; we would (or so it might seem) be at peace.

II

A number of fairly respectable schools of thought take it as more or less self-evident that religion came into existence primarily because of the dis-

2. See Martin Heidegger, *Sein und Zeit*, 8th ed. (Tübingen: Max Niemeyer, 1957), especially section II, 1, pars. 46–53, pp. 235–67.

quiet occasioned in us by our awareness of our mortality. The great modern masters of suspicion, at any rate, tended to assume that any accurate aetiology of religion would lead back ultimately to a pathetic human longing for some sort of compensation beyond the grave, some final reward or release, and that the religious impulse in human culture arises principally from a deeply felt social and psychological need to make the burdens of our existence more tolerable and the fear of death less agonizing. For Marx, religion was essentially the heart of a heartless world, the breath of pity in a universe of anguish, the tender opiate that soothes the misery of a suffering and hopeless humanity; as such, it will necessarily vanish as social alienation is progressively overcome.[3] For classical Marxist theory, admittedly, this is principally a "structural" judgment upon religion as an established and observable institution, but it is also implicitly a "genetic" account of the religious impulse as such: indeed, it must be, for otherwise Marxist theory would be obliged to acknowledge a religious dimension to society apart from and prior to the history of alienation. And for Freud, who also regarded religion as an illusion that will (or should), in the fullness of time, melt away, the origin of faith was clearly the fear of death.[4] This was not a particularly daring speculation, obviously; unlike Freud's more outlandish theories, it was neither some bizarre, unverifiable conjecture, nor the alleged result of falsified clinical cases, but followed quite naturally from simple observation and common assumptions: it was a natural—albeit banal—extrapolation from his own experience of the sort of religion he saw all around him. That said, Marx, Freud, and all those who agree with them on this point were and are most certainly wrong.

Strange as it may seem, the textual, historical, and archaeological evidence clearly shows that the religious impulse in human society has no clear connection at all with hope in an afterlife. Systems of faith vary, of course, from culture to culture and from land to land; but, when we examine the beliefs of early civilizations, anywhere in the world, we find that only a small minority of them had any concrete notion of a meaningful life beyond this life, and practically none imagined that—if there were such a life, in any meaningful sense—it was open to any but a very special few. Most ancient cultures had some vague concept of a kind of postmortem *persistence*, a shadowy, spectral half-existence beyond death, a dark, barren, joyless, and pointless underworld or otherworld; very few thought that death would bring a happier existence. The Hebrew Bible, for

---

3. See Karl Marx and Friedrich Engels, *On Religion* (Atlanta: AAR Reprints, 1963).
4. See especially Sigmund Freud, *The Future of an Illusion* (New York: Norton, 1989).

instance, contains no promises of either afterlife or resurrection until very late in its pages; indeed, not until the apocalyptic period (particularly in those books of Scripture that many traditions treat as deuterocanonical or extracanonical) does any firm concept of a recompense for the righteous beyond death emerge. For the better part of the Hebrew Bible, death is simply the end, for great and small, righteous and wicked alike; all that awaits any of us beyond this world is Sheol, a sort of abyss in which impalpable shadows of ourselves linger on amid the dust and darkness. To die is to be cut off from the land of the living—and so to be cut off from God—permanently; and one can truly live on past death only in the generations of one's children. The same is true of most ancient Greek religion, at least if art and myth are to be believed. One might mention the *Iliad*, for instance, with its repeated image of the "souls" of the dead departing for Hades squealing like bats, miserable and hopeless; or the *Odyssey* and the pathetic procession of Penelope's slain suitors being led away by Hermes, in his office as divine Psychopompos, to the shades below;[5] or the *Odyssey* again, and the visit of Odysseus to Hades, where he lures the desolate and thirsty phantoms who dwell there with sheep's blood poured into a small trench, and where he meets the ghost of Achilles, who tells him that it would be better to live the meanest life of the most wretched man upon the face of the earth than to be king over all the dead.[6] Even taking into account the Pythagorean, Platonic, and Orphic doctrines of developed Greek thought, we can still say that the indigenous *religious* consciousness of Hellas was not animated by anything like an anticipation of eternal life. And one could just as well turn to ancient Mesopotamia and look at the epic of Gilgamesh, and the vision of the house of dust described by Enkidu on his deathbed,[7] and Gilgamesh's desperate journey to find Utnapishtim (the Sumerian and Akkadian Noah) to secure from him the secret of endless life, and the tale of the serpent by the pool devouring the magic plant that might have granted such life, and the poem's bleakly unadorned closing lines, which seem to suggest that the only immortality for which any man can reasonably hope lies in his monuments and the works of his hands (the "mighty wall of Uruk," for example).[8] And yet all these cultures, and others like them, were profoundly "religious" in every sense: they worshiped and served their God or gods with offerings, hymns,

5. Homer, *Odyssey*, book 24.
6. Homer, *Odyssey*, book 11.
7. *Gilgamesh*, tablet 7.
8. *Gilgamesh*, tablets 10–11.

and prayers; they built temples and erected altars; they believed in a divine realm and in transcendent powers; they were not, in any identifiable sense, "materialist" in their conception of human existence. But, manifestly, to be religious is not necessarily to imagine that death is anything but final.[9]

This is not to deny that there is a relation at the profoundest level between the human consciousness of death and religious practice and belief; it is only to say that this relation is not the simple mechanical connection between rational misery and irrational hope that Marx and Freud imagined it was. Nor is it to deny that, as religious consciousness develops, the idea of an afterlife tends to assume more concrete and more inviting features. Rather, it is to say only that, if death is, in some sense, the "cause" of religion, it is only insofar as religion reconciles us *to* death—or, better, reminds us of death, or reminds us to die—by making death familiar, explicable, rational, and even natural to us. If our orientation toward an indefinite future, and our awareness of ourselves as mortal, and our inability to resolve the tension between the two seem to condemn us to a perpetual alienation from the natural world, the principal function of many of the more venerable forms of religious practice would seem to be one of overcoming this alienation, by reintegrating us into the circular economy of nature through recurring rituals that allow us to participate in some larger cosmic or sacral order, of which the natural cycle of life and death is merely one manifestation. The primary ritual act by which this is accomplished (as scarcely needs to be said) is sacrifice, of the most basic *do ut des* variety. No religious transaction with the divine serves better to reconcile human beings to the violence of nature, or to soothe the anguish occasioned in us by that spiritual dignity or abnormality in human nature that has estranged us from the perennial cosmic circle of life and death, and encumbered us with apprehension and grief.[10] By granting us a ritual way of return to the cycle of natural creation and destruction, and allowing us willingly and consciously to embrace that cycle as a higher spiritual mystery underlying and transcending our anomalous futurity, sacrifice allows us to overcome, in one moment, both our awareness and our forgetfulness of death: in the case of the former, by distracting us from our special and "unnatural" vocation to an indeterminate future with a sacral spectacle that announces the universal vocation of all things to a

9. John Bowker, *The Meanings of Death* (Cambridge: Cambridge University Press, 1991), pp. 18–42.

10. See René Girard, *Violence and the Sacred* (Baltimore: Johns Hopkins University Press, 1979).

holy death; in the case of the latter, by reminding us of death's transcendent necessity and inherent logic, and teaching us to see our own deaths as offerings to the absolute. Sacrifice, of a certain sort at least, is perhaps the most venerable religious gesture of all, not because it speaks of an ultimate meaning to our individual lives, beyond or despite death, but because it makes death itself meaningful to us. The meaning of life *is* death, so to speak, and life the meaning of death.

This sacrificial sense of reality, moreover, leads quite reasonably to a sacrificial cosmology and ontology: an image of the universe as itself, essentially, sacrifice, a great cycle of feeding, comprising gods and mortals both, preserving life through a complex system of balanced transactions with death, all governed and disposed by the inscrutable power of fate. Quite literally, we feed the gods (or, as the case may be, our ancestors), who require our sacrifices, and they preserve us from the forces they personify and grant us some measure of their power. An especially grand and horrible expression of this cosmology would be the interminable flow of human victims that the priests of the Aztecs slaughtered to feed the light of the sun god Tonatiuh. A far lovelier expression would be the Vedic myth of Purusa, the primordial man, by whose sacrifice—and from whose dismembered body—the cosmos first arose.[11] Even more sublime is the theophany granted to Arjuna by Krishna on the Kuru Plain in the Bhagavad Gita, in which Arjuna sees Vishnu as at once the infinite creator from whom all things flow and the omnivorous slayer into whose innumerable blazing mouths men and gods and entire worlds fly to their destruction.[12] Somewhat more abstract, but no less awesome, is the fully developed Stoic vision of the universe as a perfect, divine, harmonious, and finite plenitude, wherein each being must yield its place in time to make room for another, which must in its turn also give way to yet another; and indeed the Stoic universe is itself, as a whole, an eternal cycle, ever and again consumed in the great ecpyrosis that ends each cosmic age, only to arise again and repeat itself in its every particular, forever.[13] In a truly sacrificial vision of reality, the cosmos is a closed system, a fixed totality, within which the divine, the natural, and the human occupy places determined

11. Rig Veda, book 10.

12. Bhagavad Gita, book 11.

13. The best classic sources of Stoic logic, metaphysics, and moral doctrine are of course Sextus Empiricus, Diogenes Laertius, Cicero, Epictetus, and Marcus Aurelius; perhaps the most illuminating modern work on Stoicism is still E. Vernon Arnold's *Roman Stoicism: Being Lectures on the History of the Stoic Philosophy, with Special Reference to Its Development within the Roman Empire* (Cambridge: Cambridge University Press, 1911).

by necessity; and this totality is an economy, a precarious and oscillating equilibrium between creation and destruction, order and chaos, form and indeterminacy.

This, at any rate, is one definition of religion: a system of beliefs and cultic gestures that proclaim the absolute necessity of death and finitude, and that allow men and women to become willing and conscious participants in and contributors to the sacred order of the cosmos. Ritual sacrifice, in such a universe, is an attempt to contain nature's wanton violence within religion's methodical violence, to civilize it, to make it familiar, and to draw upon its power. Nature is resisted and controlled, by rites at once apotropaic—appeasing chaos and rationalizing it within the stability of cult—and fiduciary—recuperating sacrificial expenditures in the form of divine favor, a numinous power reinforcing the regime (sacral, social, and political) that sacrifice serves.[14] In this way, the violence of the city is legitimated by a religious appeal to the violence of nature, and humanity learns (gratefully, no doubt) to be reconciled to both. There is an ethos of sublime surrender here, and with it comes great peace: it allows for all the extravagances of the festive and the tragic, ecstasy and sorrow, rapture and resolve, but in the end teaches one to accept one's place within an order to which even the gods are subordinate. Religion, in this sense, truly is an opiate—or, better, it is the wine of Dionysus: an inebriating embrace of nature's deepest joys and deepest violences, an intoxicating nihilism. Humanity, absorbed in the terrible dramaturgy of sacrifice, learns to find the meaning of life in life's surrender to death; one learns, that is, to offer oneself, all those whom one loves, indeed the whole world of living things up to the abyss without protest, knowing that the delicate balances of the universe would fail, the sublime logic of nature and history alike disintegrate, and the very light of heaven die away but for these oblations to the night.

III

"Religion," though, like "sacrifice," is a word with a vast range of meanings, many of them only very tenuously analogous to one another. A sacrificial understanding of reality, of the sort described above, necessarily implies a certain kind of religious logic, one in which liturgical, cosmo-

---

14. See Giorgio Agamben, *Homo Sacer: Sovereign Power and Bare Life* (Stanford: Stanford University Press, 1998).

logical, and occasionally mystical concerns are paramount, while "ethical" concerns (if they are present at all) occupy only a subordinate place, and are often matters more of ritual purity than of anything else. A radically different religious logic, however—one rarely encountered in the lore of ancient cult, but now dominant among the peoples of the world—regards the moral condition of the individual soul as a matter of genuinely central religious importance, and this logic is found in its purest form most typically in faiths whose ultimate horizon is that of a final judgment upon the lives of individuals, an eschatological discrimination of the righteous from the sinful. These two logics are not, of course, exclusive of one another in practice, but they are sufficiently formally incompatible that few religious systems can reconcile them with perfect consistency or with perfect stability: the combination is almost invariably volatile and tends to invite constant internal revisions and revolutions, or even the entire overthrow of one logic by the other.

It used to be fashionable, of course, for scholars to characterize the tension between the priestly and prophetic traditions in Israel as a kind of antagonism between "ritual" and "ethical" religion; but this distinction was, needless to say, far too simplistic and was often made more in the interest of Protestant apologetics than of sound scholarship. The developed temple cult of Israel, after all, involved an understanding of sacrifice that had nothing in common with, say, the rites of the esurient gods of ancient Mesopotamia or of the Aztecs' blood-steeped charnel-house universe. The central cultic oblation made by Israel, the *qurban* of the Day of Atonement, was not a simple exchange of goods for services, but a ceremony of reconciliation and purification, of repentance and forgiveness. It was already a "moral" sacrifice, and indeed an act of divine judgment: God's verdict upon sin, a penitential return of the nation to God with an offering of its own life's blood, and a gracious reprieve, granted not out of divine need, and not because divine wrath had been "appeased," but entirely through God's mercy. Nevertheless, from the time of the prophets, through the exilic and Second Temple periods, to the time of Christ, there was a clear divergence in Israel's religious beliefs between a special concentration on temple law and worship, on the one hand, and a devotion to "the law and the prophets" and moral community, on the other: between, that is, the sacerdotal and the rabbinical, the "nomic" and the "hermeneutical," the temple and the synagogue, the Saducaic and the Pharisaic, the hieratic and the messianic. Most Jews in the Holy Land at the time of Christ were, of course, quite comfortably situated within both traditions at once, despite the rather radical differences between them (the most obvious being that the Pharisees believed in the resurrection and the life of the world to come while the Sadducees did not). There were apocalyptic sects born in the intertestamental period and after, that were, in a sense, eschatological without remainder, but these were marginal groups and were merely "acute" manifestations of a religious sensibility whose more "chronic" expressions pervaded the whole Jewish world. In the Maccabean age, apocalyptic speculation had acquired a special urgency, on account not so much of some cultural anxiety about death as of an explicit resolve that the justice of God not be impugned. Under the Seleucid ruler Antiochus Epiphanes, faithful Jews who refused to defile their faith with false worship or to violate the Mosaic code had suffered monstrous persecutions—torments and deaths of almost unimaginable cruelty—and this naturally raised the question of God's fidelity to his own covenants. The claims that God would reward the righteous after death, by taking their souls to himself or by raising them from death on the last day, and that God would send a messiah to release his people from bondage, were assertions, ultimately, of God's perfect goodness, despite all the horrors of history. And, for obvious reasons, such claims continued to flourish during the period of Roman occupation. In the wider world of the Jewish diaspora, moreover, the synagogical tradition was the only form of Judaism that was in any sense a "live option." And, of course, with the final destruction of the temple in Jerusalem, the priestly tradition essentially faded into obsolescence.

The idea of an assessment of souls in the afterlife—though rare in the most ancient religions—is nevertheless extremely old. It was certainly part of ancient Egyptian religion from a very early period. Not that Egyptian belief was uniform from age to age or region to region, but as a rule it did involve a particularly involved notion of the soul's journey after death, one that tended to include a divine judgment on the life the soul had led in this world. Most of the archaeological and textual evidence, of course, suggests that a meaningful afterlife was often seen as something possible only for the rich, who could afford to provision themselves for the journey from this world to the next; but it also suggests that this was by no means always the case. What ultimately determines the destiny of the soul in the Egyptian Book of the Dead, for instance, is the verdict passed upon it by Osiris and his court of forty-two gods in the divine realm of Amenta. Everyone who comes before this divine tribunal must submit to a trial in which his heart is weighed in a balance against an image of Ma'at, goddess of truth; and should one's iniquities be so grave or so many as to tip the scales, one is denied entry into the next life and one's heart is thrown to a beast called the "Devourer."[15] Admittedly, certain texts suggest that, for many, this trial was regarded more as an ordeal to be passed by any available means than as an encouragement to a life of righteousness. A magical ornament in the shape of a scarab, for instance, placed upon the chest of a mummified corpse, was believed to "seal" the heart so that it could not give evidence against the soul before Osiris. And apparently there were those who thought that the proper way to prepare for death was to memorize spells by which they might evade demons and persuade the divine ferryman to carry them across into the next life, whether they had earned passage or not. But the criteria by which the soul was to be judged were understood to be unambiguously moral: the Book of the Dead, for example, describes a dead man before his judges pleading that he has never defrauded others, caused others to go hungry, starved infants, or committed any other crimes against his neighbors. The Egyptian governor Harkhuf proclaims on his tomb (built more than twenty-two centuries before Christ) that he has fed the hungry, clothed the naked, ferried those without boats of their own, and borne no false witness against others; and he expresses the hope that this will stand him in good stead when he comes before the Great God. The legend of Prince Setna, composed perhaps three centuries before Christ, tells how two men buried on the same day—one a rich man interred with an immense treasure, the other a pauper unceremoniously cast into the desert—fared before Osiris: the rich man, having lived an evil life, was despoiled of his burial hoard and condemned to eternal torment, while the pauper was given the rich man's goods and allowed to enter into the world of the gods.

The first entirely eschatological faith of which we know is Zoroastrianism, established by the Persian prophet Zarathustra early in the sixth century BC (at least according to legend). The idea of a final judgment was so absolutely central to his creed, in fact, that Zarathustra abandoned the ancient sacrificial cosmology of Indo-Iranian "Aryan" culture more or less completely—even demoting the "devas" (the gods of Persia and Bharata) to the status of "devils"—in order to proclaim in its place a "cosmic history," with a beginning, middle, and end. Indeed, in the Zoroastrian vision of reality, the natural order is in no true sense a sacred reality at all, and hence it provides no proper model for religious practice or belief; it is at best ambiguous, a mixture of darkness and light, upon which both good and evil spiritual forces have worked. Nature as we know it is merely an

---

15. See *The Egyptian Book of the Dead*, ed. and trans. E. A. Wallis Budge (New York: Dover Publications, 1967).

episode within a greater story, the site of the spiritual struggle between good and evil. The true "horizon" of human and cosmic meaning lies beyond the closed circle of natural life and natural death, at the end of time; and the deepest truth of existence is to be found not through a perpetual ritual return to the circularity of organic nature, but through perseverance in the good and through anticipation of a divine future in which the cosmos and the self will be given their true forms. At the end of time, according to developed Zoroastrian thought, the world will be consumed in a great conflagration, the Wise Lord (Ahura Mazda) will pronounce his final verdict upon all things, the righteous will be raised to a new life in a perfected creation, and the wicked will be destroyed. Till then, the souls of the departed must cross the "Bridge of Retribution," upon which the good will find easy passage to heaven and from which the evil will plunge into the darkness of hell. And, in its aboriginal form, as well as in all its later, more dualistic forms (Mazdaist, Zurvanist, etc.), Zoroastrianism placed its emphasis upon the moral condition of the soul before God. Zoroastrian ideas, it is generally assumed, influenced the eschatological speculations of postexilic Judaism and, derivatively, those of Christianity and Islam; but, that said, it is difficult to establish any clear chronology for the emergence of certain ideas (resurrection, for example), or to determine exactly what the lines of influence between Persian and Jewish religious culture were.[16]

What is certain, however, is that the idea of a final judgment, no matter when or where it first arose, constitutes a radical reorientation of religious consciousness, away from the perennial repetitions of cosmic time and toward the great defining "crisis" of cosmic history, as well as toward the special crisis of the individual soul. This sort of "religion" offers none of the sublime, impersonal, tragic solace of cosmic fatalism, none of the solemn, narcotic bliss of sacrificial cult. Indeed, with its seemingly limitless requirement of moral labor on the part of the individual, it can quite easily replace religious comfort with spiritual insecurity—the sense of an obligation never met, a mission never quite discharged, a hope never entirely certain. In a sense, this sort of faith awakens human beings from the dreaming slumber of cultic religion and reminds them again that they are at most resident aliens in the world of nature. On the other hand, though, the idea of the final judgment has the power to infuse every moment of existence with an eternal significance, to raise human beings out of the

16. See Mary Boyce, *Zoroastrians: Their Religious Beliefs and Practices* (Oxford: Routledge, 2001).

turmoil of mere organic existence to the full dignity of moral creatures, and to transform the mundane contingencies of individual lives into occasions of transcendence and spiritual adventure. The idea of judgment liberates the soul, from the world and for the world, with a force not only absent from purely cultic religion, but subversive of it.

IV

In Christian thought, these themes—sacrifice and judgment, life from death and the life of the age to come—converge in a way that radically transforms them. Indeed, one might even say that, on the cross of Christ, two distinct orders of sacrifice uniquely coincide, and that at Easter one order triumphs completely over the other. From a purely pagan perspective, after all, the cross is most definitely a kind of sacrifice; within a certain vision of the cosmos and of society, the immolation of the sacrificial victim and the execution of the criminal belong to the same "economy": the preservation of "sacred" order (of the city, the empire, and the gods) through the destruction of the cause of social instability, and through the surrender of the particular to the universal. At the same time, the cross—for Christians—represents the perfection not only of Christ's self-outpouring life of love, but also of the entire "sacrificial" logic of Israel's Day of Atonement: an offering up of all things in love to God that allows us to draw near to him, and to be reconciled with him, under the shelter of his mercy. This latter order of sacrifice, again, is already an act of moral submission to the judgment of God, and of faith in his love, and as such is not an attempt to pay God tribute or "purchase" some portion of his power or secure some sort of abstract "credit" stored up in the absolute; it is, rather, the restoration of a communion with the divine glory, and what it asks of God is not merely the exchange of palpable goods for some imaginary sacral authority, but a return of all that has been lost in sin and death. And, at Easter, it is this latter order of oblation that God vindicates, while the former order is revealed as falsehood, nothing more than violence legitimating itself through more violence, a thing damnable to God. Another way of phrasing this is to say that, on the cross and at the empty tomb, two orders of judgment converge, and that, again, one is raised up by God as the true form of his justice, the other is overturned with an eschatological finality. Christ is condemned to death by the duly appointed authorities of his age, whose verdicts are no more than proper exercises of political prudence and responsible governance. And the crucifixion is an expression of a particular sort of "sacrificial justice," which is always willing to destroy the individual for the sake of social equilibrium; it is a perfect epitome of the legal, religious, and political rationality by which human society sustains and justifies itself. Yet God's verdict entirely reverses that of Christ's judges. Rather than confirm us in our devotion to the economy of social order, and our obedience to certain "tragic necessities," Easter reveals that divine justice is on the side of the particular, the rejected, the victim we are willing to offer up to the greater good.

In any event, one can scarcely exaggerate the scale of the disruption of many of humanity's most cherished religious expectations that the Christian proclamation of Easter constitutes. There could hardly be a more disorienting claim than that the resurrection—the eschatological horizon of history, the act of divine redemption that lies entirely outside the cycle of nature, the kingdom of God beyond the reign of death—has occurred (suddenly, incredibly) within the very heart of history and nature, in a way that breaks them open from within. It is, of course, obvious that Easter runs contrary to "nature" as we understand it, and utterly subverts the logic of "natural" sacrifice: after all, there is no older religious wisdom than that which teaches us the sacred necessity and irreversibility of death; and a victim once offered up to "order" (divine or human) is meant to be transformed into some higher, more abstract good, not return again in his own particularity, glorified and vindicated over against the powers that destroyed him for the sake of that higher good. But, in a sense, the resurrection is every bit as much a disruption of "sacred history" and of eschatological expectation. History, it would seem, is not simply the time prepared for us before the final judgment, the occasion of moral labor before the appointed end. The judgment has already come, out of season; history's great crisis has appeared now, in our midst, and has rendered all our certitudes concerning the cosmos and history untrustworthy. Time itself is fallen; its ultimate consummation is not simply the final expression of a truth it already possesses *in potentia*. Rather, it is enslaved to a "false story," which leads—if left undisturbed—toward absurdity and nothingness. The history that God confirms as the path to his truth is the unique story of Christ, from the incarnation to the resurrection; this is the story he raises up, and seals with an eschatological verdict; and, in so doing, he also pronounces his final verdict upon the fabulous tales that humanity tells about itself, and upon the historical "logic" that leads to the building of crosses. Time is to be redeemed, it turns out, and so it must be invaded by God's Logos, shattered and restored by the advent of God's kingdom; the judgment of God will not be a final confirmation of history's "total synthesis," or even of our various moral positions before an omnipotent justice, but the event of an unmerited salvation. Our only hope now lies in the power of the Holy Spirit to integrate our lives into that one true story told in Christ; we hope that the final judgment already pronounced upon him will include us too in its ultimate determinations.

Thus, far more radically than a more purely "linear" eschatological creed ever could, the Christian gospel deprives us of many of the most dependable sources of religious solace. Death, our immemorial antagonist, which religion had made familiar to us and even meaningful for us (at the cost of so much cultural labor and so many victims), has become a menacing stranger to us again, essentially meaningless, ultimately unjust. This undoubtedly robs us of the desperately needed comfort of a certain kind of spiritual complacency, an ease of conscience before the tragic immensity of fate and necessity, which has the power to grant us a very real respite from the turmoil and anguish of life. But we are no longer allowed to look upon death—our own, that of those we love, that of those to whom we are indifferent or whom we hate—as an expression of a higher cosmic justice or of a sacred economy. Rather, we are called to believe that sin and death are a ruinous distortion of creation, and that we can never be reconciled to the destruction upon which nature and history seem so inevitably to depend, or consent to the verdicts that nature and history alike pronounce upon us or others. The moral vocation of the soul, in light of God's judgment, has now become infinite: we are required to struggle not only in obedience to the rationality of cosmic or historical time, but in defiance of them and in absolute fidelity to an event that has inverted many of the most fundamental certainties of our existence. In a sense, the resurrection of Christ—understood as the revelation of God's final judgment within time—calls humanity to a second naïveté, a postreligious return to our most primordial intuition of death as something unnatural, obscene, and intrinsically evil, and a return consequently to our inextinguishable disquiet before the power of death to interrupt our "natural" orientation toward an unlimited future. That disquiet, it emerges, is a sign of a created predisposition to grace; it is the original agitation of a spiritual summons to a kingdom not of this world, to the eternal life of a renewed creation. In the light of Easter, however, that aboriginal anxiety is transformed into a kind of spiritual bliss. For what God raised up on Easter was the deified humanity of Christ; and he thereby revealed that the "true story" of our humanity is that of a true union between humanity and God, a marriage of the finite to the infinite, a divinization of the creature in Christ.

That is to say, God's judgment on humanity, as revealed at Easter, is a call to an inexhaustible experience of the intimate presence of God (a call that, inevitably, leaves open the possibility of the soul turning from God's love toward an indeterminate dereliction). The only truly "natural" human destiny is made known to us in our ontological vocation to the vision of God, and to the nuptial union of the divine and human natures in those who have been joined to Christ. One of the most exhilarating theological attempts to capture this mystery in a single metaphor was that of the fourth-century church father Gregory of Nyssa, who defined the union of the soul with God as one of eternal *epektasis*: an everlasting "stretching out" of the finite into the infinite, an endless ecstatic growth of the soul into that which always infinitely exceeds and infinitely beckons it. For Gregory, this pilgrimage "from glory to glory" has the character of a "pure future," so to speak, in which all memory is always being assumed into ever greater anticipation and ever grander adventure: a motion prompted entirely by love and blissful desire, rather than by tragic anxiety or painful recollection or egoism. It is, in a sense, that very futurity that renders death so tormenting a mystery to fallen humanity—the futurity from which various religious wisdoms have sought over the ages to deliver us—but rescued now from the falsehood of death, and shown to be the deepest truth of our nature, and the mark of a divine destiny. The true meaning of our life, it turns out, is its openness to God's eternity: a meaning revealed to us by a divine judgment that has made that eternity at once the proper content of our historical memory, the correct measure of our created nature, and the true object of all our hope.

FOURTEEN

The Myth of Schism

I. The Mythology of Division

The division between the Orthodox and Roman Catholic Churches—
officially almost a millennium old, but in many ways far older—has often enough been characterized as the ineluctable effect of one or another
irreconcilable and irreducible difference: political (caesars and czars as
opposed to princes and popes), cultural (Greek or Byzantine as opposed
to Latin or Frankish), theological (divergent views of nature and grace or
original sin), doctrinal (the *filioque* clause, papal infallibility, and so on),
ritual (leavened bread and icons as opposed to azymes and statuary), ecclesiological (patriarchal pentarchy and *sobornost* as opposed to universal papal jurisdiction and *monarchia*), even "ontological"—to cite the somewhat
hermetic language once employed by the ecumenical patriarch (I hope
that this last was a case of mistranslation, as I should be inconsolable if I
discovered that we do not even now have being in common). And, because
these various distinctions have been drawn only rarely in a spirit of critical
detachment, uncontaminated by some element of squalid recrimination,
it has usually proved difficult to separate matters of real significance from
those raised for purposes either purely polemical or ultimately frivolous.
Every serious ecumenical engagement between the Orthodox and Catholic
communions reveals depth upon depth of substantial agreement, and yet
always fades upon the midnight knell, as each side ruefully acknowledges
the perplexing refractoriness and stubborn persistence of differences that
lie (apparently) deeper still. Always an abiding sense of some ever more
determinative—and yet, curiously, ever more indeterminate—essential

difference overshadows every conversation (however charitable) that attempts to span the divide. And this sense serves constantly to temper our elation over whatever meager accords we strike, to imbue our continued division with an almost mystical aura of inevitability, and to resign us fatalistically to our failures and to the failure of our love.

By all rights, however, Pope John Paul II's *Ut unum sint* should have inaugurated a new era in the ecumenical relations between Orthodoxy and Roman Catholicism. There is, of course, nothing remarkable in the author of *Orientale lumen*—that hymn of love to Eastern Christianity—expressing so fervent a desire for reconciliation with the East; but nothing, I think, could have prepared anyone for the extraordinary overture John Paul made in stating that he wished for a conversation with other Christians (especially, it seems obvious, with those of the East) regarding papal primacy, one in which the issue of the pope's ecclesial jurisdiction would be open. Indeed, it was so surprising a gesture that neither the Orthodox Church nor the Catholic Church seems yet to know how to react to it. And yet, of course, it touches upon the one real issue that the two churches must address directly. If we are sufficiently reflective and free of absurd prejudices, most of us would grant that the truly central question that we must approach together is how we are to understand church authority, apostolic authority, and episcopal authority in relation to the Petrine office and to the papal privilege regarding enunciation of dogma. If we were allowed to discuss this, free from any anxiety regarding other concerns, many other issues surely would resolve themselves, as obviously subordinate to this one great concern. But here, as it happens, is the very question I wish to raise in what follows: Will we ever indeed be allowed really to have that conversation? I ask this because the most intransigent and extreme members of our respective communions—and those, I fear, who in the East are usually at present the most impassioned and obstreperous among us—seem often incapable or unwilling to acknowledge any recognizable distinction between substantial and accidental differences, between real and imagined difficulties, between obvious and merely suppositious theological issues, and between matters of negligible import and those that lie at the heart of our division.

As regards my own communion, I must reluctantly report that there are some Eastern Christians who have become incapable of defining what it is to be Orthodox except in contradistinction to Roman Catholicism; and among these are a small but voluble number who have (I sometimes suspect) lost any rationale for their Orthodoxy other than their profound hatred, delirious terror, and encyclopedic ignorance of

Rome. For such as these, there can never be any limit set to the number of grievances that need to be cited against Rome, nor any act of contrition on the part of Rome sufficient for absolution. There was something inherently strange in the spectacle of John Paul asking pardon for the 1204 sack of Constantinople and its sequel; but there is something inherently unseemly in the refusal of certain Eastern polemicists to allow the episode to sink back to the level of utter irrelevancy to which it belongs. (In any event, I eagerly await the day when the patriarch of Constantinople, in a gesture of unqualified Christian contrition, makes public penance for the brutal mass slaughter of the metic Latin Christians of Byzantium—men, women, and children—at the rise of Andronicus I Comnenus in 1182, and the sale of thousands of them into slavery to the Turks. Frankly, when all is said and done, the sack of 1204 was a rather measured response, one might argue.)

Now, on the one hand, I am obviously talking about a certain kind of ecclesial extremist, of the sort who can imagine no version of the Catholic faith that does not conform in every detail to the practices and prejudices of his childhood; and all of our churches contain such persons. Of course, in almost every case, the great oddity of such persons—whether they be ultramontanist Catholics or what we call the "ultra-Orthodox"—is that what they generally take to be the immemorial heritage of the Catholic faith is the distinctly modern form of the church that happened to hold sway in the days when their minds still luxuriated in infant pliancy. Thus when a certain kind of militantly conservative Catholic priest is heard to claim that the celibate priesthood was the universal practice of the early church, established by Christ in his apostles, and that therefore even married Catholic priests of the Eastern rites possess defective orders, the historically astute among us should recognize that such a delusion is possible only for a person having no understanding of the priesthood more sophisticated than his pristine boyish memories of Father O'Reilly's avuncular geniality, and the shining example of his contented bachelorhood, and the calm authority with which he presided over the life of the parish church of Saint Anne of Green Gables. And when this same priest ventures theological or ecclesiological opinions, it is almost certain that what he takes to be apostolic Catholicism will turn out to be a particular kind of post-Tridentine Baroque Catholicism, kept buoyantly afloat upon ecclesiological and sacramental principles of an antiquity not much hoarier than 1729. Similarly, when a certain kind of Greek Orthodox antipapal demagogue claims that the Eastern Church has always rejected the validity of the sacraments of the "Latin schismatics," or that the real church schism dates back to the eighth century when the Orthodox Church became estranged from the Roman over the latter's "rejection" of the (fourteenth-century) distinction between God's essence and energies, the historically literate among us should recognize that what he takes to be apostolic Orthodoxy is in fact based upon ecclesiological and sacramental principles that reach back only to 1755, and upon principles of theological interpretation first enunciated in 1942, and upon an interpretation of ecclesiastical history that dates from whenever the prescriptions for his medications expired.

On the other hand, though it is true that such persons are extremists, it is also true that they represent merely the acute manifestation of a chronic pathology. In reality, the most unpleasant aspect of the current state of the division between East and West is the sheer inventiveness with which those ardently committed to that division have gone about fabricating ever profounder and more radical reasons for it. Our distant Christian forebears were content to despise one another over the most minimal of matters—leavened or unleavened eucharistic bread, for instance, or veneration of unconsecrated elements—without ever bothering to suppose that these differences were symptomatic of anything deeper than themselves. Today, however, a grand mythology has evolved regarding the theological dispositions of Eastern and Western Christendom, to the effect that the theologies of the Eastern and Western Catholic traditions have obeyed contrary logics and have in consequence arrived at conclusions inimical each to the other—that is to say, the very essence of what we believe is no longer compatible. I do not believe that, before the middle of the twentieth century, claims were ever made regarding the nature of the division as radical as those one finds not only in the works of inane agitators like the always angry John Romanides, but in the works of theologians of genuine stature, such as Dumitru Staniloae, Vladimir Lossky, or John Zizioulas in the East, or Erich Przywara or Hans Urs von Balthasar in the West; and until those claims are defeated—as well they should be, as they are without exception entirely fanciful—we cannot reasonably hope for anything but *impasse*.

Now, speaking only for my tradition, I think I can identify fairly easily where Orthodox theology has fallen prey to this mythology. Eastern Orthodox theology gained a great deal from the—principally Russian— neopatristic and neo-Palamite revolution during the last century, and especially from the work of Vladimir Lossky. Indeed, in the wake of the Bolshevik Revolution, the very fate of Orthodoxy had become doubtful to many, and so the energy with which Lossky applied himself to a new patristic synthesis that would make clear the inmost essence of Orthodoxy is certainly understandable; but the problems bequeathed to Orthodox scholarship by the "Russian revolution" in theology are many. And the price exacted for those gains was exorbitant. For one thing, it led to a certain narrowing of the spectrum of what many Eastern theologians are prepared to treat as either centrally or legitimately Orthodox, with the consequence that many legitimate aspects of the tradition that cannot be easily situated upon the canonical Losskian path from the patristic age to the hesychastic synthesis of the fourteenth and subsequent centuries have suffered either neglect or denigration. But the most damaging consequence of Orthodoxy's twentieth-century pilgrimage *ad fontes*—paradoxically—has been an increase in the intensity of Eastern theology's anti-Western polemic, or at least in the confidence with which it is uttered. Nor is this only a problem for ecumenism: the anti-Western passion of Lossky and others has on occasion led to severe distortions of Eastern theology; and it has often made intelligent interpretations of Western Christian theology all but impossible for Orthodox thinkers. Neopatristic Orthodox scholarship has usually gone hand in hand with some of the most excruciatingly inaccurate treatments of Western theologians that one could imagine. The aforementioned John Romanides, for instance, has produced expositions of the thought of Augustine and Thomas Aquinas that are almost miraculously devoid of one single correct statement; and while this might be comical if such men spoke only for themselves, it becomes tragic when instead they influence the way great numbers of their fellows view other Christians.

In any event, I want to consider, in turn, three areas where this mythology has metastasized to unprecedented proportions in the past half century—theology, doctrine, and ecclesiology—and to suggest a few possible (if unlikely) solutions to the difficulties that each presents.

II. Theology

This is the most spacious of the three categories, and the most fabulous. Theology, inasmuch as it need not possess the hard lucidity of doctrine nor claim for itself much authority or probative power beyond the stochastic, is fertile soil for false distinctions. It is here, consequently, that those who have devoted their lives to the perpetuation and apocalyptic mythologization of the division of the ancient churches are most indefatigable in their efforts. No sooner is one fantastical theological obstacle surmounted by the cool rationality of the historian or the impeccable logic of the theologian than another is erected; no sooner is one of the interminably pullulating vines of theological legend hacked away than another springs up from its inextirpable roots. There is no area of Christian speculation where the truly creative *agent provocateur* is unable to find some vital difference between East and West, the profundity of which we have only now begun to grasp: the Trinity, nature and grace, sacraments, human nature, the divine image, heaven and hell, sanctification, original sin, soteriology, iconography, the vision of God, spirituality, even Christology. And any suggestion that perhaps differences in terminology (say, between talk of "created grace" and talk of "divine energies") might not necessarily betoken an irreconcilable antagonism between the two traditions is quickly lost in the ceaseless, swift, agile shifting of the conversation from one incorrigible difficulty to another. I shall take one example—Trinitarian theology—to illustrate two things: the power of interested scholarship to create false dilemmas whose only function is to keep contentious debates alive, and the power of such scholarship to distort the theological tradition of both sides of the divide in the process.

Since at least the time of Vladimir Lossky, it has become something of a fixed idea in modern Orthodox theology that Western theology has traditionally forgotten the biblical truth that the unity of the Trinity flows from the paternal *archē* and has come to believe instead that what constitutes the unity of God is an impersonal divine essence prior to the Trinitarian relations. It was Théodore de Régnon who, in 1892, first suggested a distinction between Western and Eastern styles of Trinitarian theology: the tendency, that is, of Latin thought to proceed from general nature to concrete person, so according priority to divine unity, and of Greek thought to proceed from person to nature, so placing the emphasis first on the plurality of divine persons. This distinction was not made in order to suggest a dogmatic superiority on either side, of course; nor, I think, was it very true. But it was seized upon, rather opportunistically, by a number of twentieth-century theologians, and now we find ourselves in an age in which we are often told that we must choose between "Greek" personalism and "Latin" essentialism. And, supposedly, this is a difference that goes all the way back to the patristic period (at least, if certain extremely misleading interpretations of Augustine and Gregory of Nyssa are to be believed). It has become so lamentably common among my fellow Orthodox to treat this claim that Western theology in general posits some "impersonal" divine ground behind the Trinitarian hypostases, and so fails to see the Father as the "fountainhead of divinity," as a simple fact of theological history (and the secret logic of Latin "filioquism"), that it seems almost rude to point out that it is quite demonstrably untrue, from the patristic through the medieval periods, with a few insignificant exceptions. In fact, I would go so far as to claim that the understanding of the generation of the Son and the procession of the Spirit found in Augustine is not only compatible, but also identical, with that of the Cappadocian fathers—including Gregory's and Basil's belief that the generation of the Son is directly from the Father, while the procession of the Spirit is from the Father only *per Filium* (*sed*, to borrow a phrase, *de Patre principaliter*). I have no wish to dwell very long upon the matter here, but I might observe that both Augustine and Gregory of Nyssa even distinguish generation and procession within the Trinity in terms primarily of the order of cause: that is, both claim that the procession of the Spirit differs from the generation of the Son principally in that the former occurs *through* the Son. As Gregory writes (in a passage that would fit very well in, say, book 5 of Augustine's *De Trinitate*),

> [W]hile confessing the immutability of the [divine] nature, we do not deny difference in regard to cause and that which is caused, by which alone we discern the difference of each Person from the other, in that we believe one to be the cause and another to be from the cause; and again we conceive of another difference within that which is from the cause: between the one who, on the one hand, comes directly from the principle and the one who, on the other, comes from the principle through the one who arises directly; thus it unquestionably remains peculiar to the Son to be the Only Begotten, while at the same time it is not to be doubted that the Spirit is of the Father, by virtue of the mediation of the Son that safeguards the Son's character as Only Begotten, and thus the Spirit is not excluded from his natural relation to the Father.[1]

This is the very argument—made by Augustine in *De Trinitate*—that scores of Orthodox theologians in recent decades have denounced as entirely alien to Eastern tradition.

Again, I do not want to venture too far into purely technical matters, but I can think of no better example of an almost entirely imaginary theological problem, pursued with ferocious pertinacity solely because it serves to exaggerate and harden—or, rather, to rationalize—the division between

---

1. Gregory of Nyssa, *Ad Ablabium: Quod non sint tres Dei*, Gregorii Nysseni Opera, ed. Werner Jaeger et al. (Leiden: Brill, 1958–), 3/1:55–56.

Christian East and West, but that succeeds only in distorting the tradition of both almost beyond recognition. And I cannot emphasize this last point too forcefully. Since the time of Lossky, various modern Orthodox theologians have adopted an exaggerated "Photianism" and have, in their assault on "filioquism," argued that—though, within the economy of salvation, the Spirit is breathed out by Christ upon the apostles—the Trinitarian relations as revealed in the economy of salvation are distinct from the eternal relations of the immanent Trinity. This is theologically disastrous, and in fact subversive of the entire Eastern patristic tradition of Trinitarian dogma. Were this claim sound, there would be absolutely no basis for Trinitarian theology at all; the arguments by which the Cappadocians defended full Trinitarian theology against Arian and Eunomian thought—in works like Basil's *De Spiritu Sancto* and Gregory's *Adversus Macedonianos*—would entirely fail. Orthodoxy would have no basis whatsoever.

In any event, as I say, this is only one example among many. In the abstract, theology as such should throw up no impediments to the ecumenical enterprise between East and West; whatever differences may exist between the two traditions, none of them is of any appreciable magnitude, and even if they were they would still constitute only differences between *theologoumena*, not between *dogmata*. And yet it is in fact in the realm of theology that the greatest number of obstacles to intelligent and charitable dialogue appear; for, where there remains some desire to rationalize and deepen the division between the churches, the sheer speculative plasticity of theological reflection and language allows for an endless multiplication of ever newer "ancient" differences. As for how to remedy this situation, I can offer only the weak recommendation of better education: perhaps we might find a way to force young Orthodox theologians to read Augustine and Aquinas, rather than belligerent treatments of Augustine and Aquinas written by dyspeptic Greeks, or to force young Catholic theologians to immerse themselves in Byzantine scholasticism and Eastern ecclesiology, and to force everyone involved to learn the history of the church in all its ambiguity. But, whatever we do, we have too long allowed bad scholarship and empty cant and counterfeit history to influence and even dictate the terms of the relation between Orthodoxy and Rome.

III. Doctrine

Doctrine presents us with another kind of obstacle, at once more concrete and more minimal in form. These differences, once one puts aside purely tendentious attempts to magnify or multiply the doctrinal divergences of the two traditions, are very few indeed, easily identified, and in some cases easily resolved (if there is a will to do so). One of the great virtues of the Roman Catholic approach to doctrinal pronouncements is that, in their official formulae, these pronouncements are often so scrupulously pure of detail that they are capable of a vast variety of theological receptions. Of the two modern Marian dogmas—the assumption of Mary and the Immaculate Conception—the first is obviously perfectly in accord (though too vague to be identical) with the story that the Orthodox Church celebrates every Feast of the Dormition; the second, it has often been noted, seems to imply a doctrine of original sin quite different from that common to the East, but here two points need to be made: first, theological differences are not doctrinal differences and, second, the doctrine is again stated with such chaste minimalism that it is an error to imagine that any particular historically conditioned understanding of original sin must necessarily attach to it. In truth, it is not so much the substance of such doctrines that must remain issues of contention between us, but simply the question of whether there was ever sufficient authority to promulgate them in the first place: and that, of course, takes us back to the issues of papal infallibility, and papal primacy, and the nature of ecumenical councils.

That said, doctrines do divide us, and I think that, in the nature of things, the Eastern Church inevitably has a keener sense of this. I have among my Roman Catholic theologian friends, especially those who have had little direct dealings with Eastern Christianity, some who are justifiably offended by the hostility with which the advances of the Roman Church are occasionally met by certain Orthodox, and who assume that the greatest obstacle to reunion of the churches is Eastern immaturity and divisiveness. The problem is dismissed as one of "psychology," and the only counsel offered is one of "patience." Fair enough: decades of communist tyranny set atop centuries of other, far more invincible tyrannies have effectively shattered the Orthodox world into a contentious confederacy of national churches struggling to preserve their own regional identities against every "alien" influence, and under such conditions only the most obdurate stock survives. But psychology is the least of our problems. Simply said, a Catholic who looks eastward *should* find nothing to which to object, because what he sees is the church of the seven ecumenical councils (but—here's the rub—for him, this means the first seven of twenty-one, at least according to the definition of ecumenical council bequeathed the Roman Church by Robert Bellarmine). When an Orthodox Christian turns his eyes westward, however, he sees many elements that appear novel to him: the *filioque* clause, the way in which papal primacy is articulated, purgatory, etc. Our divisions do truly concern doctrine, and this problem admits of no immediately obvious remedy, because both churches are so fearfully burdened by infallibility. And we need to appreciate that this creates an essential asymmetry in the Orthodox and Catholic approaches to the ecumenical enterprise. No Catholic properly conscious of the teachings of his church would be alarmed by what the Orthodox Church would bring into his communion—he would find it sound and familiar, and would not therefore suspect for a moment that reunion had in any way compromised or diluted his Catholicism. But to an Orthodox Christian, inasmuch as the Roman Church does make doctrinal assertions absent from his tradition, it may well seem that to accept reunion with Rome would mean becoming a Roman Catholic, and so ceasing to be Orthodox. Hence it would be unreasonable to expect the Eastern and Western Churches to approach ecumenism from the same vantage: the historical situations of the churches are simply too different.

To show what I mean, I suppose I should point to the two areas where I suspect the most important dogmatic progress needs to be made, one of which is very obvious—the *filioque* clause—and the other of which is less so—the doctrine of purgatory. In the first case, actually, doctrinal concord should not (in ideal circumstances) be elusive. Indeed, were this simply a matter of theology, my impulse would be to defend the clause, so long as it is understood to mean that the Spirit proceeds from the Father through the Son (the Father being, as Scripture clearly reveals, the sole wellspring of Godhead), because I believe that that is the authentic Eastern teaching as well, and the only teaching that can at once be made congruent with the evidence of Scripture and the logic of Orthodox theological tradition. Not everyone agrees: as I have said, Vladimir Lossky and others have argued the opposite; but I find their arguments not only unpersuasive, but also historically absurd and theologically catastrophic. But this is not solely a matter of theology, and where doctrine is concerned a much narrower set of standards must apply. That the insertion of the phrase in the creed was irregular Rome freely acknowledges, and John Paul II as much as said that it should be taken as no more than a theological gloss upon the Spirit's procession from the Father, and he was himself obviously quite happy to revert to the Greek half of the diptychs in his own usage. But, given that we are talking about doctrine, I must be honest and point out that, on this matter, half measures will avail us nothing, and anything short of a total ablation of the phrase from all Catholic rites will prove fruitless. For really, it does not matter how sophisticated we become in our grasp of theological history, or how subtle in our dogmatic negotiations with the past; it is simply a fact that so long as the clause is used in any quarter of the Roman communion, there will not be reunion with the East. It has too long served as the historical symbol par excellence of what divides us, and around the ambiguity and irregularity of its insertion in the universal symbol of Catholic faith, without the assent of the Eastern churches, cluster so many of the most divisive issues of theological history, that it will remain an insurmountable obstacle to unity for not only the foreseeable, but also the imaginable, future. Orthodox hierarchs could undertake reunion only at the price of massive internal schisms—and what then would be gained? It may seem unfair to ask Rome to make so immense and possibly disruptive a gesture without any reciprocal move on the part of the East, but—given the asymmetry of the ecumenical situation mentioned above—this cannot be treated as an occasion for a *quid pro quo*. A decision must be reached about what is most important: if it is unity, the phrase must be expunged from all confessional use; if the phrase is, however, to remain, we may as well resign ourselves to disunity in perpetuity.

On the second matter, purgatory, it may seem somewhat counterintuitive to place this issue alongside something of such enormous consequence as the *filioque* clause, but here I think is one area where Roman doctrinal pronouncements have not been as marked as one might wish by that formulary minimalism I praised above. The Eastern Church believes in sanctification after death, and perhaps the doctrine of purgatory really asserts nothing more than that; but Rome has also traditionally spoken of it as "temporal punishment," which the pope may in whole or in part remit. The problem here is, it is difficult, from the Orthodox perspective, to see how it could be both. That is, if it is sanctification, then it is nothing other than salvation: that is, the transformation of our souls, by which the Holy Spirit conforms us to God, through all eternity, and frees us from the last residue of our perversity and selfishness. The Orthodox and Catholic Churches are as one, after all, in denying that salvation is either a magical transformation of the human being into something else or merely a forensic imputation of sinlessness to a sinful creature: it is a real glorification and organic transfiguration of the creature in Christ, one which never violates the integrity of our creatureliness, but which—by causing us to progress from sin to righteousness—really makes us partakers of the divine nature. Very well then: What then could it mean to remit purgation? Why, if it is sanctification, would one want such remission, and would it not then involve instead the very magical transformation of the creature into something beyond itself that the Orthodox and Catholic Churches both deny? These are not, granted, unanswerable questions, but they are questions as yet unanswered, and there is genuine need for a serious engagement on what the doctrinal formulation regarding sanctification after death should be, and whether Roman and Orthodox traditions can be reconciled in a more than superficial way on this one issue.

IV. Ecclesiology

Let me turn, finally, to the real root of our division, ecclesiology. It may be the case that the one singular failure of the early church was in not convoking a council to deal with the matter of ecclesiology as a properly doctrinal locus. It is here, perhaps, where all other problems come to rest. Papal primacy, and especially the doctrine of papal infallibility, of course, remain at the very center of what separates us: Does the one imply universal jurisdiction, and if so of what sort? Does the other absolve the pontiff of any responsibility to conciliar authority? And so on.

Catholic ecumenists, I should point out, often misconstrue the nature of the Orthodox distrust of their good will. It is not simply the case that the Orthodox are so fissiparous and jealous of their autonomy that the Petrine office appears to them a dangerous principle of homogeneity, to which their fractious Eastern wills cannot submit. Rather, it more often than not appears to be a dangerous principle of plurality. After all, under the capacious canopy of the papal office, so many disparate things find common shelter. An obvious example: three men are called patriarch of Antioch in the Roman communion (Melkite, Maronite, and East Syrian)—which suggests that the very title of patriarch, even as regards an apostolic see, is merely honorific, because the only unique patriarchal office is the pope's. To Orthodox Christians it often appears as if, from the Catholic side, so long as the pope's supremacy is acknowledged, all else is irrelevant ornament. Which yields the sad paradox that the more the Catholic Church strives to accommodate Orthodox concerns, the more disposed many Orthodox are to see in this merely the advance embassy of an omnivorous ecclesial empire. Now, of course, this plurality of patriarchs is an accident of history; but it is also an insufferable situation. We surely must acknowledge that the apostolic dignity of a patriarchate should not be reduced to an honorary title attached to a metropolitan responsible for one rite among others within his jurisdiction. And the very notion that the pope could possibly possess the authority to "appoint" a patriarch in another see is a historical and theological nonsense for which the Orthodox should rightly have no patience whatsoever. So this too we must address: What is the unique dignity of the apostolic office of patriarch, and what is its jurisdictional authority, and how does it relate to the preeminent patriarchate occupied by the bishop of Rome?

As regards the doctrine of papal infallibility, and especially the claim that the definition of dogma by the pope proceeds *ex sese et non ex consensu ecclesiae*, two comments seem worth making. The first is that, taking the doctrine again in its most minimal form, the claim of infallibility is inoffensive: if indeed the Holy Spirit speaks to the mind of the church, and the church promulgates infallible doctrine, and the successor of Peter enjoys the privilege of enunciating doctrine, then whenever he speaks *ex cathedra* of course he speaks infallibly; this is almost a tautology. It is the question, obviously, of how one gets to that point that is the object of our contention. As for the claim that it is not reached *ex consensu*, the only real question is whether this is a prior or a posterior condition. That is to say, what does it imply regarding the authority of councils, or other patriarchates, or tradition? Obviously Rome denies that the pontiff could generate doctrine out of personal whim. And, after all, clearly it is true that no doctrine could possibly follow from the *consensus* of the church, if for no other reason than that the church is not a democracy, and truth is not something upon which we vote. That said, I do not wish to conjure this issue away, and I would that the definition had never been pronounced; but this I can say: it is not clear to me that, as formulated, the doctrine destines us to perpetual division. It can, I suspect, be integrated into a fully developed teaching regarding conciliarity, one that can accommodate a certain magisterial privilege that is unique, but not isolated from the charisms of episcopal collegiality.

These, however, are familiar questions and need not be more fully addressed here. There is, though, one final ecclesiological issue that it seems to me should be raised, and that rarely is, and that bears directly upon the way in which the matter of papal jurisdiction is phrased in *Ut unum sint*. It is no great secret that the popular picture of the division between East and West—the myth, that is, of a sudden definitive catastrophic breach between the churches that immediately created two distinct communions—bears little relation to history. We know that, even after the excommunications of 1054, both Rome and Constantinople were—as far as anyone could tell—in communion with the patriarchate of Antioch, for instance; that this estrangement between two patriarchs affected next to nothing in the northern Balkans; that even after the sack of Constantinople the boundaries between Catholic and Orthodox were fluid in much of the *oecumene*; that as late as the time of Nicholas Cabasilas, and well beyond, the sacramental validity of the Western Church could not credibly be challenged, or vice versa. As I have said, it was only in the eighteenth century that denigrations of the orders or sacraments of the respective "other" church became part of theological discourse; and those who still cling to this view of a hermetically sealed sacramental order—Orthodox or Catholic—over against a now invalid antichurch are in fact not defenders of tradition, but rank modernists. The worst manifestation of this is the practice among some Greek parishes—which I would not call irregular but heretical, if I had the authority so to do—of rebaptism. The attempt of certain modern Orthodox to justify this practice from Cyprianic principles would be compelling were it not so manifestly a thoroughly contemporary development, out of keeping with the thinking of the Eastern Church right through the high Middle Ages, and if it were not for the absolute absence of any analogy between the two situations.

Chrysostom Frank published an article some years ago that laid out quite compactly, but with a wealth of detail, how porous (or, in some cases, nonexistent) the partitions were between the churches for centuries after the excommunications of 1054.[2] *Communicatio in sacris* between Orthodox and Catholics, Frank notes, continued in some places till the seventeenth century. At the Council of Florence (1438–1439), for instance, both sides spoke of the division between East and West as a wall of separation erected *within* the one Catholic Church. In various reaches of the Ottoman Empire, Frank observes, great numbers of Orthodox and Catholic believers— among the clergy no less than among the laity—proceeded as if there were no division. Latin missionaries were even known to regard the local Orthodox bishop as their ordinary, and Catholic priests were allowed to preach in Orthodox churches, catechize, hear confessions, and even on occasion administer the Eucharist. Orthodox Christians did not hesitate to show their reverence for the Catholic sacrament at *corpus Christi* processions, and on the island of Andros the Orthodox bishop and his clergy—fully vested and bearing candles—participated in the procession itself. In the seventeenth century, Frank shows, there were abundant signs of cordiality between the communions: a former Athonite abbot in 1628 asking Rome to open a school on the Holy Mountain, the Orthodox patriarch of Antioch in 1644 inviting the Jesuits to open a house in Damascus, the metropolitan of Aegina in 1690 petitioning the pope for Jesuits to undertake pastoral work

2. Chrysostom Frank, "Orthodox-Catholic Relations: An Orthodox Reflection," *Pro Ecclesia* 7, no. 1 (Winter 1998).

in his diocese. And then, Frank sadly observes, in the eighteenth century both churches hardened in their positions, and soon this history of accord was forgotten. That said, it is still not the case, even in the modern period, that an absolute division between the two communions has ever existed. Under communist rule in Russia, for instance, Orthodox and Catholic communicants out of necessity sometimes received from the same chalice, with tacit episcopal consent, and there are parts of Syria today where this fluidity of boundaries is an open secret and intercommunion a simple fact of life. In fact, I know of two Syrian parishes in the United States that have passed from the jurisdiction of an Orthodox to a Catholic bishop or in the opposite direction whose communicants consider themselves either Catholic or Orthodox while belonging to one parish and one altar. To put it simply, there has never been a time when a perfect and impermeable wall has stood between the sacramental orders of East and West.

Perhaps none of this is very important: local irregularities, after all, are not an index of church discipline. But all of this raises a question for me: to wit, When and where can we really locate the schism? Not only in time and space, that is, but within dogmatic and canonical norms. We are divided, we know, but how, when, and by what authority? And, while it is a social and cultural and political fact that we are divided, what is its theological rationale? Can the failure of communion between two patriarchs or bishops—a frequent event in the early church—create a real division of sacramentally united communions from one another? Could, for instance, the Orthodox really believe that the pope could excommunicate another patriarch and his flock? By what provision of Eastern canon law? And if Rome cannot, how much less Constantinople? And if communion has never truly wholly ceased, how can we actually identify the moment, the cause, or in fact the possibility of that division? And this, I think, may be the real question that a discussion of papal jurisdiction must ultimately broach, the least obvious or expected question of all: not how we can possibly discover the doctrinal and theological resources that would enable or justify reunion, but how we can possibly discover the doctrinal and theological resources that could justify or indeed make certain our division. This is not a moral question—how do we dare to remain disunited?—but a purely canonical one: Are we sure that we are? For, if not, then our division is simply sin, a habit of desire and thought that feeds upon nothing but its own perverse passions and immanent logic, a fiction of the will, and obedience to a lie.

In any event, my last remark is only this: reunion of the Orthodox and Roman Churches has become an imperative, and time is growing short.

I say this because I often suffer from bleak premonitions of the ultimate cultural triumph in the West of a consumerism so devoid of transcendent values as to be, inevitably, nothing but a pervasive and pitiless nihilism. And it is, I think, a particularly soothing and saccharine nihilism, possessing a singular power for absorbing the native energies of the civilization it is displacing without prompting any extravagant alarm at its vacuous barbarisms. And I suspect that the only tools at Christianity's disposal, as it confronts the rapid and seemingly inexorable advance of this nihilism, will be evangelical zeal and internal unity. I like to think—call it the Sophiologist in me—that the tribulations that Eastern Christianity has suffered under Islamic and communist rule have insulated it from some of the more corrosive pathologies of modernity for a purpose, and endowed it with a special mission to bring its liturgical, intellectual, and spiritual strengths to the aid of the Western Christian world in its struggle with the nihilism that the post-Christian West has long incubated and that now surrounds us all, while yet drawing on the strengths and charisms of the Western Church to preserve Orthodoxy from the political and cultural frailty that still afflicts Eastern Christianity. Whatever the case, though, we are more in need of one another now than ever. To turn away from ecumenism now may be to turn toward the darkness that is deepening all about us. We are called to be children of light, and I do not think that we will walk very far in the light hereafter except together.

FIFTEEN

Remarks in Response to Father Lawrence Dewan

My thanks, first and foremost, to Father Dewan for a presentation at once so very concise and yet so marvelously comprehensive of its topic. I have to admit, though, and rather peevishly, that he has put me at something of a disadvantage. However concentrated his address, there is a magisterial quality about it that leaves me with the feeling that to interrogate its premises or to take exception to its conclusions would be nothing less than to contend with Aquinas himself, a task for which I am neither qualified nor eager. Nor, moreover, do I want to reduce Father Dewan to the role of medium at my private séance. Still, it seems incumbent on me to begin our discussion by raising what I hope are a few genuinely probative questions. So I am afraid I am going to do the tediously obvious thing and ask about the real applicability of the all-embracing vision with which we have just been presented to the world that lies about us, and to proceed *etsi deus non daretur*—or at least *etsi Thomas non daretur*. I hope this will prove a useful way of proceeding, and one that is not too impertinent.

So let me make three rather large and leisurely remarks, each culminating in a small and overly hasty question.

I

A rather pregnant sentence appears midway through Father Dewan's paper: "If we wish to make Thomas's standpoint our own, we must realize the importance of the knowledge that nature is a cause which acts for an end." Indeed—but we cannot deduce an "ought" from an "if" unless the "if" has already been decided. I am not sure how conditional that conditional clause is, but every conditional implicitly comprises its own negation. So what if we do not wish to make Thomas's standpoint our own? Or, at least, are not persuaded as yet that we should? More to the point, what if we do not share in this knowledge of nature's *causal* finality? I ask this not for myself. For, while it is true that I have no particular desire to share Thomas's perspective on much of anything, neither do I have any particular aversion to doing so in particular instances; and I, unlike the vast majority of my contemporaries, start from a powerful sympathy with Thomas's metaphysics. Let us say that I am asking from the vantage of some anonymous modern man: say, some post-Kantian, post-Nietzschean, semi-Heideggerean, universalist, crypto-perennialist, confessionally Eastern Orthodox cynic from Maryland, skeptical of the demonstrability of formal or final causality at the purely dialectical level— or, rather, let us just say I am asking from the vantage of any person raised in the world after Darwin.

As Father Dewan says, everything depends upon understanding nature as a cause that operates for an end. Seeing the world thus, we can observe a natural continuity among cosmology, ethics, and metaphysics. There are forms that determine the emergence of substances, and ends— proximate, ultimate, or transcendent—that guide the particularities of existence and unite the totality of things into a whole: a *universum*. The entire ensemble of these causes is then embraced within the all-disposing and all-sustaining finality of God's governance and providence. All these causes are ontologically—if not necessarily chronologically—prior to their consequences; and thus the universe is a spiritual, physical, moral, social, political continuum, obscure in some of its details, perhaps, but resplendently obvious in its totality. And, from the universe, we can draw legitimate conclusions not only about the "is" of a thing, but about its "ought." Recognizing the causal priority of finality, nature itself—through its evident forms—instructs us in elements of moral fulfillment; a legitimate analogy can be drawn that is more than mere metaphor between natural and social order, or between natural and social ends, as complementary manifestations of a single divine order. And so on.

Needless to say, however, formal and final causes have fallen on hard times in recent years. And, in my admittedly inadequate and desultory survey of modern Thomist authors, I have often run across scholars who attempt to dismiss the problem merely by adverting to the demonstrable reality of form and finality within nature. But this, of course, accomplishes nothing; modern science does not for a moment deny either form or finality; it denies only that they should be conceived as causes, rather than as consequences: emergent phenomena that represent not the supereminent source of all things, but merely the residue of a process. This is especially clear at the ontogenic level, where formal constraints operate in the most fruitful of ways, but where these constraints are seen as the result of an incalculably vast series of fortuitous phylogenic mutations and attritions. And this, of course, makes all the difference: for, in the absence of that causal priority, all moral analogy—every claim that the social participates in a natural order, which is itself a manifestation of divine government—is suppositious at best, and strikes the ears of many like the distant rumor of an ancient music.

So, at last, my question: Is it possible to argue with any cogency for the real causal priority of finality in nature, or is the Thomist position possible only under the fully unfurled canopy of faith? And, if the latter, does Thomas's standpoint become, viewed from the outside, a "system" in the Hegelian sense, sealed within the seamlessness of its immanent logic—a system that is, moreover, as Hume observed of Berkeley's thought, susceptible of no refutation but impotent to command assent?

II

My second, briefer question follows directly from the first. Let us assume that final causality *is* rationally demonstrable (I tend to think it is); we still have not at that point determined what moral analogy, if any, can be drawn between the final causes resident in nature and human motive or action. Another pregnant passage from Father Dewan's address reads: "Thomas presents the existence of God as *naturally* known to all, even though naturally *reasoned to*. That someone professes ignorance of the existence of God stems from moral disorder. . . . Given that one has knowledge of God as the author of being, one has knowledge of him as lovable by us, indeed as more lovable than ourselves." Now I will grant that there is something appealing in this assertion, purely in the abstract; at least, it seems obvious to me that the refusal to acknowledge the ontological dependency of finite reality on a transcendent source is evidence of a defect of understanding, which may well proceed from some perversity of the will. And yet, after all—or so it seems to me—there is so very much that mitigates the culpability in this "failure," given that we have all grown up within a narrative of reality that understands the natural as something accomplished through immense ages of monstrous violence, mass extinction, the extraordinary profligacy of an algorithmic phylogenic logic that will squander tens of thousands of lives to fashion a single durable type; a process of evolution that advances not despite—but because of—disease, warfare, predation, famine, extinction, and so on. And the result? A world of elemental caprice, natural calamity, the pitilessness of chance, children consumed by cancer . . . (this is a potentially interminable list).

So my second question: Even if we acknowledge the reality of an organizing finality, given the nature of the efficient causes it prompts into action, can we really claim that this cause is transparent in its moral or social implications, or that it operates as a moral cause—in any sense we understand at all—that commands imitation, obedience, or (most unlikely of all) love?

III

And, lastly, even assuming we can establish the existence of a kind of moral imperative in the very orderliness of the world, it may not really be possible—apart from simple declaration—properly to discern the hierarchy of goods within societies.

I ask this out of a very real sense of frustration at the few texts I have lately read by Thomists of the old persuasion, laying out with extraordinary precision arguments regarding the relative preponderance of diverse moral ends. In many instances, perhaps, the decisions regarding the relative ultimacy of certain goods—which, that is, take teleological precedence over others in the grammar of moral action—are obvious and uncontroversial. But, beyond a certain, very rudimentary level of practical ethical deliberation, it becomes fairly obvious that the determination of which ends—and hence of which imperatives—command our prior obedience is not only touched, but thoroughly polluted, by arbitrariness, and is sustainable only by the most circular kinds of argument; and that the very premises upon which such deliberations necessarily rest can often be reduced, by any truly scrupulous analysis, to the character of sheer assertion. At the most crucial junctures, precisely where prescriptive clarity seems most needful, teleology fails us and a kind of purely intuitive prudence—always shaped by a host of insupportable prejudices—begins to predominate. So, in a world that is able to understand itself *etsi Thomas non daretur*, is there really any way of translating the apprehension of a final cosmic cause that is also the Good into a moral language that is ever anything more than an interminable succession of peremptory moral assertions without any ascertainable rule for adjudicating among them?

Which, I suppose, is another way of asking whether in the disenchanted world of modernity, even for Christians, the idea of natural law can ever be much more than a fond desire and a willful fiction—unless, of course, by natural law we mean only a general instruction in particular natural goods and a general guide to the content of moral judgments whose character as imperatives emanates from some mysterious realm wholly outside the entire continuum of nature. Such an idea of natural law would be, of course, severely minimalist, and would rather rapidly—I would think—dissolve back into indefinition when challenged to justify itself. But maybe, after all, the very idea of natural law is at most an edifying nonsense so long as it is conceived as a "law" that is truly "natural."

SIXTEEN

Thrift

The road of excess leads to the palace of wisdom.

—William Blake,
The Marriage of Heaven and Hell

I. Thrift and Virtue

No child dreaming in idle innocence of valiant deeds or splendid accomplishments or enduring works has ever had occasion to spare a thought for thrift; in the opulent golden mornings of our lives, when all things seem possible, we do not—if we are sane—surrender our fantasies of castles, battlefields, banquets, explorations, conquests, trophies, and transfigurations for the dry, astringent, colorless images the word "thrift" summons to mind to bore us into the resigned docility of adulthood: immaculate interiors sparely adorned and sensibly furnished, ill-lighted corridors, gardens dedicated entirely to edible vegetables, larders as unappetizing as they are replete, cupboard shelves lightly laden with unpatterned plate and service, plain garments with simple seams, parlors only judiciously heated, and meals adequate, nourishing, and accompanied by the poorest of wines. As a value, thrift is devoid of any element of the majestic or the mysterious, and so is impotent to stir our imaginations or inspire our wills; it does not enchant, beguile, or inveigle us. G. K. Chesterton, in his best book, *What's Wrong with the World*, entitled a brief, diverting, but unpersuasive chapter "The Romance of Thrift,"[1] but this is merely another example of his often annoying delight in paradox; the phrase strikes us as whimsical because we all know that "romance" and "thrift" are practically antonymous. A culture perfectly devoted to thrift would produce nothing prodigious or astonishing, would allow the arts to languish, would leave behind no magnificent palaces or glorious temples or mighty monuments to teach later generations humility before their ancestors, and would require nothing more from itself than material sufficiency and a wise use of resources. And an individual perfectly devoted to thrift could never become a hero, a saint, or a monster, since thrift is the enemy of all grand gestures—of recklessness, generosity, fealty, defiance, prodigality, risk, and contrition alike—and acts as a restraint upon any desire that threatens to exceed the rigid bounds of moral and fiscal economy. Thrift, therefore, can have no absolute value in itself; if pursued as an absolute, it can only destroy and render inert; taken as an end in itself, it must become an ethics of lifelessness. It is a philological irony that, though "thrift" is the substantive that corresponds to the verb "thrive," the meanings of the two words have today been rendered—by the vagaries of usage and association—all but irreconcilable: one who thrives is one who flourishes, who is vigorous and robust, rude of health and possibly of manner, prosperous and perhaps a bit profligate, who does not worry over each expenditure, but increases even where he squanders; one who is thrifty, by contrast, is one who must jealously guard his substance against dissipation and abuse, who measures out his goods and his hours according to an inflexible calculus of need and due proportion, and who must consequently cultivate in himself a kind of habitual calm anxiety. The thrifty man does not "thrive"; he merely survives, and that is his triumph. To perfect the practice of thrift, one must aspire to a condition of almost mystical drabness.

It might well be asked, then, why thrift should possess any interest as an object of critical inquiry. It most certainly is *not* one of the classical virtues, as enumerated in either pagan or Christian sources, nor is there evidence of it having ever occupied any prominent place among the spiritual or social concerns of later Christendom. It is at best a neutral and purely pragmatic value, a practical strategy for preserving one's resources against the perils of privation or the temptation to ruinous extravagance. But it possesses no moral nature of its own; it is equally at the service of prudent stewardship or heartless parsimony, providence or theft, charity or greed. It is princi-

---

1. G. K. Chesterton, *What's Wrong with the World*, 2nd ed. (London and New York: Cassell and Co., 1910), pp. 135–42.

pally the art of domestic economy, and while classical and medieval cultures both tended to praise, say, the woman who could run a household well without falling into debt, wasting her husband's wealth, or failing to have enough stores to feed her family through the fallow seasons, thrift lacked that quality of heroic (and, to be exact, *virile*) exertion that, in one sense or another, was an aspect of the recognized virtues of pagan or Christian culture. And yet, thrift is genuinely worthy of our attention, as an ethos or practice or personal discipline, if we are interested in the moral and cultural sources of American society; for it was a distinct and surprisingly central value in the early formation of America, and to understand its nature, its origins as a recognized good, its religious and ethical character, and so on, is to gain a truly probative perspective upon the forces that shaped and still shape American culture, for good or ill. In fact, it is precisely the *enigma* of thrift—how, that is, so mundane and (really) negligible a value could ever have come to be regarded as a moral duty or achievement—that makes it illuminative of certain lingering mysteries of America's cultural and social oddity. To determine what thrift is or has been in American cultural history, however, one must first identify what it is not and has never been.

Thrift should not, first of all, be confused with or mistaken for the classical virtue of prudence, which is something far more expansive. Prudence is a kind of practical wisdom, sustained and inevitably surpassed by a higher, "theoretical" wisdom whose aim is the contemplation—the *theōria*—of divine things. In Aristotelian terms, prudence is the art of balance in all of life's contingencies, a hewing to the "golden mean," an intellectual habit that allows one to recognize the virtuous and vicious paths that open up before one and to elect the former; it involves a proper sense of what one owes to another, what is due to oneself, where various persons fit in the scale of society, and what each occasion demands of us. The prudent man may be cavalierly generous, if the situation requires it, or utterly uncompromising; he may be imperious or suppliant, bold or cautious, inflexible or yielding, cunning or guileless, restrained or lavish, as circumstances dictate; he should be moderate in most things, but conscious of what is expected of him and willing to undertake whatever effort or expense is required to meet those expectations; he should, if he is a gentleman (and only gentlemen are capable of true prudence), be magnanimous in his dealings with inferiors; and he should govern his emotions. Cicero calls prudence "the knowledge of what is good, what bad, and what neutral," and says it is composed of memory, intelligence, and foresight.[2]

---

2. Cicero, De inventione 2.53.159.

Thrift is nothing so immense or consequential. Of the four classic virtues upon which various pagan and Christian sources agree—prudence, justice, fortitude, and temperance—thrift comes nearest perhaps to the last, but it would be an unwarranted aggrandizement of thrift to suggest that the two are identical. According again to Cicero (and Aristotle, Seneca, and Aquinas would all agree), temperance is the wise restraint of lust, anger, and brazenness, and is composed of continence, clemency, and modesty.[3] Thrift is far smaller and far more specific than this. At most, I think we can say that thrift, in a palliated and diluted way, bears some resemblance—and has some tenuous connection—to ancient ideals of personal restraint, sobriety, and the equilibrium of the gentlemanly mean: the wise and cautious comportment of the Aristotelian aristocrat, the Stoic ideal of seemly simplicity and self-governance, the Christian distaste for gross indulgence and dissipation, and so on. Nonetheless, it is not an aristocratic ideal, an interior discipline of the "chaste spirit," or a species of Christian humility. It is something simpler, homelier, and more concrete—yet more ambiguous—in nature.

By the same token, one should avoid imagining that thrift is a distinctly Christian value. Nowhere in the literary remains of Christian late antiquity or of the Middle Ages is there any evidence that thrift was thought to entail any notable moral or spiritual qualities, or was even recognized as a distinct category of ethical behavior or achievement. Randle Cotgrave, in his *A Dictionarie of the French and English Tongues* of 1611, several times quotes the old French proverb "Après la feste et le jeu, les pois au feu," which he renders in various ways: for instance, "When costlie Feasts and Games are ended, fond wast[e] by thrift let be amended"; or, again, "Those that will make good shift, must after play use thrift." This is probably as close to a definition of the nature and value of thrift as one could hope to extract from all the folklore, high philosophy, and spiritual wisdom we possess of the premodern culture of Christendom. Insofar as thrift is ever invoked in medieval texts, as anything more than the tribute debauchery must pay to necessity, it is as a preparation or remedy for the necessary expenditures of feasts and charity; as such it is a purely material economy that occupies a penumbral (and somewhat profane) interval between the extravagance of the festal periods and the daily, animal exigencies of sheer *conservatio in esse*. And I do not think it would be correct to interpret the absence of any high valuation of thrift as simple neutrality toward it; nor, I think, should one simply say that the economic conditions necessary for thrift

3. Cicero, *De inventione* 2.53.163.

to emerge as an actual "virtue" were not yet in place and so, as yet, thrift had not been given adequate thematic treatment. Rather, there was an intrinsic antagonism in Christian culture toward any celebration of thrift as a species of virtue (an antagonism, obviously, that had no occasion to become explicit or conscious); the entire rhythm by which medieval Christian society lived militated against it. The whole Christian year—and so the whole flow of communal life—was governed by the church's calendar of celebration and penance, an oscillation between feast and fast, each of which represented a distinct form of exorbitance, excess, or extravagance. The former was, ideally, unrestrained so long as sin was avoided, and the latter was a form of mortification well beyond anything necessity might impose (during Lent and Advent, for instance, the duty of almsgiving was vastly increased, and so neither could be regarded as a period of frugality as such, and neither was necessarily any less onerous to the householder than periods of feast). Even ordinary time was seen as a preparation for the Lenten or festal seasons and was measured out by days of indulgence (Sundays especially) and days of abnegation (Wednesdays and Fridays); and eleemosynary obligations were never wholly relaxed at any point in the Christian year. This does not mean that, as a matter of practical routine, houses were not governed by the same laws of scarcity and plenty that have held invincible sway in every age; but, if we wish to define the ethos of the Middle Ages, we can do so only by ascertaining what medieval persons praised as virtues and abhorred as vices, which values they thought morally or spiritually important and which they thought nugatory, and what practices they considered organic expressions of their faith. It should be clear, at the very least, that there was simply no room for a "virtue" of the middle ground in an age whose entire spiritual and cultural reality was given definition by an oscillation between twin extravagances of "release and restraint," or in an age in which it was often considered rather shameful to keep one's resources to oneself (an age, that is, when economy was only a private regimen and excess was a public good).[4]

Above all, thrift ought not to be mistaken for a form of Christian asceticism, for the simple reason that there is nothing more extravagant, profligate, and (in a purely practical sense) useless than the ascetic life. Throughout the Christian centuries, ascetic discipline—for the religious and secular priests both—was seen properly as a kind of Lent undertaken

---

4. For a good discussion of the disciplines and liberties of the Christian calendar in medieval society, see Bridget Ann Henisch, *Feast and Fast: Food in Medieval Society* (University Park: Pennsylvania State University Press, 1976), especially pp. 28–58.

by those of special vocation, for the good of the whole body, but not as a model of simple self-restraint applicable to all. Max Weber burdened us with the largely worthless concept of Protestantism's "this-worldly asceticism," which is a category mistake: not because it is a contradiction in terms (the premise that asceticism is typically unworldly is profoundly mistaken), but because it suggests that there is some sort of continuity in sensibility and intention between asceticism and a sober life of prudent moderation—which there certainly is not. The ascetic is never moderate, nor does he or she strive to conserve material resources as such, nor certainly should he or she ever be conscious of cost. The austerities of Simon Stylites or Evagrios Pontikos or John of the Cross were every bit as exorbitant in their way as the decor of Versailles. Asceticism is a giving of the self without reserve: it should be jealous of nothing but purity; it produces nothing profitable; it contributes nothing that can be weighed, measured, or stored; it is a pouring out of one's entire substance into the sands of the desert or the chill of an isolated cell. Its principal fruits are spiritual progress, bodily inanition, and prayer. The Christian ascetic does not merely deny himself certain pleasures so as to be certain that his goods will not vanish prematurely; he denies himself even the just wages of his labor and even necessary things, in order to place himself in a—quite precisely—"exorbitant" relation to all normal society, all common responsibilities; this allows him to devote himself to the life of sanctification and perfection in the Holy Spirit. The desert fathers of the fourth century left the city and went into the wastes in obedience to Christ's command to take no thought of the morrow; and theirs was the pattern that all subsequent Christian monasticism imitated. Of course, cenobitic monasticism required—as all self-sustaining establishments do—rigid economies and practical discretion; but these, in themselves, are not ascetic *ideals*. And later medieval monastic establishments in the West (especially those of the Cistercians) became great centers of technological innovation and production; but no one ever mistook economic activity for a spiritual labor *in itself*. More to the point, to regard the withholding of goods as something ascetical—especially when the temptation to possession of goods can be every bit as powerful and as vicious as the temptation to prodigality—is to fall victim to a grave confusion; and to mistake the sobriety, diligence, and moderation of the secure, thrifty, provident householder for the utter extremity and infinite expenditure of ascetic discipline is practically to conflate opposites.

II. Thrift and Religion

It is unlikely one could find much evidence that, before the early modern period, there was any distinct concept of thrift as, in any proper sense, a religious value. A person of perverse temperament might perhaps argue that, if thrift is to be found within the religious realm at all, its supreme manifestation would be human sacrifice. Certainly one could scarcely conceive of a more deliberate and conscientious use of an easily replenished and often otherwise useless resource to secure a profitable return. All cultic sacrifice is, after all, a form of investment, a prudential transaction, an offering of something precious but superfluous in exchange for something of greater and more enduring worth, or of a concrete but finite good in exchange for a sort of transcendent credit stored up in the absolute. This, some might even say, is what *religion* is in its most venerable form. The whole mythos of Indo-European cult, it has often been suggested, was first and foremost one of sacrifice (most majestically expressed, probably, in the Vedic story of Purusa), and described a cosmos that was a closed and inescapable system, within which gods and mortals alike occupied places determined by fate; and this system was necessarily an economy, a cycle of creation and destruction, order and chaos, life and death: we fed the gods, who required our sacrifices, and they in exchange preserved us from the forces they personified and granted us some of their power.

This sort of sacrifice, though, pertains only to our understanding of religion in the abstract, and to a variety of cultures dependent upon a certain kind of sacral order. The Christian story is very different. At least, Christian scripture shows little sign of any proper awareness of the *economy* of sacrifice. The Hebrew Bible does, of course, recount many stories of sacrifice, some of them having the character of a fiduciary transaction. But the most important cultic oblation made by Israel, the *qurban* of the Day of Atonement, was not a simple *do ut des* exchange of goods for services, but a rite of reconciliation and purification, of repentance and forgiveness. The principal "sacrificial" moment in the patriarchal narratives, moreover, is the story of the *aqedah*, the binding of Isaac, which is no prudential exchange: Abraham's offering of his son is not, after all, a limited, rational transaction with the divine, for the purpose of gaining benefits for its people, but would—if it were brought to pass—extinguish the very possibility of Israel at all. The angel of God sparing Isaac simply emphasizes that the gift of Israel has been given with a transcendent gratuity that exceeds any exchange of divine and human services, or any cycle of equivalence and indemnity. As for the Christian understanding of sacrifice, it belongs entirely to the story of Christ's offering upon the cross, which would seem to shatter the older rationality of sacrificial economy altogether: an offering of infinite worth, made by God himself, out of boundless love, one that renders all other sacrifices unnecessary, and one that—far from sustaining the exquisitely calibrated cosmic balance of life and death—overthrows the power of death entirely, and thereby shows it to be something alien to the true order of creation as God intends it. There is, if nothing else, a certain notable want of frugality in this picture of things.

At a somewhat less abstract level, one can scarcely fail to notice that Christian scripture in general, though it abounds in extravagant gestures and bold counsels, is fairly poor in what most of us would recognize as practical advice.

> Take therefore no thought for the morrow: for the morrow shall take thought for the things of itself. (Matt. 6:34 KJV)

> Why take ye thought for raiment? Consider the lilies of the field, how they grow; they toil not, neither do they spin: and yet I say unto you, that even Solomon in all his glory was not arrayed like one of these. . . . Therefore take no thought, saying, What shall we eat? or, What shall we drink? or, Wherewithal shall we be clothed? (Matt. 6:28–29, 31 KJV; cf. Luke 12:27–29)

> And if any man will sue thee at the law, and take away thy coat, let him have thy cloak also. And whosoever shall compel thee to go a mile, go with him twain. Give to him that asketh thee, and from him that would borrow of thee turn not thou away. Ye have heard that it hath been said, Thou shalt love thy neighbour, and hate thine enemy. But I say unto you, Love your enemies, bless them that curse you, do good to them that hate you, and pray for them which despitefully use you, and persecute you. (Matt. 5:40–44 KJV)

> Sell all that thou hast, and distribute unto the poor, and thou shalt have treasure in heaven: and come, follow me. (Luke 18:22 KJV; cf. Matt. 19:21)

The Christian vision of reality seems necessarily to presume an inexhaustible plenitude, whose source may not always be visible, but is always somehow in reach; and, as a consequence, anxiety over a scarcity of resources or of time is clearly something of a sin: either a failure to trust in our Father in heaven, who will supply all our wants if we but ask him, or a failure to love our neighbor—to whom we should give without reserve—with sufficient charity. Christ approves even of the "waste" of an ointment that might have been sold to feed the poor so long as this is an act of genuine love and devotion. The prodigal son, when he returns from his debauches, is greeted not by stern reproof and a cleansing hygiene of plain victuals and honest labor, but by unconditional forgiveness and the further unwarranted (and even slightly unjust) expenditure of the fatted calf. Christ feeds the multitude not by judiciously rationing and carefully distributing what little food he has to give, but by a miraculous generosity that is so heedless in its apportionment that, even when everyone has eaten his fill, the superflux far exceeds what was originally available; like the manna of old, the good things that flow from God are always more than sufficient. If there is any regimen of moderation that we are supposed to learn from the Gospels, it certainly is not evident on the surface of the story they tell. We see Christ in Scripture at the wedding feast in Cana and we see him fasting forty days in the desert; we see him sharing wine with his disciples on the night before his death and we see him enduring the torments of the cross; as for how well he would have fared as an entrepreneurial carpenter, we are told nothing. And the entire story of the gospel might be said to involve a "metaphysics of excess": God creates *ex nihilo* out of the free overflow of his love; he loved us while we were yet sinners; he desires that all human beings should be saved and come to a knowledge of his truth; the divine Son evacuated himself of his eternal glory to become one of us and to die on our behalf simply out of the immensity of his love; he granted us the "free gift" (Rom. 5:15–16) of a salvation we could not merit on our own; he promises the transfiguration of the world in a kingdom of deathless joy, and he commands his followers, "be ye perfect" (Matt. 5:48).

It is perhaps worth lingering over this last injunction for a moment, if only to note that the Christian understanding of perfection is of a particularly uncompromising kind; at least, the spiritual life recommended by the gospel would seem to be one of unreserved commitment, a total surrender to grace, even a kind of holy recklessness. As a purely moral imperative, the dominical commandment of perfection was traditionally understood as an entirely unambiguous requirement not that one guard but that one give freely of one's possessions: it was seen as a command to charity, that is to say, to boundless generosity, to overflowing expense on behalf of others, no matter what their stations or characters—but never to "thrift." And it was this "perfectionist" maxim that, in some sense, shaped the ethical edifice of Christendom. I spoke above—in deploring Weber's talk of "this-worldly asceticism"—of the ascetic impulse as being, in its sheer exorbitance, productive of nothing *profitable*; but this is not to say it produced nothing *material*. There was, for instance, a long tradition of Christian monastic hospitals for the destitute and dying, going back to the days of Constantine, extending from the Syrian and Byzantine East to the Western fringes of Christendom; in the Eastern Christian Roman world, at least as early as the sixth century, there were free hospitals served by physicians and surgeons, with trained monastic staffs, and offering convalescent care;[5] in the West, during the Middle Ages, the Benedictines alone were responsible for more than two thousand hospitals; in the twelfth century, the Hospitallers were devoted almost entirely to the creation of such establishments. And these hospitals were also almshouses, which fed the hungry, provided for widows and orphans, and gave to all who came in need.[6] One could go on. By comparison, to be honest, the meager achievements of Puritan culture in this regard seem rather embarrassing; indeed, one wonders whether, by so excessively celebrating obedience to pragmatic necessities that just about everyone everywhere has had to observe at one time or another (frugality, sobriety, conservation of resources), certain forms of Protestant thought succeeded only in a positively "unworldly" neglect of many aspects of society that Christendom had made into regions of moral labor (nothing was more disastrous to free hospital care in northern Europe, for example, than the Reformation's dissolution of monastic establishments). Many Puritan conceptions of the "common good," frankly, would be difficult to distinguish in their palpable consequences from sheer self-interest;[7] and many forms of Puritan charity were not only severely limited in scope, but also contingent upon the presumed obligation of the poor to be docile subjects of moral and spiritual reform, under the guidance of their benefactors. Hence the ease with which Puritan culture could discriminate between the "deserving" and "undeserving" poor (not necessarily a false distinction, maybe, but certainly one that the ancient and medieval church—to say nothing of Christ's teachings—never encouraged individuals or almshouses or monasteries to believe themselves competent to make).[8]

5. Historians of medicine used to claim that ancient and medieval Christian hospitals were just hospices and shelters, offering no real systematic medical treatment; this, we now know, is false. See Timothy S. Miller, *The Birth of the Hospital in the Byzantine Empire*, 2nd ed. (Baltimore: Johns Hopkins University Press, 1997).

6. See Guenter B. Risse, *Mending Bodies, Saving Souls: A History of Hospitals* (Oxford: Oxford University Press, 1999).

7. See Stephen Foster, *Their Solitary Way: The Puritan Social Ethic in the First Century of Settlement in New England* (New Haven: Yale University Press, 1971), pp. 121–24.

8. Some classic and particularly illuminating histories of New England's Puritan

Understood, moreover, as a specifically spiritual vocation, this call to perfection has been seen as (if anything) an even more uncompromising imperative: God summoning us to the utter abandon of love. One can look anywhere in the church's spiritual tradition, really, to confirm this. There is something—one is almost tempted to say—endemic to Christian devotion that requires an atmosphere of extremes, of ecstasy and desolation, rejoicing and remorse, total surrender and infinite endeavor. One might mention Saint Gregory of Nyssa, in the fourth century, who saw the Christian life as an *epektasis*, a perpetual "stretching out" of the soul into the infinity of God's goodness, an eternal pilgrimage into ever-greater depths of divine glory. Far from manifesting any anxiety over time as a dwindling resource to be jealously marshaled, Gregory could scarcely even be bothered to notice the existence of death, except as a transitory stage—now that death is overthrown—in the infinite adventure of the soul's journey into God, compelled not by its fear of dearth, but by its blissful immersion in the infinite plenitude of divine beauty. The soul partaking of divine blessings, he said, is a vessel endlessly expanding as it receives what flows into it inexhaustibly;[9] its only satisfaction is its ever rekindled desire for more of God's goodness.[10] Or one might mention John of the Cross, in the sixteenth century, for whom the life of the soul reborn in Christ is one of terrifying or radiant extremes: sorrow and bliss, wrath and mercy, dereliction and divinization. He spoke often of the soul's terror in the dark night of purgative affliction, its sense of its own dissolution before the fire of divine wrath against sin;[11] and he spoke just as often of the soul's union with God, its ecstatic transformation in the beloved, its blissful surrender to God's love;[12] but nowhere does he seem to descry some moderate, virtuous mean between these extremes. One might even mention Søren Kierkegaard, whose attempt to give voice to the pathos of Christian faith (in a particularly pure Protestant register) led him to speak of "infinite

---

culture and ethos are Darrett B. Rutman, *American Puritanism: Faith and Practice* (Philadelphia: Lippincott, 1970); Perry Miller, *The New England Mind: From Colony to Province* (Cambridge, MA: Harvard University Press, 1953); Miller, *The New England Mind: The Seventeenth Century* (New York: Macmillan, 1939); Samuel Eliot Morison, *Builders of the Bay Colony* (Boston: Houghton Mifflin, 1930).

9. Gregory of Nyssa, *De anima et resurrectione*, Patrologia Graeca 46:105b–c.

10. Gregory of Nyssa, *De vita Moysis* 2; Gregorii Nysseni Opera, ed. Werner Jaeger et al. (Leiden: Brill, 1958–), 8/1:116–17.

11. See, for example, *The Dark Night of the Soul* 2.6.1–2, in *Collected Works of St. John of the Cross*, trans. Kieran Kavanaugh and Otilio Rodriguez (Washington, DC: IS Publications, 1979), pp. 337–38.

12. See *The Spiritual Canticle* 22.3, in *Collected Works of St. John of the Cross*, p. 497.

resignation," belief "on the strength of the absurd," the "knight of faith" who has given up all only to receive the finite back again as a gift of God, the absolute incommunicability of faith, the "teleological suspension of the ethical," the terrible solitude of the man who exists—outside the logic of the universal—by the singular passion of his faith.[13]

None of which is to say that Christian teaching has never recognized a kind of piety of ordinary life (or of ordinary time), but one should note that this piety has traditionally been concerned with the extraordinary demands of faith that arise *within* the ordinary: moments of extremity—on one's deathbed, say, or in the throes of a potentially fatal fever—when one might, by one's perseverance, imitate the fortitude of the martyrs of old. There is something in the doctrinal, metaphysical, and moral language of Christianity that seems at times jarringly incompatible with attempts to make the realms of civic and domestic responsibility spheres of spiritual achievement in and of themselves, rather than mere occasions for the exercise of charity, justice, or temperance. We look in vain if we go searching through the works of Christian antiquity and the Middle Ages for warm disquisitions on "family values," or fiery exhortations to sound and scrupulous stewardship of our possessions, or lustrous portraits of home, hearth, and the hushed sanctity of the dining-room table. The early church's view of marriage, to be perfectly honest, often verged upon the mildly hostile;[14] and even those church fathers who had indulgent or kind words to say of the domestic sphere still never suggested that it provided any unique opportunities for Christian virtue or that it was comparable to the monastic life as a path of holiness. Saint Augustine, for example, may have been more of a realist than, say, Saint Jerome in acknowledging that the Christian life was lived principally by married men and women, and not by celibates; but his own view of sexual desire within marriage was far more pessimistic than that of almost any other father,[15] and nowhere

13. See especially *Fear and Trembling*, trans. Alastair Hannay (Harmondsworth, UK, and New York: Penguin Books, 1985), pp. 74–75. See therein the "Speech in Praise of Abraham," the preamble of the *Problemata*, and *Problema* II.

14. See Peter Brown, *The Body and Society: Men, Women, and Sexual Revolution in Early Christianity* (New York: Columbia University Press, 1988).

15. Brown, *The Body and Society*, pp. 387–427. Augustine's arguments against the Pelagians, we should recall, entailed no rejection of Christian perfectionism. The Pelagian controversy did not concern the nature of the Christian moral life, but only the doctrinal issue of the formal relation between grace and nature *in* the moral life. Neither Augustine nor Pelagius thought sin somehow "excusable" on the grounds of moral infirmity, even if Augustine thought sin "inevitable," and neither thought that failing to strive for perfection was permissible for the Christian.

in his writings does he speak of any special Christian virtues specifically proper to the life of the family. As for the medieval Christian world, it may have known an extremely efficient and lively domestic order, but the only true "household of faith" it recognized was the church, which was nothing less than the whole Christian polity. Moreover, medieval culture believed that it was Adam's curse that a man should feed himself by the sweat of his face; thus the hardships of common life, the exigencies of economy, the constant duress of providing for a family, and all the other burdens of daily life were seen principally as fruits of sin and signs of our alienation from God and of our exile from paradise, from which the church's feasts brought times of blessed relief: a sweet foretaste of the wedding feast of the Lamb and the eighth day of creation, when we shall rest from all our works. As a consequence, there was small scope for any great "romance"— or for any distinct morality—of ordinary life. The realm of true spiritual achievement was, in the end, to be found elsewhere; the life of the freeman's household might have been blameless and godly, but it was neither particularly noble nor holy; and the family was not, in any identifiable sense, a distinct moral category.

And yet it is most definitely true that the once humble *artes domesticae*—including thrift—did become actual *goods* in early modernity, at least in Protestant culture; and there are any number of plausible explanations for why this should have been so. In part, surely, it had much to do with the obvious material realities of the rise of bourgeois culture and the new social and pecuniary enfranchisement of an entrepreneurial middle class; in classical terms, the great social transition of the modern period was the gradual displacement of an aristocratic order by a "banausic," and it is only natural that, with the ascendancy of the new class, its native practices and prejudices should assume a new dignity, social and religious, its *ethos* should assume the character of a genuine ethics, and its *mores* should assume the dimensions of a positive morality. But this new high estimate of the moral nature of such things as thrift also, undoubtedly, had something to do with the broad rejection within Protestant culture of the ascetic life, of a unique priestly ministry, and of many of the penitential and festive customs enshrined in the Christian calendar. Once distinct sacerdotal vocations and periods of restraint had ceased to exist, there was no longer any office of mediation or any communal activity anywhere within the Christian *civitas* that could in any way be undertaken on behalf of the dissolute, the prodigal, the "ordinary," or those torpid souls who at the end of the day will be found to have labored but an hour. Nor was the profound comfort of a clearly enunciated and irreversible absolution anywhere to be found. Here, most certainly, we see something of the vast, cold loneliness of the individual conscience in Protestant religion, supposedly secure in the simplicity of faith, and yet also deprived of many of those tangible signs and corporate rhythms that once had assured the baptized soul of its participation in a living, social body of salvation. With the repudiation of monasticism and priestly discipline, the moral life of the individual must necessarily fall subject to a far more rigorous set of obligations; and where feast and fast have been dissolved into a single, largely monotonous life of sober piety, ordinary time becomes the model of spiritual life. Sydney Ahlstrom speaks of the new ideal of the "gospel of work" that arose within that particular style of Reformed English religion that the Puritan colonists of the seventeenth century brought with them to North America: "Most influential was the new emphasis on serving the Lord in one's vocation—as a tradesman, as a merchant, as an artisan, or as a magistrate or 'citizen.' Formerly it was thought necessary to withdraw from the tainted world in order to develop the highest spirituality; monasticism was the surest way to perfection. Now it was the life of withdrawal which was regarded as tainted and opposed to God's will. In the Reformed tradition especially, an additional premium was put on austerity, frugality, and sober living."[16] Economy—in the modern sense of the word—became a kind of Christian virtue in itself in Reformed culture; and perhaps there is a certain theological logic in this. At least, it is somewhat tempting to see a subtle connection between the Calvinist celebration of sober and frugal living and, say, the hideous doctrine of "limited atonement" that disfigures certain prominent strains of Reformed thought (a doctrine that suggests that even God's love for his creatures is obedient to some greater law of divine thrift). Ahlstrom writes also of the "awesome doctrine" of predestined election, and upon the question it almost necessarily excites: Am I among the chosen? "Rare would be the person who, taking the question seriously, would proclaim his unfavored status by profligacy, dishonesty, or laziness. Reformed theology unquestionably encouraged rectitude, probity, and industry; and it did so even among those who in no way entertained the 'bourgeois heresy' that worldly success is a sure sign of election, or worse still, a means of earning redemption."[17] A suspicion of works righteousness and a rejection of any priestly office of intercession other than Christ's own led almost inevitably to a greater insistence on the necessity of labor and discipline.

16. Sydney E. Ahlstrom, *A Religious History of the American People* (New Haven: Yale University Press, 1972), p. 118.

17. Ahlstrom, *A Religious History*, p. 118.

None can do penance for me or live a righteous life on my behalf; none has the sacramental power to assure me of forgiveness; where there is only the priesthood of all believers, each soul is a city unto itself, and there are no larger structures of mediation whereby the faithful can bear one another's spiritual burdens, or whereby excess can be fruitfully reintegrated into the organic complexity of a living hierarchical community. This form of Christianity seems vaguely Gnostic: in its repudiation of a sacral vision that had united heaven and earth by innumerable strands of analogy and by intricate hierarchies of participation, it placed the soul before God in a world emptied of sacramental shelters, in a state of almost perfect isolation. In such a world, one's ability to live in self-sufficiency, contained within one's own plenitude, set apart from the fallen world, squandering neither goods nor time, might be the only discernible sign that one has also been set apart by God, and been chosen to enter into his plenitude.

One should also take note of the somewhat remarkable reviviscence of Stoicism in early modernity, and of its influence upon Christian thought, not only among Catholic humanists, but also among many of the Reformers. Certain of the latter found, for instance, Stoic natural law theory especially suited to a defense of a divinely ordained secular order, independent from and in some areas supreme over the church. Granted, the logic, physics, and metaphysics of the Stoa exercised little influence over sixteenth- and seventeenth-century humanists and theologians; but the later Stoic understanding of the ethics of the "cosmopolis," particularly as enunciated by Epictetus and Seneca, struck a great number of responsive chords among the Christian scholars of early modernity who were seeking an ethical grammar for a society increasingly detached from the moral authorities of the old Christendom. Many found the Stoic ideal of *autarkeia*—self-rule—especially appealing as a model for the sober and rational life of Christian piety. Melanchthon's views on the constitution of society and on Christian civic virtue were openly Stoic in much of their inspiration. Calvin's first publication was his commentary of 1532 on Seneca's essay on clemency, and aspects of his moral doctrine of later years seem obviously marked by—at the very least—a Stoic sensibility. This makes perfect sense. The Stoic vision of reality, after all, was one of utter fatedness, according to which one's place in the cosmos was assigned by eternal necessity, and was sealed by the eternal recurrence of all things; and Stoic ethics was not so much an active striving for perfection as a practice of equanimity and justice toward all one's fellow citizens in the cosmopolis, as a sign of one's rational assent to the universe as a whole and one's place within it. In Calvinist thought, similarly, the sovereignty of God has determined all things from everlasting, according to God's inscrutable counsels and unchanging decrees, and one's place within the universal drama by which God shows forth his righteousness and power—in wrath and mercy, dereliction and election—has been fixed from before the foundation of the world; the moral life of the elect, therefore, can contribute nothing to justification or sanctification, and there is no righteousness but the righteousness of God manifesting itself in us. Thus the life of sobriety, humility, and pious industriousness is, primarily, a sign of God's grace: by one's consent and obedience to the will of God, one reveals to oneself and to others that one is a vessel of God's preordained mercy and saving grace.[18] Admittedly, "thrift" was not one of the virtues explicitly named by Epictetus, Marcus Aurelius, or Seneca, but the Stoics' distaste for empty pomp and ostentation, their love of serene simplicity, and their constant emphasis upon the ethical responsibilities incumbent upon every citizen of the cosmos were exquisitely well fitted to a Protestant society intent upon shedding the more exotic, "irrational," and sacral elements of Catholic culture. This new, more "Stoical" version of Christian virtue remained a powerful current of American moral culture through the nineteenth century, in both the Protestant antebellum South and in the once Puritan northeast. In the colonies of New England, the homely moralism of the seventeenth century was in many ways perfectly consonant with the northeastern liberal and (broadly speaking) deist tradition of the later eighteenth century, which imbibed from various fashionable European strains of thought another style of modern Stoicism.

---

18. It may seem peculiar to liken the determinism of Calvinism to that of Stoicism, given their apparent metaphysical and moral incompatibility: Stoicism's metaphysics of immanence and morality of *apatheia* on the one hand, Calvinism's emphasis on God's transcendence and gratitude to God on the other. But Stoic "immanentism" concerned the omnipervasiveness of the divine mind, which is benevolent and infinitely wise in its disposition of all things, and Stoic *apatheia* is the cultivation of a serene immunity to the perturbations of external passions that requires gratitude to God. By the same token, the early Reformed notion of divine transcendence could not be characterized as transcendence in the full ontological sense one finds in patristic and high medieval thought, but only as the mere supremacy of an omnipotent will determining every eventuality; and certainly there is a tendency in Reformed tradition to see a kind of resigned *consent* to God's will as an admirable Christian quality. If Stoicism is a form of pantheism, Calvinism might well be called a form of what Erich Przywara named "theopanism," a kind of "dialectical immanentism" premised upon the sole infinite sovereignty of God, who is the supreme supracosmic agency. See Erich Przywara, *Analogia Entis: Metaphysik; Ur-Struktur und All-Rhythmus* (Einsiedeln: Johannes-Verlag, 1962), pp. 70–78, 128–35, 247–301.

III. Thrift and Culture

There is no great mystery, I think, to most of the ways in which the new moral "value" of thrift shaped the evolution of American society. One sees it at work in many of our most distinctive myths and ideals: the rugged obduracy of the colonial settlers, the self-sustaining polity and church of the colonial family, the intrepid pilgrim or pioneer enduring the scarcity and extremity of savage winters or burning wastes or intractable soils, the flinty independence of the "self-made man," the unadorned honesty and dependable decency of the average American, and so forth. We have made heroes in our national lore of persons whom earlier ages would have seen as representing the very antithesis of heroism: farmers, homesteaders, migrants, speculators, "peasants," craftsmen, entrepreneurs, merchants, and all those who "made something of themselves" through labor and (of all things) diligent economies. "Virtue," in classical culture, was the exclusive property of the aristocratic class; Christianity was profoundly subversive of the antique social order in imagining an entirely new kind of virtue—charity among persons drawn from every station and race—and in demonstrating the power of even the base-born to exhibit virtues that philosophers frequently extolled but rarely practiced with comparable zeal; but, even then, the highest Christian virtues were still understood to be the province of a sort of aristocracy of the spirit—martyrs, virgins, bishops, ascetics—and were not easily attainable by those walking the broad pathways of the great world. What occurred in early modernity, though, was—for want of a better term—a kind of "democratization" of Christian virtue, a translation of sanctity from the realm of extraordinary effort to the world of ordinary labor and sane moderation.

At a very concrete level, a high valuation of thrift allowed for a new appreciation of the dignity of both labor and enterprise, and for some sense of the moral seriousness and moral perils possible in both. An emphasis upon freeholds and the inalienability of property helped to sustain a broad cultural distrust of large profligate structures of government, and of any claim to usurpatious, confiscatory, or dispositive authority on the part of the state. The birth of thrift as an actual ideal certainly helped not only to remove any element of shame from economic liberalism and commerce (for better or worse), but even to imbue them with a faint air of sanctity. It assisted also in the discovery of the "law" of supply and demand and provided a kind of moral license for the exploitation of that law. It helped to define the marshaling and deployment of resources as a preeminent rule of economic life—so much so that even labor could come to be considered as a commodity, and the value and expense of labor could be figured into the organization of mass industrial production (in contrast to the independent labor of the old artisanal and technical guilds). Most crucially, it rendered the private accumulation and investment of capital entirely respectable—indeed, morally admirable. Constant technological revolution; a material philosophy that construes the world almost exclusively as regions of resources, investment, acquisition, and development; a culture that regards business as a social good and the regular consumption of goods and services as intrinsically virtuous; and indeed the whole edifice of modern material culture rest in part upon the new "Christian" value of sober private economy and "godly thrift."

This also, perhaps, accounts for certain of the large contradictions of American society—principally its almost miraculous combinations of austerity and profligacy, prudery and wantonness, charity and greed— some of which may be amounting to a fiscal crisis, if the dourer prognosticators are to be believed. The national rate of personal savings has fallen far below that of personal indebtedness. Many live almost entirely upon credit. America's industrial base continues to disintegrate while its rate of consumption continues to accelerate. A great deal of our wealth rests precariously poised upon an uncertain real estate market. And so on. Perhaps this is because we have simply abandoned the principles of our forebears, cast aside the example of their industriousness and thrift, and surrendered ourselves entirely to the sway of appetite. But perhaps it may be just as true to say that we are suffering from these cultural and fiscal pathologies not simply because we have ceased to value thrift, but because historically we have valued it far too highly. A culture that treats thrift as a moral good can easily become one that encourages profligate expenditure; an economy or society that believes in the ethical duty to accumulate and jealously to guard one's material substance is an economy or society that can believe in the sanity of the ceaseless acquisition and disposal of possessions. Hoarding, after all, is not thrifty, but supremely wasteful, since it reduces wealth to an inert sum that must, over time, shrink away. And, of course, when thrift is understood as something good in itself, it must also be regarded as a law applicable not only to scarcity, but also to surfeit. Thus it may demand simply that wealth be ever in movement, lest the economy fail in general, and so impoverish us all, even if the requirement of endless growth is an economic illusion and a material impossibility. Americans are not necessarily an especially sensuous people—if one judges these things according to refinement of tastes—but we surpass all others in our capacity for consumption and accumulation. Indeed, much of our economy runs not so much upon the manufacture of goods—we seem content to allow that to pass into other hands—but upon the manufacture of the "needs" that correspond to these "goods" (which, one would think, can be neither culturally nor morally healthy).

Perhaps because of a certain ambiguity inextirpable from the idea of thrift as a moral value—the ambiguity, that is, of an ethic of sober restraint that is also an ethic of the blameless acquisition of wealth—we have succeeded in creating a culture of hedonism without redeeming irony, libertinism without style, a kind of decadence so naïve and democratized as to be utterly tedious, lacking any of the crepuscular glamour that more civilized forms of decadence generally tend to possess. Logically speaking, this was probably inevitable from the days of the Puritan settlement of New England: a moral vision that makes acquisition more or less irreproachable, but the enjoyment of goods an object of moral suspicion and opprobrium, is one that has deferred the moral odium from the "root of all evil" (the love of money) to the mere flowers of that evil (degraded luxuriance)—or, in fact, to something intrinsically innocent and even admirable (an appreciation of leisure and games and the good things of creation). Such an ethics may encourage industriousness and wealth, but only at the cost of a rather destructive defamation of the created world and of sane human happiness. In a society formed at a deep level by such an ethics, to turn toward enjoyment and ease is already to have turned toward a "lower" or "contemptible" realm, without any moral gravity—or moral grace—of its own; thus "graceless extravagance" is practically a pleonasm, and refined or morally commendable enjoyment is something somewhat incredible and indistinct to the moral imagination. Or, to put the matter even more concisely, we may be the first culture in the history of the world to have created a genuinely "barbarous decadence" (at least, one might conclude as much from our current popular culture). After all, our "thrift ethos" was hostile from the beginning to so many of the pillars of higher civilization: extravagance, contemplative indolence, lavish patronage, aristocratic disdain for mere utility, the willingness to squander time on needless detail or languid appreciation, and so on. The Puritans were in many ways a tribe of drab barbarians, content to turn away from the magnificence of the European past to eke out bland lives of frugal mediocrity and cultural penury, and to call it virtue; and we are their heirs.[19]

---

19. For the classic text on the place of "time wasted" in the creation of civilization and the living of a fully human life, see Josef Pieper, *Leisure: The Basis of Culture*, trans. Gerald Malsbary (South Bend, IN: St. Augustine's Press, 1998); see also Pieper, *In Tune with the*

At the same time, one must note that, because of our unprecedented combination of general wealth and Christian scruple (or vestigial Christian scruple), we are perhaps the most spontaneously generous people in the world; statistically, at least, our charitable largesse as individuals is without rival. Almsgiving may not have for us the ritual and sacral significance it had for medieval culture, but perhaps it is our sense that the accumulation and use of wealth are inherently a moral activity that prompts us to give so ungrudgingly. But, then, the reverse of this reality seems to be a culture unable to halt the decay of community or the advance of a vapid and corrosive materialism into every sphere of social life. Precisely because the use of material possessions has no ritual or sacral grammar, it is subject to no ritual or sacral restraint. Our excesses are those of neither feast nor fast, but are in the most exact sense profane: a cycle of pure acquisition and expenditure, *in infinitum*. For thrift, when taken as a value in itself, comprises its own inversion, and tends to destroy its own moral basis (it is scarcely a novel observation, for instance, that Puritan frugality ultimately subverted itself). And this makes it that much more obvious that "thrift" is not really a virtue, but only a material strategy, morally neutral and with an essentially dialectical structure: virtues admit of no dialectic; they are pure of their opposites; prudence does not breed recklessness, fortitude cowardice, or charity hate. And so, again, perhaps we have as a society forgotten the wisdom of thrift; but perhaps this is in part because we first forgot the vast, glorious chasm separating Shrove Tuesday from Ash Wednesday, and the art of living fully now on one side of that chasm, now on the other, with grace and by grace. We retreated to a purely material middle long ago, and learned to value the power of wealth to beget wealth too highly, and to rejoice in unexceptional accomplishments as though they were forms of heroism or sanctity, and to cease seeking certain truths that cannot be found in the middle, but only at the extremes.

The early modern "consecration" of the ordinary was, it seems fair to say, a mixed blessing at best. No one, surely, should regret the modern recognition of the dignity of work and of the nobility that inheres in building businesses that employ persons and allow them to provide for their families. But it is hard not to lament the displacement of true virtues in our scale of values by mere pragmatic exigencies, and our consequent failure (at times) to recognize what is truly good, honorable, or admirable in any vocation or way of life. It is hard not to suspect that a culture that

---

World: A Theory of Festivity, trans. Richard Winston and Clara Winston (South Bend, IN: St. Augustine's Press, 1999).

could ever have mistaken trivial (if practical) values like thrift for virtues of a certain moral pusillanimity: surely its spiritual and material expectations of itself must be depressingly unadventurous. And it may be true that we should celebrate the modern "discovery" of the domestic sphere as a realm of moral striving, and the return of Christian sanctity to daily life; but, that said, to "democratize" holiness or virtue is also frequently to cheapen both, and to ignore the demands they make upon us. Goodness becomes mere decency, and then in time mere respectability, and then an ethics of individual conscience, and then finally one of personal "choice" (which is the poorest social morality imaginable). And, while it does indeed honor the laborer to see his or her labor as "godly," this can easily be mistaken as a license to believe that one becomes godly simply in enriching oneself. It would be convenient, naturally, to think that, rather than all those searing sanctifications that were once the Christian ideal— mortifications, martyrdoms, heroic feats of charity—righteousness were really a matter of living well. We should probably all like to believe that in providing for our children or in avoiding overdrafts we were also obeying Christ's injunction to be perfect, or that in storing tinned vegetables and dry goods in our cellars we were also storing up treasure in heaven. But, while it is one thing to affirm the abundance of grace in every area of life, it is another thing altogether to reject the heroism of virtue as a kind of "works righteousness" and to pretend that sobriety, frugality, and sartorial dreariness are truer expressions of personal sanctity. And while it is ennobling to affirm that the sacred penetrates every dimension of the secular realm, it is an impoverishment of our moral imaginations to mistake the secular for the sacred and thereby to banish the sacred from the world. From a classical Christian perspective, the elevation of thrift to the level of moral or religious achievement might well appear to be simply another form of a materialist error—one with potentially devastating cultural and spiritual consequences.

In any event, this much at least seems certain: though we might occasionally speak of thrift as a virtue, it is nothing of the sort—except, perhaps, in an ironic sense (Nietzsche's "virtues of the Last Man," for instance). Thrift is neither penance nor rejoicing, neither charity nor gratitude. It is at most an ethos, poised between the bright daylight of feast and the chill night of fast, one that discourages Lenten destitution and festal exorbitance alike. In itself it merits neither praise nor condemnation: it is equally at the service of creation or destruction, benevolence or miserliness, moral effort or absolute antinomianism, community or petty individualism; it can be a sign of prudence and temperance or an especially unctuous euphemism for avarice. Taken by itself, it leans a little to the sinister side, since it can never be an unconditional good but can easily degenerate into an unqualified evil. It is formally prior to neither virtue nor vice. It often provides, however, the efficient or material basis that makes either virtue or vice possible: it is, that is to say, a form of power. Like any sound discipline of the will, it engenders a purely neutral strength that can be turned to any number of ends. At the level of the individual, it is the way in which one acquires the means to do what one would do—to house the homeless or to take homes away from the poor; to feed the hungry or to build a private replica of the Petit Trianon; to create a business or to prosper from the destruction of businesses others have built. At the level of society, it is that accumulation of material wealth and vital energy that makes our culture so prodigally creative and destructive, so pitilessly forgetful of the past and so blissfully enchanted with the future, able to work such prodigies of weal and woe in the earth, so plenteous in its beneficence and so dreadful an engine of cultural annihilation. It is our constant if often secret ethos, and our most general value (even when we are at our most wasteful and dissolute). It is worthy, therefore, of our most precise attention, as a way of trying to understand what we have been and what we are becoming.

SEVENTEEN

Christianity, Modernity, and Freedom

1. Modernity—to the degree that it was or is a kind of cultural project or epochal ideology—understands itself as the history of freedom. Or rather, I suppose I should say, the one grand cultural and historical narrative that we as modern persons tend to share, and that most sharply distinguishes a modern from a premodern vision of society, is the story of liberation, the story of the ascent of the individual out of the shadows of hierarchy and subsidiary identity into the light of full recognition, dignity, and autonomy. And a powerful narrative it is, whether we prefer it in the simple form embraced by the *philosophes* (freedom from the constraints of tradition and the discovery of an ethos obedient to universal reason), the more rigorous form of Kant (the discovery that this rational ethos is ultimately founded upon the individual's own rational autonomy), the more speculative form of Hegel (freedom as the positive achievement of the rational civil state, which creates liberty by situating it within the poetic limits of the law), the more enthusiast form of Romanticism (return to the innocent spontaneity and goodness of nature, uncorrupted by culture), the more libertarian form of that great gnostic adventure called America ("Thanks, I don't need your help"), or some eclectic mixture of all of these (which is the norm). It does not, obviously, amount to a single ideological program; rather, it gives rise to a bewildering variety of analogous but often incompatible ideologies; but it does determine what our highest or central value is, to which all other values are subordinate and in comparison to which they are always provisional.

2. It has become something of a commonplace in recent years to observe that the modern understanding of freedom differs qualitatively and

rather radically from many of the more classical or medieval conceptions of freedom. According to these latter, so the story goes, true freedom is the realization of a complex nature in its proper ends, both natural and supernatural; it is the power of a thing to flourish, to become ever more fully what it is. But to think of freedom thus, one must believe not only that we possess an actual nature, which must flourish to be free, but also that there is a transcendent Good toward which that nature is oriented. To be fully free is to be joined to that end for which our natures were originally framed, and whatever separates us from that end—including even our own personal choices—is a form of bondage. We are free, that is to say, not because we can choose, but only when we have chosen well. Thus ultimate liberation requires us to look to the "sun of the Good" in order to learn how to choose; but the more we emerge from illusion and caprice, and the more perfect our vision becomes, the less there is to *choose*, because the will has become increasingly inalienable from its natural object, whether that object lies within or beyond itself. The power of choice, however in-dispensable it may be to this pilgrimage toward the Good, is nothing but the minimal condition for a freedom that can be achieved only when that power has been subsumed into the far higher power of one who is natu-rally "unable to sin": a paradisal state in which the consonance between desire and its proper object is so perfect that goodness is hardly even an "ethical" category any longer. Within these terms, it once made perfect sense to say that God is infinitely free because, in his infinite actuality and simplicity, he cannot be alienated from his own nature, which is the Good itself, and so is "incapable" of evil.

Today, though, such language would strike most ears as a little bi-zarre, and even perhaps willfully perverse. What the word "freedom" has generally come to mean for most of us now, when our usage is at its most habitual and unreflective, is libertarian autonomy and spontaneous vo-lition, the negative freedom of the unrestrained—or at least minimally restrained—individual will. If we conceive of it at all as the realization of our nature, this is only because we have already come to think of human nature primarily as free spontaneity. Thus, though many of the seminal modern narratives of liberation—Enlightenment and Romantic alike—often understood freedom as the release of an aboriginal human nature from the fetters of tradition, the modern conception of freedom achieves its most logically consistent form only when practically all constraints have come to be seen as arbitrary and extrinsic, and when the very idea of natural or intrinsic constraints has come to be regarded as an intolera-ble imposition upon the sovereignty of the will. In this sense, the modern notion of freedom is essentially nihilistic (using that word in its most technical and least polemical sense): it is a liberty whose intentional horizon has been purged of all prior identifiable goods—all prior objects—and one that thus lies open before the indeterminate. For us to be as free as we possibly can be, there must be *nothing* transcendent of the will that might command it toward ends it does not choose or even fabricate for itself, no value higher than those the will imposes upon its world, no nature but what the will elects for itself. Thus we cannot even speak of a society ordered toward the transcendental structure of being—toward the true, the good, and the beautiful—and still be understood to be speaking about freedom. If true liberty is by definition prior to or utterly beyond nature, there can be no coherent understanding of the law as a shared mediation between individual and common good, or between a community of free souls and the Good as such. Law can be only constraint or permission, a determination of the relative preponderance of the power of the state and the license of the self, a greater or lesser aid to the realization of private ends or the suppression of conflicting desires. Thus, everything in the interval between state and self—community, affinity, natural association, all of culture—is a "lawless" realm, a sort of shared privacy or elective localism, subject to the law's powers of restraint, but otherwise irrelevant to the law's primary function, which is to fortify the state and regulate the individual, securing both against the claims of anything that falls outside that naked dialectic they constitute.[1]

Needless to say, perhaps, such a concept of freedom is at some level irreducibly mythical. Desire is never purely indeterminate, but is always directed toward an end that is desired before it can be willed. The very first movement of the will—and any scrupulous phenomenology of action reveals this to us—is always toward some object of intention; and any distinct and finite object can appear to the intellect as desirable only because the will has already been wakened, and desire has already been evoked, by a "transcendental" object, the Good as such, the very desirability of being itself, toward which every appetite is always primordially turned. Thus an absolutely "negative liberty"—even assuming such a thing could really be created within the realm of civil law—still cannot make anyone free in the modern "pure" sense. One cannot simply choose what to desire, or choose either to desire or not to desire; and the fiction that such perfect

---

1. I would argue that even the Hegelian tradition, right or left, ultimately falls into this pattern—even Marxism, despite its best intentions—but that is a matter that can be deferred to another time.

spontaneity lies within the powers of any rational being, if truly believed, may very well leave one dangerously susceptible to any number of external manipulations or accidental "traumas" of the will. Only a wisdom that allows one to distinguish worthy ends from worthless, or to recognize the relative value of diverse desires, can actually make one in any meaningful sense *free*. Only the acquisition of useful constraints and powers, upon which one can reflect in relation to the Good as such, allows one consciously to act toward a meaningful end; and this, one might very well conclude, is as much a social as a personal project, which must give shape to a realm of positive law. But the modern, libertarian, mythical concept of freedom—simply by virtue of its soothing vacuity and plasticity—makes it rather difficult even to imagine what a community of "lawful freedom" might look like. And it often makes it even more difficult to notice how, veiled behind the language of mere negative liberty, certain powers and enfranchised interests (the state, capital, ideology) have largely supplanted those mediating realities of community and culture and faith in which positive law should be situated, and have taken over the task of shaping our desires for us.

3. It is also now something of a commonplace to assert that this modern understanding of what it means to be free is, to a great extent, a late product or indirect derivative or fortuitous metamorphosis of late scholastic voluntarism. A great deal of late medieval and early modern Christian thought, in its anxiety to protect divine action against any imputation of necessity or compulsion, either external or internal to the divine will, progressively altered the very concept of divine freedom. Divine sovereignty came to be imagined as such an abyss of pure power that God could even act in a way unrelated to his own essence; indeed, this mysterious, sublime, unimaginable, *pure* power—in which no creature can participate, and over against which every movement of creaturely will is as nothing at all—became in some sense the very definition of what it is for God to be God. In this way, divine liberty was progressively equated with sheer spontaneity; and, in at least one picture of God, elective *arbitrium* was elevated over rational *voluntas*. Inevitably, this understanding of freedom migrated from theology to anthropology—from God to the creature fashioned in God's image—and began to shape moral, political, and social thought. And, of course, this could lead only in the direction of an ultimate atheism, whether fully conscious or merely practical. If God's freedom is primarily his infinite power to elect what he will—if, in fact, this abyssal liberty is not only not bound to the dictates of his nature, but in the most radical sense *is* his nature—and if human freedom is merely a finite instance of

the same kind of liberty, then there is no ontological liaison between infinite and finite freedom. In the older model of freedom, there could not possibly be a *real* conflict between the divine and human wills, because the power of the human will was understood as a finite participation in the perfect and infinite power of God's freedom, his knowledge and love of his own infinite goodness. Even sin was understood as only the misused—the poorly aimed—operation of this imparted movement toward the Good, a disordered love still sustained by a more primordial love of the divine. In the newer model, however, the only relations possible between the divine and human wills are either conflict or surrender, embraced within an irresoluble tension between incommiscible spontaneities. Thus all genuinely *modern* stories of liberation, presuming as they do some version of this model of freedom, perhaps *must* terminate in a final rebellion against God: for he is the one intolerable rival who must be slain if humanity is ever truly to be free. And thus, also, much of the history of modern secularism, along with many of its humanist or collectivist or libertarian tales regarding the freedom of a humanity "come of age," might very well be regarded—from a Christian perspective—as doubly damnable: as both a rejection of the God who declares himself in all of being and the illegitimate offspring of a degenerate theology.

One does not, incidentally, have to subscribe to what a traditional Marxist would call ideology in order to take this story seriously. One certainly need not believe that the whole of modernity was obscurely born in the darkness of monastic cells or in the flickering candlelight of scriptoria, in complete abstraction from the new material conditions that emerged in western Europe on the threshold of the modern age. On the other hand, though, ideas are not only shaped by material conditions, but they also shape them. This story of how we came to think of freedom as we now usually do, and of why so much of modern history has been the history of conflict between different visions of liberation, is undoubtedly true, even if it is subject to countless qualifications and complications. But it is not the whole story.

4. Christianity began not as an institution, not even as a creed, but as an event that had no proper precedent or any immediately conceivable sequel. In its earliest dawn, the gospel arrived in history as a kind of convulsive disruption *of* history, a subversive rejection of almost all the immemorial cultic, social, and philosophical wisdoms of the ancient world. And the event that the gospel proclaimed—the event within the event, so to speak—was the resurrection of Christ, which was neither a religious event, nor a natural event, nor even an event within the history

of religion, but a moment of almost pure interruption. According to Paul, it had effectively erased all sacred, social, racial, and national boundaries, gathered into itself all divine sovereignty over history, and subdued all the spiritual agencies of the cosmos: the powers and principalities, the thrones and dominions, the "god of this world." It was a complete liberation from the constraints of elemental existence (the *stoicheia*), but also from the power of law; for even the law of Moses, holy though it was, was still only delivered by an angel, through a human mediator, in order to operate as a kind of probationary "disciplinarian" (*paidagōgos*), and had now been replaced by the law of love. Thus Christianity entered human consciousness not primarily as a new system of practices and observances, or as an alternative set of religious obligations, but first and foremost as apocalypse, the visionary annunciation of the kingdom and its sudden invasion of historical and natural time alike. And, as René Girard rightly observes, the nature of this apocalypse was, in a very profound sense, irreligious. It was a complete reversal of perspective in the realm of the sacred, the instant in which the victim of social and religious order—whom all human wisdom has always been prepared to hand over to death as a necessary, and so, legitimate sacrifice—was all at once revealed as the righteous one, the innocent one, even God himself. So, in its original form, the gospel was a pressing command to all persons to come forth, out of the economies of society and cult, and into the immediacy of that event: for the days are short. And, having thus been born in the terrible and joyous expectation of time's imminent end—its first "waking moment" utterly saturated by the knowledge that the end was near—the church was not at first quite prepared to inhabit time except in a state of something like sustained crisis. There was no obvious medium by which a people in some sense already living in history's aftermath, in a state of constant urgency, could enter history again, as either an institution, or a body of law, or even a religion. It would take some time, and some degree of adjustment of expectations, and perhaps a considerable degree of disenchantment, for so singular an irruption of the eschatological into the temporal to be recuperated into stable order again.

From the beginning, consequently, there has been a certain paradoxical tension at the very core of Christian belief. In religious terms, accommodation with and adaptation of cultic forms was possible, even within as radically novel an association as the church; and, to a large degree, it came about quite simply as a kind of natural "pseudomorphism," a crystallization of Christian cult within the religious space vacated by earlier cults, even as the church strove to generate new kinds of community within the shelter of the culturally intelligible configurations it had assumed. This was, of course, inevitable and necessary. A perfectly apocalyptic consciousness—a consciousness subsisting in a moment of pure interruption—cannot really be sustained beyond a certain, very brief period. The exigencies of material existence demanded that Christianity would in time have to become "historical" again, "cultural" again, which is to say "cultic." What began primarily as force could not endure except as structure. But, as was also inevitable, the results of this accommodation between apocalypse and cult were very frequently tragic. As a religion, Christianity has provided many guises by which the original provocation of the Christian event has been made more bearable to historical consciousness, but under which it has far too often been all but entirely hidden. The religious impulse has served as the necessary vehicle by which an essentially apocalyptic awareness has been conveyed through the alien element of "fallen" time, but has also frequently enough striven to suppress that awareness. The alloy, moreover, has probably always been a somewhat unstable one. At least, at times it seems as if the Christian event is of its nature something too refractory and volatile—the impulse to rebellion too constitutive of its own spiritual logic—to be contained even within its own institutions. This, at least, might explain why Christianity over the centuries not only has proved so irrepressibly fissile (as all large religious traditions, to some degree, are), but has also given rise to a culture capable of the most militant atheism, and even of self-conscious nihilism. Even in its most enduring and necessary historical forms, there is an ungovernable energy within it, something that desires not to crystallize but rather to disperse itself into the future, to start always anew, more spirit than flesh or letter. As the proclamation of time's invasion by eternity, and as the seal of finality upon the annunciation of the presence of the kingdom in and among us, the gospel of Easter must remain—within the limits of time as we know it—an event that is always yet to be fully understood.

5. All of modernity's tales of liberation, in all their variety and frequent contradictoriness, are variations within or upon or in the shadow of this very particular history. Resistance to or flight from the authority of the law—or, rather, a sense of the law's ultimate nullity—lies at the heart of the gospel. In every modern demand for social and personal recognition as inherent rights, there is at least a distant echo of Paul's proclamation of the unanticipated "free gift" found in Christ. The peculiar restlessness, the ferment, of modern Western history—great revolutions and local rebellions, the ceaseless generation of magnificent principles and insidious abstractions, politics as the interminable ideological conflict between Edenic

nostalgias and eschatological optimisms, the ungovernable proliferation of ever newer "innate" rights and ever more comprehensive forms of "social justice"—belongs to the long secular aftermath of the declaration that the kingdom has arrived in Christ, that the prince of this world has been judged and cast out, that the one who lies under the condemnation of the powers of this age has been vindicated by God and raised up as Lord. It is a sort of "oblivious memory" of Paul's message that all the powers of the present age have been subdued, and death and wrath defeated, not by the law—which, for all its sanctity, is impotent to set us free—but by a gift that has canceled the law's power over against us.

For the only law by which it is possible for the church truly to live is Christ's commandment that his followers must love one another; and this law of love is anarchic in its universal embrace: so much so that, in Christ, there is no longer a division between Jew and Greek, free and slave, man and woman. Paul, moreover, is adamant, even fierce: those who have been emancipated from the law's power may not now turn back to the law for shelter, on pain of subjecting themselves again to the elements of the age that is passing, and of thus excluding themselves from the age that is coming to birth.

6. Perhaps Christian culture has always been haunted by a certain, seemingly irresoluble dilemma: the mystery of an impossible mediation between the kingdom's charitable lawlessness (which is a higher law) and the practical necessities of social life within fallen time. Historically, the only communities that have attempted to form societies obedient to the apocalyptic consciousness of God's "anarchic" love have been monastic. Their ideal, at least, has always been to live not according to a *lex*, but according to a *regula*, a sort of lawless law agreed upon by all, enforced only by gestures of love, shared service, statutes of penance and reconciliation, and the absolute rule of forgiveness. And only a precious few of these communities have succeeded to any appreciable degree, for any respectable length of time. For those, moreover, who cannot and should not retreat from the world where positive law must operate—society, the family, all the commanding heights and sheltered valleys of culture—the mediation of the law is of its nature something always imperfectly defined, always something of a hermeneutical and creative struggle, and always somewhat alien. That a truly Christian society can exist, guided by the law of love, is more or less an article of faith—otherwise the historical venture of the church would be pointless—but its political and legal configurations are anything but obvious, and are subject to constant revision, not only in response to extrinsic material developments, but also on account of a

certain spiritual dynamism intrinsic to the gospel. There is perhaps an admirable clarity to Islam's refusal to erect any impermeable partition between spiritual and social community, or between the prophetic and the political realms; certainly, Islam traditionally does not find itself in the predicament of trying to inhabit two frames of time simultaneously, the apocalyptic and the ordinary. But there could never be such a thing as a Christian body of law and legal interpretation analogous to Islam's Sharia, not simply because of the difference between Christian cultural history and Muslim cultural history, but because it would be impossible within the terms of the gospel. In a very profound sense, Christians should inhabit history not only as pilgrims, but also as resident aliens—or as fugitives.

7. Of course, were it not for this essential ambiguity in the Christian approach to civil law—this inexact, tentative, conjectural, endlessly corrigible sense of how a just or free society might be cultivated in the light of the kingdom—Western history would be missing much of its exhilarating and tragic dynamism. And this includes much of both the creativity and destructiveness of modern Western society, which is a consequence not simply of the disintegration of a "Christian cultural consensus," but of an ancient and perhaps irresoluble tension within Christian culture itself.

One sees it from the very beginning of the Christian tradition, in the church's approach to the institution of slavery. On the one hand, it is doubtful that slavery could even have been recognized *as* an institution—as, that is, a practice entirely contingent on human custom—by pre-Christian culture, inasmuch as the latter lacked any concept of the history of sin. On the other hand, the first generations of Christians, living not only on the margins of society, but also at the end of days, clearly had no occasion to imagine a human society this side of the eschaton from which the institution had been deracinated. Paul's letter to Philemon is a plea to a master to recognize his slave as his brother in Christ, not his chattel, and in that sense its moral prescriptions are no less—and really somewhat more—radical than those of the Stoics; but, of course, it says nothing about what political or social realities should follow from the knowledge that, in Christ, the difference between slave and free had been annulled. And so, as the event of the apostolic church gradually coalesced into the institution of the imperial church, the general Christian attitude toward slavery became one of pragmatic accommodation with economic and social reality, only somewhat colored by a certain apocalyptic irony—a tacit recognition that the practice was the result of the Fall—which at first resulted, apart from a few significant but limited legal ameliorations, in very little. There were exceptional figures, of course, like Gregory of Nyssa and his sister Macrina: the former produced the only ancient text still extant seeming to condemn the very institution of slavery (and on entirely theological grounds), and the latter persuaded her mother to manumit her slaves. But the typical view of educated Christians was probably that of their brother Basil of Caesarea, who regarded slavery as a regrettable necessity inasmuch as, in a fallen world, there are certain souls that cannot govern themselves justly. And, while theologians such as John Chrysostom took it for granted that a Christian master could not humiliate and beat his slaves, Augustine—always more dour—morosely recommended chastisement if it was needed to dissuade a wanton servant from injurious sin. This is understandable, perhaps. An appeal to "natural" hierarchy has always been credible within Christian culture; in the body of Christ there are many members, as the apostle said.

On the other hand, however, what has always been utterly *incredible* within the New Testament's picture of reality is that anyone can justly be denied the "aspect"—the face and form and dignity—given him or her in Christ (in whom there is neither slave nor free). Most good historians of the period know that the gradual disappearance of chattel slavery in western Europe during the Middle Ages was occasioned not simply by economic and political changes (crucial though they were), but by the emergence of a wholly baptized populace, and of the consequent trans-formation of the entirety of society into the one body of Christ, of which every member was a coheir presumptive of God's kingdom. Of course, when chattel slavery was revived in the early modern period—the age of the nation-state, colonies, and commercial empires—there were many who attempted (quite plausibly, they thought) to defend the practice in theological terms, as a stewardship of untutored souls, a kind of mission to heathens and savages, and so on. But, in the end, it was theology—and most definitely *not* economics—that carried the cause of abolition to vic-tory (even in the one nation where the issue would be resolved finally only by war). And it is arguable that, apart from the assumptions and grammar of Christian theology, the movement would not have been intelligible.

Something similar might be said in regard to the history of the polit-ical emancipation of women. At the very least, one has to grant that, as a living cause, it was of uniquely Western provenance; and whether any-thing like it could have arisen in a non-Christian culture is an open ques-tion. More importantly, though, anyone who takes the time to explore the debates that surrounded the early campaign for women's suffrage, in the press and in popular journals, will discover that the terms of the ar-guments were to a surprising degree deeply theological, and on both sides (especially in the United States). Needless to say, there were many who opposed the cause simply out of fear of change or contempt for women, but there were also many—no less adamant in their opposition—who were clearly moved by an anxiety for the organic integrity of the "body of love": they believed that the removal of the franchise from the household as a whole and its uniform extension to both sexes would, simply by introducing the divisions of political interest into the family and thereby into the whole of society, hasten the dissolution of Christian culture. And yet no argument in favor of women's suffrage was more solvent or ultimately more persuasive than the claim that the dignity conferred by Christ upon all who had been baptized into his death was apportioned without preference to men and women alike, and that therefore no Christian nation could justly relegate women to a position of only secondary dignity.[2]

8. All this being said, however, the fact remains that the narratives of liberation that most powerfully shape society today, whatever their remote theological antecedents or religious causes might be, presume an understanding of freedom that is not only no longer explicitly Christian, but perhaps in many ways incompatible with a Christian view of the human being. And this, by itself, has to be taken as evidence of Christian culture's failure, over the course of its history, to give durable form or adequate content to a vision of society that could actually translate the anarchy of Christian love into positive law or civil order. We live now under the regime of negative liberty, which is admittedly a frequently very comfortable situation to find ourselves in, but which also means that we have all become the sovereign possessors of an ever emptier liberty, and citizens of a social order that, on principle, does not aspire to the "pedagogy of the Good." And this, of course, means that we enjoy precisely the kind and degree of liberty that best serve the interests of state and market. It is, after all, very much at the heart of the "modern project" that both should enclose our cultural commons as thoroughly as possible, while banishing to the realm of private fixations and eccentric associations any cultural forces that might prove intractable to their aims. The ideal citizen of the modern civil order is both dependent upon the state for the whole of his or her legal and social identity and also a wholly liberated consumer, with the resources to choose whatever and as much as he or she will. Any ideas or

2. I realize that the story of the women's movement is rarely told in this way, but that is because we usually tell it "backwards," entirely from the perspective of early twentieth-century progressivism. For those who doubt me, I recommend, as a particularly illuminating exercise, reading through the editorials and articles concerning women's suffrage that appeared in *Harper's Magazine* from the 1850s through the turn of the century.

loyalties that might dilute this dependency or inhibit this liberty must not be allowed to enter the world of law, or really even of licit public discourse; they must remain safely sequestered in the world of personal psychology.

Whatever the future of Christian social thought may be, it must begin from this situation. Its primary task, it seems to me, must be to enunciate a vision of freedom that neither "idealizes away" the injustices of the past nor surrenders to the soporific nihilism of mere negative liberty. And, as always, any worthwhile Christian theology of culture must confront, ever anew, its own baffling and fruitful and dangerous inner tension between an apocalyptic consciousness, somehow "beyond the law," and the sacramental reality of a fallen world that groans in anticipation of its transformation into the kingdom. The question of freedom for Christians must always be how to live corporately and "lawfully" within the anarchic prodigality of divine love and the light of divine goodness without attempting to collapse that tension or to flee from it to a liberty that "makes not free."

EIGHTEEN

The Encounter between Eastern Orthodoxy
and Radical Orthodoxy

A Brief Foreword

Apart from an obvious and largely accidental homonymy, and perhaps something of a shared tendency toward combativeness, there seems little uniting Eastern Orthodoxy and the Radical Orthodoxy movement. The former is chiefly marked—or so it often seems—by its historically fated conservatism, its broad indifference to any but the Eastern church fathers, its diffidence in regard to philosophical schools and debates outside its own tradition, and its at times admirable and at times deplorable insularity; the latter by its frissons of theological and political radicalism, its militantly "Latin" and "Augustinian" approaches to theology, its fascination with everything *au courant* in the world of Continental thought, and its cheerful openness to an endless variety of influences (the unwholesome on some occasions along with the wholesome). More to the point, perhaps, the former is an ancient church, comprising (at least, on optimistic estimates) a quarter-billion souls, and carrying within itself some two millennia of traditions and memories, while the latter is a theological movement of recent vintage, the adherents of which can be numbered (at most) in the hundreds, and the purpose of which is to influence the development of speculative theology in all Christian communions. It is, needless to say, difficult fruitfully to compare creatures of such disparate species.

That said, there is—it seems to me—a natural affinity between the two, and a sphere of interests common to them. Both are, if nothing else, expressions of a single metaphysical and theological tradition. One is a more organic, continuous, ramifying, and floriferous expression, with all the strengths and weaknesses of any purely natural phenomenon, and the other a more reflective and critical expression, nurtured under the conservatory conditions of the academy, with all the security and fragility that entails. But both subsist in an element of what should be described—honestly and proudly—as the Christian Platonist tradition. (Some among the Orthodox take exception to this designation, principally because it is so obviously correct, but it is a fact that Orthodoxy is never more Platonist than when denouncing "Platonism.") Everything the Orthodox treasure in the Eastern patristic tradition—its emphasis upon the metaphysics of participation, the deification of the creature in Christ, the ascent of the soul to the vision of God, the spiritual reality of the divine image in the soul, the mystical coinherence of the body of Christ, and the real will of God to save all human beings, as well as its salutary ignorance of any real partition, conceptual or ontological, between nature and grace—constitutes the native atmosphere in which Radical Orthodoxy has evolved. Even the latter's "Augustinianism" is devoid of any of those special features of the late Augustine's catastrophic misreading of Paul that are so profoundly distasteful to Eastern Christians: the doctrine of predilective predestination *ante praevisa merita*, the morbidly forensic understanding of original sin, the thrashing legions of unbaptized babies descending to their perpetual and condign combustion, and so on. The "radically orthodox" Augustine is the saner, more Platonist soul of the earlier theology, rather than the author of *De correptione*, the *Retractiones*, and the *Enchiridion*.

All of that, however, amounts to little more than saying that Eastern Orthodox tradition and the theology of Radical Orthodoxy reflect many of the same broad currents of ancient Catholic tradition. The more crucial rationale, though, for the sort of serious engagement between the two parties this volume represents, is that they are already involved in a sort of tacit alliance against a single enemy. Each is, in its distinctive way, a kind of evasion of or rebellion against modernity. Granted, in the case of the Orthodox Church, the "evasion" has been more a matter of omission and of historical circumstance than of a conscious resistance to the pathologies of modern thought and culture, and so the "rebellion" sometimes degenerates into a depressingly imprecise hostility toward "the West" as a whole. And granted, also, in the case of Radical Orthodoxy, both the evasion and the rebellion at times seem almost utopian in their abstraction from the concrete particularities of communities and nations and ecclesial traditions. But, in both cases, one encounters an ethos naturally antagonistic to post-Christian understandings of the self, of freedom, and of society, and to the dehumanizing and ultimately nihilistic consequences toward which they lead. And, in both cases also, one encounters an awareness that the most destructive forces within modernity were in some sense incubated within theology (though again, in the case of some Eastern Christians, this awareness is sometimes diffused into a more general, and somewhat vacuous, distrust of "Latin" theology as a whole).

It is a commonplace (though, happily, a sound one) to observe that much of the modern vision of reality—the "mechanical philosophy," the reduction of the concept of freedom to that of pure spontaneity of will, the politics of the absolutist state, and so on—was to some extent obscurely born in the late medieval collapse of the Christian metaphysical tradition as it had developed over more than a millennium, and especially in the rise of nominalism and voluntarism. The original impulse guiding these developments, of course, was a desire by certain theologians to affirm as radically as possible the sovereign transcendence of God; but the image of God thus produced—as hardly needs to be said—was ultimately of a superrational and even supermoral God, whose divinity consisted entirely in the omnipotence and arbitrariness of his will, and who was not truly transcendent of his creation, but merely the supreme power within it. In detaching God's freedom from God's nature as Goodness, Truth, and Charity—as this theology necessarily, if not always intentionally, did— Christian thought laid the foundations for many of those later revolutions in philosophy and morality that would help to produce the post-Christian order. It was inevitable, after all, that the object of the voluntarist model of freedom would migrate from the divine to the human will, and that a world evacuated of its ontological continuity with God's goodness would ultimately find no place for God within itself. And, in early modernity, when the new God of infinite and absolute will had to a very great degree displaced the true God from many human minds, the new technology of print assured that all Christians would make the acquaintance of this im- poster, and through him come to understand true liberty as a personal sovereignty transcending even the dictates and constraints of nature. Moreover—more crucially—the God thus produced was monstrous: an abyss of pure, predestining omnipotence, whose majesty was revealed at once in his unmerited mercy toward the elect and his righteous wrath against the derelict. And he was to be found in the theologies of almost every school: not only Jansenism, Lutheranism, and Calvinism, but the theology of the Dominican Thomists, such as Bañez and Alvarez as well (though the Dominicans, through their superior faculty for specious rea- soning, did a better job of convincing themselves that their God was a good God). That modern Western humanity came in large measure to refuse to believe in or worship such a God was ineluctable, and in some sense extremely commendable (no one, after all, can be faulted for preferring atheism to Calvinism or the old "two-tiered" Thomism).

In any event, these are old arguments, and there is no need to rehearse them here. All I wish to point out is that Eastern Orthodoxy—through its innocence of these theological deformations—and Radical Orthodoxy—through its rejection and abhorrence of them—are already in some way bound together in a single destiny; and, as the community of believing European Christians continues to dwindle away (as it certainly will, far into the foreseeable future), they should not hesitate to lend their strengths each to the other, and to mend their own infirmities thereby. What such an interaction might produce is difficult to say, but one might venture a few guesses. Perhaps certain Eastern Orthodox theologians might be moved to reconsider the Eastern hostility toward Augustine (the largely good, earlier Augustine, that is) that has become such a vogue among the Orthodox in the past five decades, and that has made many of them insensible to the brilliance even of works such as *De Trinitate*, and that continues to produce offensively silly caricatures of Augustine's theology in Orthodox scholarship. Perhaps, by the same token, certain of the radically orthodox could be weaned from their preposterous refusal to acknowledge that Augustine's late theology of nature and grace, sin and election, must be accounted the chief cause within the Latin tradition of that tradition's susceptibility to the appeal of voluntarism. Some Eastern theologians might be emboldened partly to abandon the neo-Palamite theology that has become so dominant in their church since the middle of the last century, and frankly acknowledge the incoherence of some of its most influential expressions, and come to recognize that in some ways Augustine or Thomas was closer to the Greek fathers in his understanding of divine transcendence than was the neo-Palamite version of Palamas (who is Palamas as he has come to be understood by many); these theologians might even feel freer to avail themselves of many of the speculative riches of their own tradition that have been forgotten as a result of the fruitful but narrowing triumph of the neo-Palamite synthesis (Byzantine scholasticism, Sophiology, and so forth). And perhaps some of the radically orthodox, taking the example of modern Eastern theology more to heart, might learn better to integrate the mystical and spiritual dimensions of the faith into their expositions of doctrine and into their theological speculations. Most importantly, perhaps, the Eastern Orthodox might be reminded by their encounters with Radical Orthodoxy that a true defiance of the more nihilistic currents of modernity should take the form not simply of a retreat into liturgical and spiritual tradition, but of a social and political philosophy as well. And perhaps the radically orthodox might profit from an exposure to the sheer obduracy of Eastern Christianity—the effect of decades and centuries of misfortune and oppression—and learn to fortify themselves against the almost certain failure of their project as a social and political force.

One could go on, of course, but the endless addition of one "perhaps" to another leads nowhere, except in the direction of an ever more random association of ideas. Suffice it to say that the time is ripe for a collection of this sort,[1] and—both for the conversation it comprises and for the further conversations it portends—this book is a worthy object of celebration.

1. This piece was written as a foreword to *Encounter between Eastern Orthodoxy and Radical Orthodoxy*.

NINETEEN

Remarks in Response to Gianni Vattimo

Within the particular act of hermeneutical retrieval in which, at present, Gianni Vattimo is engaged, an opening to theology has appeared; in attempting to unite (or reunite) the history of the decline of every "strong thought of Being" to the history of the Christian proclamation of God's *kenōsis* in Christ, Vattimo has made the genealogy of philosophical nihilism a theme within the greater hermeneutical transmission of "salvation history" (as today's paper demonstrated). Vattimo has also made it quite clear in various recent writings that he does not hereby suppose some form of hermeneutical supersessionism, as if "weak thought" accomplishes what theology failed to do; this would, among other things, mean that weak thought is a kind of truth somehow objectively real apart from its own hermeneutical transmission, toward which there can be various independent approaches, some more correct, some more deficient. His interest, simply enough, is in an act of recollection, or of *Andenken*, that will rescue philosophy from a certain forgetfulness. The invitation to theology—which is, after all, nothing but a practice of hermeneutical retrieval—to respond to this project is frequently quite explicit in his work. What I wish to do here, then, is interrogate the use he makes of the language of "salvation history" and to do so in fairly classical theological terms; for however far Western philosophy may yet go in remembering its originary "mission," theology may still remember otherwise—alongside "nihilism" perhaps, but always also from a different direction (to put this differently, theology perhaps can remember only from the future that it has already been given, and so can only recall, in some sense, its future). In any event, I hope I shall be indulged on three counts: for proceeding entirely from a certain theological vantage (though scaffolded within a hermeneutical question only); for doing so in terms too condensed and briefly stated; and for beginning anecdotally.

A few years ago, I met Prof. Vattimo at the University of Virginia—I do not know if he recalls me—where, over the course of two days, I fear, I plagued him with questions situated somewhere between urgency and impertinence, until he finally brought a close to our sporadic conversation by suggesting that we would meet each other in infinity. A lovely phrase actually, and one that called to my mind two models of eschatological reconciliation or harmony: that of Nicholas of Cusa, who thought that different lines of thought, converging upon the mystery of God, could in the calculus of the divine infinity come to lie together in peace without actually competing or being reduced one to the other (for God is the *infinite* complication of differences); and that, simply enough, of the Bible, which promises that we all may meet in some final Zion, when the God of Israel will rule as a blessing to all nations, in the dispensation of an ultimate peace (the hope perhaps most poignantly invoked at every Passover: "Next year in Jerusalem"—a phrase expressing at once both a pious desire to eat the seder in the Holy City and also an anticipation of the messianic day of redemption). I knew that Vattimo's thought was moving ineluctably toward deeper encounters with theology, but whether according to a logic of infinite *discrete* complication or according to one of ultimate convergence, I could not say; then I assumed the former, now I think quite plausibly the latter.

But, to paraphrase what Isaiah, Jesus, Saint Paul, and Jacques Derrida have at various times and in diverse places told us, we are not yet in Jerusalem, but only in Disney World. I admire much of Vattimo's account of the genealogy of nihilism, secularization, the decline of metaphysics, and the weakening of thought as belonging to salvation history; at least it seems to me not only persuasive but eminently theologically sound to say that Western thought comes to relinquish many a strong thought of Being—and so comes to understand Being as event—as the hermeneutical issue not only of the transmission or *Überlieferung* of Western philosophy as such, but as the consequence of the *kenōsis* of God in Jesus of Nazareth, and the history of that announcement. But I suffer from two adherences—one a commitment to a kind of Orthodox Christianity and the other a sentimental attachment to a kind of heterodox Marxism—that perhaps make me prey to certain metaphysical nostalgias and that prompt me to ask certain questions of his argument, or at least to voice certain hesitations. Certainly the most provocative formula in his address today was:

"the history of Being is the history of nihilism, that is, the very history of salvation that we have come to know from the Bible." The *very* history of salvation? Surely something has been left out at this point. Surely some element—which I feel obliged to say is the eschatological element—has received inadequate attention.

I should note immediately that Vattimo wisely rejects the sort of fashionable tragic apocalypticism that understands redemption only as a violent rupture within history, or as a sort of timeless and featureless negation that can be brought only over against history as the abyssal or persecuting appeal of the ethical: eschatology, that is, reduced to a structure that simply impends upon every moment within a history that, obedient to a gnostic logic, it invades but also abandons as intrinsically irredeemable and unredemptive. His vision is essentially comic, and never lapses into a tragic Levinasian peremptoriness or anguish. All for the best: he has not lost sight of the darkness of history in resisting the despair that history engenders; he has merely taken up the properly Jewish and Christian belief that it is history that is to be redeemed, and that redemption is a history. Still, if it is indeed the history *of salvation* with which we are concerned, redemption and the weakening of thought cannot simply be equated one with the other; there must yet remain an interval between, an eschatological suspense—properly understood—if the weakening of thought, and indeed divine *kenōsis* itself, are not to be converted into simply another tragic economy. And it is very doubtful one can do here without the theological tropologies of eschatological judgment, divine transcendence, and divine power. Of course, to invoke these terms is to invite apprehension: Are they not contaminated with the worst kind of metaphysical violence, or with a yearning for the stability of a strong structure of Being, or of a strong structure of history . . . ? I think what I am saying is innocent of dangerous tendencies; but, if not wholly so, I still must plead the inevitability of these terms, if not their tractability.

So I shall voice my hesitations in three moments: roughly called ontological, eschatological, and ideological (though the last is really soteriological).

1. Vattimo recognizes that divine *kenōsis*, in the Bible, is not a punctiliar irruption of God, in Christ, into the alien element of time, but is how it is from the beginning: the God who creates, as opposed to a god immanent within and dependent upon the cruel sacrificial economies of nature, already pours himself out from his transcendence and gives being freely to that which was previously nothing at all; being, given as event, is a gracious weakening. But then, in classic Christian theological

terms, for reasons proper to its reflections on the economy of salvation in relation to Trinitarian doctrine, this is still not the *first* moment of divine *kenōsis*. If it were, then God's identity and the world's would be achieved in the eventuation of the world; a convertibility and so interdependence between divinity and worldliness, under the canopy of being, would take shape; a metaphysics would be born, along with a tragic aporia concerning whether salvation history redeems the world or God. Christian thought inevitably posits—given its textual and dogmatic concerns—an eternal outpouring of the Father in the Son, and a further, different outpouring through the Son in the Spirit; because God enjoys a life of this eternal and joyous giving, without thereby ceasing also to be the one who gives, it requires no tragic alienation for him to give and also to be the place (the *chōra*) of another giving. I should note that Vattimo has himself amply addressed the Trinitarian provenance of the history he describes, and how the Christian God is clearly not simply a divine origin recalling us to unshakable metaphysical foundations; all I wish really to insist, with whatever onto-theological perils it may appear to entail, and however differently various schools of theology construe the matter, is that it is necessary to say that the event of God's being is first for himself, without need of us or the tragic probations of our history to achieve his peace. If thus, in him, those things that our habits of thought necessarily oppose—strength and weakness, love and judgment, power and emptiness—are always already one life and reconciling motion, then the creation of the world from nothingness is the first redemptive act, and the God who made himself one with what was as nothing, and became a place for it, the lamb slain from the foundations of the world, can also come—and will come—to redeem his creatures. Even in pouring himself out entirely he is not exhausted, but always possesses the power of raising up.

Perhaps this is a retreat into antique metaphysics, or into irrelevancy, but for theology to interpret the biblical language of redemption, it has always proved necessary to imagine both a primordial and an ultimate coincidence of Being and peace—as the event of the God who gives himself to the as-nothing, not tragically, not exhausting his divinity, but confirming it as the power to redeem. One must, in short, speak of God's transcendence: not, to be sure, the threatening vertical transcendence of what Vattimo defines as metaphysics, which can belong only to Being conceived as a totality, with the divine placed at the summit of its hierarchy, the founded and founding god, the speculative completion and surety of our world, which a *kenōsis* would indeed exhaust; this is, after all, not really transcendence, but merely the foundation of all immanence.

Nor is this to speak of the equally threatening negative transcendence of God conceived merely as the Wholly Other. Between the cataphatic and apophatic voices of transcendence—between a "metaphysical" and a dialectical theology—there remains an open way of analogy: imagined not in terms of a simple scale of metaphysical sympathies, but as the discourse of a God who is most near in his otherness and most strange in his intimacy. After all, what Vattimo has called an "amiable" continuity between God and world, which he rightly prefers to a paradoxical and dialectical transcendence, can reside only in this open interval of the analogical, which never collapses into simple equivalence or univocity and so never reduces the action of God with us to the "fate" of God in us. The Christian God is inexhaustibly kenotic, so to speak, pouring himself out in—but still there beyond—our history; and so there is, indeed, a history of *salvation*.

2. This may perhaps gain clarity if I turn to eschatology. For a theologian, what might be most immediately disorienting in Vattimo's discourse is its almost exclusive identification of salvation history with *kenōsis*, because, of course, in Christian tradition, the language of abasement has always been wedded quite indissolubly to the language of exaltation; the church preached first the resurrection of Christ, his lordship over history, and only in this light gave shape to a theology of the divine Son's descent from the form of God to the form of a slave. And this is not merely incidental to the story; for in the paschal vindication of Jesus of Nazareth over against those who put him to death, and in no other way, it was precisely the form of a slave that became visible for perhaps the first time ever: visible, moreover, as the object of God's love and as, indeed, the very form of God. And this is so because the resurrection is already an eschatological event, the promised eschatological redemption of creation already accomplished and yet still somehow present now within history itself, as in some very real sense a disruption of all our immanent teleologies, whether those of nature, society, city, household, or history. It disrupts, that is, that sacrificial economy that builds crosses to preserve its stable orders of destiny, privilege, power, and class against the elements of nature and culture that might upset those orders—the criminal, the colonial barbarian, the enemy, and other agents of civic disorder. It deprives thought of those first and "evident" principles and foundations by which it might construct a world to accommodate our violences, by discriminating among the essences of things: noble from base, ideal from simulacral, master from slave, even judge from criminal. And none of the founding gestures of the old metaphysics can resist this disruption. The verdict of God is on the side of the slave. No tableau in the New Testament is more wonder-

ful or terrible than that of Christ, scourged and mocked, standing before Pilate, as it is laid out in the Fourth Gospel: one figure vested with all the glory and power of the ancient order, all the prerogative of empire, demanding a show of pedigrees—"Whence art thou?"—and proclaiming the singular truth of his world—"I have power to crucify thee"; and another figure, quite absurd, beaten, crowned with thorns, derided, a criminal and slave prating madly of his otherworldly kingdom. Where else, before the Gospels, would the order of truth in this scene have been so thoroughly inverted, and God shown to be on the side of the condemned, the civic sacrifice? Nor could this slave be brought before our eyes as God's truth, God's place, but that God came also with power to redeem and to judge. God is on the side, again, of the as-nothing, the metaphysically empty being of the slave, who truly has no substance, no *ousia* (which also, like *substantia*, means both substance and wealth), no homeland, no autochthony or prerogative, no *face* (*non habens personam*, as Roman law defined the slave). Vattimo, deeply influenced by René Girard, is certainly well aware of where the Gospels find the grace of God. But I wish nonetheless to emphasize that only in this eschatological light of Easter—this defiant and perhaps ironic display of divine power—are we made able to see what formerly we never saw, what was invisible: the slave, the person, my God.

It is no accident, I think, that the first uncompromising attack upon the institution of slavery in Western history, written in the fourth century by Gregory of Nyssa, was a Lenten sermon preparing a congregation for Easter (on which day Gregory would also go on to demand that his congregation manumit their slaves). Gregory's theology was uniquely dominated by eschatology, as it happens, and as a consequence it was he who, first among the fathers, explicitly denied that there is such a thing as a metaphysical "essence" of the human, to which some attain and of which others fall short—rather, there is only the whole of humanity gathered into Christ at the end of time, and this entire community is alone what the truly human is. It was he also, incidentally, who first described salvation history as a gradual *akolouthia* or unfolding of Christ's charity in time, an unfolding that will ultimately be at one with our history as a whole. But in every case, this was because his theology was profoundly paschal, profoundly—so to speak—triumphalist.

Is this not also the story of the decline of metaphysics: not merely a weakening of thought released by God's *kenōsis*, but the irresistible and revolutionary transcendence visited upon thought by the proclamation of Easter? For the resurrection was definitely a revolution against, and conquest of, the powers, principalities, thrones, and dominions; it accomplished not the death of God, but the death of immanence, in the sense of an enclosed and self-justifying totality: the death of many metaphysical gods, certainly, and of that vertical hierarchical transcendence that is still only the completion of immanence, but not of the one who will be where he will be, who can identify himself with the as-nothing and yet also still redeem them and raise them up. Everything now is lifted up into an inescapable transcendence, and we obscure this *hermeneutical* truth when we continue to think of strength and weakness, or mercy and justice, or the form of the slave and the form of God as merely opposed; to speak only of weakness and say nothing of strength leaves us still within the logic of the immanent order of power—or the powers.

3. Which brings me to my final hesitation: the ideological or, more properly, soteriological. I confess that my first encounter with "weak thought" some years ago immediately aroused a sort of suspicion in my mind, so much then a creature of Frankfurt School thinking, to the effect that this was perhaps just a kind of twilight thinking that completed the project of the West (the twilight land, the *Abendland*) and confirmed its privilege of inscribing the finality of its narrative over every other story: Is there not, I wondered, a peculiar strength in the yielding passivity of this thinking, a power of dissolving every intractable or local narrative into its own fluid "truthlessness"? And was this not then merely the ideological superstructure of the free market, that truly transparent society in which all things dissolve into a kind of univocal flow of commodification, into that flux of perpetual transvaluation expressed so exquisitely well by the ubiquity of the price tag? And so on. I have since put this suspicion away as the sullen paranoia of an indolent academic radical, but some trace of my initial apprehension does remain. Does a weakening of thought always, even within the ambit of our peculiar Judeo-Christian *Überlieferung*, simply weaken into charity? Is charity its own light, its own visibility? Are there not always more exuberant and violent nihilisms waiting to fill in the empty spaces left where what we thought were strong, enduring edifices of truth once stood? Because the decline of every strong structure of Being—as Vattimo, following Heidegger, knows—is a possibility of liberation within a condition of risk: the technological *Gestell*. And more and more, having put aside (for good reasons) the metaphysical humanism that arrayed itself as a science of the human essence or as the dialectics of subjectivity, we too dissolve into an order of visibility that requires of us that we be pure, punctiliar instances of acquisitive power and indeterminate appetite, gazing out upon a region of indifferent instances and occasions of the use of that power. History delivers us to the market, and within this

order of visibility, so many things can be reduced to a new invisibility: that which we have been taught to see as formerly we could not—the "slave," the homeless person, the physically or mentally disabled, the pauper—can so easily be hidden again behind such visible and stable essences as the commodity of cheap labor, the economic burden of the unemployed, the irrelevance of those who lack the power of purchase. Much of the story of secularization remains quite unredemptive, after all. We exist in the heart of this fluid, inessential, but still oppressive spectacle; in this age, it is not only today, but every day, that we are gathered—in ways too numerous and terrible to tell—in Disney World. And so it constitutes something other than metaphysical nostalgia to call always on that eschatological light— the particular history of God in Christ, seen from the vantage of Easter— continually to make the otherwise invisible irresistibly appear. And this light must indeed be a visibility, a particular thematization according to the story of Christ: the abyssal darkness of a featureless eschaton, provoking us supposedly to sheer ethical obligation, will never quite make us able to see where charity should be directed, or why it should persist. Against the tendency to mistake any history—even one as liberating as the decline of metaphysics—for salvation history *tout court* (the Constantinian fallacy of finding God's peace unproblematically present in the peace we can achieve), but also against the empty provocations of an eschaton without content (which could confirm no aspect of our actual history as redemptive), must be placed the absolute content of God's redemptive will, both manifestly accomplished and mysteriously to come: the resurrected slave. Otherwise we have not quite listened to the transmission of this history; we are wanting in *pietas*. It cannot be simply that our history, even in this continuing decline, *is* salvation history; rather, it belongs to—by accord or resistance—a particular history still unfolding in its midst, which only eschatologically may be seen to unfold to the blessing of all: the history, that is, of the as-nothing, who had no story at all until God both poured himself out in their midst and raised them up again in himself. For Christian thought, at least, this is the very heart of any reflection upon what is meant by "salvation history." Against the power of the market, against every order of closure—even one that imagines it has established justice upon the earth—the light of God's verdict on Christ, with the unique optical inversion to which it subjects all our histories, must always be invoked as a power different from our power, revered as a justice infinitely more merciful than our justice, and called upon as redemption.

So, having said all this, I am not entirely sure what these remarks accomplish, or sure whether they are immeasurably remote from Vattimo's language or for the most part so close as to mark only a difference in emphasis and terms (a preference, that is, for a more openly triumphalistic and revolutionary intonation, with all the attendant dangers of such a preference). I am still thinking out the work that Vattimo is producing on this matter, and truly cannot say whether and to what degree there is either a discrete but harmonious complication or even a peaceful convergence between his history of nihilism and what I take to be the particular hermeneutical burden of theology: the real antagonism between continuous secularization and the eschatological arrival of redeeming judgment, or between a peacefully interminable immanence and an irresistible transcendence. I occasionally *feel* very close and, at other times, I feel nothing of the kind.

At any rate, I know this: it is good to meet Prof. Vattimo again, even here, under the overshadowing ears of the all-conquering mouse; but it is certainly possible to hope, and even in some real sense to expect: next year—*Deo volente*—in Jerusalem.

TWENTY

God, Creation, and Evil

The Moral Meaning of *Creatio ex Nihilo*

Romans 5:18–19: Ἄρα οὖν ὡς δι' ἑνὸς παραπτώματος εἰς πάντας ἀνθρώπους εἰς κατάκριμα, οὕτως καὶ δι' ἑνὸς δικαιώματος εἰς πάντας ἀνθρώπους εἰς δικαίωσιν ζωῆς· ὥσπερ γὰρ διὰ τῆς παρακοῆς τοῦ ἑνὸς ἀνθρώπου ἁμαρτωλοὶ κατεστάθησαν οἱ πολλοί, οὕτως καὶ διὰ τῆς ὑπακοῆς τοῦ ἑνὸς δίκαιοι κατασταθήσονται οἱ πολλοί.

Romans 11:32: συνέκλεισεν γὰρ ὁ θεὸς τοὺς πάντας εἰς ἀπείθειαν ἵνα τοὺς πάντας ἐλεήσῃ.

1 Corinthians 3:15: . . . ζημιωθήσεται, αὐτὸς δὲ σωθήσεται, οὕτως δὲ ὡς διὰ πυρός.

1 Corinthians 15:22: ὥσπερ γὰρ ἐν τῷ Ἀδὰμ πάντες ἀποθνήσκουσιν, οὕτως καὶ ἐν τῷ Χριστῷ πάντες ζωοποιηθήσονται.

1 Corinthians 15:28: . . . ἵνα ᾖ ὁ θεὸς πάντα ἐν πᾶσιν.

1 Timothy 2:3–4: . . . θεοῦ, ὃς πάντας ἀνθρώπους θέλει σωθῆναι καὶ εἰς ἐπίγνωσιν ἀληθείας ἐλθεῖν.

1 Timothy 4:10: . . . θεῷ ζῶντι, ὅς ἐστιν σωτὴρ πάντων ἀνθρώπων, μάλιστα πιστῶν.

1. I have to confess to a certain unease with this topic. Something tells me that, treated candidly, it confronts us with a very obvious equation, of crystalline clarity, whose final result will be either all or nothing (neither of which is a particularly tractable sum). I also fear repeating arguments I have made in the past, and thereby retaining both their strengths and their deficiencies. I am especially keen to avoid arguments that rely in a very particular way upon the classical metaphysics of transcendence, to which I remain ever faithful, but which can also constitute something of an easy escape from troubling problems. The temptation, to which I have often yielded, is to invoke the ontology of ontological supereminence, or impassibility, or the eternal plenitude of the absolute (or what have you) to remind us that God *in se* is not determined by creation and that, consequently, evil does not enter into our understanding of the divine essence. All of this is true, of course, but left to itself it inexorably devolves toward half-truth, and then toward triviality—a wave of the prestidigitator's hand and Auschwitz magically vanishes. And so I should prefer here to address the other side of that metaphysical picture: the unavoidable conclusion that, precisely because God and creation are ontologically distinct in the manner of the absolute and the contingent, they are morally indiscerptible.

The first theological insight I learned from Gregory of Nyssa—and I suspect the last to which I shall cling when all others fall away—is that the Christian doctrine of *creatio ex nihilo* is not merely a cosmological or metaphysical claim, but is also an eschatological claim about the world's relation to God, and hence a moral claim about the nature of God in himself. In the end of all things is their beginning, and only from the perspective of the end can one know what they are, why they have been made, and who the God is who has called them forth from nothingness. And in Gregory's thought, with an integrity found only also in Origen and Maximus, protology and eschatology are a single science, a single revelation disclosed in the God-man. There is no profounder meditation on the meaning of creation than Gregory's eschatological treatise *On the Soul and Resurrection*, and no more brilliantly realized eschatological vision than his *On the Making of Humanity*. For him, clearly, one can say that the cosmos has been truly created only when it reaches its consummation in "the union of all things with the first good," and that humanity has truly been created only when all human beings, united in the living body of Christ, become at last that "Godlike thing" that is "humankind according to the image."

My topic, though, is not Gregory's theology, but only the principle that the doctrine of creation constitutes an assertion regarding the eternal *identity* of God. It is chiefly an affirmation of God's absolute dispositive liberty in all his acts: the absence of any external restraint upon or necessity behind every decision of his will. And, while one must avoid the pathetic anthropomorphism of imagining God's decision to create as an arbitrary choice made after deliberation among options, one must still affirm that it is *free*, that creation can add nothing to God, that God's being is not dependent on the world's, and that the only necessity in the divine act of creation is the impossibility of any hindrance upon God's expression of his goodness. Yet, paradoxically perhaps, this means that the moral destiny of creation and the moral nature of God are absolutely inseparable. For, as the transcendent Good beyond all beings, he is the transcendental end of any action of any rational nature; and then, obviously, the end toward which God acts must be his own goodness: he who is the beginning and end of all things. And this eternal teleology, viewed from the vantage of history, is a cosmic eschatology. As an eternal act, creation's term is the divine nature; within the orientation of time, its term is a "final judgment." No matter how great the autonomy one grants the realm of secondary causes, two things are certain. First, as God's act of creation is free, constrained by neither necessity nor ignorance, all contingent ends are intentionally enfolded within his decision. And, second, precisely because God in himself is absolute, "absolved" of every pathos of the contingent, his moral "venture" in creating is infinite. For all causes are logically reducible to their first cause; this is no more than a logical truism, and it does not matter whether one construes the relation between primary and secondary causality as one of total determinism or utter indeterminacy, for in either case all "consequents" are—either as actualities or merely as possibilities—contingent upon their primordial "antecedent," apart from which they could not exist. Moreover, the rationale—the definition—of a first cause is the final cause that prompts it; and so if that first cause is an infinitely free act emerging from an infinite wisdom, all those consequents are intentionally entailed—again, either as actualities or as possibilities— within that first act; and so the final end to which that act tends is its *whole* moral truth. The traditional ontological definition of evil as a *privatio boni* is not merely a logically necessary metaphysical axiom about the transcendental structure of being, but also an assertion that when we say "God is good," we are speaking of him not only relative to his creation, but also (however apophatically) as he is in himself; for in every sense being *is* act, and God—in his simplicity and infinite freedom—*is* what he does.

2. Between the ontology of *creatio ex nihilo* and that of emanation, after all, there really is no metaphysical difference—unless by the latter

we mean a kind of gross material efflux of the divine substance into lesser substances (but of course no one, except perhaps John Milton, ever believed in such a thing). In either case, all that exists comes from one divine source, and subsists by the grace of impartation and the labor of participation: an economy of donation and dependency, supereminence and individuation, actuality and potentiality. God goes forth in all beings and in all beings returns to himself—as, moreover, an expression not of God's dialectical struggle with some recalcitrant exteriority, but of an inexhaustible power wholly possessed by the divine in peaceful liberty. All the doctrine of creation adds is an assurance that in this divine outpouring there is no element of the "irrational": something purely spontaneous, or organic, or even mechanical, beyond the power of God's rational freedom. But then it also means that within the story of creation, viewed from its final cause, there can be no residue of the pardonably tragic, no irrecuperable or irreconcilable remainder left at the end of the tale; for, if there were, this too God would have done, as a price freely assumed in creating. This is simply the logic of the truly absolute. Hegel, for instance, saw the great slaughterbench of history as a tragic inevitability of the Idea's odyssey toward *Geist* through the far countries of finite negation; for him, the merely particular—say, the isolated man whose death is, from the vantage of the all, no more consequential than the harvesting of a head of cabbage—is simply the smoke that rises from the sacrifice. But the story *we* tell, of creation as God's sovereign act of love, leaves no room for an ultimate distinction between the universal truth of reason and the moral meaning of the particular—nor, indeed, for a distinction between the moral meaning of the particular and the moral nature of God. Precisely because God does not determine himself in creation—because there is no dialectical necessity binding him to time or chaos, no need to forge his identity in the fires of history—in creating he reveals himself truly. Thus every evil that time comprises, natural or moral—a worthless distinction, really, since human nature is a natural phenomenon—is an arraignment of God's goodness: every death of a child, every chance calamity, every act of malice; everything diseased, thwarted, pitiless, purposeless, or cruel; and, until the end of all things, no answer has been given. Precisely because creation is not a theogony, all of it is theophany. It would be impious, I suppose, to suggest that, in his final divine judgment of creatures, God will judge himself; but one *must* hold that by that judgment God truly will *disclose* himself (which, of course, is to say the same thing, in a more hushed and reverential voice). Even Paul asks, in the tortured, conditional voice of Romans 9, whether there might be vessels of wrath stored up solely for destruction *only* because he trusts that there are not, that instead *all* are bound in disobedience *only* so that God might prove himself just by showing mercy on *all*. The *argumentum ad baculum* is a terrifying specter, momentarily conjured up only so as to be immediately chased away by a decisive, radiant *argumentum ad caritatem*.

3. But this creates a small problem of theological coherence, for a rather obvious reason. To wit—and this should be an uncontroversial statement—the God in whom the majority of Christians throughout history have professed belief would appear to be evil (at least, judging by the dreadful things we habitually say about him). And I intend nothing more here than an exercise in sober precision, based on the presumption that words should have some determinate content. Every putatively meaningful theological affirmation dangles upon a golden but fragile thread of analogy. It must be possible to speak of God without mistaking him for a being among beings, an instance of something greater than himself. Between God and creatures lies an epistemological chasm nothing less than infinite, which no predicate can span univocally. Even Scotists believe that, within the weak embrace of a largely negative *conceptum univocum entis*, the modal disproportion between the infinite and the finite renders the analogy between God and creatures irreducibly disjunctive. But neither can theological language consist in nothing but equivocal expostulations, piously but fruitlessly offered up into the abyss of the divine mystery; this would evacuate theological language not only of logical but also of *semantic* content; nothing could be affirmed—nothing could *mean* anything at all. And yet, down the centuries, Christians have again and again subscribed to formulations of their faith that clearly reduce a host of cardinal Christian theological usages—most especially moral predicates like "good," "merciful," "just," "benevolent," "loving"—to utter equivocity, and by association the entire grammar of Christian belief to meaninglessness. Indeed, so absolute is this equivocity that the only hope of rescuing any analogy from the general ruin would be to adopt "evil" as the sole plausible moral "proportion" between God and creatures.

Nor am I speaking of a few marginal, eccentric sects within Christian history; I mean the broad mainstream: particularly, I suppose it pleases me to say, but not exclusively in the West. Let us, briefly, dwell on the obvious. Consider—to begin with the mildest of moral difficulties—how many Christians down the centuries have had to reconcile their consciences to the repellent notion that all humans are at conception already guilty of a transgression that condemns them, justly, to eternal separation from God; and that, in the doctrine's extreme form, every newborn infant belongs to a "*massa damnata*," hateful in God's eyes from the first moment of existence. Of course, the very idea of an "inherited guilt" is a logical absurdity, rather on the order of a "square circle"; all the doctrine *truly* asserts is that God imputes to innocent creatures a guilt they can never have contracted, out of what from any sane perspective can only be called malice. But this is just the beginning of the problem. For one broad venerable stream of tradition, God on the basis of this imputation delivers the vast majority of the race to perpetual torment, including infants who die unbaptized—though one later, intenerating redaction of the tale says the children, at least, though denied the vision of God, will be granted the homely beatitude of the *limbus infantium* (which mitigates but does not dispel the doctrine's moral idiocy). And then the theology of "grace" grows grimmer. For, in the great Augustinian tradition, since we are somehow born meriting not only death but also eternal torment, we are asked to see in God's narrow choice *ante praevisa merita* to elect a small remnant for salvation, and either to predestine or infallibly consign the vast remainder to everlasting misery, a laudable generosity. When Augustine lamented the softheartedness that made Origen believe that demons, heathens, and (most preposterously of all) unbaptized babies might ultimately be spared the torments of eternal fire, he made clear how the moral imagination must bend and twist in order to absorb such beliefs. Pascal, in assuring us that our existence is explicable only in light of a belief in the eternal and condign torment of babies who die before reaching the baptismal font, shows us that there is often no meaningful distinction between perfect faith and perfect nihilism. Calvin, in telling us that hell is copiously populated with infants not a cubit long, merely reminds us that, within a certain traditional understanding of grace and predestination, the choice to worship God rather than the devil is at most a matter of prudence. So it is that, for many Christians down the years, the rationale of evangelization has been a desperate race to save as many souls as possible *from God* (think of poor Francis Xavier, dying of exhaustion trying to pluck as many infants as possible from the flames). Really, Reformed tradition is perhaps to be praised here for the flinty resolve with which it faces its creed's implications: Calvin had the courage to acknowledge that his account of divine sovereignty necessitates belief in the predestination not only of the saved and the damned, but of the Fall itself; and he recognized that the biblical claim that "God is love" must, on his principles, be accounted a definition not of God in himself, but only of God as experienced by the elect (toward the damned, God is in fact hate). And it is fitting that, among all models of atonement, Reformed theology so securely fastened upon a particularly sanguinary version of "substitution"—though one whose appeasements avail only for a very few, leaving the requirement of an eternal hell for the great many fully to reveal the glory of divine sovereignty.

Very well. Say that Calvinism is nothing but a cruel *reductio ad absurdum* of the worst aspects of an immensely influential but still deeply defective theological tradition. (And, as an Orthodox, I would simply be keeping up tradition if I were merely to denounce all of these doctrinal deformations as just so much Western Christian "barbarism" and retreat to the pre-Augustinian idyll of Byzantine theology.) Surely, though, we need not grant that the larger Christian understanding of God is morally contradictory. Would that the matter were quite that simple. For all of this follows from an incoherence deeply fixed at the heart of almost all Christian traditions: that is, the idea that the omnipotent God of love, who creates the world from nothing, either imposes or tolerates the eternal torment of the damned. It is not merely peculiarity of personal temperament that prompts Tertullian to speak of the saved relishing the delightful spectacle of the destruction of the reprobate, or Peter Lombard and Thomas Aquinas to assert that the vision of the torments of the damned will increase the beatitude of the redeemed (as any trace of pity would darken the joys of heaven), or Luther to insist that the saved will rejoice to see their loved ones roasting in hell. All of them were simply following the only poor thread of logic they had to guide them out of a labyrinth of impossible contradictions; the sheer enormity of the idea of a hell of eternal torment forces the mind toward absurdities and atrocities. Of course, the logical deficiencies of such language are obvious: After all, what is a *person* other than a whole history of associations, loves, memories, attachments, and affinities? Who are we, other than all the others who have made us who we are, and to whom we belong as much as they to us? We *are* those others. To say that the sufferings of the damned will either be clouded from the eyes of the blessed or, worse, increase the pitiless bliss of heaven is also to say that *no* persons can possibly be saved: for, if the memories of others are removed, or lost, or one's knowledge of their misery is converted into indifference or, God forbid, into greater beatitude, what then remains of one in one's last bliss? Some other being altogether, surely: a spiritual anonymity, a vapid spark of pure intellection, the residue of a soul reduced to no one. But not a person—not the person who was. But the deepest problem is not the logic of such claims; it is their sheer moral hideousness.

4. Among more civilized apologists for the "infernalist" orthodoxies these days, the most popular defense seems to be an appeal to creaturely freedom and to God's respect for its dignity. But there could scarcely be a

poorer argument; whether made crudely or elegantly, it invariably fails. It might not do so, if one could construct a metaphysics or phenomenology of the will's liberty that was purely voluntarist, purely spontaneous; though, even then, one would have to explain how an absolutely libertarian act, obedient to no ultimate prior rationale whatsoever, would be distinguishable from sheer chance, or a mindless organic or mechanical impulse, and so any more "free" than an earthquake or embolism. But, on any cogent account, free will is a power inherently purposive, teleological, primordially oriented toward the good, and shaped by that transcendental appetite to the degree that a soul can recognize the good for what it is. No one can *freely* will the evil as evil; one can take the evil for the good, but that does not alter the prior transcendental orientation that wakens all desire. The "intellectualist" understanding of the will is simply the only one that can bear scrutiny. Any desire or act not directed toward its proximate object as "good," at least as "good for me," within the embrace of a constant transcendental intentionality toward the Good as such, would be by definition teleologically irrational, and so not an act of the rational will at all. To see the good and truly know it is to desire it insatiably and to obey it unconditionally; one who is truly free cannot fail, then, to seek the Good itself, while not to desire it is not to have known it, and so never to have been free to choose it. "Then you shall know the truth, and the truth shall set you free": for freedom and truth are one. "Father, forgive them, for they know not what they do": not seeing the Good, says God to God, they did not freely choose evil, and must be pardoned. This is why, under normal conditions, we recognize any genuinely self-destructive impulse in any person as a form of madness, of bondage to ignorance and delusion and despair, but not an expression of liberty. It makes no more sense to say that God allows creatures to damn themselves out of his love for them or of his respect for their freedom than to say a father might reasonably allow his deranged child to thrust her face into a fire out of a tender respect for her moral autonomy. And the argument becomes quite insufferable when one considers the personal conditions—ignorance, mortality, defectibility of intellect and will—under which each soul enters the world, and the circumstances—the suffering of all creatures, even the most innocent and delightful of them—with which that world confronts the soul. Again, Reformed tradition is commendable for the intellectual honesty with which it elevates divine sovereignty to the status of *the* absolute theological value, and sovereignty understood as pure inscrutable power. But, alas, the epistemological cost is extravagant: for Reformed theology is still dogmatically obliged to ascribe to God all those predicates (except "love") that Scripture supplies, and so must call God "good," "just," "merciful," "wise," and "truthful." But, transparently, all have been rendered equivocal by the doctrines that surround them; and this equivocity is necessarily contagious; it reduces *all* theological language to vacuity, for none of it can now be trusted; the system, in the end, is one devoid of logical or semantic content: it means nothing, it can be neither believed nor doubted, it is just a formal arrangement of intrinsically empty signifiers, no more true or false than any purely abstract pattern. And obviously no refuge is offered by the stern teaching of the human intellect's "total depravity," as that merely reiterates the problem of equivocity, but with the appropriate dressing of ceremonious cringing. In the words of John Stuart Mill, "To say that God's goodness may be different in kind from man's goodness, what is it but saying, with a slight change of phraseology, that God may possibly not be good?"

Again, however, it is not only Reformed theology that suffers from this contagion of equivocity; it infects every theology that includes the notion of an eternal hell—which is to say, just about the whole Christian tradition.

5. I suppose I might be accused not only of overstatement, but of having strayed far from my topic. To me, however, this all follows inexorably from the doctrine of creation. This is not a complicated issue, it seems to me: the eternal perdition—the eternal suffering—of any soul would be an abominable tragedy, and so a moral evil if even conditionally intended, and could not possibly be comprised within the ends intended by a truly good will (in any sense of the word "good" intelligible to us). Yet, if both the doctrine of *creatio ex nihilo* and that of eternal damnation are true, that evil is indeed comprised within the intentions and dispositions of God. And, while one may hope that some limited good will emerge from the cosmic drama, somehow preponderant over the evil, at such an unspeakable cost it can be at best a relative and tragically ambiguous good. And what, then, would any damned soul be, as enfolded within the eternal will of God, other than a price settled upon by God with his own power, an oblation willingly exchanged for a finite benefit—the lamb slain from the foundation of the world? And what then is God, inasmuch as the moral nature of any intended final cause must include within its calculus what one is willing to sacrifice to achieve that end; and if the "acceptable" price is the eternal torment of a rational nature, what room remains for any moral analogy comprehensible within finite terms?

The economics of the exchange is really quite monstrous. We can all appreciate, I imagine, the shattering force of Vanya's terrible question to

Alyosha in *The Brothers Karamazov*: If universal harmony and joy could be secured by the torture and murder of a single innocent child, would you accept that price? But let us say that somehow, mysteriously—in, say, Zosima's sanctity, Alyosha's kiss, the million-mile march of Vanya's devil, the callous old woman's onion—an answer is offered that makes the transient torments of history justifiable in the light of God's everlasting kingdom. But *eternal* torments, *final* dereliction? Here the price is raised beyond any calculus of relative goods, and into the realm of absolute—of infinite—expenditure. And the arithmetic is fairly inflexible. We need not imagine, in traditional fashion, that the legions of the damned will far outnumber the cozy company of the saved. Let us imagine instead that only one soul will perish eternally, and all others enter into the peace of the kingdom. Nor need we think of that soul as guiltless, like Vanya's helpless child, or even as mildly sympathetic. Let it be someone utterly despicable—say, Hitler. Even then, no matter how we understand the fate of that single wretched soul in relation to God's intentions, no account of the divine decision to create out of nothingness can make its propriety morally intelligible. This is obvious, of course, in predestinarian systems, since from their bleak perspective, manifestly, that poor, ridiculous, but tragically conscious puppet who has been consigned to the abyss exists for no other purpose than the ghastly spectacle of divine sovereignty. But, then, for the redeemed, each of whom might just as well have been denied efficacious grace had God so pleased, who is that wretch who endures God's final wrath, forever and ever, other than their surrogate, their redeemer, the one who suffers in their stead— their Christ? Compared to that unspeakable offering, that interminable and abominable oblation of infinite misery, what would the cross of Christ be? How would it be diminished for us? And to what? A bad afternoon? A temporary indisposition of the infinite? And what would the mystery of God becoming man in order to effect a merely partial rescue of created order be, as compared to the far deeper mystery of a worthless man becoming the suffering god upon whose perpetual holocaust the entire order of creation finally depends? But predestination need not be invoked here at all. Let us suppose instead that rational creatures possess real autonomy, and that no one goes to hell save by his or her own industry and ingenuity: when we then look at God's decision to create from that angle, curiously enough, absolutely nothing changes. Not to wax too anthropomorphizing here, like some analytic philosopher of religion, but let us say God created simply *on the chance* that humanity might sin, and that a certain number of incorrigibly wicked souls might plunge themselves into Tartarus forever; this still means that, morally, he has purchased the revelation of his power

THE HIDDEN AND THE MANIFEST

in creation by the same horrendous price—even if, in the end, no one at all happens to be damned. The logic is irresistible. God creates. *Alea iacta est.* But, as Mallarmé says, "un coup de dés jamais n'abolira le hasard": for what is hazarded has already been surrendered, entirely, no matter how the dice fall; the aleatory venture may be intentionally indeterminate, but the wager is an irrevocable intentional decision, wherein every possible cost has already been accepted; the irrecuperable expenditure has been offered even if, happily, it is never actually lost, and so the moral nature of the act is the same in either case. To venture the life of your child for some other end is, morally, already to have killed your child, even if at the last moment Artemis or Heracles or the Angel of the Lord should stay your hand. And so, the revelation of God's glory in creatures would still always be dependent upon that evil, that venture beyond good and evil, even if at the last no one perishes. Creation could never then be called "good" in an unconditional sense; nor God the "Good as such," no matter what conditional goods he might accomplish in creating. And, here too, the losing lot might just as well have fallen to the blessed, given the stochastic vagaries of existence: accidents of birth, congenital qualities of character, natural intellectual endowments, native moral aptitudes, material circumstances, personal powers of resolve, impersonal forces of chance, the grim encumbrances of sin and mortality . . . Once again, who would the damned be but the redeemers of the blessed, the price eternally paid by God for the sake of the kingdom's felicity?

To be clear: I am not attempting to subject God to an "ethical" interrogation, as though he were some finite agent answerable to standards beyond himself. That would be banal. My concern is the coherence of theological language in light of the logically indispensable doctrine of *creatio ex nihilo*. The golden thread of analogy can stretch across as vast an apophatic abyss as the modal disjunction between infinite and finite or the ontological disproportion between absolute and contingent can open before us; but it cannot span a total antithesis. When we use words like "good," "just," "love" to name God, not as if they are mysteriously *greater* in meaning than when predicated of creatures, but instead as if they bear transparently *opposite* meanings, then we are saying nothing. And, again, the contagion of this equivocity necessarily consumes theology entirely.

6. Of course, theological language is determined by Scripture; which is why I began with some of the New Testament's most famously universalistic verses, including those asserting a strict equivalence between what is lost in Adam and what is saved in Christ; I could have added several more. It is odd that for at least fifteen centuries such passages have been

all but lost behind so thin a veil as can be woven from those three deeply ambiguous verses that seem (and only *seem*) to threaten eternal torments for the wicked. But that is as may be; every good New Testament scholar is well aware of the obscurities that throng every attempt to reconstruct the eschatological vision described in Jesus's teachings. And, really, plucking individual verses like posies from the text here and there is not the way to see the entire landscape. The New Testament, to a great degree, consists in an eschatological interpretation of Hebrew Scripture's story of creation, finding in Christ, as eternal Logos and risen Lord, the unifying term of beginning and end. For Paul, in particular, the marvel of Christ's lordship is that all walls of division between persons and peoples, and finally between all creatures, have fallen; and that ultimately, when creation is restored by Christ, God will be all in all. There is no more magnificent meditation on this vision than Gregory of Nyssa's image of the progress of all persons toward union with God in the one "pleroma" of the *totus Christus*: all spiritual wills moving, to use his lovely image, from outside the temple walls (in the ages) into the temple precincts, and finally (beyond the ages) into the very sanctuary of the glory—as one. By contrast, Augustine, in the last masterpiece produced by his colossal genius, wrote of two cities eternally sealed against one another, from everlasting in the divine counsels and unto everlasting in the divine judgment (the far more populous city destined for perpetual sorrow). There is no question to my mind which of them saw the story more clearly. Or which theologians are the best guides to Scripture as a whole: Gregory, Origen, Evagrius, Diodore, Theodore, Isaac of Nineveh . . . George MacDonald.

Here however, again, the issue is the reducibility of all causes to their first cause, and the determination of the first cause by the final. If we did not proclaim a *creatio ex nihilo*—if we thought God a being limited by some external principle or internal imperfection, or if we were dualists, or dialectical idealists, or what have you—the question of evil would be an aetiological query only for us, not a terrible moral question. But, because we say God creates freely, we must believe his final judgment shall reveal him for who he is. And as God is act—as are we all in some sense—and as God is what he does, if there is a final irreconcilable dual result to his act in creating, then there is also an original irreconcilable dual premise stretching all the way back into the divine nature. So, if all are not saved, if God creates souls he knows to be destined for eternal misery, is God evil? Well, why debate semantics? Maybe every analogy fails. What is not debatable is that, if God does so create, in himself he cannot be the Good as such, and creation cannot be a morally meaningful act: it is from one vantage an act of predilective love, but from another—logically necessary—vantage an act of prudential malevolence. And so it cannot be true. We are presented by what has become the majority tradition with three fundamental claims, any two of which might be true simultaneously, but never all three: that God freely created all things out of nothingness; that God is the Good itself; and that it is certain or at least possible that some rational creatures will endure eternal loss of God. And this, I have to say, is the final moral meaning I find in the doctrine of *creatio ex nihilo*, at least if we truly believe that our language about God's goodness and the theological grammar to which it belongs are not empty: that the God of eternal retribution and pure sovereignty proclaimed by so much of Christian tradition is not, and cannot possibly be, the God of self-outpouring love revealed in Christ. If God is the good Creator of all, he is the Savior of all, without fail, who brings to himself all he has made, including all rational wills, and only thus returns to himself in all that goes forth from him. If he is not the Savior of all, the kingdom is only a dream, and creation something considerably worse than a nightmare. But, again, it is not so. God saw that it was good; and, in the ages, we shall see it too.

Acknowledgments

1. The Offering of Names: Metaphysics, Nihilism, and Analogy
   Reprinted by permission of T. & T. Clark from "The Offering of Names: Metaphysics, Nihilism, and Analogy," in *Reason and the Reasons of Faith*, ed. Reinhard Hütter and Paul J. Griffiths (Edinburgh: T. & T. Clark, 2005), pp. 55–76. Copyright © 2005. All Rights Reserved.

2. No Shadow of Turning: On Divine Impassibility
   © 2002 *Pro Ecclesia*. Originally published in *Pro Ecclesia* 11, no. 2 (Spring 2002): 184–206. Reprinted with permission.

3. The Writing of the Kingdom: Thirty-Three Aphorisms toward an Eschatology of the Text
   © 2000 *Modern Theology*. Originally published in *Modern Theology* 16, no. 2 (Spring 2000): 181–202. Reprinted with permission.

4. From "Notes on the Concept of the Infinite in the History of Western Metaphysics": Part I
   Reprinted by permission of Cambridge University Press from "Notes on the Concept of the Infinite in the History of Western Metaphysics," in *Infinity: New Research Frontiers*, ed. Michael Heller and W. Hugh Woodin (Cambridge: Cambridge University Press, 2011), pp. 255–74. Copyright © 2011. All Rights Reserved.

5. The Destiny of Christian Metaphysics: Reflections on the *Analogia Entis*
   Reprinted by permission of the William B. Eerdmans Publishing Company from "The Destiny of Christian Metaphysics: Reflections on the *Analogia Entis*," in *Analogia Entis: Invention of Antichrist or Wisdom of God?* ed. Thomas Joseph White, OP (Grand Rapids: Eerdmans, 2010), pp. 395–410. Copyright © 2010. All Rights Reserved.

6. The Mirror of the Infinite: Gregory of Nyssa and the *Vestigia Trinitatis*
© 2002 *Modern Theology*. Originally published in *Modern Theology* 18, no. 4 (Fall 2002): 541–61. Reprinted with permission.

7. The Hidden and the Manifest: Metaphysics after Nicaea
Reprinted by permission of the publishers from "The Hidden and the Manifest: Metaphysics after Nicaea," in *Orthodox Readings of Augustine*, ed. Aristotle Papanikolaou and George F. Demacopoulos (Crestwood, NY: St. Vladimir's Seminary Press, 2009), pp. 191–226. Copyright © 2009. www.svspress.com. All Rights Reserved.

8. From "Notes on the Concept of the Infinite in the History of Western Metaphysics": Part II
Reprinted by permission of Cambridge University Press from "Notes on the Concept of the Infinite in the History of Western Metaphysics," in *Infinity: New Research Frontiers*, ed. Michael Heller and W. Hugh Woodin (Cambridge: Cambridge University Press, 2011), pp. 255–74. Copyright © 2011. All Rights Reserved.

9. Impassibility as Transcendence: On the Infinite Innocence of God
Reprinted by permission of the William B. Eerdmans Publishing Company from "Impassibility as Transcendence: On the Infinite Innocence of God," in *Divine Impassibility and the Mystery of Human Suffering*, ed. James F. Keating and Thomas Joseph White (Grand Rapids: Eerdmans, 2009), pp. 299–323. Copyright © 2009. All Rights Reserved.

10. Thine Own of Thine Own: The Orthodox Understanding of Eucharistic Sacrifice
Reprinted from "Thine Own of Thine Own: The Orthodox Understanding of Eucharistic Sacrifice," in *Rediscovering the Eucharist: Ecumenical Conversations*, edited by Roch A. Kereszty. Copyright © 2003 by Roch A. Kereszty, O. Cist. Paulist Press, Inc., Mahwah, NJ. www.paulistpress.com. Used with Permission.

11. Matter, Monism, and Narrative: An Essay on the Metaphysics of *Paradise Lost*
© 1996 *Milton Quarterly*. Originally published in *Milton Quarterly* 30, no.1 (Winter 1996): 16–27. Reprinted with permission.

12. The Whole Humanity: Gregory of Nyssa's Critique of Slavery in Light of His Eschatology
© 2001 *Scottish Journal of Theology*. Originally published in *Scottish Journal of Theology* 54, no. 1 (2001): 51–69. Reprinted with permission.

13. Death, Final Judgment, and the Meaning of Life
Reprinted by permission of Oxford University Press from "Death, Final Judgment, and the Meaning of Life," in *The Oxford Handbook of Eschatology*, ed. Jerry Walls (Oxford: Oxford University Press, 2008), pp. 476–89. Copyright © 2008. All Rights Reserved.

14. The Myth of Schism
Reprinted by permission of the publishers from "The Myth of Schism," in *Ecumenism Today*, ed. Francesca Aran Murphy and Christopher Asprey (Farnham, UK: Ashgate, 2008), pp. 95–106. Copyright © 2008. All Rights Reserved.

Acknowledgments

15. **Remarks in Response to Father Lawrence Dewan**
These remarks were given in response to an admirably lucid address on natural law theory in Thomas Aquinas delivered by Father Dewan at Providence College in 2008.

16. **Thrift**
Not previously published.

17. **Christianity, Modernity, and Freedom**
Reprinted by permission of Georgetown University Press from "Christianity, Modernity, and Freedom," in *Tradition and Modernity: Christian and Muslim Perspectives*, ed. David Marshall (Washington, DC: Georgetown University Press, 2013), pp. 67–78. Copyright © 2011. All Rights Reserved.

18. **The Encounter between Eastern Orthodoxy and Radical Orthodoxy: A Brief Foreword**
Reprinted by permission of the publishers from "Foreword," in *Encounter between Eastern Orthodoxy and Radical Orthodoxy*, ed. Adrian Pabst and Christoph Schneider (Farnham, UK: Ashgate, 2009), pp. xi–xiv. Copyright © 2009.

19. **Remarks in Response to Gianni Vattimo**
These remarks were given in response to an address on belief delivered by Gianni Vattimo at the annual convention of the Academy of American Religion in 1998 when, for reasons at once unaccountable and yet exquisitely apt, it was held at Disney World.

20. **God, Creation, and Evil: The Moral Meaning of *Creatio ex Nihilo***
© *Radical Orthodoxy: Theology, Philosophy, Politics* 3, no. 1 (2015): 1–17. Reprinted with Permission.

Index

Analogy of being (*Analogia entis*), 37–44, 97–112, 137–64; and ante-Nicene metaphysics, 144–45; and Balthasar, 98, 111; and Christology, 111–12; and *creatio ex nihilo*, 42, 84, 98–99; and divine transcendence and immanence, 74, 109–10, 142, 179, 333; and God's moral character, 342; and natural metaphysics, 10, 25, 101–3; and textuality of the world, 79. *See also Creatio ex nihilo*; Przywara, Erich

Apatheia (divine impassibility), 45–69, 167–90; contrast with divine immutability, 169; and divine wrath, 62; and God's epistemic impassibility, 172, 174, 181–82; and *kenōsis*, 63–65, 68; rejection of by modern theologians, 49–51; and sin, 45–69; Stoic roots of, 55; and the Trinity, 59–63

Apophatic (negative) theology, 2, 74, 99–100, 109, 127, 137–64

Aquinas, Saint Thomas (Thomism), 17n26, 19, 29, 42n36, 58, 102, 142, 152, 165–66, 171n6, 225, 276, 285–89, 293, 326, 344; and *praemotio physica*, 167–89

Aristotle, 19, 24, 91–92, 94, 240

Asceticism, 290–311

Athanasius, Saint, 48, 61, 64, 67, 197, 220

Atheism, 3, 187–88, 190, 315, 318, 327

Atonement: Calvinism's doctrine of "limited" atonement, 303; and Eucharist, 191–216; Israel's Day of, 67, 261, 265, 296

Augustine, Saint, 56–57, 58, 60–61, 88, 102, 129, 137, 141, 142, 151, 152, 219, 234, 301, 342–43, 349; Eastern Orthodox responses to, 139–40, 325, 327, 344; and the "*massa damnata,*" 342–43, 349; on the Trinity, 60–61, 109, 114–15, 117–19, 121, 137–64. *See also* Original sin

Balthasar, Hans Urs von, 98, 111, 246

Bañez, Domingo (Bañezians), 171–72, 174, 176–80, 184, 186–87

Barth, Karl, 37n33, 97, 98, 99, 248n35

Bulgakov, Sergius, 197, 202–3

Calvin, John (Calvinism) 177, 187, 303, 304–5, 326, 327, 343

Christ: death of, 45–69, 182, 185,